A
MOUTHFUL
OF AIR

A
MOUTHFUL
OF AIR

Language, Languages . . .

Especially English

ANTHONY
BURGESS

WILLIAM MORROW AND COMPANY, INC.   NEW YORK

Library of Congress Cataloging-in-Publication Data

Burgess, Anthony, 1917–
    A mouthful of air : language, languages . . . especially English / by
Anthony Burgess.
        p.   cm.
    ISBN 0-688-11935-2
    1. English language.   2. Language and languages.   I. Title.
PE1072.B796   1993
420—dc20   92-45117
                                                                              CIP

Printed in the United States of America

First Edition

1   2   3   4   5   6   7   8   9   10

BOOK DESIGN BY BARBARA BACHMAN

FOREWORD

LINGUISTIC

IGNORANCE

The term "analphabetic" means lacking an alphabet or, in some kind of structured and informative compilation (an encyclopedia, for instance), an alphabetic order. It is also used as a synonym for "illiterate"—unlettered, unable to read. To be illiterate, in a society fenced round by alphabetic information, is as bad as to be syphilitic or, bringing the morbidity up to date, afflicted by AIDS. In societies blessed by compulsory state education, there is not much literal illiteracy around. Hence the term is much used as a metaphor, as in the phrase "cultural illiteracy." Innumeracy is another disease, or, more properly, an elected crime, but it does not carry the same flavor of moral obliquity.

My own prejudices have led me to look for a term descriptive of an inability to read music. Music is not written in letters (save for brusque directives about speed and expression) but in notes. "Inneumacy" might have served before the fourteenth century, when music was composed in the now near-unintelligible symbols called neumes. "Immusicality" is not quite adequate, as it implies no more than a tin ear, or an inability to understand the higher music. "Musical illiteracy" is inexact, but it seems to have a meaning—the bafflement of one who looks at a score and finds it unintelligible.

Music is the exploitation of sound, and so, when you come to think of it, is language. I need, rather more desperately than an improvement on "musical illiteracy," a term to designate those to whom language as sound has little meaning. "Aphonetic" might do, or "aphonic." This seems to signify an inability to make sounds, whereas it is meant to mean an incapacity, uncured by education, to know what our vocal apparatuses, along with our brains, are doing when sounds are uttered. "Phonetic illiteracy" is not appropriate, especially when one is concerned with the vocal events that letters merely ineptly encode.

There is, of course, more to language than sounds. There are structures as well. If I use the expression "linguistic ignorance," I mean lack of scientific, or quasi-scientific, knowledge of how language behaves. The behavior of language is what this book is about. It is intended to be an easy approach to the elimination of linguistic ignorance. This ignorance does not primarily apply to language as a foreign substance—we are all ignorant of most of the languages of the world—but, very much primarily, to the English language that you and I speak, American or British. To know how English works is to know how language works. And vice versa.

W. B. Yeats wrote of one of his poems that he "made it out of a mouthful of air." All literature is made in this way, though we tend to think of it as a scratching of signs on paper. Literature gives permanence to language: people learn Greek to read Plato and Latin to read Catullus. Language is books. But it is primarily so much air, a mouthful at a time, modified by contortions of the vocal organs. It is impermanent, evanescent, highly changeable, but it is the primary reality, while writing and printing are of a secondary order. This book is a visual object and uses visual symbols, but it is dedicated to the truth that language is what we speak and hear.

Nearly thirty years ago, I published a little book called *Language Made Plain*. It was reprinted ten years later, with a correction of errors and an attempt to bring it up to date (the academic study of language is volatile and progressive, changeable in its terminology, open to new theories, increasingly reliant on new insights, and helped by new technology). A good deal of that book has been embodied in this new and larger one, though with the inevitable modifications of substance and style that are the fruit of experience. That general and somewhat simplistic study of the nature of language is now subordinated to an examination of the language that my readers and I know best. This book may not always look like it, but it is meant to be about the English language. It is also, like the earlier book, intended for the plain reader. It avoids technicalities as far as it can, though it is no more possible to write of language without occasionally introducing them than it is to produce a car user's manual that does not refer to carburetors and spark plugs.

The book is pedagogical in intent: it unashamedly tries to teach. Before I became a professional novelist, I was a teacher. In 1940 I gained a degree in English language and literature and was then inducted into the British Army. From 1942 until 1946 I was an instructor only indirectly concerned with the teaching of English. The British government had decided to educate the common soldier in the principles for which the Second World War was being fought and the pattern of the postwar future it was hoped to build—a temporal home for heroes to live in. I was engaged in propagandizing for what was termed the "British way and purpose," and modifying official instructional material in the face of soldierly cynicism. But there was a large influx into the army of products of the state educational system who had not learned to read and write. The number, indeed, was larger than had been thought possible. It was necessary to improvise very rapidly methods that, within a six-week primary training period, would enable an illiterate recruit to write a simple letter home (I AM ORLRITE OPE U R 2), doubtless to other illiterates, and understand, with slightly more vagueness than the literate, instructions posted on the company or battalion notice board. The time granted was insufficient, and little was achieved, though the War Office eventually brought out a manual for the teaching of the unlettered ("When you come home on leave it is good to sink your teeth in a good slice of beef"). I never saw this in use.

Posted to Gibraltar, where military duty consisted in a long passive waiting for the defense of the Rock, I found myself ordered to take voluntary army classes in subjects of which I had little knowledge— Russian and German, for instance, and elementary bookkeeping. The British way and purpose also continued, to loud groans, to unfold itself. Gibraltarian schoolchildren had been evacuated to the bombs of England; they returned to find that the Irish Christian Brothers who had previously taught them objected, as neutrals, to serving in a war zone and had left the schools teacherless. The army became responsible for all civilian education on the Rock, from infants up to mustached adults who wished to learn advanced bookkeeping. The teaching of English at all levels, which I was obliged to undertake, did not quite approach the language as a foreign one, though the mother tongue of nearly all Gibraltarians was Andalusian Spanish. The English they wished to improve was strictly utilitarian, without the fancy trimmings of the literary. In all their colonies, unlike the French, the British have never been eager to implant their literature, conceivably finding it, which it is, subversive. The figurative use of language was not well understood by my students. If I asked for a sentence illustrating the adage "Too many cooks spoil the broth," I would receive some such literal variant as "There were too many cooks in the kitchen and so the soup was not good."

As the war ended, the needs of regular soldiers had to be met in a specific way: peacetime promotion depended partly on success in one or other of the grades of the examinations for the army certificate of education. A general deficiency—in syntax, spelling, and vocabulary—called for stiff remedial work. Upon demobilization, I was not quite out of the army, for as a civilian instructor I taught sergeant-recruits for the army Educational Corps. Except among the Scots, who have always benefited from a rigorous educational system, I found gross deficiencies in the handling of English. The half-blind were to lead the totally so.

I moved on to an emergency training college, one of the establishments set up, usually in now-abandoned U.S. Army camps, to remedy an acute shortage of teachers in state schools. Ex-servicemen eager to join the teaching ranks were given a thirteen-month course in teaching method and the basic subjects—what used to be called the three R's—garnished with a little literature, music, history, geography, drawing, and woodwork. I specialized in speech training. A problem was already rumbling among mature students who rejected the notion of the supraregional Received Pronunciation I found it necessary to teach. Bradfordians and Glaswegians were not automatically to be posted to schools in their own localities, and Yorkshire "loov" for "love" and Scottish "fuitba" for "football" might not be well received in Croydon or Penzance. My classes were not all that prescriptive: teaching phonetics, I could at least show how sounds were made; the making of them was up to the students.

With the termination of the emergency scheme in 1950, I found a post as English master in a grammar school. This type of establishment was a cut very much below the British public school but a good way above the new secondary modern and technical schools. The comprehensive school, which was to replace all three, was still on the drawing board. The new egalitarian spirit of Great Britain made no distinction between the three modes of secondary education in terms of prestige, but parents knew better. My school was mixed in sex though not in race—the multiracial society was only just beginning to emerge—and it was triply streamed. The 'A' stream was for bright children with an academic bent who might move on to a university: usually their brightness was a reflection of a cultivated home. The 'B' stream was not quite so bright, though it was brighter than the 'N' stream. The 'N' stood for "normal," normality, as decreed by the worker's state, signifying antiacademic and, indeed, antieducational. Teachers were worse paid than skilled manual workers, and this implied a depressed status compatible with the new philosophy of equality: leveling was to be downward; intellectual distinction was considered elitist.

After four years of working in the branches of English instruction that were later to be externally examined—from basic grammar to set books—I became an education officer, or *pegawai pelajaran*, in Malaya. My work in the Malay College, modeled on the British public school and sometimes called the Eton of the East, was not greatly different from the home variety, though a great deal of remedial labor had to be expended on Malay-tinted English speech. When I transferred to a teachers' training college, where the studentship was multiracial—Malay, Chinese, Indian, Eurasian, and Japanese—I had to impart methods of instruction in Malayan schools that would treat English as a second language. Remedial work had to be performed on the potential teachers themselves, but this was not onerous. The family backgrounds of the students, professional and commercial, had ensured an almost literary knowledge of English, and, in some instances, genuine bookishness. One of my Chinese students became a university lecturer in England, with a profound specialization in Wordsworth.

With the coming of Malayan independence in 1957, I transferred myself to the sultanate of Brunei, in North Borneo, where I taught at the Omar Ali Saifuddin College. This was lowly and unstimulating work. The state was oil-rich, and the spirit of aspiration, which alone makes students willing to learn, was quelled by a torpid prosperity qualified by Islamic puritanism. I taught potential teachers of Malay in their own language, introducing the alien science of *fonetik*, along with a homemade terminology, with *bunyi bibir-bibir* ("sound lip-lip") for labial phonemes, and *fonem* and *alofon* as straightforward loan-words. My teaching career ended with frustration, the mistaken diagnosis of a brain tumor, and the decision to try to earn my living as a professional writer.

But being a professional writer has entailed willingness to teach—though only in the United States, where creative writing is regarded as an academic subject. I have held professorships in literature but have always slyly tried to introduce a little elementary linguistics. This preoccupation goes back to the beginning of my career. In the grammar school I gave my pupils at least one weekly lesson in phonetics and earned rebukes, mostly from parents who saw no use in it.

The teaching instinct is hard to quell, and long after the statutory age of retirement from the trade, I sometimes daydream of returning to the classroom. I face, without too much fear, a class of louts who do not wish to learn. I deprecate my great age and recount, as evidence of my credibility as a teacher, my bizarrely various teaching career. This ended, I say, in Borneo. An insolent but knowledgeable pupil asks if I taught orangutans. I cut mildly through the cruel laughter to pronounce that I did, and I write *orang hutan* on the blackboard in Arabic script, explaining that the term means "man of the forest" and that some of my Borneo students were straight out of primitive kampongs. The native word for the amiable ape that is found in Borneo is *mawas* or *maias*. These two terms I also write in Arabic script. I explain that the Arabic alphabet was carried to the East Indies, along with the Islamic religion, by Arab traders and missionaries.

This is supposed to be an English lesson, but it is doubtful if the English language will be so much as mentioned before the bell rings. My real, as opposed to imaginary, teaching experience has been much of this order—trying to induce an interest in the phenomenon of language in general before swooping to the particular and, even then, not neglecting the general. I have in my time been censured by school principals and the visiting officers of Her Majesty's Inspectorate for a bizarre homemade syllabus that did not seem to consult the requirements of final examinations. To have twelve-year-olds writing their names in Arabic script or trying to disentangle the radicals from a Chinese ideogram does not look much like the teaching of English. But if it promotes an interest in the faculty that separates man from the beasts, it will do its work.

* * *

A language is defined not only by what it is but by what it is not. English seems to belong to two families of languages. It is both like and unlike French, like and unlike German. Its structure, if not its vocabulary, proclaims a remote relationship to Russian. But it is not a bit like Malay or Japanese. How not? Let us at least glance at those two to see how not. Again, Russian and Greek and Arabic do at least conform to our Western writing system by using an alphabet. An alphabet may be said to be efficient if it visualizes the sounds of a language. The Roman alphabet fits Welsh and Italian and German fairly snugly; English strains under it. Why? Why has the Chinese language not eased its way out of the burden of complicated ideograms and taken the alphabetic road? We may start wondering whether our spelling system, which tells so many phonetic lies, is not closer to Chinese usage—recognizing a word by its shape, not by its sound components—than to that of its European relatives.

None of the educational reforms proposed in countries where English is the first language have paid much attention to English as a system of sounds. We are all bemused by the printed word, giving it an authority it does not really possess. I plead now for the introduction of some kind of phonetic study into the English curriculum at all levels. Children must learn to know what their vocal organs are doing when they speak their own, or any other, language. I make no apology for insisting that language is a mouthful, or several mouthfuls, of air.

But naturally I accept that speech is not everything. Those aspects of language that are best taken in by the eye are not neglected here. We would all wish that modes of sonic transmission had been invented in the Middle Ages so that we could hear Chaucer's speech and, with two centuries of technical improvement, Shakespeare's. But now that this mode of communication is with us, and some of us writers know our books as audio cassettes, I would not be happy to see the act of reading a text disappear. As a music lover, I cannot accept a Beethoven symphony as solely something for the ear. The word /lait/ is also the word "light." The phonetic spelling tells us how it sounds now; the traditional spelling tells us something about how it used to sound in English, and still sounds in Scottish and German. Chinese who speak different dialects, mutually unintelligible, can communicate through the recognition of a nationwide symbol. Language is eye and ear.

We do not know much about language, but we are trying to learn. This book dare not be too dogmatic. It dare not be too scholarly either, since scholars speak to each other in a way that the untrained reader is not equipped to understand. But I think that it contains the minimum of linguistic substance that not only the teacher of English but the speaker and reader of English ought to know. When I say "English," I mean all the forms it has taken in its haphazard travel across the globe. I write this preface in Switzerland, oppressed by workmen outside quarreling in the Italian of Ticino, while, in the house opposite, a plaintive quarrel is proceeding in the German of Zürich. I write as one brought up on a variety of British English—that of Lancashire—but I am aware of the big world outside me. If Americans or Australians or New Zealanders reading this book object to what they see as a British bias, that cannot be helped. We are what we are. But I do not think that they will be able to complain of insularity.

This, then, is a gentle rap on the door of linguistic knowledge. The door opens on a mansion with too many stories, too many rooms. But we can learn enough for our purposes on the ground floor.

A.B.
Savosa

CONTENTS

A
MOUTHFUL
OF AIR

PART ONE

*Language and
Languages*

1.

SIGNALS IN THE DARK

I shall try in this book to give, to the layman and laywoman and even the laychild, some cool information about the phenomenon of language in general and about one language in particular.

Coolness is necessary. Words—their spelling, meaning, pronunciation—frequently arouse strong if ignorant feelings. Letters to newspapers, especially the London *Times*, are sometimes apoplectic about new usages—"gay" for homosexual, "hopefully" in the sense of the German *hoffentlich*, "it is to be hoped"—and about the mispronunciations of television newscasters. People quarrel about words, heatedly and unreasonably. Very occasionally they appeal to nonexistent authorities. There is a superstitious belief that God, or some lesser being in charge of language, has laid down laws on a kind of linguistic Mount Sinai. The Chinese once posited a superhuman provenance for language. In old Mandarin the word *ku* designated a sort of drinking goblet with corners. When this vessel came to be made without corners, it was still called *ku*, and Confucius considered this outrageous—not because the word was no longer appropriate to the thing, but because the thing no longer conformed to the word. The idea that the two should conform was the doctrine of *cheng ming*, which, if it functioned in our time, would forbid forms like "tin box," because a box is essentially wooden. Professor Roy Harris, who is in charge of the Department of Linguistics at Oxford, has written of "the women's liberation lady who legally changed her name from Cooperman to Cooperperson. If she had believed in the doctrine of *cheng ming* she would have had a sex-change operation instead."

Languages are made by ordinary human beings, not by God or the pundits who stand in for him. They seem to be somewhat arbitrary collocations of sounds, symbolized as written or printed signs, whose origins belong to the mists of prehistory. There was, when man became man, clearly a social need for them. We may think of a language as a system of communication used within a particular social group. Inevitably, the emotions aroused by group loyalty obstruct the making of objective judgments about language. When we think we are making such a judgment, we are often merely making a statement about our prejudices. It is instructive to examine these prejudices occasionally. I used to have very powerful objections to the Americanization of British English. In this, of course, I was at one with "Disgusted of Leamington Spa" in the *Times* correspondence columns. I used to read with a kind of fascinated horror the effusions of an "Agony Aunt" in a popular daily paper that, by definition, was not the *Times*. I waited masochistically for her to use the locution "I guess," as in "I guess he really loves you after all" or "I guess you'd better get yourself a new boyfriend." I saw in this a threat to the British way of life, but I saw also that my seeing it as such was nonsense. I knew that "I guess" is at least as old as Chaucer, pure English English, something sent over on the *Mayflower*. But, like most of us, I do not really enjoy submitting to reason. I prefer to condemn "I guess" as an American importation and its use by a British writer as a betrayal of the traditions of my national group.

Such condemnation can seem virtuous, because patriotism (despite Dr. Johnson's description of it as the "last refuge of a scoundrel") is a noble concept. While patriotic virtue burns in the mind, adrenaline courses around the body and exhilarates. Reason never has this euphoric effect. And so patriotic sentiment justifies our contempt of foreign languages and makes us unwilling to learn them properly. Few Westerners seem able to take Chinese seriously, though the days when a comedian could raise a snigger with inanities of the "Hoo Flung Dung" variety seem to be passing. Russian terms like *glasnost* and *perestroika* have come into English, but all that many people hear in the language of Pushkin and Dostoevsky is a deep vodka-soaked rumble bristling with "vich" and "ski." As for German—this is an ugly language, brutal and aggressively guttural. We rarely admit that it seems ugly because of two painful world wars. Sometimes automatic sneers at foreign languages are mitigated by pleasant memories— warm holidays abroad, trips to the opera, *vino*. Italian is regarded as a beautiful language, full of blue skies and sexy tenors. Trippers to Paris, furtively visiting the Folies-Bergère, used to project their own guilt onto the French language and see it as "naughty," even "immoral." But, as Britain's place in Europe grows to confirmation, such xenophobic stupidity has to disappear.

Within the national group, our prejudices tend to be mixed and, because they operate mainly on the unconscious level, not easily recognizable. We can be natives of great cities and still find an urban dialect less pleasant than a rural one. And yet, hearing prettiness and quaintness in a Dorset or Devon twang, we can also despise it, associating it with rural stupidity or backwardness. The supposedly ugly tones of Manchester or Birmingham will, because of their great civic associations, be at the same time somehow admirable. The whole business of ugliness and beauty works strangely. A BBC announcer says "payday," a Cockney says "piedie," or something near it. The former is thought to contain beautiful vowels, the latter not, and yet the announcer can use those Cockney sounds in "Eat that pie and you die" without anybody's face turning sour. In fact, terms like "ugly" and "beautiful" cannot apply to languages at all. Poets can make beautiful patterns out of words, but there are no standards we can use to formulate aesthetic judgments on the words themselves. We all have our pet hates and loves among words, but these always have to be referred to matters of association. If I dislike the word "shit," it is because I have no love of the substance. Clearly, I am aware of that substance when I hear the word used metaphorically (as in "Don't give me that shit"), while to the persistent user of it the original physical denotation has been swallowed up in the metaphor. A person who dislikes beets as a vegetable is not likely to love "beets" as a word. A poet who, in childhood, had a panful of hot stewed prunes spilled on him is, if he is rather a stupid poet, capable of writing, "And death, terrible as prunes" or "I flinch at the prunes of your anger." Association, or connotation, is necessary to the poet, but the connotations should make sense in a public, not private, context. Questions of word love and word hatred had best be approached very coolly.

We are normally quick to observe regional variations in the use of the national language, but we feel less strongly about these than we do about class divisions in speech. The dialects of English—that is, those regional forms that have their own vocabulary and grammar as well as pronunciations—are dying fast, but the accent remains and is attached to some variety or other of what we term Standard English. If we speak, as I do when I feel like it, with a Lancashire accent, we will often be good-humored and only slightly condescending toward those who use the accent of Wolverhampton or Tyneside. Sometimes we will even express a strong admiration of alien forms of English— the speech of the Scottish Highlands, for instance, but perhaps not that of Glasgow. But we feel rather differently about English speech when it seems to be a badge or banner of social class. The dialect known as Standard English was, originally, a pure regional form— so-called East Midland English, with no claim to any intrinsic merit. But it was spoken in an area that was, and still is, socially and economi- cally preeminent—the area that contains London, the great public schools, and the two most prestigious universities. Thus it gained a special glamour as the language of the court and the language of learning. It has ever since—not always falsely—been associated with wealth, position, and education. It is the supraregional dialect of the masters, while the regional dialects remain the property of the men. In certain industrial areas it can still excite resentment as "posh" or "swanky," despite the fact that it no longer goes along with power or privilege. Out-of-work actors can speak it, so can underpaid school- masters; tycoons, proud of their rise to the top from humble origins, will often cling to their underprivileged mother dialect, or a slight modification of it. It has been difficult for many inhabitants of a class- ridden country like England to see virtue in Standard English or even accept that it is possible to learn it, as one learns any foreign language. Its virtue lies in its neutrality, its lack of purely local associations, its transparency, its clarity, its suitability for intellectual discourses or dispassionate government pronouncements. It is cold, tending to wit rather than humor, the airy as opposed to the earthy.

There is room for regional dialects and room for Standard English with what is termed Received Pronunciation. The place for the re- gional dialect or the strongly regional accent is the place in which it was born; it is right for the football stadium, the public bar, the village dance. Standard English, with Received Pronunciation, is for the BBC talk on structuralism or postmodernism, the cocktail party in Hampstead, the interview for a job that involves wide travel. What is dangerous is the tendency among "natural" speakers of SE with RP (I think I may use these abbreviations from now on) to despise those who cannot or will not speak it themselves. The reason for this contempt is clear. The man or woman who is limited to regional speech appears to lack experience of the great world—smart restaurants, art galleries, piano recitals, polite talk. We are always ready to look down on people: it is an abiding pleasure, a poultice for our own sore sense of inferiority. We must think of the supraregional advantages of SE with RP—universal intelligibility and neutrality—rather than its class associations.

Snobbishness as regards speech appears when least expected, often disguised as something rather different. To return to my popular daily newspaper (which I read with the same painful pleasure as I find in the probing of a bad tooth)—this consistently uses the word "mum" in its articles and news items; not "mum" meaning silent but "mum" meaning mother. During World War II, the British government stuck up posters counseling discretion in talk lest the enemy be listening: "BE LIKE DAD—KEEP MUM." Here was condescension as well as juvenile punning, also willful denial of the fact that many mothers were doing war work and bringing in more money than their husbands in the services. The devisers of the slogan would be unlikely to call their own mothers "mum." It is one of the colloquial terms that worry me. I dislike it, though reason tells me that as it is a short word, it is useful for headlines (compare "wed" for marry and "bid" for attempt). Also, it is a term full of warm human connotations, suitable for a journal that prides itself on its warm human appeal. Yet I feel revulsion when I read "MUM SEES BABY DROWN" or "DI TO BE A MUM" (meaning that the Princess of Wales is to have a baby). I try to justify this feeling by saying that "mother" is full of associations of great dignity (England can be the mother of the free but hardly the mum of it), while the popular word is limited and vulgar. Yet I doubt if this explanation is really valid. The revulsion is too violent. I suspect the great demon of snobbishness; a diabolic voice whispers, "This is the word of your working-class childhood. It reeks of the clotheshorse in the kitchen, bread and dripping by the fire. Despise it."

Yet the term "vulgar" is so often applied to language that we have to consider what it really means. The vulgar tongue was once merely the language of the *vulgus* or people. Vulgarity seems now to signify the coarsening, the bringing low, of humanity's view of itself. We all consider man to be a creature capable of nobility, driven by high aspirations. Reduce man—which seems mainly the task of television commercials—to the status of a mere consumer, a gorger of junk food, a buyer of smart cars or state-of-the-art television receivers, and the human soul disappears. Language is considered vulgar when it reduces man to his basic appetites. These basic appetites exist, but they are qualified by something higher. Society admits that there is a place for vulgarity; large dictionaries (like the great slang compilation of Eric Partridge) are crammed with words suitable for man as a gorging, copulating, vomiting homunculus. But society also forces on the users of language a notion of "registers"—what is appropriate for this social situation or that. The register that calls the Queen Mother the "Queen Mum" swamps vulgarity in affection (*The Oxford English Dictionary* accepts the usage). But it would be inappropriate, meaning vulgar, to address the Queen Mother by that term at a royal garden party. The Speaker of the House of Commons was, in the spring of 1989, heard to mumble "Fuck off" in the direction of an obstreperous member. He had moved into the wrong register. Within the same House, a bill may be approved but should not be okayed. An American professor should not say: "Now we zero in on the nitty-gritty of this particular parameter." The registers are confused. Society decrees registers, but the language from which they are drawn is indifferent. It remains cool, neutral, objective.

Before we can study language coolly, we must strangle our group prejudices; we must explode a great number of hoary fallacies, themselves derived from emotional attitudes. As no language is either beautiful or ugly, so no language is intrinsically either superior or inferior to another. The fact that English has become a world auxiliary is no evidence that it is a *better* language than Basque or Finnish; its global spread is the result of a historical accident that is based on a fact of geography. Languages are developed in social groups, and each group develops the language it needs. If certain primitive peoples (like the Temiars of Malaysia) cannot count beyond two (sometimes we cannot ourselves: *uni*lateral, *bi*lateral, *multi*lateral), they are not in the least inconvenienced: they have what they want; when they want more they will get it. We had to use the word "other" to mean "what follows after first" before the Norman French gave us "second." As for "primitive communities," the term may be in order, but it is dangerous to talk of "primitive languages." In point of richness of grammar and luxuriance of vocabulary, the languages of certain "backward" peoples like the Eskimos are highly sophisticated.

No man, however learned or powerful, can exert control over a language, despite the "Newspeak" of George Orwell's *Nineteen Eighty-Four*. Languages change, and we cannot stop them from changing, nor can we determine the modes in which they shall change. It is not even possible to legislate for a language, to say what is right and what is wrong (questions of intelligibility are a different matter). If it is wrong to say "you was," then the educated men of the eighteenth century were wrong. If it is sluttish to drop one's 'h's, then Queen Elizabeth I was a slut. What we regard as errors are often merely survivals from an earlier form of the language. Characters in William Faulkner's novels of the American South say "hit" for "it." Lancashire dialect speakers says "it" for "its" (so did Shakespeare: "Come to it grandam and it grandam shall give it a plum"). These are good Anglo-Saxon. They may not be in use in SE, but who is to say that they are "wrong"?

And so we must avoid making hot judgments, laying down the law, nursing prejudices, waving jingoistic flags, bringing a spirit of petty parochialism to the world of human language. Languages are made by the people for the people, and people must use language as their needs dictate. No academy has the monopoly of "correctness"; no dictator knows best. If we want to understand the phenomenon of language—and it is an astonishing one—we must put on the working jacket of humility.

Our ignorance about the fundamentals of language is not solely derived from willful prejudice, natural inertia, or national apathy. We nurse a long tradition of amateurishly incompetent language teaching in our schools: many a sixth-form boy can read Racine with ease but have difficulty in asking a gendarme the way to the metro. Foreign tongues are taught after a fashion, but language itself—its nature, function, psychology, physiology, history—is almost totally neglected. Our English grammar books are often shamefully out of date: inaccuracies of definition and ineptitudes in terminology are perpetuated; pointless exercises are set; the findings of linguistic specialists do not reach the level of the classroom. Our teaching of foreign pronunciation is farcical (listen to our great political leaders trying to speak French). More than all this, the tyranny of the printed or written word prevails. We forget that language is primarily sounds, and that sounds existed long before visual signs were invented. The illiterates of the Third World are not dumb.

Thus, many people think that there are only five vowel sounds because there are only five (or six) vowel letters. Some teachers of literature are convinced that "Austrian armies awfully arrayed" shows an analogous phonetic pattern to "Boldly by batteries besieged Belgrade." J. B. Priestley, in his novel *Angel Pavement*, could describe the speech peculiarity of one of his characters thus: "He softened all his sibilants, putting an 'h' after every 's'." (Actually, instead of a voiced palatal fricative, he used an unvoiced one.) C. P. Snow, who was always telling literary men to learn more about science, was capable of the same sort of descriptive ineptitude: "She left the g's off all words ending in 'ing'." (No, she did not. She substituted an alveolar nasal for a velar one.) Snow did not appreciate that the science of language was the first science a writer should know about. Ivor Brown, a self-proclaimed philologist or word fancier, could write about "Shakespeare's instinctive feeling for the letter 'r'; time after time he was to play on its emotional vibration, especially when linked with the utter 'o'." Later he speaks of the "letter's potency." The unwitting high priest of this cult of "letters" was Arthur Rimbaud, who wrote a famous sonnet on the vowels; but Rimbaud was really concerned with the significance of the vowel letters in alchemy, not in language at all.

One feels strongly (at least I do) that practitioners of literature should at least show an interest in the raw material of their art. That awareness of sound demonstrated by the opening of Nabokov's *Lolita* is rare in modern literature: "Lolita, light of my life, fire of my loins. My sin, my soul. Lo-lee-ta: the tip of the tongue making a trip of three steps down from the palate to tap, at three, on the teeth. Lo. Lee. Ta." Nabokov recognized that the two 'l's of the name are different, or allophonic. Kingsley Amis's novels are accurate records of the way people speak. The middle-aged hero of *Girl, 20* tries to ingratiate himself with the young by overdoing assimilation. He says "vogka" and "corm beef" and "tim peaches." He mishears the trendy centralization of the front vowel 'a,' so that "flat" becomes "fluht." Printing conventions, and his public's ignorance of phonetics, limit Amis to a very sketchy representation of speech sounds, or phonemes. In this book I propose that the reader become familiar with the International Phonetic Alphabet, or IPA. The reader may shudder in advance, but we have to do something about the accurate visualization of speech.

I have an idealistic vision of phonetic symbols being added to our daily stock of alphabetic signs, so that I may tap the symbol /ə/ on my typewriter or word processor when I want to represent the sound that begins "apart" or ends "Asia." I can insert an IPA floppy disk into my IBM or Apple, but I want a keyboard with /ʃ/ and /ʒ/ on it.

As the world shrinks and the need for every educated man, woman, and child to know foreign languages grows more urgent, we have to devise techniques for learning them quickly and accurately. Our best beginning is an examination of the nature of language itself. There is no reason why this should be regarded as an expert study: we need no special equipment; a laboratory is set on our shoulders. Apart from the utility of such a study, there should be in everyone a natural curiosity that our systems of education have done nothing to foster and everything to dull. We can, with only a tinge of facetiousness, regard this as a matter of life and death. There used to be a Hebrew word signifying either an ear of corn or a stream in flood that in the Book of Judges (12:4–6) Jephthah used to distinguish between his own Gileadites and the fleeing Ephraimites. An Ephraimite, being in the opposed situation of J. B. Priestley's character, had no unvoiced palatal fricative: "Then said they unto him, Say now Shibboleth: and he said Sibboleth: for he could not frame to pronounce it right. Then they took him, and slew him at the passages of Jordan." A course in phonetics might have saved his life.

No society, whether human or animal, can exist without communication. Thoughts, desires, appetites, orders, have to be conveyed from one brain to another, and they cannot easily be conveyed directly. Only with telepathy do we find mind speaking straight to mind without the intermediacy of signs, and this technique is still odd enough to seem a television trick or a property of science fiction. The vast majority of sentient beings—men, women, cats, dogs, bees, horses—have to rely on signals, symbols of what they feel and think and want, and these signals can assume a vast number of forms. There is, indeed, hardly any limit to the material devices we can use to express what is in our minds: we can wave our hands, screw up our faces, shrug our shoulders, compose poems, scrawl on walls, carve signs on stone or wood, mold signs with clay or butter, puff sky messages from an aircraft, semaphore, heliograph, telephone, run a pirate radio transmitter, stick pins in dolls. A dog will scratch at a door if it wants to be let in; a cat will mew for milk; a hostess will ring a bell for a course to be changed; a pub customer will rap with a coin for service; the people in the flat upstairs will bang with a stick if our party is too noisy. One can fill pages with such obvious examples, not forgetting the language of flowers and the dances of honeybees, but one will always end up with human speech, and its visual records, as the most subtle, comprehensive, and exact system of communication the whole wide universe possesses.

And yet even this, which seems self-evident, will be questioned by experts in other fields of communication. The musical composer will contend that his art can go deeper and wider than words. We are moved by music in ways that words cannot describe, and such emotion can drive us to action—war, murder, love. There is evidently a sort of communication in music that operates at an unconscious level of the mind, and not only the human mind: animals can be powerfully affected by organized sound. Music and speech have something in common, and the community of basic material—rhythm, duration, and intonation—is best heard in song, which heightens the expressiveness of words. It may be said that music uses everything in speech except meaning, if by that we mean dictionary meaning. We can notate speech in the symbols of music, and the approach to poetry made by Gerard Manley Hopkins (1844–1889) implied a system of quasi-musical notation to clarify prosodic stress. Music is lauded as an international language: we do not need a Russian grammar to appreciate Tchaikovsky or Shostakovich. Nevertheless, some composers do not travel well. Elgar is not well appreciated outside the Anglo-Saxon community, though when we say that his works are "typically English" we have great difficulty in demonstrating precisely what we mean. His music will not be unintelligible on the basic level to a Russian or Frenchman, but its connotations—what lies beyond the mere notes—will make no impact. This is a subtle business. We hear too much music—our daily lives are flooded with it—but we still do not fully understand it. All art preserves mysteries that aesthetic philosophers tackle in vain. But in this book we shall hardly be concerned with art. Usefulness is our main theme, and particularly the usefulness of speech. Art is important, whether it is music, literature, painting, drama, or ballet, but it takes up only a small part of the total life of a society. Without speech, and the various visual notations of speech, human society would not be possible at all.

Having lauded one sign system in particular, let me return to signs in general. These can take two main forms, which, as with many opposed things, can shade gently into each other. They can be *conventional* or they can be *iconic*. "Iconic" derives from the Greek *eikon*, meaning an image, and it is thought by some that most primitive human signs try to present a recognizable image of the thought or desire that the signaler wishes to communicate. Thus, if we are in a foreign country and cannot speak the language, we can show hunger by going through the motions of putting something into our mouths and pretending to chew. This is iconic. The phrase "I'm hungry" is understood only by those who know some English. A convention long established is that those sounds stand for that particular human need, and the convention has to be specially learned. An intelligent cat, like the Siamese I once had, will show that it wants milk by licking an empty saucer. This seems to be a piece of iconic signaling: the sign is an image of the fulfillment of a need. What can we say of the sign regularly used in ballet to indicate love—the hands over the heart? Is this conventional or iconic? In a sense it overlaps both categories, for though we no longer believe that the heart as a physical organ is the seat of love, yet we accept for the moment that that outdated crude anatomy of the passions is correct: within a conventional acceptance the sign then becomes iconic. And so with the transfixed heart of the valentine or the heart as a verb meaning "love" on T-shirts. But if choreographers decided between themselves that a slap on the thighs should indicate love, then that would be a purely arbitrary symbol, a mere piece of conventional signaling.

The conventional and the iconic appear in all the arts, though the terms "representational" and "nonrepresentational" are better known. Painting and sculpture are, or were, expected to be iconic: many people are disappointed or even outraged if they do not get, in however distorted a manner, a recognizable image of a person or thing. Music is nearly always a language of conventional signs (whose "meaning" perhaps only the unconscious mind can recognize), but with composers like Richard Strauss there is a strong iconic urge. In Strauss's symphonic poem *Don Quixote* we can hear horns imitating the bleating of sheep; a wind machine gives us pure wind. The same instrument appears in Vaughan Williams's *Sinfonia Antarctica* to represent the howling of Antarctic gales. This kind of iconic composing is rare and is frequently condemned for its alleged crudity, but no composer faced with setting the words "He ascended into heaven" is likely to make his melodic line move downward.

Human speech is essentially a system of conventional signs, though theorists like Max Müller (1823–1900) once held that all language sprang out of a desire to imitate natural phenomena (this was called the "bowwow" theory). There are, in all languages, words that attempt a sonic image of the things they represent, just as the child's "quack-quack," meaning "duck," is an image of the duck's characteristic noise. "Splash" sounds like water, "froufrou" sounds like the rustle of skirts. "Pop" is right for the bursting of a balloon, and "boom," however feebly, suggests a bomb going off. (Interestingly, although perhaps not surprisingly, different peoples use quite different sonic images to represent the same sounds. Thus what is "bowwow" to the English is *faire ouâ-ouâ* to the French, and *wan-wan* to the Japanese.)

Even with purely visual images, it is possible to find a certain appositeness in the forms of words, though often only the linguist can explain this. Take "moon," for instance. It is the 'oo' or /u:/ (the colon indicates length) that is descriptive. The lips have to imitate a moon shape in order to give the right quality to the vowel. The back of the tongue is raised high, very close to the palate (which the Malay language calls the *langit* or sky of the mouth). The moon, when full, is both round and high. Many languages have an iconic word for our beloved satellite. Spanish and Italian have *luna* and Portuguese has *lua*. The French *lune* puts the front, not the back, of the tongue high, suggesting a new moon rather than plenilunarity (forgive my fancifulness). German, with *Mond*, and also Anglo-Saxon with *mona*, bring the moon down the sky. Finnish *kuu* is high enough. Hebrew *levanah*, Yiddish *levoneh*, Japanese *tsuki*, Swahili *mwezi*, Greek *fengari*, and Arabic *qamar* are far from iconic; the Arabic seems to turn the moon into a rasping scimitar. Obviously, there is no need to make a word iconic if the language does not wish it. To return to English, a word like "little" seems apt, for the i-sound (/ɪ/ in the IPA) is made by narrowing the passage between the front of the tongue and the palate, suggesting that only something very small could creep through. To give the impression of even greater littleness, the form "leetle" is sometimes roguishly used. The ee-sound or /i:/ is even higher than /ɪ/, making the space between tongue and palate only big enough for something microscopic to creep through. With "teeny-weeny" we are on the borders of invisibility.

This class of iconic words is so small, or leetle, as to be virtually negligible. In any case, some very important words—such structural mortar as "if," "when," "so"—can never have had a corresponding image in the outside world. Language is arbitrary, conventional, and has been so from the beginning; only the poet can invent a golden age of iconic language in which thing and word enjoyed a blissful marriage. The device of onomatopoeia—sound imitating sense—is beloved of lyric poets like Keats ("The murmurous haunt of flies on summer eves") and Tennyson ("The moan of doves in immemorial elms"), but there are severe limits to what it can do. Still, a definition of poetry as "conventional language trying to be iconic" is worth arguing about.

Whatever speech does, we cannot doubt that the earliest attempts to represent words by visual signs were iconic. Chinese symbols still show, in varying degrees of clarity, ancient attempts to *draw* the referent of the word (that is, the thing in the outside world that the word represents), and, when this direct representation failed, to use metaphor for rendering the abstract concrete. And so with Egyptian picture writing, which is full of recognizable gods, lions, snakes, birds, and water pots. Our own alphabet, as we shall see later, is ultimately derived from hieroglyphics, but all picture elements have long disappeared: the essence of the alphabetic system is its conventionality. Only in the letter O, which seems to come from an Egyptian drawing of an eye, do we find anything approaching an iconic purpose: the letter represents the shape of the mouth when pronouncing the o-sound; here is the "moon" business in reverse. But it does not work in "love" or "woman." Arbitrariness is the very essence of all signs above the level of what we see on our highways.

An alphabet is a series of signs representing signs. The sounds I make when saying "man" stand for something in the outside world; the letters that make up MAN stand for those sounds. Thus, with a visual system of representation, we are two removes from reality. We are three removes from reality when we use a system like Braille or Morse: the dots and dashes or embossed symbols stand for alphabetic letters; the alphabetic letters stand for sounds; the sounds stand for what exists in the mind or the world outside. It is as well to stay as close to reality as possible; that is why the study of language is a study of sounds and what sounds can do.

Why and how and when did man start using those organizations of sounds that we call human language? We can only guess. In the days when even savants had to accept, in the manner of Christian fundamentalists in the American Deep South, the literal truth of the Book of Genesis, language had to be not a divine invention but a system of naming devised, on God's orders, by Adam. All human beings had a common language that was confounded into mutually unintelligible dialects when men had the effrontery to build the Tower of Babel. God was angry at the erection of a ladder to heaven, and though he could not make language, he could unmake it. Man lost Eden, and also lost the perfect pre-Babelian tongue. Magic could perhaps recover that language. Perhaps fragments of the Adamic system still adhered to the language of fallen man. If, the cabalists taught, you could learn the cabalistic approach to the word "gold," you might get information about the nature of gold itself. This is close to the *cheng ming* doctrine. John Locke (1632–1704), harbinger of the new rationalism, set his face against scholarly superstition and paved the road toward today's Tower of Babel—a fair term for the many-roomed mansion of language study, in which nobody agrees with anybody else.

Adamic language, like the myth of Genesis itself, assumes a sudden act of creation after an infinite silence. But all animals, and man is an animal, have always used sound to signal needs or emotions. The sounds that human beings use in speech differ from animal sounds in being fully *structured*. True, birdsong may be said to be structured, though its structures are limited. I read recently (in *Whistled Languages*, by R. G. Busnel and A. Classe) of a blackbird that "copied whistles that for years a man had used to signal his cat. The model whistled rather roughly four notes between 1 and 2 kHz, with variations of pitch and rhythm. The blackbird transposed the whole motif up a fifth and introduced ornaments as one introduces embellishments in eighteenth-century music." Parrots and mynah birds imitate human speech, though nobody understands why or even how. The nature of speech as we use it presupposes something that neither birds nor animals possess—a kind of language machine in the skull that is capable of making a literally infinite number of new structures. Birds have a repertoire of songs, but they cannot compose music. There is, potentially, an infinite number of symphonies in the world, as there is an infinite number of poems. This implies a unique structuring capacity that only man possesses.

The structuralist philosophy that has come out of France, and of which Claude Lévi-Strauss (b. 1908) must be considered the greatest exponent, states that man, in order to make sense of the world, imposes upon the swirl of phenomena outside himself a series of basic patterns. The color spectrum is a continuum, with violet merging into indigo into blue into green into yellow into orange into red. Man is capable of isolating colors, opposing one to another, and making a system of signals out of the opposition: in a traffic signal red opposes yellow and both oppose green. Speech, however, is the fundamental human structure, and the phoneme and the morpheme are the basic types of structural opposition. A phoneme is a speech sound. The phoneme /t/ opposes /d/: Both are made in precisely the same way, but there is vibration of the vocal cords for /d/, none for /t/. "The cat sat on the mat" employs two kinds of morpheme—free forms like the three rhyming words, bound forms or helper morphemes like the others. Vowel opposes consonant. A remarkably economical selection of sounds, so structured, suffices to make an infinitude of speeches and write an infinitude of books. Followers of Lévi-Strauss, like Roland Barthes (1915–1980), have attempted to apply a linguistic model to other social structures, particularly (since Barthes was a Parisian) to the haute couture and the haute cuisine. A dish can follow a language pattern, so that a meat noun can have an adjectival vegetable, and even an off-the-peg suit has segments corresponding to the parts of a statement (a tie may be considered a superfluous adjective in some contexts: much depends on the social "register" required). Dress, especially the dress of fashionable women, is more for information than for either modesty or warmth.

It may be that primitive man communicated with visual signs before he developed into a talker, but there is no reason to suppose that his meaningful movements of hands, face, and body were accompanied by silence; he was probably never a dumb gesticulator, a sort of silent Tarzan film. I imagine early human society as full of noise—babblings and gurglings diversified by grunts and howls—though such noise might be a mere by-product of tongue and lip movements corresponding to the movements of bodily gesture. It is helpful to think of the present relationship of speech and gesture in reverse. We all use nods, shrugs, arm movements, smiles, and frowns to help out speech; perhaps our ancestors used sound to help out gesture. When sound, responding to the structure-making engine being slowly set up in the skull, turned into speech, it might have been recognized as an invaluable means of establishing and maintaining social contact in the event of the speaker's being cut off from his fellows. Bodily gesture has a very limited visual range: stones, trees, whole forests, may get in the way of it; darkness will render it quite useless. Speech is a kind of light in darkness.

At this early stage in its development, it was, by our standards, a very dim light. It could not produce the twenty volumes of *The Oxford English Dictionary*. It had little to do with "meaning" as we understand the term. Speech was, and still is, a means of establishing or maintaining contact with other members of our social group. The anthropologist Bronislaw Kasper Malinowski (1884–1942) used the term "phatic communion" to describe this kind of activity. Talk about the weather rarely indicates much real interest in the weather: it is just something to say, a means of making contact or showing friendliness. We can feel strongly for primitive man in the dark; for all our science, we have not fully overcome our fear of it or, when human contact is lost, our sense of devastating loneliness in it. Our ancestors, separated from such contact in the big incomprehensible blackness, must have chattered incessantly.

Phatic communion has a great deal to do with the making of literature, which, after all, may be regarded primarily as a noninformative medium of human contact. The babbling and bubbling of Elizabethan stage clowns goes along with the puns and the euphuisms; the garrulousness of pamphleteers like Nashe and Greene is more phatic than meaningful. The products of a golden age of literature seem the natural expression of life in a small, warm, compact, very human society—that of Shakespeare's London. What was once the heart of culture no longer produces much of it: its concern is the market for culture. It is a huge depersonalized abstraction, no longer a society at all. Literature, as cities grow, becomes increasingly an expression of loneliness and exile—a cry in the dark, whistling in the dark.

Out of the chattering of primitive man, something like language as we know it was eventually to crystallize. We tend to think of a language as deliberately architectural—a blueprint grammar, a dictionary-load of bricks. This is partly because of the Genesis myth—filling a garden with words—and partly because of the way in which we learn foreign languages: we start off with a silence and slowly make it less silent. We think, in fact, of the conscious creation of a structure out of verbal atoms: our unit is the word, the smallest possible verbal form. But the unit of primitive man would be more like a phrase, a clause, a total statement. He would learn to associate a segment of the flow of speech with a particular experience to be described or expressed. When we see a sunrise, we instinctively analyze into particles: sun, east, sky, red, gold, rising. Primitive man would see the process as a single experience, indivisible. The analytical faculty comes very late in the evolution of humankind. The isolation of the word, the breaking down of language into the stuff of grammars and dictionaries, belongs to the last few centuries. The Romans are, comparatively speaking, our near neighbors in time, but they lacked the analytical equipment to dissect their language as today's grammarians have dissected it. Before the scholars devised the classificatory system on which our own is based, they had to accept the complex of Latin as it was.

Primitive language, then, must not be thought of as a sort of pidgin, with words like little painful barks all separated out. "They will be loved" is the English for the Latin *amabuntur*. The English way—and English is a progressive, self-simplifying language: the technical term is *syncretic*—is to analyze a complex experience into irreducible particles: four words to the one of Latin. Old Western languages like Latin, Greek, and Sanskrit are *synthetic*: they build up long words and express everything that appertains to time and space with inflections. We all remember, if we belong to that dying breed that learned Latin, the various inflections of the singular form of the word for a table— *mensa, mensae, mensae, mensam, mensa*. English has an unchanging singular form "table," and we express relationships by means of additional words: "to a table," "with a table," and so on. The oldest languages of all must, we think, have been highly synthetic, with verb forms and noun forms of great length.

We accept that the main function of language is to convey wishes, thoughts, and feelings within a particular social group, though its original purpose may have been mainly phatic. Our highly complex modern societies depend on the precise functioning of such communication. But, as science and technology develop, it becomes more and more evident that language as we have known it is not precise enough. Mathematicians and physicists, to say nothing of engineers, rely on signals capable of single unambiguous meanings. The words of ordinary language tend to ambiguity and vagueness: in every serious discussion much time has to be spent on redefining common terms like "love," "justice," "freedom." Language has, in fact, many of the qualities possessed by human beings themselves: it tends to be emotional when pure reason is required, it is sometimes unsure of what it means, it changes form, meaning, and sound. It is slippery, elusive, hard to fix, define, or delimit.

So, when we talk about a language—English, French, Russian, or Sanskrit—we refer to a process rather than to a thing. English consists of its future as well as its past and present, and when we discuss an English word we may be talking of things not yet known. A language consists of potentialities whose nature we can only guess at, though its genetic qualities help to determine its development. But, if we try to grasp the flow of language at that nonexistent point called "now," we are still in the dark as to its boundaries, and we cannot be sure of its content. How many words are there in English? We cannot say. It is not enough to point to the number of words in the 1989 *Oxford English Dictionary*, because no dictionary, however large, can pretend to be complete, nor can a dictionary take in all the derivatives of a word. Fresh words are coined every day; borrowing from other languages goes on incessantly. If, in my own home, my family uses invented words like "shlerp," "focklepoff," and "arpworthy," we are entitled to regard them as part of English. They certainly belong to no other language, and they are recognizable linguistic forms—just as "chortle," "brillig," and "frabjous," inventions of Lewis Carroll, belong to English. It is best to regard the language as a growing corpus of words and structures that nobody can know entirely but upon which anyone can draw at any time—a sort of unlimited bank account. It is not just the sum total of what has been spoken and written; it is also what *can* be spoken and written. It is actual and potential. In another sense, it is a code, always ready for individual acts of encoding and decoding.

I see that I am arriving at a point where clarification of the phenomenon of language had best be handed over to experts. I am, like you, merely a user of language, though, as its exploitation is my profession, I am drawn to a consideration of its mysteries every time I hit my typewriter or stroke the keyboard of my word processor. My student days were concerned with philology, which no longer seems to exist. Linguistics has been slow to enter the academic curricula. Let us make a brief survey of what, though it functions in no laboratories, must be regarded as a science.

2.

THE SCIENCE OF LANGUAGE

Linguistics as a discipline hardly existed before the nineteenth century—despite some remarkable intuitions as far back as the medieval Roger Bacon—and the nineteenth-century linguists concentrated on what is termed historico-comparative linguistics. Men like Rasmus Khristian Rask (1787–1832) and Jacob Grimm (1785–1863)—one of the two brothers who collected the appropriately grim fairy tales of the German *Volk*—were concerned with the processes that made the Germanic tongues emerge from the Indo-European mother language (more about this in a later chapter). August Schleicher (1821–1868) attempted to reconstruct that remote and unrecorded language through comparison of the features possessed by all its children. One of the great inquirers into ancient phonology—or the sound systems of early languages—was Ferdinand de Saussure. Although his dates—1857–1913—proclaim him as belonging to the age of historico-comparative studies, it is Saussure whom we take to be the father of modern linguistics. This is the age of descriptive linguistics, or structural linguistics, and the first scholar to present a full-bodied theory of the structural principle was Saussure.

He was a Swiss professor whose lectures were collected and published after his death by two of his students—Charles Bally and Albert Sechehaye—under the title *Cours de linguistique générale*. The work appeared in English comparatively recently—in 1959, as *Course in General Linguistics*—but the actual translation was probably supererogatory: the original had long since sown its seeds. Saussure's importance lies mainly in the power of the definitions he made concerning the nature of language. Thus, he attempted to define the act of speech in terms of a connection between thought and sound. A is talking to B, and the process of conversation is presented as a circuit that opens in the brain, where mental facts or *concepts* are associated with sound images used to express them. A given concept unlocks a sound image—this is a psychological event. But then a physiological event supervenes: the brain sends out an impulse corresponding to the image, aimed at the organs used in producing sounds. The sounds travel from A's mouth to B's ear—a purely physical process. The circuit continues with B, but now there is a reversal of the process, with the sound image going from B's ear to B's brain, where the psychological associations of the image lead to the corresponding concept. The concept itself is not a linguistic entity, but sound unrelated to concept is nothing but noise. Sounds are made meaningful by being related to concepts: in other words, language may be regarded as the link between a sound and a thought. To use Saussure's terms, the concept is the *signified*, and the expression of the thought the *signifier*. What comes out of the association between the two may be called the *linguistic sign*. Our task is to understand the nature of this sign.

The sign, Saussure points out, is essentially an arbitrary thing: there is no inner relationship between signifier and signified. Signs are mostly immutable, language is peculiarly inert—we receive it from the remote past and pass it on to the remote future. No one can fight against accepting the forms that it takes. "Because the sign is arbitrary," Saussure says, "it follows no law other than that of tradition, and because it is based on tradition, it is arbitrary." (I follow Wade Baskin's translation.) Yet, as we all know too well, forms and meanings do change, and Saussure attributes change to a relaxation or displacement of the tie between signified and signifier. He takes as an example the German *Drittel*, which means "one third." It used to be *Dritteil*, in which we clearly see the form *Teil*, meaning "part." The concept itself remains unchanged, but there has been a shift of relationship between the signifier and the signified: this has altered the *value* of the linguistic sign. The question of value is important, and it depends on the relationship a sign possesses to the total vocabulary. The English word "sheep," the Spanish *carnero*, the French *mouton*, have the same signification but not the same value. "Sheep" cannot mean the cooked meat of the animal—"mutton" is used for that—but the French and Spanish words make no distinction between the beast in the field and the meat in the kitchen. Thus the *values* of the Romance terms differ from that of the English term, but the *signification* is the same.

Another distinction Saussure made that has become basic to linguistic thinking is that between *parole* and *langue*, aspects of the totality known as *langage* (translation of the terms is awkward and not often attempted). *Parole* is language as the individual speaker uses it—the physical actuality that is never exactly identical between two speakers of the language. *Langue* is not spoken by anyone: it is the sum total of all the *paroles* spoken by individuals, but it remains abstract, generalized, a social phenomenon, an institution only minimally changeable by the individual speaker or writer. It is a social entity limited in time: *langue* is contemporary to the society that expresses itself through it. Once "time" is mentioned we find ourselves using two other Saussurian terms that have been fundamental to linguistic studies—*synchronic* and *diachronic*. Synchronic linguistics deals with linguistic events occurring in a given period of time—the "vertical" approach—while diachronic linguistics is concerned with language moving through time and hence changing—the "horizontal" approach. The two studies require somewhat different investigatory techniques, since what occurs in time—like a change in sound or structure—is unwilled and unconscious, while what happens in a static slab of time is conscious and willed. Thus, we can hear the difference between the vowels of *man* and *men*, but during the Great Vowel Shift (which might have started to take place while King Henry V was fighting at Agincourt, or perhaps earlier, perhaps later), nobody was, presumably, conscious that the vowel of "shine" was changing from a French or Italian /i/ in the direction of the diphthong /aɪ/ that speakers of RP use today.

The term *sign* is the great Saussurian legacy. Language is a system of signs, arbitrary in form and only to be understood in terms of the whole system that is a given language. Language is also a *structure*, whose parts can be understood only in relation to each other. The new science of semiotics, which deals with signs in general, whether linguistic or not, springs out of Saussure. Structuralism, which I referred to a few pages back, is both an anthropological discipline that examines social cultures in terms of their signs, and a mode of approach to literature that concentrates less on meaning (the most difficult part of language study) than the way sign relates to sign within a literary structure.

An important movement in linguistics that found some of its starting points in the writings (or transcriptions of lectures) of Saussure but then deviated from them was the so-called Prague School (originally *le cercle linguistique de Prague*). Their leading figure was Nikolas Trubetzkoy (1890–1938), although Roman Jakobson (1896–1982), who became a professor at Harvard, was able to do more to publicize and extend the activities of the movement. It was the original Prague scholars who called their approach to language a "phonological" one. Phonetics, as we shall see, or hear, in some detail later, is concerned with speech sounds for their own sake, as interesting entities in themselves, not as aspects of discourse. Phonology deals with those sounds in terms of their function, the manner in which they behave within the total structure of a given language. Trubetzkoy said that this approach was perhaps wholly Slavic in origin, and he expressed himself as indebted to J. Baudouin de Courtenay, a Polish professor at the University of Moscow, who saw as early as 1870 the need to distinguish between what a sound is in itself and how that sound is used in the structure of a language. Languages, according to the Prague School, have their own special and idiosyncratic ways of ordering speech sounds into patterns—*Sprachgebilde*—but essential to all such structures is that principle of opposition or meaningful contrast that in the study of culture generally, is seen to be an aspect of all sign systems. We learn about /p/ through contrasting it with /b/ in such word pairs as pole:bowl, rip:rib. Differences between sounds that do not signify differences of meaning are not phonemic or (a term they originally preferred) phonematic. They are outside the field of phonological study. The phonetician is interested in the fact that English has two 'l' sounds—the "clear l" that begins "lily" and the "dark l" that ends "dull." But the phonologist knows that it makes no difference to the conveyance of meaning which of the two is used. The Welsh get on well enough with a clear 'l' in all positions, and the Americans—this is one of the salient characteristics of their speech—never use any 'l' but a dark one. The phonetician cares but the phonologist does not. It was Trubetzkoy's mission to develop a set of "contrast criteria" for identifying phonemic oppositions.

The point primarily made is that while a middle C played on a flute is a fixed and absolute and wholly measurable sound (we can count the vibrations per second), there is nothing so solid about the speech sound we call a phoneme. A *significant* sound—a sound, that is, concerned with determining meaning—is only *relatively* different from other significant sounds. Modes of opposition can vary from the very wide to the very narrow. For example, /a/ and /i/ (the first sound is in the French *patte*, the second in the French or English *machine*) are alike only in that they are vowels. This is "multilateral opposition." German /k/ (as in *Katze*) and German /x/ (the rasp at the end of *Bach*) are totally alike except for the one distinguishing factor of the first's being a stop (back of tongue and soft palate meet and then part; the temporary stoppage of air is followed by a small explosion: another word for it is "plosive") and the second's being a fricative (back of tongue and soft palate rub each other: there is audible friction). This kind of opposition is called "bilateral." "Proportional opposition" occurs when one pair of contrasting phonemes has as its contrasting feature a property that is the distinguishing mark of other pairs. Thus, /p/ and /b/ differ only in being respectively unvoiced and voiced (the vocal cords vibrate for /b/ but not for /p/): this is termed a contrast of "sonority."

But /t/ - /d/ and /k/ - /g/ exhibit exactly the same difference. We get "isolated opposition" between the Spanish /r/ of *pero* ("but"), and the /r̄/ of *perro* ("dog"). The second r-roll is longer than the first. Length of sound is not a contrastive feature of any other pair of phonemes in Spanish. Phonemes can contrast in some positions but not in others (those two Spanish phonemes oppose each other only between vowels), and then "neutralization" occurs. This kind of pairing leads to an accurate and economical inventory of the speech sounds of a language, and it also helps in the study of the history of a language, indicating why certain sound changes took place or, presumably, are likely to take place.

Saussure had said that the diachronic and synchronic approaches to language must be distinct and separate, but the special preoccupations of the Prague School led its most distinguished scholars to maintain—in 1928, at the First International Congress of Linguistics at The Hague—that the phonological approach was as applicable to diachronic as to synchronic linguistics. A language, so it would appear, wishes to observe certain principles of economy and symmetry—so the synchronic examination of the phonologists indicates—and the history of a phonemic system may show a movement in the direction of establishing an ever more harmonious and economic sound pattern. If, for example, a language has /p/ - /b/ opposition in it (*pok:bok*, say, *sap:sab*, and so on) and also /t/ - /d/ opposition (*tuk:duk*, *sut:sud*, etc.) but a /k/ that does not significantly oppose to /g/ (*kus* but no *gus*, *sok* but no *sog*), then three possible results in the fullness of time are foreseeable. A /k/ - /g/ opposition may appear to complete the pattern. All oppositions will disappear, leaving only /p/ and /t/ and /k/. Or, the third possibility, /k/ will disappear, leaving /p/ - /b/ and /t/ - /d/. Italian can make no significant, or clearly audible, contrast between *gli* in *famiglia* and *li* in *Italia* (or the *gli* in *aglio*—"garlic"— and the *li* in *olio*—"oil"). Consequently one of the two has to go. As one sees today from illiterate scrawls of "ITAGLIA" on Roman walls and monuments, the *li* may be leaving the language, though literate spelling will not show it for a very long time. The opposition of "high functional yield"—like the /p/ - /b/ of English, which produces a very large number of "minimal pairs" (peat:beat, pit:bit, pack:back, and so on)—is less subject to decay than one of "low functional yield." In the Spanish of Andalusia, the fact that no meaningful contrast exists between the *y* of *vaya* ("go!") and the *ll* of *calle* ("street") has meant the virtual disappearance of *ll* as a phoneme if not as a written sign. Uneducated workers in Algeciras spell *yo* as *llo* and *llegar* as *yegar*.

One of the problems of linguistic studies resides in that area where a phoneme identifies itself through the kind of opposition that determines difference of meaning. The study of meaning, semantics, tends to take the inquirer out of the area of language and drop him in the world of "culture," where the establishment of meanings depends on the disciplines of such sciences as psychology, sociology, and anthropology. The linguistic anthropologist may find it difficult to reconcile the two sciences he has yoked together and may end up—like Claude Lévi-Strauss—as a structuralist looking in primitive societies for the kind of pattern he has already found in language (the general may then come out of the special). Leonard Bloomfield (1887–1949), perhaps the greatest linguistic scholar America has produced, was logical in rejecting an approach to language analysis that depended on nonlinguistic criteria for its results. He insisted that meaning had to be investigated through formal—that is to say, structural—differences in a language. It is, according to him, structural differences that determine semantic differences.

This sounds mechanistic. It cuts out the Saussurian "concept." Like the behavioristic psychology of Watson in America and Pavlov in

Russia, it is distrustful of the "soul." Bloomfield redefined the phoneme so as to cleanse it of its semantic significance at the same time
he saw that it could not, like the raw materials of the exact sciences,
be measured accurately by instruments. If a phoneme is neither a
determinant of meaning nor an acoustic entity, what can it be? Bloomfield described it as a "feature of language structure": the phonemes
of a language, seen as a bundle of abstractions (though a rather
elegant bundle), are used to describe various properties of the utterances of that language. This does not mean that Bloomfield was
indifferent to semantic inquiry. He saw merely that the "statement
of meanings is . . . the weak point in language study." We define
meanings by demonstration, by circumlocution, by translation, but
none of these techniques is really satisfactory. "We can define the
names of minerals, for example, in terms of chemistry and mineral-
ogy . . . but we have no precise way of defining words like *love* or
hate." He saw meaning as the situation in which utterance on the part
of A and response on the part of B takes place, and perhaps this is
as far as the study of language should go in this difficult field. The
importance of Bloomfield lies precisely in his desperate desire to
make linguistics as glorious a discipline as physics or chemistry.

The best-known name in modern American linguistics is, without
doubt, that of Noam Chomsky (b. 1928), whose theories have superseded the behaviorist approach of Bloomfield. Chomsky's fame rests
not only on his linguistic pronouncements but on his political radical-
ism, expressed in highly critical utterances on American foreign policy. There are some admirers of Chomsky who see his linguistic and
political sides as emanations of a single conviction. For as Chomsky
emphasizes the fundamental structural similarity of all languages,
despite surface differences to which too much attention is commonly
paid, so, by extension, he wishes to emphasize the fundamental one-
ness of humankind and the criminality of trying to impair this unity
through wars, whether hot or cold.

Chomsky has provided the theoretical basis of what is termed
"transformational-generative grammar"—or just "transformational
grammar"—which seems to derive from a view held as far back as
the Middle Ages, to the effect that all languages have roughly the
same sort of grammar. In the sense that a statement made in ancient
Sanskrit and one made in modern Chinese both exhibit such features
as substantive categories (parts of speech) and formal categories (subject and predicate), this is evidently true. True, Japanese does not

properly recognize the part of speech we call the adjective, seeing it as a kind of verb (as in *Sono kutsu wa atarashii*—"Those shoes are new"—the verb element being contained in *atarashii*, "new"), but its statements function in a way that admits the description of things. Chomsky is near enough right in pronouncing a basic structural unity for all languages. The German philologist Karl Wilhelm von Humboldt (1767–1835), who was a Chomskian before his time, used the term "inner form" to describe the basic makeup of all languages. Chomsky prefers "deep structure," to which he opposes "surface structure"—meaning the superficial divergencies that mask the basic identity. Out of this notion glimmers the possibility of fulfillment of the old dream of a world language, based on the establishment of a corpus of "linguistic universals."

If we step back and look at the complexity of the language we ourselves use, it seems rather astonishing that we have been able to learn it at all with comparatively so little fuss. Add two or three or more foreign languages to our endowment, and the astonishment is greater still. For a language seems to contain an infinitude of structures, and one can go through life, apparently, without repeating oneself unduly. I have written fifty-odd books, and I should imagine that all their sentences are different. And there is the sense that there is always some new statement to create. The potentialities of a language are so vast that we must wonder sometimes at ourselves: how do we manage to know so much? Language learning has little to do with exceptional intelligence, and one has to conclude that what seems so complex is really quite simple—or else the rules of language are built into the human brain, as much a human endowment as the instinct of self-preservation.

Chomsky says that linguistic competence is achieved when a speaker has mastered the set of rules by which language is generated. The rules are comparatively straightforward, and the human brain is somehow disposed to the mastering of them. To learn a language is not to memorize a vocabulary but to acquire a set of rules. To the transformational grammarian, a complete grammar of a given language is the full corpus of operational procedures needed for producing all the acceptable sentences of that language. This grammar would be a copy, or rather a model, of the "grammar mechanism" already built into the human organism. Let us see how such a model is made.

A language, according to Chomsky's definition, is "a set—finite or infinite—of sentences, each finite in length and constructed out of a finite set of elements." He does not define a sentence, assuming, fairly enough, that such a structure can be recognized intuitively. Any "well-formed" sentence in English (we can call the sentence S) contains a noun phrase (NP) and a verb phrase (VP)—in other words, a subject and a predicate. A noun phrase must have at least a noun—like "man" or "horse"—or a pronoun—like "I" or "you"—but it can also have determiners (D) like "this" or "the" or "every." A verb phrase has to have a verb, but it can also have complements of various kinds (Compl), such as adjectives, adverbs, and noun phrases. In the following we have a set of "rewrite rules" for generating basic sentence patterns in English. The arrow means "rewrite" and the items bracketed are optional.

Rule 1: S
Rule 2: S → NP + VP
Rule 3: NP → (D+) N
Rule 4: VP V → (+ Compl)
$$\text{Rule 5: Compl} \rightarrow \begin{bmatrix} \text{(NP+) NP} \\ \text{Adj} \\ \text{Adv} \end{bmatrix}$$

This "grammar" machine can determine most of the basic sentences in the language. If we follow all the procedures indicated, these rules will give linear sequences of terminal symbols or markers—what Chomsky calls "terminal strings"—in this manner:

1. D + N + V + Adj   ("The man is old";
                                        "His horse is strong")
2. D + N + V + Adv   ("All babies cry frequently";
                                        "The girl smiles sweetly")
3. D + N + V   ("The dog barks";
                                        "Every man dies")
4. D + N + V (+ D + N)   ("The boy writes [his brother]
    + D + N   a letter")

With a complete list of terminal strings, all the basic sentences possible to English can be worked out. By means of *transformations*, the phrase-structure grammar can be expanded to cover all combinations, rearrangements, additions, and deletions of the basic sentence. So far, however, we have in mind only sentences in the "active voice." To create a passive version of the example in (4) above—"A letter is written by the boy"—we need a formula like this:

$$Np^1 + V + NP^2 \text{ Tpas} \qquad NP^2 + be + V\text{-}en(+ by + NP^1)$$

NP^1 stands for the first $D + N$ in (4), and NP^2 stands for the second. Tpas is the symbol for "passive transformation." V-*en* means the past participle of the main verb and *be* stands for the auxiliary verb that goes with it to make the passive construction.

Since Chomsky, who may be said to have started a quiet revolution, professional linguists have been ferociously busy at the work of propounding linguistic rules—not the prescriptive rules of the classroom but laws intended to have scientific validity. Thus, we pronounce "telegraph" with a stress on the first syllable but "telegraphic" with a stress on the penultimate, and so for telescope:telescopic or atom: atomic and so on. The old way was to list the pairs, showing the stress shift but not explaining it. Now we can say: "Stress in the adjective is regularly attracted toward the syllable immediately preceding the adjective-forming suffix -*ic*." Given a new word, say "agronome," we will know how to pronounce "agronomic." But how about "arithmetic"? "Arithmetic" with the antepenult stressed is a noun, but the adjective "arithmetic" obeys the general rule. As Neil Smith and Deirdre Wilson put it in their book *Modern Linguistics: The Result of Chomsky's Revolution*, "Descriptive adequacy here involves providing an explanation for facts at one level of analysis, phonology, by reference to constructs at a different level, syntax." Perhaps you had better read that several times.

The terminology of modern linguistics can be formidable, although no more so than a word-processor manual, but it can also be endearingly down to earth. "A meaningless element which has syntactic but no semantic function"—in other words, is needed for a well-made sentence but means nothing—is called a "dummy." "It upsets me that he left" or "It gives me a pain to eat cold fried fish" has an "it" that is part of the structure but that adds nothing to the meaning: the "it" is a dummy. A "tough-movement" relates the object of an embedded clause to the subject of a higher clause, as with "It is hard to lasso elephants" and "Elephants are hard to lasso" (for "hard," if you will, read "tough"). Deep structures are now argued about a great deal.

Chomsky said that "John gave a book to Bill" and "Bill was given a book by John," being synonymous statements, shared a common deep structure. But "Bill received a book from John" clearly means the same as those two and yet, because of the lexical, or verbal, difference ("receive," not "give"—active or passive), cannot be paired with either in terms of deep structure. Now Chomsky's successors are saying that it is not a matter of the word but of the meaning, or, to be exact, of generative semantics. But how about "John killed Bill" and "John caused Bill to die"? Do these have a deep structure in common?

Chomsky's contribution to modern linguistics is regarded by some scholars as of no great importance. The British linguist Robert Dixon has said that "his linguistics is mostly concerned with formalizing previous ideas of linguistics in terms of logical rules, and making explicit various intuitions about language patterns." But this may in itself be a major advance—the provision of new tools for grammarians. Chomsky himself has stressed the implications of his theory for a deeper knowledge of the nature of language itself, not just any given language. We can hardly doubt the importance of "the discovery that certain features of a given language can be reduced to universal properties of language, and explained in terms of these deeper aspects of linguistic form."

I have mentioned, very superficially I fear, a few of the major names in linguistics. There are many more, and there are many books, most of them very forbidding to the amateur. The study of language is no longer an easily penetrated province. It is as tough a science as nuclear biology or astrophysics. But, in this book, we can more or less ignore the science and concentrate on the technology. We do not want to disassemble and reassemble an internal combustion engine; we merely wish to drive a car.

3.

LANGUAGE IN ACTION

A word in a dictionary is very much like a car in a mammoth automobile show—full of potential but temporarily inactive. To get the car on the road, a whole complex of things is required—fuel and a driver at the wheel, direction, and traffic signs. To get a word moving we need the devices that come under the heading of grammar. Grammar is a technique for describing words in action. We can divide it into two compartments—morphology and syntax. Morphology gives us the inventory of word forms in any given language and shows us how to construct them; syntax provides us with the rule for combining words into "higher-order structures" like phrases and sentences. The two aspects of grammar are very closely connected. For instance, if it is a rule in English morphology that the present third person singular of a noun ends in '-s,' as in "likes" or "loves," this makes little sense until the principles of syntax are invoked, with, say, "John" as a singular noun (or noun phrase or NP, to follow Chomsky) governing "likes" or "loves" and completing that state of being with another NP, such as "Jill" or "grilled kidneys." As the modern grammarians put it, Roger Lass, for instance, in *The Shape of English* (1987), "Inflectional morphology generally can't be interpreted except in relation to the syntactic structures that it represents." I shall try to make things less technically frightening.

Because grammar looks like a science and yet does not behave like one (words often jump out of their classificatory cages), teachers and textbook writers have been wary of digging too deeply into it. A lot of out-of-date conceptions used to lie fossilized in grammar books, and their makers—who often had stockbroker incomes—did not like to admit this. Nor did the inertia of teachers or the examiner's love of the unambiguous encourage the revision of the thirty-third impression. It was best to let things carry on as they were: let sleeping dogmas lie. The pupil-examinees have not wanted fresh light on grammar; they have merely wanted to get rid of it.

Grammarians like the one whose funeral Robert Browning celebrated in a famous poem made their appearance at the time of the New Learning. They wanted to analyze the linguistic data offered by Greek and Latin (an English grammar school was, strictly speaking, a Latin grammar school); inevitably when they turned to the description of the way the vernacular behaved, they brought their classical grammatical apparatus with them. Most of the languages of Europe were then analyzed as though they *ought* to be the tongue of Homer or of Cicero. Some grammarians smacked the bottom of English because it had carelessly lost its genders and most of its case endings. This was not cricket, meaning not Latin. Fortunately for them, few European grammarians were ever called upon to examine a language like Chinese or Tibetan and equip it with a descriptive apparatus. The fact is that English, French, and the rest of the European tongues (except Basque, perhaps) will, to some extent, yield to the classical categories because, like Greek and Latin, they are Indo-European languages (more about this in a later chapter). But Japanese and Eskimo, not having had a classical upbringing, refuse to play the game.

Smug scholars like John Stuart Mill (1806–1873), who saw in the "eight parts of speech" fundamental categories of human thought, required, and still require, the cold douche of contact with an Asiatic language. There is nothing universal about those weary old Western grammatical compartments, and, at best, they were, and remain, somewhat shoddy and makeshift when applied to the languages for which they were formulated. There were too many assumptions, there was too little desire (there never is when vested interests are involved) to look linguistic facts in the face.

Some of us are not even too happy with the assumptions about the "well-formed sentence" that have come in with Noam Chomsky. Any such sentence in English must have a noun phrase (NP) and a verb phrase (VP) or, as used to be said, a subject and predicate, on the order of "Dad drinks" or "Mum nags." But many complete statements do not obey this rule. "Fire!"—"Away!"—"Oh, no!"—"Go!"—all are totally intelligible. The characteristic dialect of retired major generals ignores the opening NP or subject in statements like "Met the fellow in Bombay. Never liked him. Obviously up to no good. Never cared for the cut of his jib. Saw him again at Lord's. Turned my face the other way." I see no point in positing "deep structures" that take for granted an "understood" but suppressed form. I do not believe that when I shout "Help!" or "*Aiuto!*" I am making an abbreviated version of "(You) bring me help!" or "*Dammi un aiuto!*"

An exploding of the traditional doctrine that every sentence must contain a verb occurs when it is seen that languages like Russian, Malay, and Chinese get along well enough without the *copula*—the verb "to be"—as in sentences like "He is a good man." Malay renders this as "*Dia* (he) *orang* (man or person) *baik* (good)" and Russian as "*On* (he) *-dobriy* (good) *chelovyek* (man)," though that dash after "On" has a kind of algebraic signification, a ghost of a copula unheard in speech. The verb "to be" is not "understood," since it does not exist. Let us, without using Chomskian descriptive devices, make up some typically "grammar book" sentences—that is, sentences that would not give a Latinist palpitations—and examine the functions of the words within them.

The girl is pretty.

She is pretty.

If you want to show this as a "terminal string," the formula is D + N + V + Adj, where D stands for "determiner," a word like "the" or "this" or "every." "Girl" is a noun. For "girl" we can substitute "she": this makes "she" a pronoun. "Pretty" is an adjective: it qualifies the noun if placed next to it; it is predicated of the noun if it comes after the copula "is." Its behavior is manifestly different from that of "the." "Girls are pretty" makes sense; "Girls are the" does not. This applies to all the determiners (a useful enough term) and prevents our saying "Girls are every" or "Girls are these." "Is" is a verb of a special kind. As, like "seems" or "becomes," "is" cannot in itself express total meaning—unless used theologically or metaphysically—it can be called a synsemantic verb. "Be!" makes no sense, nor does "Become!" or "Seem!" but "Glow!" or "Go!" make sense enough.

Before we expand adjectives into phrases and clauses, let us note their anomalous behavior. "He is easy to please" is structured in the same way as "He is eager to please," but we require a terminology that will demonstrate the difference not merely in meaning but in form. In "He is easy to please" ("Pleasing him is easy"), the "to please" is subject-orientated. In the other sentence, it is "he" who is to do the pleasing: "to please" is object-orientated. Reconstruct it as "Pleasing him is eager," and it makes no sense.

This pretty girl shall be my wife.

The girl with the flaxen hair shall be my wife.

That girl, whom I have adored ever since my early manhood, shall be my wife.

These three sentences are identical in their essential structure—"Girl shall be my wife." The phrase "with the flaxen hair" in the second sentence is doing the same sort of work—descriptive—as the adjective "pretty" in the first. It can be called an adjective phrase. Phrases of this kind begin with a preposition—a colorless sememe that links noun and noun. Here are other examples.

THE GIRL   with the hazel eyes
            on the bus
            of my dreams
            from Walthamstow
            at the house on the corner

In the third sentence, the word group "whom I have adored ever since my early manhood" is performing an adjectival or descriptive task: it is interchangeable, more or less, with the adjective "adorable" or "long-adored." It is not quite an adjective phrase, for it contains two pure sentence elements—a verb with a subject—and can be termed an adjective clause. Such clauses begin with a relative pronoun, a kind of personalized conjunction or joining word, that refers back to a noun in the main sentence and links that main sentence to the adjective clause itself. Here are other examples:

THE GIRL   whom I see every day on the bus
who lives next door
whose mother works in my office
with whom I play tennis OR
whom I play tennis with OR
I play tennis with

This last adjective clause is genuinely elliptical: "whom" is really understood. This omission of a relative pronoun is rare in other languages.

He will come tonight.

He will come at about quarter past nine.

He will come when the sun is setting.

In the first of these sentences, "tonight" tells more about the proposed action expressed in the verb "will come." Helping the verb, it can be called an adverb. "At about quarter past nine" (note the preposition at the beginning) is an adverb phrase. "When the sun is setting" or "While the sun is going down" or "As soon as the sun sets" contains a NP-VP combination—"sun sets." The introductory word or phrase ("when" or "while" or "as soon as") glues two sentences together. It is a join device or conjunction, like "and" or "but" or "also." The adverb "tonight" and the two adverb substitutes express time, answering the question "When will he come?" but a number of other adverbial machines can be used:

MANNER   COME   quickly
with all haste
as if your life depended on it

PLACE   WAIT   here
in the pub on the corner
where the three roads meet

REASON	I KILL	motivelessly
		for kicks
		because I nurse an ineradicable rage

CONCESSION	Nevertheless	HE IS WRETCHED
	Despite his wealth	
	Although he is rich	

We must note that adverbs of manner—"quickly," "beautifully"— and adverbs of degree—"more," "most," "rather"—can modify an adjective ("beautifully warm"; "most kind") or an adverb ("exceptionally badly"; "rather coldly"). "Very" is an adjective and adverb helper, too ("very cold"; "very coldly"), but it cannot modify a verb. It obviously requires to be slotted somewhere, so some such term as "nonadverbial modifier" might serve. There are other such modifiers that, admirable with adjectives or adverbs, are somewhat tremulous when they have to help a verb. "Conceivably correct" is in order, but the modifier will not work in a statement like "I did it conceivably"; "Conceivably he's a fraud" will do. We still have some way to go before we can classify with total satisfaction the elements that make up sensible statements.

I like	WOMEN	don't like me
I like	TO DANCE	is to know the poetry of motion
I like	WALKING IN THE FIELDS	is good exercise
I like	WHAT YOU DID THEN	was uncalled for

The forms in capitals above can act as object of "I like" or as subject of what comes after. "Women" is a noun; "to dance" is a noun phrase (infinitive form: verb without subject preceded by the preposition "to"); "walking" is a verbal noun (a noun made out of a verb, identical with the present participle in "I am walking"). The final noun substitute is a noun clause: Note the subject-predicate "you-did" preceded by the relative pronoun "What."

There is no room here for a fuller account of syntax. We ought, however, to add that the odd interpolated forms like "Of course," "not likely," "most emphatically not," "with all my heart," as well as plain "yes" and "no" can be termed affirmative and negative words and phrases, while expressions like "Er . . ." and "Well . . ." and "you see . . ." may be called fillers or stabilizers. There used to be a ragbag category called the interjection, created to accommodate otherwise unclassifiable elements of speech. Some of history's great cries of agony, like "My son, my son!" or "Light, light!" or Faustus's "Ah, Mephistopheles . . ." are not what Chomsky would call well formed. It may be that both life and literature are too big for grammar.

Terms like "noun," "adjective," "verb," and so on are useful tools that help us to cope with the problems of learning foreign languages. The noun is pretty well a universal form, as things and people are universal entities, and the universality, likewise, of states and actions finds its linguistic counterpart in the verb, which appears in all languages. Adjectives are a different matter: as we shall see later, they do not properly exist in Japanese. To discuss the adjective and adverb as separate categories in German leads to awkwardness, since they take the same form: *Der Mann ist gut* ("The man is good"); *Ich schreibe gut* ("I write well"). While we are on adjectives, we may note a disconcerting logic about German that, putting the adjective before the noun as in all Germanic languages, puts the whole of an adjective phrase there, too. English has "buttered bread" but "bread spread with butter and jam"; German has "with butter and strawberry jam spread bread." In other words, in speaking German, one must have the entire content of one's adjective phrase ready before the noun that it qualifies makes its appearance.

This preparation of a phrasal entirety finds a counterpart in the German procedure with noun, adjective, and adverb clauses, for in these the verb is always shunted to the end. A sentence like "This is the girl with whom I to the cinema went" calls for precise formulation of the clause before utterance; so does "He told me that I forgiven was." Note this separation of the subject from the verb, seen at its most idiosyncratic with a compound verb like "I shall have gone." This consists of (a) subject "I"; (b) finite (or subject-taking part of the verb) "shall"; (c) infinitive "have"; (d) past participle "gone." In a German noun clause, that English order is reversed. "He tells me that by that time I gone have shall"—giving the formula (a) (d) (c) (b). Similarly, one has "I think that he it done have must." One ought to practice such seeming perversions in English before trying them out in German. Even in very straightforward sentences, German seems to split up its compound verbs very curiously: "I have to him spoken"; "He has it arranged." This is analogous to outmoded English poetic forms like "Him have I often seen, with torso bare," where English, remembering the very Germanic constructions of the language as it was a thousand years ago, also takes on the adjective position of the Romance languages—*torso nudo, torse nu.*

There are two aspects of morphology that cause distress when languages of a conservative type—like German or Russian—or old languages—like Latin and Greek—have to be learned. These are (a) a rich system of inflections, whereby a noun or verb changes its ending according to the work it does in a sentence and (b) a complete panoply of genders, so that some nouns are masculine, others feminine, others neuter. More progressive languages, like English, have discarded genders and most of the noun inflections, while Italian and Spanish, regaining something of the wealth of verb endings bequeathed by Latin, have simplified the noun and made gender no real problem. Persian, Malay, and Chinese have no gender and no inflections: through studying these languages we learn how much useless luggage the grammar books of the progressive West still have to carry.

Gender, in fact, is a luxury that contributes nothing to meaning. If I say *le bière* and *une cognac* I am breaking fundamental French rules but not thereby rendering myself unintelligible: the waiter will bring what I ask. In English, where gender persists only with seagoing craft and, generally, with cars and airplanes that are loved by their owners or pilots, it may be a breach of etiquette to call a ship "it" and not "she," but no semantic law is transgressed against. It may seem wasteful that English needs "he" and "she" only for sexual differentiation (and not always then: I have still to hear a snake called "he" or "she"), while "it" has to embrace everything else, but English has at least resolved the old confusion between sex and gender, which need have nothing at all to do with each other. In German *das Mädchen* is neuter, though it means "the young girl," and "the horse"—*das Pferd*—is also neuter, whether gelded or not. In Russian *sobaka* ("dog") is feminine even when male, and Latin *poeta* ("poet") belongs to one of the feminine declensions.

It has been suggested that gender had its origins in animism—that primitive attitude to nature that gave everything a soul and saw biological sex as a necessary attribute of the animate. It is rather more likely that gender is an attempt—at a later stage of human development—to impose order on disorder, to herd a mass of primitive particulars into a few general groups, using the sexual categories—of which neuter, which posits the absence of sex, is logically one—as the best known and most convenient. Such categories have also been applied to metals, and dies, screws, and templates are still given a male or female appellation. With a bastard file the whole sexual business is taken even further.

The only motive for categorizing nouns according to gender is a syntactical one: gender is important in nouns when other words are affected by it. In Latin, *murus* ("wall") is masculine, *porta* ("door") is feminine, and *tectum* ("roof") is neuter. This involves a particular choice when we want to apply the adjective "good" to these words. *Murus* must be *bonus, porta bona*, and *tectum bonum*. Words are, so to speak, aware of each other in environments where they breathe the same air. Old English had a full set of genders in nouns and corresponding endings in adjectives; these have disappeared because, with the phonological changes of Middle English, the endings that indicated gender have dropped off: *Mona* has become "moon," *ealu* has become "ale," *sunu* has turned into "sun," and so on. Endings have disappeared in German, too, but the gender system persists. It is hard to know from a German word whether to make it *der, die*, or *das*. As a German professor of English said to me, "It's always the one you don't expect." He added that he was glad he had learned German in childhood, since he did not have to cope with its often bewildering gender system in his questioning maturity.

Gender learning is a nuisance to us Anglophones because of our complete emancipation from it in our own tongue. It does not matter to us when we are reading a genderful language, so long as that language has a clearly defined word order, so that we know, from its position, which adjective qualifies which noun. But in Latin, where word order is fluid, especially in poetry, agreement between noun and adjective may be our only way of making sense of a passage. In learning to speak enough of a foreign language to find our way about, we ought not to tie up our tongues because we have forgotten the gender of, say, *Frühstück* ("breakfast"). The satisfying of morning hunger is more important than morphological exactitude. But native speakers of gendered languages can be horrified by the ignorance or ineptitude of the gender-emancipated. The French will show their horror, the Italians not. The Germans may gently sneer.

Morphology, or accidence, is concerned with examining patterns of word endings as they appear in that total meaningful structure we call a sentence. Nouns in Latin are very fully "inflected": a noun will vary its ending according to its relationship with other words. So, *mensa* (nom.) is a table (the English "mess" in its military sense is ultimately derived from it), but only if it is the subject of a verb. For the rest, I kick the *mensam* (acc.), admire the color (of the) *mensae*, give a good polish (to the) *mensae*, take a leg from the *mensā*. There can be many *mensae* in a shop, and we can admire all these *mensas*. The colors (of the) *mensarum* can be admirable, and we would like to add leaves to or walk off with all the *mensis*. This seems complicated and confusing, but it is only a matter of using a glued-on ending instead of a free preposition in front. If English fastened its prepositions to the end of "table," we would have something like this:

SINGULAR	CASE	PLURAL
tableof	(genitive)	tablesof
tableto	(dative)	tablesto
tableby,	(ablative)	tablesby,
tablewith, or		tableswith, or
tablefrom		tablesfrom

The noun in English used to have a whole set of such cases, and Modern German still uses them. Here is the word for "day" in Old English and Modern German (it is masculine in both languages):

OLD ENGLISH

	NOM.	ACC.	GEN.	DAT.
SINGULAR	*daeg*	*daeg*	*daeges*	*daege*
PLURAL	*dagas*	*dagas*	*daga*	*dagum*

MODERN GERMAN

	NOM.	ACC.	GEN.	DAT.
SINGULAR	*Tag*	*Tag*	*Tages*	*Tage*
PLURAL	*Tage*	*Tage*	*Tage*	*Tagen*

The genitive singular survives in Modern English, always acceptable for nouns denoting living things—like "John's," "boy's," "girl's," "dog's"—though strictly speaking, ' 's' turns a noun into an adjective. We are not too happy about expressions like "the apple's core," "the door's handle," "the box's lid," though there is no true rule against them. By an act of simple extension, the ancient genitive singular has become also a possessive marker in the plural—"men's clothing," "boys' books," "women's sorrows."

The Romance languages have dropped all noun inflections except for a plural indicator. This is straightforward in Spanish, where an -s is invariably used, and straightforward enough in French, where -s (homme:hommes) or -x (bureau:bureaux) is so often a purely visual sign. Here the plural article is the true indicator of plurality—l'homme versus les hommes. Italian plurals follow the Latin pattern, changing -o to -i and -a to -e (ragazzo:ragazzi; donna:donne), but one must beware of words of Greek derivation ending in -a. Problema, for instance, is not feminine but masculine, and the plural is problemi. English, so progressive in other ways, uses a very mixed bag. "S"—indicating either /s/ or /z/—we may regard as the regular pluralizer; but forms like "ox:oxen," "child:children," "brother:brethren," represent an older and very Teutonic way of making plurals, as do "man:men," "woman:women," "mouse:mice," "tooth:teeth," "goose:geese," and so on.

Children and comic songs ("Ours is a nice house, ours is:/ We've got no rats nor mouses") rationalize English plurals, and the few eccentric-seeming ones we have either fascinate foreigners (who delight in the "child:children" pattern) or are easily avoided by them. We hear little of children these days and much more of kids. German, however, is happier with this mutation of vowels on the "man:men" principle than with any other of the pluralizing devices available, and plurals like the following are regular and normal: Bach:Bäche; Bogen:Bögen; Chor:Chöre; Drang:Dränge; Genuss:Genüsse. The two dots (or dieresis or Umlaut) are a fronting signal: the tongue obeys the order to form the vowel not in the back but in the front of the mouth.

Personal pronouns remain complicated in most Western languages, and they show a strange unwillingness to "generalize" that must be traced back to some primeval alienation or schizophrenia. John may love John, but I have to love me and she her, he him. There is no phonetic unity. Jeg bears no relationship to mig in Icelandic, nor ya to mne in Russian, nor ego to me in Latin. We see the same lack of sound pattern in "we:us," Russian mi:nas, German wir:uns, and Icelandic vjer:oss. This is no law of linguistic nature, for Malay has saya and Chinese has wo as invariable "I-me" forms. English has tried to simplify its personal pronouns over the centuries, though earlier forms survive in dialect and colloquial speech. "Bash 'em" and "Give 'em hell" contain an unaspirated form of the old "hem" (not "them"), and the rural "Tell un" ("Tell him") goes back to "hine." The Lancashire word for "she" is "oo" /ɯ/, which is a survival of Old English, "heo," abandoned in favor of the demonstrative "sio," whence "she."

English now recognizes only two inflections for all pronouns—the subjective (or nominative) "I," "you," "he," "she," "they," and the objective (or accusative) "me," "you," "him," "her," "them." The possessives, as in "his face" or "her hair" or "their cheek," are adjectival. The objective form is used after transitive verbs like "hit," "kick," "love," and also after prepositions like "after," "for," "between." It is because "you" has become an invariable form—in number as well as case—that the solecisms "Between you and I" and "Let you and I talk" are committed. It is through the operation of such analogies (if "you" can be invariable, why not "I" as well?) that languages can be simplified. It remains to say that not all speakers of English are happy about the invariability of "you" as both singular and plural. "Thou" was once the regular singular (as *tu* was in Latin) until it became a signal of purely intimate address. "You" took its place. The same thing happened in French: you have to be very familiar with a person to *tutoyer* or use *tu* and *toi*. In Spanish, *Usted* (which is highly polite) opposes *tu*; in Italian it used to be *voi*, a genuine "you" plural, until it became *Lei*. When we hear the plural "youse" or "you-all" (in the English of Tamils as well as of American Southerners), we are being told that "you" has wholly passed over to the singular and that a new plural is needed.

The greatest richness of inflection is to be found in the verbs of the Indo-European languages, such richness seeming just and necessary if we note that the verbs of the older tongues, like Latin, were not helped by personal pronouns. If we pervert an English verb, as we perverted an English noun, fastening the pronouns to the end, we can see that the corresponding Latin verb is not so unreasonable after all.

ENGLISH	LATIN
loveI	*amo*
lovesthou	*amas*
loveshe, lovesshe, lovesit	*amat*

lovewe	*amamus*
loveyou	*amatis*
lovethey	*amant*

The tendency in the Germanic languages has been for the inflections of the verb to become simplified, leaving the work of personalization to pronouns. The terminal "-s" of the third person singular in English is not strictly necessary, since "he" or "she" or "it" does the work of saying who is performing the action or suffering the condition. "May" and "must" get along without inflection, and there is a possibility that someday we shall all be saying "he love," "she eat," "it bark." Black English has the right idea.

Latin grammarians (meaning the classifying men of the Renaissance) never found it as easy to categorize verbs as to categorize nouns. This is why students of Latin have so many pages of principal parts of irregular verbs to learn by heart, some of them—like *fero, ferre, tuli, latum*—so fantastic as never to be forgotten. The insistence on setting irregular verbs to be memorized, which blighted my boyhood, is often misguided. It sets sheer form above meaning and forgets that one may go through life without having to use—or even to recognize in speech or literature—the more irregular of the irregulars. One may go a long way in French with the auxiliaries *être* and *avoir* and the verbs whose infinitive ending is *-er*. The beginner in English can subsist equally well on the "weak verbs" (those that make their past forms by adding "-ed") until he is sufficiently familiar with the flavor of the language not to be scared of irregularities.

Indeed, foreign learner and native speaker alike can get through a great part of the day with only one verb—though a "strong" one—"get." It is "strong" because it changes its vowel in the past tense to "got." I get up in the morning, get a bath and a shave, get dressed, get my breakfast, get into the car, get to the office, get down to work, get some coffee at eleven, get lunch at one, get back, get angry, get tired, get home, get into a fight with my wife, get to bed. For some reason, "get" is regarded as vulgar, perhaps because it can make life so easy.

"To understand all is to forgive all." We may invoke this maxim in connection with all the illogicalities of language, and especially English. We can invoke it when considering "go" and "went," which do not seem to belong to the same verb at all. "Go" is defective and has had to borrow the past tense of "wend" ("I wend my way"; "I went my way"). We say "I sing," "I sang," "I have sung" and wonder how this strong verb can inhabit the same linguistic world as "I walk," "I walked," "I have walked." The truth is that all languages like to conserve, hate to discard, and the strong verb belongs to an earlier stage of development, while the weak one belongs to a later—and more amenable, or logical—phase. Only by creating artificial languages like Esperanto or Novial can we hope to achieve perfect logic and perfect regularity, and then we soon become sated with mechanical perfection, longing for something more human and imperfect— the complexities of Russian grammar, the waywardness of English orthography.

Chomsky pronounced that knowledge of grammatical construction constituted the true mastery of a language. "With a complete list of terminal strings all the basic sentences possible can be worked out." I am not happy about this. Chinese and Malay do not impose this kind of obligation. Vocabulary is far more important in both than rules of syntax. German has its own fascination and, in a ghostly manner, its own peculiar truth. We may not know what the verb "grobble" means, but we can be pretty sure that if I grobble, he grobbles, and that, some time in the past, several people grobbled. If "grobble" is a noun, then its plural is probably "grobbles." There is a satisfactory boniness about grammar that the flesh of vocabulary, or lexis, requires before it can become vertebrate and walk the earth. But it is probably unrealistic to stress its importance. It leads us to a world of dreams:

> When I corkled the veriduct in morful wurtubs and, prexing the coroflock, chonted the furpool by crerlicoking the fark, wottled the duneflow by fonking the raketoppled purnlow and then asserticled the prert (in both slonces) through a clariform rarp of werthearkers.

That is good grammar. But it is not anything else.

4.

THE THINGS
WE SPEAK WITH

The lips are very visibly involved in speech, and rather less visibly, so are the teeth, tongue, and palate. The sounds all these make are sometimes orchestrated by the buzzing of the vocal cords, sometimes not. Speech, of course, is not the only meaningful sound emitted by the human body. The stomach and viscera frequently announce to the world the progress of what is called peristalsis. We can cough, sneeze, and make noises indicative of impatience, anger, fatigue, agreement, disagreement. But none of these sounds is within our present province. The rasping noise we make when trying to dislodge a fish bone from the throat may be identical with one of the guttural consonants of Arabic, but that must be considered fortuitous. Only speech sounds are dignified with the name of *phones*, and these are the province of the phonetician.

Before we go any further, we have to distinguish between two kinds of speech study. I have already mentioned these in discussing the Prague School of linguistics; but now we have to dig deeper. Phonetics examines speech sounds without direct reference to how these are structured into meaningful statements. It is interested in the mechanics and acoustics of speech but regards the *semantic* aspect (the one that deals with meaning) as the field of quite different specialists. Phonetics, then, is one thing, but *phonology* is another. Phonology, you may remember, relates speech sounds directly to their linguistic function. It deals not in phones but in *phonemes*. Both the phonetician and the phonologist find it necessary in a written discourse such as this to use a scientific mode of notation. The ordinary alphabet, especially as used in English, is not very helpful when it comes to the visual symbolization of sounds. As George Bernard Shaw delighted in saying, you can write "fish" as "ghoti" with total alphabetic logic— "gh" as in "laugh," "o" as in "women," "ti" as in "nation." (Another whimsical Irishman, James Joyce, has, in his *Finnegans Wake*, a poetic extension of this: "ghoti smells fish," where the goat and the finned swimmer combine into a Christian symbol—scapegoat and Christ as the Greek fish ichthus. Forgive the irrelevance.)

I have already slyly insinuated into my text certain phonemic symbols—regular or strange alphabetic signs enclosed in slashes. These belong to the International Phonetic Alphabet or IPA. For the moment take it that the sign /k/ stands for the sound you already know or think you know. But pronounce the three words "cool," "kill," and "keel" and you will discover that the three /k/ sounds are alike but not identical. They are all recognizably /k/, but for "cool" the sound is made farther back in the mouth than for the /k/ of the other words. And the /k/ of "keel" is nearer the teeth than the one in "kill." Similarly, take the vowel /ɪ/ that occurs five times in the word "incivility." The sound seems to get progressively lower in pitch, but our recognition of the /ɪ/ is not impaired. It appears that we have a general class of /k/, or of /ɪ/, that can be divided into constituent members. We can thus speak of the /k/ or /ɪ/ phoneme and refer to the constituent members as *allophones*.

Kingsley Amis, as I noted earlier, is one of the few novelists with a technical interest in the processes of speech. In an early novel of his, *I Like It Here*, he has a character who, switching off the radio, cuts off Frank Sinatra "in mid-phoneme." This is not quite right: he should have written "in mid-allophone." For, though we may study phonemes, we cannot strictly pronounce or hear them. A phoneme is realized only through its allophones. It may be a unit of speech, but it is totally abstract, an idea rather than an event. The phonologist realizes this, but he is not very interested in allophones. He knows that allophones are a fact of phonetic life, but the phoneme is good enough for him. For, in any given language, the substitution of one allophone for another will make no difference to the meaning. The one spectacular allophonic division we have in RP is to be found in the /l/ phoneme. I have mentioned this already—the fact that the /l/ at the beginning of a word like "lull" is different from the one at the end. The phonetician is interested enough in the difference between the light and dark 'l' to wish to use two distinct symbols—/l/ for light /l/ and |ł| for the dark variety. We use vertical lines to enclose allophonic symbols. But the phonologist is satisfied with /l/ for both varieties; he leaves |l| and |ł| to the phonetician.

What is allophonic in one language may be phonemic in another. This is an important point to consider when learning a foreign language. There is a tendency among English learners of French to regard /y/—the vowel in *lune*—as a rather eccentric allophone of the phoneme. This may be because they have heard Glaswegians use /y/ instead of /u/ in the word "you." So an Englishman may think that /tu/ is good enough when he means /ty/, forgetting that *tout* and *tu* have totally different meanings. Similarly, the distinction in Russian between *brat* meaning "brother" and *brat'* meaning "to bring" may be lost on the English learner. The first /t/ is like the one he knows, and the second, which drags the /t/ on to the palate in the process known as iotization, seems to him a mere fantastic variant. But what to him is allophonic is to the Russian phonemic—a difference of meaning is involved.

Let us now see where phones come from. They will be dignified into phonemes only when we have passed the highly physical stage of examining them as mere noises. Speech sounds are made out of out-breathed air. This air is molded into different shapes, or obstructed and then released, or allowed to escape to the outside world under pressure. In other words, the air from our lungs is modified by the various organs that lie in the throat and the mouth. We can take it as a near-invariable rule that speech is made from out-breathed air, though certain African languages use an in-breathed—or *imploded*—sound. In the name "Mboa" we start off with an in-breathed /m/. Sometimes our English "yes" seems to start off with an imploded /m/ when our affirmation is casual. Swedish girls, asked if they would care for a cup of coffee, sometimes say /mja:/, with the /m/ faint, a mere ghost of implosion, if they do not wish to appear too eager.

In the upper part of the windpipe lies the *larynx*, which contains and protects the *vocal cords*. The larynx is prominent in men and is called the Adam's apple, denoting a regret at committing the primal

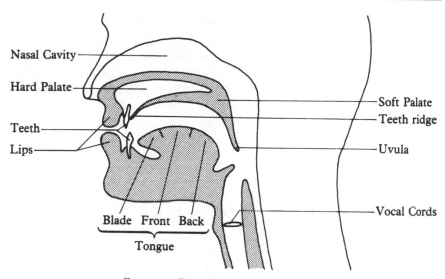

Nasal Cavity

Hard Palate

Teeth

Lips

Soft Palate

Teeth ridge

Uvula

Vocal Cords

Blade Front Back

Tongue

FIGURE 1. THE ORGANS OF SPEECH

sin of disobedience that is not evident in the smooth female throat. The vocal cords, smaller in women than in men, resemble a pair of lips. Stretched across the larynx, from front to back, they are tough pieces of membrane capable of approaching each other, meeting, and then separating again. The space between them is called the *glottis*—the Greek word for "voice"—but it is really the cords themselves that constitute the voice. Air makes them vibrate, and this vibration is the rich musical sound we hear in song. The vibration of the vocal cords is not enough in itself to provide richness, any more than a violin string removed from the violin body can give us much more than a thin screech. The voice requires resonators, like any musical instrument, and resonance is provided by the chest, the throat, the mouth and nose cavities, and the sinuses. These hollow chambers of various sizes magnify the fundamental sound that the voice produces.

We can, then, bring the vocal cords together in the same way that we can bring our lips together. It is a process normally left to the unconscious, but we can learn conscious manipulation easily enough. The out-breathed air coming from the lungs forces its way through the two membranes and makes them vibrate. The vibration goes on when we pronounce a vowel sound or articulate a consonant such as /b/, /d/, /m/, or /z/. These sounds, made with the vocal cords brought together and vibrating away with the impact of air from the lungs, are called *voiced* sounds, that is, sounds made with the voice. There would not be much speech without the voice—for a start, there would be no vowels—and we have some notion of what it is like to have no voice when we suffer from laryngitis. When the vocal cords are diseased and have to be removed, there are two ways of creating a substitute: one can learn to send up "voiced" air from the stomach (this is true ventriloquism or belly talk) or one can be equipped with an artificial larynx.

When the vocal cords are apart from each other—like parted lips—the air is allowed to come up through the windpipe without meeting any obstruction in the larynx. This gives us pure breath, which we hear in the English aspirate /h/. When we utter sounds like /p/, /t/, /k/, /f/, and /s/, the vocal cords are wide apart, untouched by air from the lungs and hence incapable of vibration. Sounds like those are termed *unvoiced*. The unvoiced-voiced opposition (or U/V) is fundamental to most languages. If one alternates sounds like /s/ and /z/ very rapidly, one is forcing the vocal cords into athletic opening and shutting. You can tell the difference between an unvoiced sound and a voiced one by covering your ears with your hands when you speak. If you can feel a vibration, then the sound is voiced. The vibration of the vocal cords has communicated itself to the bones of your head.

Another thing that the vocal cords can do is to come together tightly, presenting a shut double door to the air that is clamoring to come up from below. This is known as *closed glottis*. When the vocal cords suddenly separate, the air—formerly compressed underneath—rushes out in an explosion of some violence. This effect is known as a *glottal stop*—really, of course, a stop followed by a release—and it is far more common in English than people realize. A demagogic politician crying "This land is ours" is almost certainly going to begin the "ours" with a violent glottal stop. There is no letter for this speech item in the ordinary Roman alphabet, and this blinds, or deafens, many of us to its existence. We can hear it in the Glaswegian's "Sa'urday" or the Cockney's "Wha' a lo' of li'l bo'les." As I write, its incidence in British English is increasing. The IPA represents it as a question mark without a dot, thus: /ʔ/.

The other vocal organs are visible in a mirror or even capable of being touched. Some are movable, as the vocal cords are; others stay still. Let us look at the movables first. Open your mouth to a mirror, and you will see a small fleshy organ hanging at the back. This is the *uvula* (Latin for "little grape"). It is, as it were, a tail lightly attached to the *soft palate* or *velum*. The soft palate is capable of moving down to meet the back of the tongue or up away from it. It is a door connecting the mouth with the nose cavity or *nasal pharynx*, and it determines whether the air breathed out from the lungs shall escape by the mouth or by the nostrils. If the soft palate moves up, then there is a space between the uvula and the back of the tongue, and the air can come into the mouth and then proceed between the lips to greet the great world without. Most of the sounds we make are made with this mouth air. But if the soft palate moves down, so that it rests on the back of the tongue, then the air cannot enter the mouth from the windpipe: it meets a closed door. All it can do is to move into the nose cavity, or nasal pharynx, and then make its exit through the nostrils. The sounds /m/, /n/, and /ŋ/ (this last is the "ng" of "sing") are made by allowing the air to come out via the nose (by courtesy of the soft palate) and are hence termed *nasal* sounds. Vowels can be nasalized as well, and the French language has a plentiful supply of these. In very casual English speech, nasalization of a vowel takes the place of a following /n/. I knew a man who entered the public bar of a pub with the one vocable /pā:/. (The little sign called a *tilde* that appears over the vowel signifies nasalization.) This meant "Pint." Over the years the speaker had simplified the word in the following stages: (1) /paint/, (2) /pain/, (3) pāīn/, (4) /pā:/. Children with adenoid growths—spongy matter obstructing the passage of air into the nasal pharynx--cannot pronounce nasal sounds and are unable to recite with any clarity passages like the following: "Do not be afraid. I am only the sandman, and with my bag of golden sand I bring sleep to everyone." What we get instead is something like "Du dot be afraid, I ab odly the sadbad, ad with by bag of golded sad I brig sleep to everywud." When we have a bad cold, mucus clogs the nasal pharynx, and we have the same difficulty. For some reason this is popularly called "speaking through one's nose," which is precisely what it is not.

The most lively of the movable speech organs is the tongue, and it is by far the most important of them. Indeed, "tongue" is a synonym for "language" in many languages, and "language" itself derives from the Latin *lingua*, meaning "tongue." We can, for convenience, divide this meaty organ into three segments—the blade, including the *tip*; the *front*; and the *back*. When the tongue is lying at rest, the blade is opposite the ridge of the upper teeth, the front is opposite the hard palate (or roof of the mouth), and the back is opposite the soft palate. These three parts of the tongue govern, so far as speech is concerned, those three corresponding parts of the mouth. The remaining movable organs are the lips: we know something about those and will soon know more.

The fixed organs are the *hard palate*, that concave, rocky, rather ticklish dome of the mouth against which, in the poem by Keats, joy's grape is pressed; the *teeth*; and the *teethridge* or *alveolus*—that convex portion of the roof of the mouth that lies immediately behind the roots of the teeth. If you can bear to examine this apparatus frequently in a mirror, you will experience a sense of wonder that it should be able, with the aid of the concept-breeding brain, to create all the languages of the world. The whole structure is so damnably simple.

Almost from the very beginning of recorded human language, it seems to have been recognized that there are two complementary elements in the total body of speech sounds—vowels and consonants. The ancient Hebrews found the consonants earthy and the vowels airy or heavenly, and they were reluctant to allow the latter to come down to earth and be represented in visual symbols. There is no doubt something gross and brash and materialist about consonants: they are noises made by banging things together, rubbing, hissing, buzzing. Vowels, on the other hand, are pure music—woodwind to the consonantal percussion—and, because they are produced by the creation of space between the tongue and the hard or soft palate (these spaces are not measured scientifically but arrived at by a sort of acoustic guesswork), they tend to be indefinite and mutable. The history of the sound changes of a language is mainly a history of its vowels.

Again, our difficulty in learning a foreign language is chiefly a difficulty of enunciating the right vowel sounds. The problems offered by the /x/ at the end of *Bach* or the shch-sound in a Russian word like *tovarisch* (/ʃtʃ/ in the IPA) are easily solved. You retch briefly for /x/; you practice on "smashed china" for the Russian phoneme. But to make the u-sound French *lune* or German *über* requires a complete reorientation of vowel habits. We have to change our phonemic thinking.

The Roman alphabet that the whole West employs is kinder to consonants than to vowels. The five symbols it uses—A E I O U— are adequate for Italian and must have been adequate for Latin, but even with the addition of Y, they are inadequate for rendering the vowels of English. The Russians, who use the Cyrillic alphabet with its reasonable supply of vowel symbols, are in no hurry to be romanized and one cannot blame them. The range of English vowels is well illustrated by two mnemonic phrases—"Who would know aught of art must learn, act, and then take his ease" and "Fear the poor outside the door; beware of power, avoid desire." The first contains the fourteen English vowels; the second displays the English diphthongs and triphthongs (not exactly multiple vowels, more the journey the tongue makes from one vowel position to another), with—in "power" and "desire"—an extra lap added. The total number of vowels and composite vowels is twenty-three. And yet, bemused by the limitations of the regular alphabet, the uninstructed are forced into believing there are only five. We will put that right, but not yet. First come the consonants.

THE BUZZES AND HISSES AND BANGS

One way of producing a consonant is to hold back the air that rises from the lungs and then suddenly release it. The release is signaled by a mild explosion. The kind of consonant thus produced is called a *plosive* or a *stop consonant*.

If we close our lips, imprisoning air in the mouth, then suddenly permit our lips to part, we get the sound /p/ as in "pip." This is termed the unvoiced bilabial plosive. The description sounds pretentious, but it is exact. The vocal cords are not vibrating, hence there is no voice. There is a definite, though slight, explosion. Both lips are used, hence the "bilabial." If we switch on the vocal cords and perform the identical operation, we get the voiced bilabial plosive /b/ as in "bib."

We must now forget about the lips and consider what happens when the tongue tip is pressed against the teethridge or alveolus. We hold back the air and, on releasing the tongue, emit the sound /t/ if the vocal cords are not vibrating and the sound /d/ if they are. Thus we have an unvoiced alveolar plosive and a voiced one. But the use of the teethridge is perhaps peculiarly English. Many other languages prefer to let the tongue tip strike the teeth, not the roots of the teeth. The sounds are then dental plosives. The Irish, brought up on an inherited Celtic sound system, use a dental /t/ that is especially noticeable when it precedes a trilled /r/. This is so much on the teeth that British listeners hear it as the sound /θ/ (the Greek theta is used to represent the initial sound in "thin" and "thick"), and novelists and playwrights like to spell the Irish "true" as "thrue."

Our third pair of plosives belongs to the back of the mouth, when the air from the lungs is impeded by the pressing of the back of the tongue against the soft palate or velum. The sudden release of the air produces the sounds /k/ and /g/, depending on whether the vocal cords are vibrating or not. The unvoiced velar plosive is /k/, and the voiced equivalent is /g/.

We are accustomed to the full and firm opposition between the unvoiced /p/, /t/, and /k/ and the voiced /b/, /d/, and /g/: this is characteristic of the European languages. But the opposition in most Chinese dialects is more subtle, for it is between a fully voiced and a partially voiced plosive. If, in a Chinese coffee shop, you ask for ice— *ping*—you have to half-voice the /p/ and perhaps think of it as /b̥/, with the symbol ○ under the voiced consonant signifying an unvoicing. It is a compromise symbol but adequate. The half voicing requires practice, but it has to be taken seriously. The Chinese are entitled to their own phonemic system.

There are subtleties and refinements even in our native use of the plosives of which we are rarely conscious. Sometimes we content ourselves with the stop and ignore the release. This always happens when two plosives come together, as in "stopped" or "licked." Note the ineptness of our spelling there, by the way. The '-ed' marks a past form of the verb and is invariable. It is pronounced /d/ in "loved" but /t/ in "liked." It depends on whether the preceding consonant is voiced or unvoiced. Neighbouring sounds influence each other. "Stopped" has /pt/ at the end and "licked" has /kt/, despite the conventional spelling. For the first stop in each instance, only the first phase of the operation is fulfilled; release is left to the second consonant. This happens also in phrases like "bad boy" (/db/) and "good girl" (/dg/). When Italians say "bad a boy" and "good a girl" they clearly have not been taught the rule. But they are perhaps overscrupulous, by English-speaking standards, in their approach to plosives. English words like "rubbed" use the double 'b' as a signal that the preceding vowel is a short one. Italian words like *repubblica* and *tetto* and *acca* double the plosive consonants to indicate pronunciation. For the first of the twin plosives a stop, for the second a release, so that both announce their presence. Some Italian dialects ignore the rule, but English learners of Italian (meaning Tuscan) had better pay attention to it.

In some languages a stop consonant is initiated but not released. The stops of Malay (they can hardly be called plosives, since they do not explode) merely catch the air and then let it die, as in *sedap*, *kulit*, *balek*. This happens also in a good deal of colloquial English, so that "sit" or "get" ends with a token stop position but no plosive sound. Such dead-stop consonants are increasingly being assimilated to glottal stops, as in "Ge' a' i' " for "Get at it." One dare not be censorious about this: one must merely note that it is happening.

English plosives are breathy, especially in initial positions, so that, despite the spelling, there are four sounds in words like "pin," "ten," and "can," a definite aspirate following the plosive (/ph/, /th/, /kh/). Initial /t/ is assertive, but it becomes curiously weak when it gets into a medial position, as in "butter" or "water": this is especially true of American English. The unvoiced stop becomes voiced under the influence of the surrounding vowels. I had a conversation with a distinguished American scholar who was writing a book about Dr. Samuel Johnson. He was dealing, he told me, with Johnson as a rider. I made various inept remarks about the importance of equestrian exercise in the eighteenth century, seeing the scholar's eyes grow glassy. Then I realized that "rider" meant "writer." Sometimes this voicing of /t/ is more radical, so that it is transformed into a feeble /r/. We have all, in our time, said "Shurrup" to low people who did not deserve meticulous articulation. The process is, historically speaking, respectable enough. "Porridge" was once "pottage." When the /t/ is turned into an /r/, it is assuming some of the nonpercussive quality we associate with a vowel. The British /r/ is, in fact, so feeble that it has become the vowel /ə/ in words like "four" and "lore," when, that is, it has not disappeared entirely.

In very young children, the presence of a plosive in a word is more evident than the point of articulation of that plosive. Hence childish forms like "lickle" and "bockle." Ernest Pontifex, in Samuel Butler's *The Way of All Flesh*, is savagely punished for saying "tum" instead of "come." Told to say "come," he tearfully protests that he is saying "tum." This confusion of plosives is not always infantile. "Apricot" should be, as it is in Shakespeare's *Richard II*, "apricock," derived from the Arabic *al-precoq*, itself derived from the Latin *præcox*.

* * *

The three voiced plosives /b/, /d/, and /g/ are, as we know, made with air that proceeds up the windpipe into the mouth and then out of it. When they are sounded through the nose (by courtesy of the soft palate, which drops to allow this to happen), we get the three common nasal consonants /m/, /n/, and /ŋ/. The first two nasals can be pronounced sharply, as in a child's call for its mama. They can also take on the continuous quality of a vowel, as in the expression of content (a warm fire, a sofa, a box of chocolates) that can be written as "mmmmmmm." The third nasal—/ŋ/—never appears at the beginning of a word in any of the European languages, though Eastern languages are happy to use it initially (Malay: *ngada, ngap, ngeri*) and Chinese has it as a word complete in itself—*Ng*. In the English of Chaucer's time (1342–1400), it was always followed by /g/, as it still is in the North of England, where "singing" is pronounced "singgingg." Even in the South, teachers tell children who say "singin'," "talkin'," and "goin' " that they are dropping their 'g's. This shows the primacy of spelling over pronunciation: people see two letters in the spelling and believe there are two corresponding sounds. So-called 'g' dropping is merely the substitution of one nasal (/n/) for another (/ŋ/). Its ancestry is most respectable. Social judgments on it are, as must be expected, self-contradictory. It is vulgar for Cockneys to say "singin' and dancin' " but genteel for the country folk to talk of "huntin', shootin', and fishin'."

There is an oral deformity that imposes perpetual nasalization. People born with a cleft palate, whose outer manifestation is a harelip, are unable to shut off air from the nasal pharynx until they are fitted with the prosthesis known as an obturator. This closes the gap in the hard palate. Even then they have to learn the technique of denasalizing, so that "sing a song" does not sound like "hning a hnong." The practice of deliberate yawning is the answer, so that the soft palate or velum is encouraged to become athletic. It takes time.

In normal English speech, there is an interesting phenomenon in which plosives and nasals cooperate. Say "kitten," "garden," "button," "shopman," and you will find that you are exploding the /p/ or /t/ or /d/ through your nose. The tongue or lips remain in the position for the plosive and the soft palate drops to let the air rush out through the nose for the nasal consonant that follows. Some people pronounce "mutton" and "garden" more or less as they are spelled, insisting on a vowel between the plosive /t/ or /d/ and the nasal /n/. Oscar Wilde, in his youth, mocked this refinement with a little rhyme beginning, "Parding, Mrs. Harding, is my kitting in your garding, a-eating of a mutting bone?" Let the brilliant economy of the natural articulation prevail and remember the term *faucal plosion*, the fauce being the narrow passage between the soft palate and the base of the tongue.

I have already briefly referred to nasalization and noted that one of the great phonetic characteristics of French is its tendency to nasalize vowels. This nasalization is the result of dropping nasal consonants but allowing a kind of nasal ghost to haunt what is left of the word. In *un*, for instance, the final /n/, present in the original Latin *unus*, has long disappeared from the pronunciation (except before a vowel, as in *un homme*), but the *u* remembers it and, as a kind of memorial tribute, nasalizes itself. French is fond of dropping final consonants, but while it is ready to forget the final /t/ in *restaurant*, it is always faithful to the departed nasal: the final *a* comes straight out of the nostrils. Cyrano de Bergerac is, in reminding Frenchmen of the importance of the nose, a great Gallic hero.

Certain consonants are made by "rubbing" the airstream between two vocal organs that have been brought into very close proximity. These are *fricatives* (the root is the same as in "friction"). The effect is that of gas escaping through a tiny aperture: we are aware of pressure; we are aware of duration. Fricative consonants can be continued as long as the breath lasts, and hence they are very different from plosives, which are instantaneous, gone with the wind. Let us start with the lips.

By rubbing air between the nearly closed lips we are able to produce two sounds that are not official English phonemes, though they are to be found in other languages. The unvoiced lip fricative is, to the anglophone ear, like a combination of /p/, /f/, and /h/. It was a common sound in ancient Greek, and the IPA uses the old Greek letter phi to represent it, thus: /ɸ/. The Romans heard it as an aspirated /p/, and so such Latinized Greek words as *philosophia*, *Phoebus*, and so on. We, who use the Roman alphabet, continue the custom, and the very name of our present study begins with an aspirated /p/ that has become a pure /f/: "phonetics." If you voice this bilabial fricative you produce the *v* of Spanish *vaso*. It is also the sound that has, in Greece, replaced the /b/ that was once represented by beta—β. The IPA uses this symbol for the fricative. Modern Greeks uttering the name of their hero Byron seem to be saying "Vyron" to English ears, but the /β/ has no v-bite in it: it is a pure vibration of the lips.

It seems (at least to me) likely that the voiced bilabial fricative existed for a long time in colloquial English, especially that of lower-class Londoners, and that it was used indifferently where we would now use /v/ and /w/. To Charles Dickens, who wrote before the discipline of descriptive linguistics had come into existence, it appeared that the Wellers, *père et fils*, said /v/ when they meant /w/ and /w/ when they meant /v/. It seems unlikely that Tony Weller said, "Be wery careful o' vidders," but probable that he said, "Be /β/ery careful o' /β/idders." And so, when his son Sam, asked whether he spelled his name with a V or a W, replied, "That depends on the taste and fancy of the speller," he was as good as saying that the English alphabet had no letter for the voiced bilabial fricative /β/. Certainly, the /v/-/w/ opposition seems to make little sense to German speakers. And the /v/ has no place in Arabic, Chinese, or Malay: the bilabial fricative is as common in the speech of English-speaking Orientals as it seems to have been in the speech of nineteenth-century London.

More familiar than the two bilabial fricatives are the labiodental fricatives, sounds made by pressing the upper teeth on the lower lips and allowing the air to filter through the tooth gaps. These two phonemes are /f/ and /v/, the second voiced, the first not. The difficulty encountered by students of English who do not have the /v/ in their native phonemic inventories is easily overcome. They must be told to bite the lower lip and then sing. Two fricatives that may be regarded as typically English (though they once existed in all Germanic languages and are still found in Icelandic) are those made by placing the tongue tip between the teeth and (a) blowing for the unvoiced fricative and (b) singing for the voiced one. The unvoiced sound is the "th" of "thin," "thick," "path," and "eighth"; the voiced sound appears in "this," "that," "them," and "those." We use only the one digraph (two letters—'th') to represent the two phonemes in the regular alphabet; this is confusing. In the IPA the Greek theta /θ/ presents the unvoiced sound. The Anglo-Saxon (and modern Icelandic) rune /ð/ serves for the voiced one.

This, the voiced linguodental fricative, is found in Welsh disguised as *dd—gorwedd, cerdedd*. An approach to it is made in the Castilian dialect of Spanish (*cuidad, madre*), which also has the unvoiced /θ/, represented, before *i* or *e*, by *c*, as in the name Cervantes, or else by

FIGURE 2

THE PRINCIPAL ENGLISH CONSONANT SOUNDS				
PLACE OF ARTICULATION	SOUND	INITIAL	MEDIAL	FINAL
Place I	p	pin	caper	cap
Bilabial	b	been	cabin	cab
	m	my	swimmer	came
	ʌʌ	where	anywhere	—
	w	wear	queen	—
Place II	f	fish	suffer	calf
Labiodental	v	vine	lives	love
Place III	θ	thin	ether	bath
Dental	ð	thou	other	bathe
Place IV A	t	tie	bitter	sat
Alveolar	d	die	bidder	sad
	n	no	runner	shine
	l	law	lily	tall
	s	so	taste	miss
	z	zoo	using	dogs
	ʃ	shoe	precious	wash
	ʒ	Zhivago	pleasure	rouge
	r	row	sorry	—
Place V	ç	huge	—	—
Palatal	j	yard	tune	—
Place VI	k	cod	except	lock
Velar	g	god	exact	log
	ŋ	—	singer	song
Affricates	tʃ	chin	catching	scotch
Combined sounds	dʒ	June	ageless	judge

z, as in *luz* or *lapiz*. Inability to say them, as with some members of the Edwardian aristocracy, is termed *thetatismus* by speech therapists. The cause is less mechanical than acoustic. To some ears they sound like allophones of /f/ and /v/ respectively, and this is particularly true of Cockney speech, where the riddle "How many fevvers on a frush's froat?" is answered with "Five fahsand free undred and firty-free." Yet such speakers do not lack the mechanical equipment to make the two sounds: they have tongues, many of them have teeth—it is a matter of their not finding /θ/ and /ð/ significant or phonemic.

A pair of fricatives made by putting the tongue tip on the teeth-ridge or alveolus and rubbing the airstream between gives us a near-universal hiss (/s/) and buzz (/z/)—the unvoiced and voiced alveolar fricatives. Spanish possesses the letter z but not the phoneme /z/. German avoids /s/ initially, pronouncing words like *Sohn* and *Sommer* with a /z/. English has a healthy distribution of both phonemes, but British English hates representing /z/ phonetically, even where usage allows it. Many people consider spellings like "civilized" uncivilized, although my American publisher prefers it; they agree with King Lear that "whoreson zed" is an "unnecessary letter." This is a pity. The spellings "cloze" and "close" would distinguish two different words; "boyz" and "girlz" would be helpful to English-learning foreigners.

Let us now give the point of the tongue a rest and place the *front* of the tongue on the hard palate (a piece of meat on an inverted butcher's slab). The squeezing of the airstream between gives us our two palatal consonants—the unvoiced fricative in "fish," "shell," "fission," and "passion," and the voiced one in "pleasure," "leisure," and French *je*. We require two outlandish symbols for these—/ʃ/ for "sh" and /ʒ/ for what a rough-and-ready phoneticization renders as "zh." These two sounds are often substituted by drunks for the corresponding alveolar fricatives /s/ and /z/, as in "Yesh, that'sh absholutely true, conshtable. I wazh jusht shnatching a little shnooze in the front sheat." This is because less delicacy of control is required to articulate with the front of the tongue than with the tip of the tongue, and drunkenness, or Korsakov's syndrome, does not permit much delicacy.

The unvoiced /ʃ/ is common enough in English, though conventional spelling disguises it. The voiced version /ʒ/ is rather rare and is never to be found at the beginning of a word, though the film *Doctor Zhivago*, almost overnight, was able to implant a new speech custom that did not appear unduly exotic. Two far more common phonemes—or phoneme clusters—consist of combinations of those two sounds with plosive consonants—/tʃ/ and /dʒ/. The first one is heard in words like "chicken," "cheat," "fetch," and "kitchen." The second appears as 'j' in words like "jam" and "joke," as 'g' in "gentle," "gin," and "pigeon," and as 'dge' in words like "dodge," "wedge," and "gadget."

This combination of a plosive with a fricative is a feature of English well worth examining. The plosive, instead of terminating in an explosion, allows the two articulating organs to separate gradually, so that we hear a neighboring fricative. The forms /tʃ/ and /dʒ/ are not the only examples of this; we have also /tθ/ in "eighth," /dθ/ in "width," /ts/ in "bets," and /dz/ in "beds." The form—plosive ending in a fricative—is known as an *affricate*. The only two affricates we associate with the beginning, as well as the middle and end, of an English word are /tʃ/ and /dʒ/, but various regional forms of English substitute /ts/ in words like "too," "ten," or "tell." I have just seen a television commercial in which a young housewife, recommending a detergent, says "Keeps my hands pretty, /ts/oo." I have heard, more than once, "Drop /dz/ead!" The Z in German words like *Zeche*, *Zeug*, *Ziel*, is a /ts/. In German words that have the same distant origin as certain English words, this /ts/ is equivalent to English /s/ (*Zelle* = "cell") or English /t/ (*zu* = "to" or "too").

We move to the soft palate (or velum) and the back of the tongue for our last fricatives. If the back of the tongue rubs against the velum, without any vibration of the vocal cords, then we have the fricative heard in German or Welsh *Bach*, *bach*, or in Scottish *loch*. The Greeks had a letter for this sound—χ—which the Romans, hearing it as an aspirated /k/, bequeathed to us in the German or Welsh or Scottish form. We find /x/ a reasonable symbol. The corresponding voiced sound /ɡ/ is a gargling sound heard in Arabic and, with some German speakers, at the end of words like *Pfennig*, *Honig*, *Leipzig*.

All these consonants we have glanced at are fairly straightforward in the ways they are articulated and the way they jet out the air from mouth or nose. The 'l' sound is rather more mysterious. Primarily, it is made by stopping mouth air with the tip of the tongue against the teethridge and allowing the air to sneak out along one or both sides

FIGURE 3

CHART OF CONSONANTS ACCORDING TO THEIR ORGANS OF ARTICULATION

Horizontal rows indicate Manner of Articulation	PLACE I Bilabial — Two lips articulating against one another		PLACE II Labiodental — Lower lip articulating against upper front teeth		PLACE III Dental — Tip of tongue articulating against edge of upper front teeth		PLACE IVA Alveolar — Tip of tongue touching teethridge behind front teeth		PLACE IVB Alveolar — Edge of the tongue against the upper teeth at sides; tip of tongue free, pointing toward, but *not* touching: 1 Extreme front of upper gums or upper teeth		2 Middle of upper gums		3 Extreme back of upper gums		PLACE V Palatal — Front of tongue articulating against hard palate		PLACE VI Velar — Back of tongue articulating against soft palate	
	VS	VD	VS	VD	VS	VD	VS	VD	VS	VD	VS	VD	VS	VD	VS	VD	VS	VD
STOP PLOSIVES	p	b					t	d									k	g
NASALS		m						n										ŋ
LATERALS							l̥	l										
FRICATIVES	ɸ	β	f	v	θ	ð			s	z	ʃ	ʒ		r	ç		χ	ɣ
GLIDES	ʍ	w														j		
AFFRICATES							tʃ tθ	dʒ dθ										

Based on a chart by Margaret Prendergast McClean.
NOTE: VS = voiceless; VD = voiced.

of the tongue. This side element bids us term /l/ a lateral consonant. Sometimes, because the airstream can be divided into two separate side currents, it is called also a *divided* consonant.

The /l/ phoneme in British English has two distinct allophones. The /l/ we hear before vowels or after consonants has a thin, clear quality, suggesting somehow the resonance of the vowel /i:/ in "see." We hear it in "long," "flight," and "cling." It is rightly called clear 'l' (|l|) and it is the /l/ we hear in every possible position in French, Italian, Spanish, and German words. But there is another kind of /l/—the one we hear in "tell," "ale," "milk," and "film"—in other words, the /l/ that comes after a vowel and before a consonant. This is called dark 'l' (|ł|). What makes them sound different?

Both |l| and |ł| have a *primary* articulation of tongue tip against teethridge; but they have also a *secondary* articulation, and this is what makes them sound different. With the clear 'l,' the front of the tongue is raised toward the hard palate; with the dark 'l,' the back of the tongue is raised toward the soft palate. Clear 'l' is a palatized sound, dark 'l' is velarized.

Most dialects of British English (Tyneside is one exception that springs to mind) use both varieties. American English, as I have already said, uses only the dark 'l.' When we are learning most foreign languages, it is safe to assume that the clear variety of /l/ is in use whenever the letter 'l' appears. What makes French *ville* different from English 'veal" is partly the length of the vowel, but chiefly the quality of the /l/—clear in French, dark in English. We can represent the French word as /vil/, the English word as /vi:ł/. Dark 'l' sometimes becomes so dark in English that it changes into a vowel. We have all heard Cockneys pronounce "milk" as /miok/. In some words, the dark 'l' becomes the semivowel /w/, so that "eels" is pronounced not as /i:łz/ but as /ɪwz/. Sometimes the dark 'l' grows so obscure that it disappears entirely. Ponder on "walk," "talk," and "calm."

Both clear and dark 'l' are voiced: the vocal cords vibrate steadily while they are being uttered. Welsh has the distinction of possessing an unvoiced 'l' sound, one of the distinguishing badges of the language. It is spelled consistently as *ll*. It is found in such common place-names as Llanelly, Llewellyn, Llandudno, and the near-rude Llareggub of Dylan Thomas. It is an insult to a noble language to ignore this special Welsh phoneme and treat it as an allophone of the English /l/. Unvoiced 'l,' which the IPA represents as /ļ/, is an easy enough sound to hear. Put your tongue in the position for clear 'l' and blow instead of singing. In other words, aspirate your /l/. There is no need to take special lessons in Cardiff or Ynys Ddu.

It is proper to consider the various 'r' sounds immediately after examining the laterals. The fates of 'l' and 'r' have often been closely linked in the history of language. Western people expect the Chinese to say "flied lice" for "fried rice" (some, but not all, do). The Malay word for "English" is *Inggeris*. Japanese prison-camp personnel would say "broody" for "bloody." "Glamour" is derived from the Middle English "gramarye," meaning nothing more glamorous than grammar. "Flagellation" comes from Latin *flagellum*, which is a diminutive of *flagrum*—"a whip." Modern Romans call *il calcio*, which is Tuscan for "football," *er carcio*. *Blanco* ("white") in Spanish, is *branco* in Portuguese. It would seem that both 'l' and 'r' have something of the indefinite quality of a vowel, and when they do not change into vowels, they sometimes change into each other.

That the English 'r' is generally read to change from caterpillar-consonant to vowel-butterfly is shown in a very large number of words. "Here," "there," "father," "park," and "shirt" are just a few. The 'r' in a final or near-final position in English can turn into a "slack" vowel sound like /ə/ or /ɜ:/—"here" is /hɪə/ and "shirt" is /ʃɜ·t/—or become a lengthener of the preceding vowel—/park/ has been turned into /pɑ·k/. (Note that a long vowel is only half-long—a single dot instead of a full colon—before an unvoiced consonant.) The British English 'r' sound is, in fact, a very weak fricative, so weak that it can hardly stand upright and is, indeed, an upside-down symbol in the IPA: /ɹ/. This is the usual sound we hear at the beginning of words like "right," "wrong," and "rose" in many parts of England. The point of the tongue curls up and feebly engages the hard palate.

The Americans and Irish have not allowed the 'r' sound in words like "hard," "girl," "other," and the rest to disappear completely. They make the tongue tip curl up considerably—a kind of back-twisting movement that is called *retroflex*—and this gives us the obscure sound we can represent as /ɻ/. But, in a great deal of American pronunciation, we get the impression that the tongue is curling up without engaging the palate, and that the vowel that comes before the 'r' in words like "are," "dark," and so on is pronounced merely with the tongue in a retroflex position. An Englishman will say /pɜ:ł/

for "pearl," but an American is more likely to say /pɜːɻl/ or /pɝːl/, the dot in the latter transcription signifying that the tongue has gone retroflex during the utterance of the vowel.

One may note before passing on to further types of 'r' sound that it is traditional for babies and members of the British aristocracy in old-type films or stories to have difficulty in pronouncing /r/ and to substitute for it either /w/—as in "a wed, wed wose"—or the bilabial fricative /β/. This is regarded, somewhat belatedly, as a sign of the decadence of the British aristocracy. But it is generally true that few native English speakers can manage the trill or roll that is found in Scottish speech. This is the vigorous /r/ produced by repeatedly and rapidly tapping the tongue tip against the hard palate in the alveolus. It is used by Scots in every possible position. Speakers of English south of the border do, in fact, manage an /r/ with a single tap of the tongue on the teethridge when 'r' comes between two voiced sounds—as in "barrel" or "quarry." It is not a fricative; it is a ghost of the Scots trill. We need a special sign for it—/ɾ/. Americans listening to upper-class British English seem to hear the /ɾ/ as /d/, as in "veddy veddy British." It is a mishearing.

There is another kind of 'r' sound that we have to learn if we wish to attain an acceptable French pronunciation. This is the *grasséyé* or *uvular* version, made by rolling the uvula against the back of the throat. It is represented in the IPA as /R/. We hear this also in Northumberland and Durham: listen to any singer of the song "Blaydon Races." A similar kind of 'r' sound is produced when there is merely a narrowing of the space between the back of the tongue and the uvula. This is the uvular fricative symbolized as /ʁ/.

A vowel sound, as we shall soon see, is made by leaving a space between the tongue and the palate—hard or soft—and then allowing air to pass through the space. At the same time, the vocal cords are made to vibrate. But the quality of a vowel sound is partly determined by what the lips are doing. For /u/, for instance (the vowel of "soon," "fool," and "true"), the lips pout, kisswise. If we pronounce /u/ vigorously, prolonging the sound, and then suddenly leave off, there will often be an aftersound produced by the lips themselves—the sound /w/ as in "well" and "wit." This is not quite a consonant and not quite a vowel: it is convenient to think of it as a semivowel. It is a voiced sound, but there is an unvoiced version of it that we represent by

using "wh" in regular English spelling—"why," "what," and "which"
—but by an inverted "w" (/ʍ/) in the IPA.

We have already seen, when discussing the bilabial fricative, how
some foreign speakers of English tend to distrust its /w/ and even
consider that it does not exist. Some Welsh speakers have this same
notion and give us " 'oman" for "woman" (this is at least as old as
Shakespeare). But English itself has occasionally thrown away its /ʍ/
in words like "who" and its derivatives "whom" and "whose" (/hu:/,
/hu:m/, /hu:z/). It is as though, when the vowel /u/ appears immediately after /w/, the mouth decides that there is no need for mockeries
like unvoiced semivowels that are a mere ghost of /u/. But the reverse
process has taken place with the word "one" (/wʌn/). The voiced
semivowel seems to be there to remind us that the historically earlier
vowel in "one" (/o/) was one that required lip work.

If we pronounce the vowel /i/ as in "see" with some vigor, there is
a tendency for the front of the tongue to hit the palate for an instant
at the end, producing the aftersound we hear in its own right as
the first element in "yes," "yoke," and "yacht." It seems somewhat
unreasonable that the IPA should use /j/ to represent this sound, but
it will seem just to the *ja*-saying Germans. Besides, as we shall see,
/y/ is required for another purpose. This palatal semivowel is voiced,
but it has an unvoiced companion /ç/—the sound at the beginning of
"huge" and "humor," and at the end of German *ich* and *dich*.

We have completed our short survey of the most important consonants and semivowels. There are, of course, others—some of them
outlandish—which are best considered in other contexts (some of the
clicks of the African languages, for instance; a particular semivowel
in French that requires prior knowledge of the corresponding vowel
sound). Before we move on to the flutes of speech, leaving the noises
behind, we ought to note an interesting phenomenon that is perhaps
less common in English than in the languages of Europe. It is called
palatalization. It happens sometimes that a sound associated with the
teeth or teethridge is dragged farther into the mouth to be articulated
on the hard palate. We have seen how a drunken English speaker
will palatalize "seat" to "sheat" and "please" to "pleazhe." In the Latin
languages this palatalizing process works on the nasal /n/ and the
lateral consonant /l/. The palatal nasal /ɲ/ sounds to English ears like
/nj/, as in "canyon." The French and Italians write it as *gn* (*agneau*,

agnello—both meaning "lamb"); Spanish has *ñ* (*la uña*—"the finger-nail") and Portuguese prefers *nh*: the Spanish words appear as *a unha*. The palatalization of /l/ used to exist in French words like *fille* and Versailles, but now only the semivowel /j/ quality remains there. Palatalized /l/ continues in Italian—*gl* as in *megliore*, Spanish—*ll* as in *llena*, and Portuguese—*lh* as in *galhina*. Represented as /ʎ/ in the IPA, it strikes the anglophone ear as an /l/ followed rapidly by /j/—as in "million" pronounced quickly.

The Russian language enjoys palatalization, which it refers to as iotization. It will palatalize everything, and frequently does. Thus, international words like "telegram" and "telephone" appear (I am using the Roman alphabet for greater clarity) as *tyelyefon* and *tyelye-gramma*. The word for "no" strikes some ears as very like a sneer—*nyet*. The big secret of learning Russian pronunciation lies high in that rocky dome called the hard palate. But more of this later.

6.

FLUTINGS

There are people around who do not believe that the vocal cords are used to produce voiced sounds; they hand the task of sonorous vibration over to the sinuses. The devotees of sinus tone production liken the human voice to a flute, whereas the vibration of the membranes in the larynx puts others in mind of the reedy tone of the oboe. To bring music into a discussion of vowels is altogether apt. The voice as a musical instrument sustains itself through manipulation of the vowels at various pitches, and vowels themselves, according to the researches of Sir Richard Paget (1869–1955), are the product of an unconscious sense of absolute pitch. The vowel /u/, for example, is the result of intoning two notes—F-sharp and D-sharp, a major sixth, and /i/ sounds a low D-sharp with a D-natural three octaves higher. This is perilous territory. Questions like Why can some sing and some not? and Why can some sing superbly? lie outside our scope. But the aesthetic judgments we make on speaking voices have to do with those we make on singing voices. There are mysteries here that have never been fully explicated. Voice production, which involves voice placing, is an important aspect of acting as well as singing, but it has little to do with the linguistic inquiries we are making.

Vowels oppose each other—front against back, high against low, rounded against spread—but all vowels have in common the fact that they are voiced. But vowels can be whispered, as we know, and it is certain that much of our aspiration, our enunciation of /h/, is a kind of unvoiced preparation for the vowel that follows. Thus, "he" may be transcribed as /hi:/, but a more accurate representation would be /i̥i:/.

We all know what vowels sound like. We must also learn what they feel like. Sleepless nights can profitably be beguiled by going through the gamut of the English vowels—"Who would know aught of art must learn, act, and then take his ease"—silently if need be, five-finger exercises on a dummy keyboard. One finger at least can be used to check the tongue positions and find out what the lips are doing. The first thing this finger will discover is that the tip or point of the tongue is not used in the making of vowel sounds: the tongue tip can be tucked behind the bottom teeth and forgotten. We are concerned with the front of the tongue (which, at rest, faces the hard palate), the back of the tongue (which faces the velum or soft palate), and the middle or central part, which lies between front and back. Let us first see, feel, and, of course, hear what happens at the front of the mouth.

Here is a sentence: Tea is *thé* in French. This can be shown in IPA script as: /ti:ɪz te ɪn frɛnʃ/. There are four vowels here: /i/, /ɪ/, /e/, /ɛ/. The vowel /e/ is not found in English RP as a separate entity, though it is common enough in various dialects of English and in other languages. When we hear it at all in RP, it is as the first element of the diphthong /eɪ/, as in "way" and "day." Let us, for a reason that will come clear later, concentrate on the /i/, /e/, and /ɛ/, ignoring /ɪ/ for the time being. Say /i/ several times, and you will discover that the front of the tongue is raised almost to the limit; if it were to be raised any more it would touch the hard palate and the resultant sound would be the semivowel /j/ as in "yes." So /i/ is our high or close front vowel: you cannot have a higher tongue position, the tongue cannot be closer to the palate without losing the vowel altogether. The lips are spread. It is a "smiling" vowel. It is contained in the word "cheese," which photographers sometimes ask their subjects to enunciate and, more, hold, so that the vowel is overlengthened into /i::::::/.

If now the front of the tongue is lowered—the jaw goes down and takes the lower lip with it—we get the half-close front vowel /e/ (as in

French *thé* and *café*). If the tongue is further lowered (and the jaw with it), we have the vowel in "French," "ten," "debt"—the half-open front vowel. The lips are still spread. In Continental languages, as once in English in Shakespeare's time, there was a kind of creative opposition between the half-close and half-open front vowels /e/ and /ɛ/. The opposition is to be heard in Italian *e* (/e/), which means "and," and *è* (/ɛ/), which means "is." The French acute and grave accents mark the opposition—'é' and 'è.' In English, when all words containing "ea" had /ɛ/ in them, the opposition was marked in the spelling by "ee," where the second 'e' tells the tongue to stay high, and "ea," where the 'a' is a "tongue down" signal.

The opposition is disappearing everywhere, since it no longer seems to serve a structural purpose. The French *parlé* officially opposes *parlais* (half-close versus half-open), but I have seen French schoolchildren write *parlais* as *parlé*. The opposition between "see" and "sea" no longer exists in London, though it does in Dublin. In Italian it seems you can use /e/ and /ɛ/ indifferently, with no danger of being misunderstood, except for the *e* ("and") and *è* ("is"), though even there context clarifies: a conjunction is not likely to be mistaken for a verb, or vice versa.

We have, then, three front vowels—close, half-close, half-open— and we need a fully open front vowel to complete the sequence. This will be the /a/ in French *café*, German *Mann*, and the Lancashire and Yorkshire versions of "cat," "fat," "tan," and so on. It is not the sound in the RP rendering of these words, though it does appear as the first element in the diphthongs /aɪ/ and /aʊ/, in "fine" and "found" respectively. This /a/, then, is our open front vowel. You will perhaps agree that there is something satisfyingly elegant in this vowel pattern. There are two English vowels that seem to disrupt the pattern. They are /ɪ/ and /æ/, which are not to be found in the Latin languages. The first, you will remember, comes in "sit" and "fit." The second, which you will associate with the ligature or joined 'a' and 'e' of "Cæsar," stands for the very unstable vowel in RP "tan" or "man." Unstable, because, though it was a regular vowel in Anglo-Saxon, it got lost in the Middle Ages and, ever since, has had to resist a tendency to become /ɛ/, so that "man" turns into its plural. As a northerner, I still find the vowel foreign. I would be happier to join the Germans and Dutch and say /man/. We can write down the sequence of front vowels something like this:

1. i
2. e ⁱ
3. ɛ
   æ
4. a

I have numbered only what I will call the Continental vowels, regarding the two English ones as foreign intruders. Our /æ/ lies halfway between (3) and (4). Our /ɪ/ is not quite front: the tongue pulls back a little. Foreigners hear it as an allophone of /ĭ/, which makes them say, "keek eem." All these sounds are short in the Latin languages, but /i/ in English is long—/si:d/, /mi:n/. This full length, indicated by the colon, is, however, modified when /i:/ comes before an unvoiced consonant. "Seat" is shorter than "seed," and the IPA transcription shows it: /si·t/. It is because the French /i/ is short, and so is the RP /ɪ/, that the "keek eem" solecism is made possible. Length is a differentiator to the English ear but not to the French, Spanish, or Italian.

Let us now try to make a complementary sequence of vowels at the back of the mouth. We raise the back of the tongue toward the hard palate for the first of them, which is /u/—a good clear "moon-croon-June" sound made with the tongue well back and the lips rounded as for a kiss (the vowel is, and no wonder, associated with romance). In RP, matching its opposite number /i:/, it is long—/u:/—though losing half its length before an unvoiced consonant. If we now open the lips slightly, allowing the tongue to drop from this high or close position to a half-close stage, we get the pure round 'o' or /o/ that hardly exists in RP, except as the quick initial sound in "obey" or "Othello." French has it commonly in *eau*, *beau*, and so on. Let the tongue sink to the half-open position, with the lips still round, and the vowel /ɔ/ will sing out. It is normally long in English, and we hear it in words like "jaw," "for," "bought," and "taught" (note the mess of inconsistency that is English spelling). Finally if we spread the lips (no more rounding) and utter the sound that doctors ask for when they wish to explore the throat for ulceration, we have the most open back vowel of them all—/ɑ/—which appears long in English "tar," "bar," "father," and so on. It is a pity that strict spreading of the lips should enter here to spoil the sequence.

We can now represent all the vowels we have so far glanced at—and one we have not, not yet—in a diagram with numbers:

1. i			8. u
	I	ʊ	
2. e			7. o
3. ɛ			6. ɔ
	æ		
4. a			5. ɑ

You will notice the symbol /ʊ/, which stands in the same relation to /u/ as /ɪ/ does to /i/—namely, somewhat toward the middle of the mouth. It is the sound in RP "bull," "full," and "should." Like /ɪ/, it is a short vowel. It seems to me logical to resume the numbering after (4) with the bottom, rather than the top, of the mouth. After all, the vowels numbered from (1) to (5) have in common the spreading of the lips, while (6), (7), and (8) are all, in various degrees, uttered with 'o'-shaped lips.

Lurking in very nearly the dead middle of the mouth are two vowels that are very common in English. The first is a long one represented as /ɜː/, and we hear it in "word," "sir," and "shirt." It naturally loses half its length before an unvoiced consonant, so that while "bird" is shown as /bɜːd/, "skirt" has to be /skɜ·t/. Very close to, indeed just a little lower than, this long vowel is a short one called *schwa* or *shwa*. The term was first used by German philologists, who borrowed it from the Hebrew *shewa*, meaning a diacritic or written sign, indicating the lack of a vowel sound. Far from lacking, schwa is by far the commonest sound in English. It is heard in the second syllable of "father," "sister," "brother," and "supper," and in the first syllable of "apart" and "canoe." It is the indefinite article in "a boy," "a girl," and "a love affair." It is the tongue at rest in the middle of the mouth, it is colorless and lazy-sounding. All vowel sounds in slack English speech tend to move toward schwa. Yet this, the commonest sound, has no alphabetic letter of its own. The IPA symbol is /ə/. As early as 1912, when he published *Pygmalion*, George Bernard Shaw tried to set an example to readers and typesetters by using it freely in his representation of the speech of Eliza Doolittle. It still has not caught on. It is to be found on no typewriter or word-processor console. In the absence of a conventional alphabetic sign, the uninstructed cannot see how the sound may exist, though they utter it thousands of times a day. Schwa is the foreigner's clue to learning natural-sounding English.

I now pose a difficult question. At what point does the range of tongue positions available for one vowel phoneme meet the range of

tongue positions available for another? After all, vowels are not divided from each other by steel fences; they represent a continuum
of sound. If I start with the front close vowel /i/ in my ranging of all
the possible vowel positions, and then move the tongue imperceptibly
down, still producing types of /i/—theoretically an unlimited number
of them—I must sooner or later become aware of having moved into
a different phonemic area. This, at least, is true in theory. But practice
works differently, and we soon find ourselves at the heart of the
phonemic mystery. For phonemic recognition is based on what sound
opposes what. The science of phonetics may be concerned with acoustic measurement, but this does not apply in the empirical world of
speech. The vowel in "man" (/mæn/) may, with some speakers, rise
to the level of /ɛ/ as in "men," but they will compensate for this by
raising the /ɛ/ to the level of /e/, thus sustaining a clear opposition.
Foreign students of English, hearing the vowel in "man" as an allophone of the one in "men," must be made aware of the phonemic
difference by practicing on minimal pairs—that is pairs of words
differentiated only by one sound—until they realize they are working
with a phonemic system not at all like what they are used to in their
native tongues:

dead/dad   lend/land
said/sad   send/sand
fed/fad   pedal/paddle

and so on.

The recognition of phonemes, the allotment of boundaries to phonemic areas, is not a mechanical matter but a psychological one. We
all carry mental images of vowel sounds, and these images can persist,
whatever the tongue is doing. Thus, an Englishman will say /fɪt/, a
Frenchman /fit/, and a Scotsman /fet/ or even /fɛt/, but all will hold the
same mental image of "fit." Because of the extreme fluidity of vowels,
and the lack of physical obstacles to the wandering tongue, languages
tend to change. We shall see later how drastically they can—for the
moment think of the Spanish city Saragossa, which used to be called
Caesar Augustus.

Let us, before moving on, digest the eight numbered "Continental"
vowels, noting that for (l) (the sound in "see") the lips are spread and

that they are still spread, though the mouth is progressively more open, as we move through (2) (the vowel in French *thé*) and (3) (the vowel in "men") to (4) (the sound in the Lancashire or Yorkshire pronunciation of "man"). These four vowel sounds are all enunciated with the mouth set for smiling or grinning, or (as with [4]) even laughing—"hahahaha." When we move to (5), the back vowel uttered for the doctor's benefit, we feel that the lip spreading is extreme— the mouth is as wide and square as a letter box. Numbers (1), (2), (3), (4), and (5), then, are vowel sounds made with the lips spread. This should not take much digesting.

The remaining numbered vowels are made with the lips rounded. Numbers (8) (as in "moon"), (7) (as in French *beau*), and (6) (as in "saw")—all are pronounced with the lips rounded. For (8) the lips pout, for (7) they express slight surprise, for (6) they show disappointment or pity. Now we must effect some remarkable transformations, demonstrating the wonderful economy that the mouth uses to build up a vowel system.

Pronounce (1) with the lip-rounding of (8). It is best to do this by holding on to a long /i:/ and then pouting as for /u/. The resultant sound used to be an official one in Old English, but we have it no longer. Nevertheless, it will be recognizable as the vowel in French *lune* or German *Münze*—a rounded close front vowel represented in the IPA as /y/.

Pronounce (2) with the lip-rounding of (7). This is more difficult. The tongue holds the position of /e/ in *thé* and *café*, but the lips show a pure /o/. This is the sound to be heard in French *bleu* and *Dieu*, and in German *hören* and *möglich*. It appears in Danish as ø, and the IPA has borrowed this symbol—/ø/.

Pronounce (3) with the lip-rounding of (6). This again is not easy: it will take some time before the image of the sound is fixed in the mind. The lips will try to keep the vowel short and say /ɔ/ as in "saw" or "for," but the tongue will be in the position for /ɛ/ in "men." This is represented as /œ/—a symbol derived from the French. Indeed, this is the sound we hear in French *oeuf, oeuvre*. The symbol rather neatly shows a fusion of lip and tongue positions—/œ/. In *un* it is nasalized—/œ̃/.

There is one more piece of lip-rounding to do, and this is not on (4), the remaining front vowel (/a/), but on (5)—the /ɑ/ of "father." Here there cannot be any borrowing of lip-rounding from a back vowel, for (5) is itself, of course, a back vowel. So we bring pretty wide lip-rounding from nowhere, uttering a short /ɑ/ while our lips form a great circle. This gives us the short vowel in "not," "clod," "want"—in their British pronunciation, not the American. Americans do not know the sound, sharing that ignorance with the Pilgrim Fathers and, for that matter, William Shakespeare. American actors, when they need to learn the sound for use in dialect plays, are taught to imitate Roger Moore's familiar "Bond. James Bond." The IPA symbol is /ɒ/.

Having brought over lip-rounding to (1) from its opposite number (8), and from (7) and (6) to their respective opposites (2) and (3), we must practice a little more magic. This time we bring over *lip spreading* from (1) to (8), from (2) to (7), and from (3) to (6). We are letting the front vowels work on the back vowels for a change.

If we say (8) (/u/) with lips spread (as for [1], /i/), we make a sound not normally heard in the polite version of any language. It is the "boo-hoo" vowel we use when we are crying. Say /u/ as in "moon," prolonging the sound; consciously spread the lips. Ponder on the resultant vowel /ɯ/. You will have heard it in allegedly vulgar English speech, where the speaker does not trouble to round his lips for statements like "You sued him for a new blue suit." It is not up to us to condemn this vowel. I came near to probably justifiable disgust, however, when, in a television program on the moon, the vowel /ɯ/ was used consistently. It had the effect of making the moon seem flat and square.

If we say (7) (/o/) with the lip spreading appropriate to (2) (/e/), we get a strange vowel represented as /ɤ/. This is not to be found in the inventory of RP except in certain pronunciations of the word "good." "Good" is normally pronounced with the vowel /ʊ/, which is round like /u/ but made a little farther forward. But some speakers unround the vowel, or spread it, and drop their tongues to a position where we seem to hear something between "good" and "gud." I recently heard a rather sinister voice-over on a television commercial gloating over some brand or other of "/gɤ::::d/ chocolates." Before I say any more about this vowel, let me deal with the last of these hybrids in which a tongue position proper to a round sound is squashed by the spreading of the lips. If we pronounce the /ɔ/ (as in "awe") as a short vowel (it is normally long in RP) with the lip spread appropriate to "men" or "then," we hear the sound of "love" and "mother" and "putt" (as opposed to "put"). The IPA shows this as /ʌ/. It is a sound of comparatively recent origin, meaning that it was unknown in Shakespeare's time (he rhymes "love" and "prove"), and it still puzzles people of the English Midlands and the North. Even Cockneys, who belong to the heart of English culture, say /lav/ for "love." As a Mancunian, I still find the sound exotic; I am drawn to /ɤ/ as a means of dealing with the vowels in both "put" and "putt." "Put your club upon the putting green" has, in RP, one /ʊ/ and two /ʌ/s, but Manchester will prefer to use three /ɤ/s. Southerners think that they hear "a /kʊp/ of /ʃʌgə/" for "a cup of sugar" in the speech of a Northerner who is trying unsuccessfully to come to terms with RP. But in both the key words the vowel is /ɤ/. The situation is analogous to that of Charles Dickens hearing a bilabial fricative in "very" and "wherry" and interpreting it as a perverse (and comic) displacement of /v/ and /w/.

Having glanced at the vowels, we may now understand better what a semivowel is. I said earlier that /j/ in "yes" is a kind of /i/ carried to extremes—the tongue touching the palate instead of merely being close to it—and that /w/ is the lip-rounding of /u/ as an audible smack. Add to these a semivowel that we had better know if we wish to attain a perfect French pronunciation of words like *muet*, *huit*, and *lui*. The *u* in these represents the sound of /j/ with the lip-rounding of /y/. If you meet, in a French dictionary, the IPA symbol /ɥ/, we must be prepared to purse our lips as for a *petit baiser* and try to utter the semivowel /j/.

One characteristic of very careful English speech—that of the trained "elocutionist"—is the tendency to make all front vowels as far forward in the mouth as possible and all back vowels as far back—in other words, to emphasize the essential frontness or backness of the phonemes in question. It is true of Continental speech, Italian especially, that the tongue darts energetically in this manner. The middle area of the mouth produces no sound that interests Europe greatly. The situation with English, wherever it is spoken, is rather different. In the central area we have the two important sounds /ɜ/ as in "shirt" and /ə/ as in the indefinite article "a." Both the front and back vowels of everyday English speech tend to approach this zone, giving a schwa coloring to /i/ and /u/ and the rest of the vowels that the Italians and Spaniards and Welsh pronounce with a luminous purity. To represent centralized vowels, as in a Cockney rendering of "blue"

and "boot," we can place two dots over the regular IPA symbol—
/ü/, /ɔ̈/, and so on—or borrow the wiggly line of dark 'l' (/ɫ/) to pierce
its body—/ɨ/, /ɫ/. Thus the Cockney "boot" can be rendered as /bü·t/
and "he" (usually 'h'-less) as /ɨ/. Even with so-called cultivated speakers, forms like "you" and "due" show centralization, owing to the
influence of the palatal /j/. All such centralized forms are, in English,
allophones of the primal front or back phoneme. But the Russian
letter ьι represents a genuine central phoneme, in which the tongue
tries to utter the /ɪ/ of "sit" as far back as possible.

It is not for us to denounce the extreme centralization that marks
a great deal of uneducated British regional speech. Prescriptiveness
is for the classroom, but only social arguments can support the condemnation of a form like /bəɯʔ/ for "boot." This is not a rendering
traditionally acceptable at a Mayfair cocktail party or on the lecture
platform, but it is in order in those social strata where the referent
itself is put in. If remedial work on speech is ever needed—the
elevation of a rock singer to talk-show host might call for it—it is
always a matter of making the subject, or patient, more tongue- and
lip-conscious than merely ear-conscious. Eliza Doolittle can learn to
recite "The rain in Spain stays mainly in the plains" by understanding,
with her tongue more than her ear, the constitution of the /eɪ/ diphthong. It will not suddenly dawn on her as a divine revelation (despite
My Fair Lady) what the acceptable RP form is; it will be evident as
soon as she becomes mouth-conscious. To learn to speak in a new
way is a motor matter, not primarily an auditory one. The engine has
to be mastered. Very few can play by ear.

Mention of "the rain in Spain" brings us to *diphthongs*. For some
languages, English in particular, a battery of pure vowels—that is,
vowels made with a firm and unwavering tongue position—is not
enough. Sometimes the tongue will start at one vowel position and
then move in the direction of another: whether it actually reaches
the second vowel position is not important, for the journey counts
more than the arrival. If a language favors long vowels—as English
does and Italian and Spanish do not—it is disposed already to favor
diphthongs too. A long /i:/ can be written as a diphthong, in the
sense that it is one vowel followed by another, even when that other
happens to be itself, thus—/ii/. But the tongue will waver, unwilling
to maintain the same position for too long, and then produce a

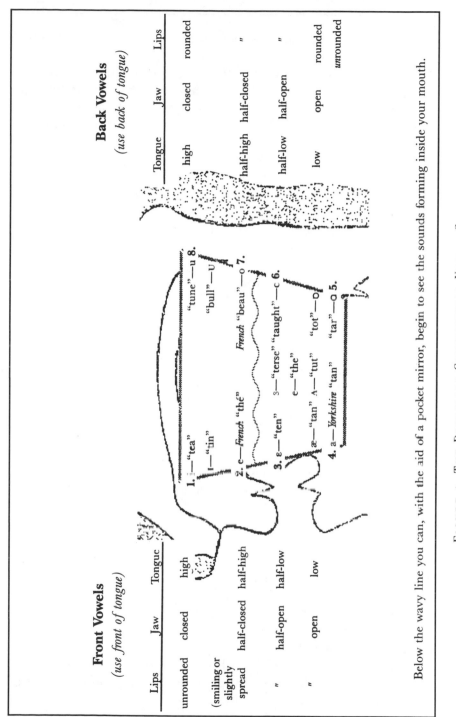

Front Vowels
(use front of tongue)

Lips	Jaw	Tongue
unrounded	closed	high
(smiling or slightly spread	half-closed	half-high
"	half-open	half-low
"	open	low

Back Vowels
(use back of tongue)

Tongue	Jaw	Lips
high	closed	rounded
half-high	half-closed	"
half-low	half-open	"
low	open	rounded
		unrounded

1. — "tea"
— "tin"
2. e — *French* "thé"
3. ε — "ten"
æ — "tan"
4. a — *Yorkshire* "tan"

"tune" — u 8.
"bull" — ʊ
French "beau" — o 7.
ɜ — "terse" "taught" — ɔ 6.
ə — "the"
ʌ — "tut"
"tot" — ɒ
"tar" — ɑ 5.

Below the wavy line you can, with the aid of a pocket mirror, begin to see the sounds forming inside your mouth.

FIGURE 4. THE PRINCIPAL CONTINENTAL VOWEL SOUNDS
BASED ON A CHART BY WILLIAM TILLY.

true diphthong or sound journey from one phoneme to another somewhat different.

The diphthongs of English will always end in the direction of a centralized vowel—/ɪ/, /ʊ/, or /ə/. The phonetic transcription will show the start of the journey and the direction, if not the end, of the journey. Thus the personal pronoun "I" starts at /a/ in RP and moves toward /ɪ/. It can be written as /aɪ/. The first element in other dialects is frequently not /a/ but some other vowel—/ɔ/ or /ʌ/ or even /ə/. On the other hand, speakers in the North of England may ignore the journey altogether and merely state the first element, which happens to be the one used in the RP diphthong. "Ave seen im" in Yorkshire stands for /aɪv siːn ɪm/ in RP. Let us now list the diphthongs according to the direction of their travel.

(a) Diphthongs moving toward /ɪ/:
 /eɪ/—as in "way," "hay," "eight"
 /aɪ/—as in "die," "high," "cry"
 /ɔɪ/—as in "toy," "foil," "noise"

(b) Diphthongs moving toward /ə/:
 /ɪə/—as in "ear," "beer," "mere"
 /ɛə/—as in "air," "bare," "scarce"
 /ɔə/—as in "oar," "bore," "coarse"
 /ʊə/—as in "poor," "sure," "tour"

(c) Diphthongs moving toward /ʊ/:
 /aʊ/—as in "cow," "house," "loud"
 /oʊ/—as in "no," "know," "bone"

Most modern dictionaries (including the 1989 edition of the *OED*) present the RP version of the diphthong in "no" and "toe" as /əʊ/. This diminishes the rounded element and, to many, will sound affected. My own pronunciation of the diphthong, though probably acceptable as a variety of RP, is, I think, equipped with a kind of /o/ at the beginning, though I may modify this according to the company I am in. There are degrees of acceptability for all the diphthongs. Thus the /aɪ/ of "white wine" may become /ɛɪ/ or even /eɪ/, resulting in the much-parodied "whate wain" of a certain class of young moneyed London female. And the /eɪ/ of "way" and "drain" may drop to /ɛɪ/ or even /æɪ/. With this last, further dropping to /aɪ/, we are in the

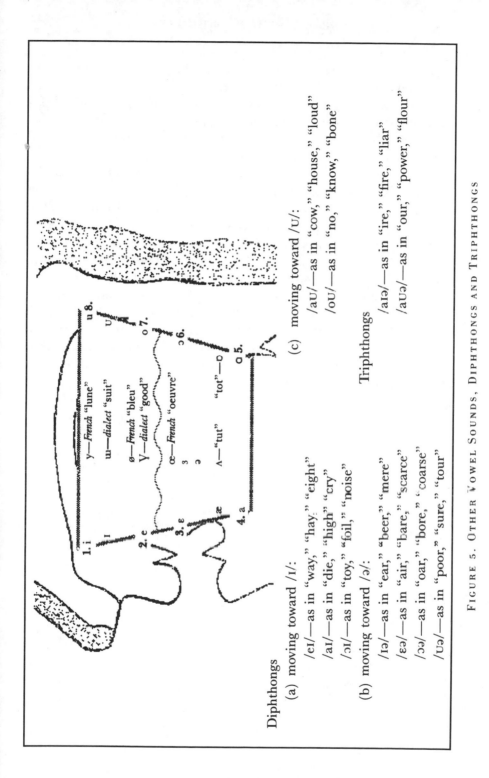

Diphthongs

(a) moving toward /ɪ/:

/eɪ/—as in "way," "hay," "eight"
/aɪ/—as in "die," "high," "cry"
/ɔɪ/—as in "toy," "foil," "noise"

(b) moving toward /ə/:

/ɪə/—as in "ear," "beer," "mere"
/ɛə/—as in "air," "bare," "scarce"
/ɔə/—as in "oar," "bore," "coarse"
/ʊə/—as in "poor," "sure," "tour"

(c) moving toward /ʊ/:

/aʊ/—as in "cow," "house," "loud"
/oʊ/—as in "no," "know," "bone"

Triphthongs

/aɪə/—as in "ire," "fire," "liar"
/aʊə/—as in "our," "power," "flour"

FIGURE 5. OTHER VOWEL SOUNDS, DIPHTHONGS AND TRIPHTHONGS

region of Cockney speech, with "the rine in Spine stying minely in the plines."

In learning foreign languages we may try to impose our own diphthongal habits on very different sound systems, but we can avoid this if we remember that English is nearly unique in possessing the central and near-central vowels that form the second element in our diphthongs. Moreover, what sound like diphthongs in such languages as Italian are more often two vowels, fully enunciated, following each other rapidly, as in /ai/. And the German diphthongs of *klein* (/klain/) and *Haus* (/haus/) tend to reach toward a second element that is a full forward /i/ or a fully back /u/. Welsh English—as in "I haven't time now"—favors two uncentralized second elements: /taim nau/.

It remains to add a couple of triphthongs, namely the two a-diphthongs /aɪ/ and /aʊ/ followed by /ə/. In "ire," "fire," and "liar" we have /aɪə/; in "our," "power," and "flour" we hear /aʊə/. Note that all diphthongs and triphthongs ending in schwa have, in their regular orthography, the letter 'r.' In rhotic dialects of English (those, that is, that have retained the 'r' that RP has lost, specifically between vowels and at the end of them), you will not hear final schwa. "Poor" will be /pur/ and "fire" will be /fair/. In the dying upper class of Great Britain you will hear final schwa droped to /ɑ/. "Come here" pronounced /kʌm hɪɑ/ is the peremptory summons of an ancient and long-retired general. It is not now much heard, or, if heard, much obeyed.

7.

PUTTING SOUNDS

ON THE ROAD

So far we have been examining, in a very cursory way, the sounds of language as though they existed in a void, probing them as on some pathologist's cold slab. To talk of /p/ and /b/ and /i/ and /u/ is to talk of abstractions, things removed from the warm current of speech. We must see them as components of the machine of communication, assemble the parts, and get the car on the road.

We have already referred, in passing, to that attribute of vowels that is called length. Some phonemes take longer to say than others: /si:d/ takes about twice as long to say as /sɪt/; /sɪt/ is twice as long as /sɪt/. Length of vowel varies from dialect to dialect in English. An Englishman will, for instance, accept /mæn/ as the normal native pronunciation of "man"; he will regard /mæ:n/ as "transatlantic." And indeed there is an American tendency to "drawl" or lengthen vowels that is in traditional contrast to the so-called clipped British habit. In Southern dialects of American English there is both lengthening and raising of that phoneme to /ɛ:/, and following a process that goes back to about 1400, the lengthening leads to diphthongizing, so that "man" can be pronounced as /meən/. Put within the limits of one's own *idiolect*—or personal mode of speech—there will be shortenings or lengthenings of vowel sounds according to context. For instance, if I say "Give it to her"—stressing the "give," as though the person addressed is holding the thing back—the vowel of "her" will be a short /ɜ/. If I now stress the "her" ("Give it to *her*, not to him"), the vowel will take on full length—/ɜ:/. And so, in "Where has she *been?*" the /i/ of "been" is quite long—/i:/, while the short form of "She's been to *London*" shows a shortening and retraction of "been" to /bɪn/. "I asked you what you heard, not what you saw" gives us the last word with a fully long /ɔ:/. "I saw nothing at all of the film" has a "saw" with a short /ɔ/.

Still, we tend to think of certain vowels in English as *naturally* long: /i:/ as in "see," /u:/ as in "you," and so on. We think of a shortening of these as a kind of perversion of their essential quality, just as we regard a lengthening of /æ/ to /æ:/ as a deformation of that sound. And so, with the notion of a *long* vowel in our mental ears, we have difficulty in mastering the short /i/ and /u/ of languages like Spanish and Italian.

Length is allophonic, not phonemic: "seed" can be pronounced as /si:d/ or as /sid/ and still be recognizably the same word. But an Englishman hearing a Frenchman pronounce "peace" as /pis/ instead of /pi•s/ may be unsure what vowel the Frenchman intends—whether the short /ɪ/ (which will transform a word of noble connotations to a crude lavatory one) or the right phoneme /i:/. Length is a vowel attribute that asks for careful listening.

Another important attribute of certain languages—important, that is, from the standpoint of meaning—is that known as *stress*. French is one of the rare languages in which stress is of no great significance: what stress there is tends to come at the end of words, but it is not violent. One of the problems of translating French opera libretti into English is coping with what seems to be perverse stress in proper names—"Joseph" and "Carmen" are stressed on the second syllable and the music exaggerates the stress. Stress in Spanish is firm enough, but it does not, as it does in English, either determine meanings or affect the quality of the phonemes that make up the word. Every English word has—if it possesses more than one syllable—its own characteristic stress or even stresses. A primary stress represented as /'/ before the syllable concerned contrasts with a secondary stress—/,/—in a word like "feverishness," which we can represent phonetically as /'fi:vərɪʃ,nəs/. The shifting of primary stress can affect meaning. Thus, "increase" as /'ɪŋkri•s/ is a noun denoting "addition or enlargement," whereas /ɪŋ'kri•s/ is a verb meaning "to enlarge, to add to." "Compact" can appear as /kəm'pækt/, an adjective meaning "firmly united or joined together"; it can also be /'kɒmpækt/, a noun with various meanings, one of which is "a lady's portable vanity box." So also is "conduct" a verb as /kən'dʌkt/ and a noun as /'kɒndʌkt/.

This lexical differentiation, as we may call it, makes the stress of a number of English words very important, but the shifting of stress may—without actually altering meaning—bring about profound phonemic changes. The "correct" pronunciation of "controversy" has its stress on the first syllable, while a British pronunciation that has gained wide currency, and hence cannot really be judged "wrong," has shifted the stress to the second. Compare the two: /'kɒntrəvɜ:sɪ/—/kən'trɒvəsɪ/: the two vowel sequences are quite different.

Stress is heavy in English words and heavier still in Russian. In neither language does ordinary spelling give any indication as to where emphasis should be thrown. That is why it is a relief to go back to the unemphatic flow of French after tussling with the capricious hammer strokes of the tongue of Dostoevsky. The daughters of Latin, in general, are not as tempestuous and fist-banging as one would expect. Greek, whose only daughter is Modern Greek, seems not to have been any more concerned with stress than Latin: the poetry of both is based on vowel length and not on the recurrence of accent. Greek derivatives in English show a good deal of stress variability:

photograph	/'foutəgrɑ·f/ (or græf/)
photographic	/'foutə'græfɪk/
photographer	/fə'tɒgrəfə/

Stress has an important part to play in those meaningful groups of words we call sentences or phrases. We have to use a new set of signs to show emphatic syllables and weak syllables here—a kind of Morse (dash for stress, dot for no stress):

— · · — · — ·

Where do you think you're going?

But as soon as we start considering the rhythms of whole statements, we are inevitably led to that other attribute of speech—intonation, speech melody, the rise and fall of the voice. I feel we need full musical notation to convey this most subtle and meaningful aspect of our daily talk. Take the following, in which the curve within a single

word represents a falling tone, while the dots and dashes merely
sketch out the total melody:

· · — ·   — · ⟍

I expect you'll want a wash.

· · — ·   — · —

I expect you'll want a wash.

The first seems inoffensive enough—an offer of ablution facilities to
a guest who has just arrived from a long journey. The second implies
several things: the speaker is not very willing to give anything (even
water, soap, the use of a towel); yet at the same time there is a
faint suggestion that the person addressed is habitually dirty, not just
travel-stained.

On the level of pure lexical meaning, intonation can turn a statement into a question:

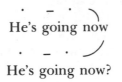

He's going now

He's going now?

The intonation patterns of other languages can be learned, though
with some difficulty, by listening. The absence of a system of notation
on the analogy of music is a handicap. When one comes to a tonal
language like Chinese, one faces very large difficulties indeed. What
we may call (though the time has not yet come to define the term
accurately) the *words* of Chinese are all formed in the same way: they
are monosyllables, either closed (consonant at the end) or open (vowel
at the end). Thus the sentence "A teapot is used for making tea and
a kettle for boiling water" is rendered as "Ch'a hu shih p'ao ch'a yung
ti, shui hu shih shao shui yung ti." (This is the national Chinese dialect
known as Kuo-yu, or Mandarin.) If you consider the limited number
of phonemes available to the human mouth, you will see that there
are not enough different monosyllables available to make all the
words that even the simplest language needs. We English users would
be in difficulties if all our sentences were like "My friend John says
that it is high time you went to the bank to get some cash to pay him
what you owe him." Already we have a fair number of monosyllables

that have the same sound but different meanings—like know - no; way - weigh; I - aye - eye. Consider how many of these homophones, as they are called, there must be in Chinese. The sentence *Ma ma ma ma ma ma* can mean "Has mother scolded the horse?" This sounds like a joke analogous to the Latin *Malo malo malo malo* ("I would rather be in an apple tree than a bad man in trouble"), but it is no joke.

In order to differentiate between monosyllables made up of the same sounds, Chinese makes use of tones. In Kuo-yu, there are five, though the fifth is falling into disuse. These are:

1. *Shang P'ing Shêng*—a sharp falling tone
2. *Hsia P'ing Shêng*—a curt upper rising tone
3. *Shang Shêng*—a long rising tone "broken in the middle"
4. *Ch'u Shêng*—a "departing tone" or falling-away melody
5. *Ju Shêng*—an abrupt intonation that shortens the vowel

Tone systems vary from dialect to dialect, and the speaker of Hakka will have difficulty in understanding a speaker of Cantonese. This is why the Chinese ideogram is important. Not being a phonetic mode of transcribing a word, it rides over dialectal differences: if a spoken word is not understood, it can always be written down. The adoption of an alphabet in China would gravely disrupt a sense of linguistic unity.

In learning a sentence like *Mên k'ou yu jên* ("There is someone at the door") we have to learn the tone that determines the meaning of each monosyllable, thus: *Mên* 2, *k'ou* 3, *yu* 3, *jên* 2. The difficulties involved in learning a tonal language are great but not insuperable. The unlearning of tonality can be equally difficult for a Chinese student of English, who may regard purely decorative tones as phonemic. In teaching minimal pairs, the Western instructor may tend to intone a "catalog pattern" that the student may take to indicate an essentially meaningful attribute to the words heard. Before we teach a language we must know something of the language of the taught.

The reader may wish now to try the transcription of the things he says into the IPA. He will first discover that he has two ways of speaking—one careful and sometimes formal, the other slack, colloquial, and unbuttoned. Careful slow speech is, following music, termed *lento*; the other variety is *allegro*. In *allegro* speech we take a lot of short cuts and utter allophones that we did not previously know existed. Thus, if we pronounce "even" *lento*, we will hear /i:vn/ (the old classroom dogma about every syllable necessarily containing a vowel is here seen to be untrue: the /n/ is syllabic and, the better to show this, it may be written with a subscript sign thus—/n̩/). If we pronounce "even" *allegro* we are more likely to hear /i:vɱ/, where the last sound is a voiced labiodental nasal: the /v/ has assimilated the /n/ to itself as far as it could, producing what may be thought of as a nasal /v/. This assimilation process is true of all speech but especially true of rapid speech. It may be interesting to note that one of our regular modern phonemes—the /ŋ/ of "sing"—began as an allophone of /n/, appearing only before /g/. When I said in an earlier chapter that Geoffrey Chaucer's "singing" was really "singgingg," as in modern Lancashire, I was not really telling the truth in seeming to imply the addition of a wanton /g/ to a phonemic /ŋ/. The situation was really the other way about, with the /ŋ/ separating itself from an inseparable /ŋg/ during the long dark history of English phonology. You use /ŋ/ more than you think—in "think," for instance, and in (*allegro*) phrases like "in God's name" and "in Glasgow." *Lento* speech will undoubtedly give a distinct /ɪn/ in both phrases.

The phonetic notation of what one says oneself and what other people say should be a staple of all courses of instruction in the mother tongue (whatever the mother tongue happens to be). This auditory training is totally neglected in our schools. In Great Britain, which has become a polyglot country, there are fine opportunities in our classrooms to notate the phonemes of Urdu, Hindi, Gujarati, and other exotic tongues, alongside the dialectal forms of English and, one assumes, the instructional RP that belong to the native tradition. This is regarded as unimportant. No governmental pronouncement on the teaching of English even alludes to it. For that matter, instruction in the use of the IPA is considered to be a remote academic luxury unrelated to the pragmatics of studying English. This view is probably sinful.

The second edition of *The Oxford English Dictionary* (1989) has replaced the homemade system of phonemic representation invented by the great Murray, father of the *OED*, with the IPA, which enjoins self-instruction in elementary phonetics on even the most amateur user of the work. And smaller dictionaries like the *Collins* use the IPA, to say nothing of foreign language dictionaries. It has to be said repeatedly that there is no magic in a phonetic alphabet, that knowledge of its symbols, ability to convert "feet" into /fi·t/ and "moon" into /mu:n/, means nothing in itself. The IPA makes sense only in terms of being an unambiguous shorthand for certain acoustic effects whose organic formation represents the only real phonetic knowledge. The important thing is the learning how to make sounds. It is not easy to pick up the phonemes of a foreign language by listening—despite the claims of the commercial organizations that put out tapes and discs. Children, if they are young enough, can pick up foreign sounds accurately: it was instructive, when Britain had her colonial responsibilities, to listen to the perfect mastery of Urdu or Chinese tonalities evinced by British children with native *amahs* or *ayahs*. Rare mimics—and all mimics are rare—can grasp a foreign sound system almost instinctively, but the great majority of language-learning adults cannot imitate exotic sounds with any approach to exactness. Told to say /y/ in French *lune*, they will produce something like /i/ or else something like /u/, but never the compromise sound that is required. To ask most adults to imitate the phonemes they hear is like asking a nonpianist to listen to a Bach fugue on the radio and then sit down at the keyboard and rattle the music off.

Nobody who has been kind enough to read this book even up to this point is, I hope, likely to be satisfied with those matchbox-sized amateur lexica that give "approximate" pronunciations in a variant of ordinary English orthography—like *kaffay* for *café*, or *bam-bee-noh* for *bambino*. The foreign language dictionaries I possess cost each rather more than a bottle of whiskey, but it is worth spending money on a professional performance. I look up the word *homme* and find, before the definition, the phonetic rendering /ɔm/. I know that the first of two symbols stands for a sound in the region of the vowel in "or" greatly shortened. I probably would be better advised to think of the sound as rounded and made with the back of the tongue about three quarters of the way down from the soft palate. I have no difficulty with /m/. I want to say not just *homme* but *un homme*, not "man" but "a man." I look up *un* and find /œ̃/ here. I have a phoneme in the tongue region of the /ɛ/ in "men" with the lip-rounding appropriate to the vowel of *homme*. I revise the technique for saying it —noting that the superscript tilde signifies snorting the vowel rather than singing it—and I practice the difficult exotic until it seems natural.

But learning to pronounce *un homme* correctly is not just a matter of getting two dictionary entries right. Add one word to another word and the answer is not two words but a new entity, a phrase. So now I have to get outside the dictionary, which deals with lexis, to confront the phenomenon of word linkage, discovering that the /n/ of *un*, silent before a consonant, comes to life before a vowel. The equation is /œ̃/ + /ɔm/ = /œ̃nɔm/.

The problem that English speakers of French encounter when trying to differentiate between *femme* ("woman") and *faim* ("hunger") is overcome if a little phonetic thought is taken. The dictionary gives the following pronunciations: *faim*—/fɛ̃/; *femme*—/fam/. The second word is straightforward enough: the /f/ and the /m/ belong to the English sound system as well as the French; the /a/ is lower than the /æ/ in "man," the jaw drops more for its enunciation. As for /fɛ̃/, we know that the vowel is somewhere near our own /ɛ/ in "men," and that it is nasalized, or snorted. To fix the difference between the two words one must practice a whole phrase—*La femme a faim* ("The woman is hungry")—/la fam a fɛ̃/. Change the *la* to *ma* and you have "My wife is hungry," which is not altogether an academic phrase if you arrive at your French hotel too late for dinner.

If we can use some basic phonetic knowledge to break down foreign words in this manner, we ought also to be able to study the allophonic differences within the English language—what, for instance, makes an Australian pronunciation of "no" different from that of an RP or American eastern seaboard version of it. Experiment is required: the tongue has to travel about, searching, and the ear keep on the alert. The diphthong in "no" is very variable as far as the first element is concerned, but the second element—/ʊ/—is usually pretty stable. Thus, British English is capable of /ʒʊ/, /əʊ/, even (though this is extreme) /eʊ/. What gives the diphthong its "oh" quality is the second element—the tongue reaching toward /ʊ/. But it seems certain that no user of a diphthong in a word like "show" or "though" allows the first element to drop as far as the /a/ of French *café* or the /ɑ/ of "car" pronounced short. To do so would be to risk producing a diphthong proper to words like "now" and "house"—a variant of /aʊ/. This limits the area in which the tongue can reach a first element in Australian "no." Try /ʌʊ/. That seems to be something like it. Try also a total unrounding—/ʌÿ/—with centralization. That will do for cracking a frostie on Bondi Beach.

Finally we must remember that all sounds of all languages are available to use. A phonemic system is not circumscribed by racial blood or isolated by a national flag. If you want the clicks of the Zulu dialects—front, middle, and back, represented in the IPA respectively as /ɪ/, /ʔ/, and /ɤ/—you can learn them. Sounds you consider yourself incapable of making are often, without your conscious knowledge, part of your daily *allegro* discourse. You cannot pronounce the 'll' or unvoiced 'L' of Welsh? You say it when you utter "Get lost" quickly. The beginning of "lost," normally voiced, begins as an unvoiced lateral under the influence of the preceding /t/. And the noise of "tut-tut" is pure Africa.

A postscript. Readers who have seen, heard, and admired ventriloquists performing may be skeptical about my phonetic dogmata. The dummy opens and shuts a letter-box mouth, affirming that lip-rounding has nothing to do with back vowels, while the lips of the artist himself make no movement. And yet the recognizable inventory of English phonemes comes comically out. Comically, yes, meaning deformed or heavily dialectal. We can speak with lips almost completely closed if we ignore rounding and avoid the bilabial consonants. I do not think any ventriloquist's dummy has yet recited "Peter Piper picked a peck of pickled peppers." The craft can, clearly, be learned. As for "throwing the voice," or making sounds seem to come from nowhere, this I do not well understand.

Another trick of utterance is not in the service of entertainment but concerned with serious communication. I refer to the whistled languages in use among the Mazateco Indians of Oaxaca in Mexico, the peasants of Gomera (one of the Canary Islands), and certain Turks.

Whistling, like riding a bicycle, is best not inquired into too curiously. Think about it, and you cannot do it. It is conceivably a medium of communication older than speech, and it relates man to birds, otters, and guinea pigs. Taboos are attached to it—"A whistling woman, a crowing hen/ Whistled the devil out of his den." Witches whistle (thrice), also whores. Yet *siffleuses* have achieved an acceptable music-hall art as *siffleurs*. Elizabeth Mann shocked me into awe by whistling a florid Bach top line with fine tone and expression. The violinist in her father Thomas's novel *Doktor Faustus* has the same gift. Whistling enables a man to be his own ensemble. I was once able to hum "Swanee River" and whistle Dvořák's *Humoresque* at the same time but have lost the knack. Dr. André Classe recalls, in his book *Whistled Languages*, written in collaboration with Professor René-Guy

Busnel, hearing Sir Richard Paget perform four-part music with his daughter, both simultaneously whistling and humming. Whistling is music, but it can also be speech. In this latter form it is either crude or comic—the American soldier's "wolf whistle" (two whistled notes a tritone or augmented fourth apart), Harpo Marx's urgent revelations to his brother Chico, which Chico laboriously has to hit-and-miss into words.

A certain Professor G. Cowan pioneered study of the Mazateco Indian method of communicating "both at close quarters and at a distance by means of modulated whistles, with the same ease, speed and intelligibility, as when using speech in the ordinary manner." I quote from an article he published in *Language* in 1948. The wonder of this faculty is diminished somewhat when we consider that Mazateco is a tonal language, like Chinese, and to make a whistle speech out of it is a matter of extracting from the vocal speech continuum those parameters that come closest to music—tone and duration.

But how, one asks, can intelligibility subsist when all those elements of language that we are taught to regard as of primary importance are eliminated? It does subsist, as it does with the drum, flute, and horn signals in central Africa. In the film of *Pygmalion*, where Leslie Howard as Professor Higgins played D-E-G on a xylophone, the audience, to its surprise and pleasure, heard the phrase as "Throw him out." But there was a question asked first, and a mere intonation curve proved a sufficient answer. We have to know how Mazateco works before we know how its whistled version works. I do not think that many of us have the time.

But in Gomera we have a dialect of Spanish to be transsibilated, and we can if we wish, like Busnel and Classe, go and hear how the thing is done before modern technology obliterates it. In 1891 R. Verneau published a book called *Cinq ans aux Îles Canaries*. It described how the peasants of Gomera whistled at each other over the deep valleys or *barrancos* that cross the island radially. Though Verneau had scientific training, he did not observe with any accuracy the technique of the *Silbo*, as it is called, or the *Silbadores*, who practice it. This has all now been put right by Professors Busnel and Classe. There are various methods of emitting the basic whistling sound— the fingerless, one-finger, two-finger, knuckle, and so on, with subtle variations within each category. Busnel and Classe give us a full inventory of the phonemes of Canary Spanish and show how these can be adapted to the whistling technique. Vowels are fairly easy, but consonants raise problems. Whistled speech is, of necessity, voiced, like vowels, so that the unvoiced-voiced opposition we have noted in pairs like /p/ - /b/ and /t/ - /d/ is mainly neutralized. "It is somewhat startling," we are told, "that in practice no ambiguity should arise from this." The making of a plosive with the lips stops the air in speech. The lips are immobilized in whistling, so that the Silbadores check the air flow by means of the thorax muscle and the diaphragm.

Something of a mystery, then, to us cold-eyed observers. But a mystery that has worked, though it is dying out as telephones and loud hailers increasingly span valleys. Yet whistling has a future as a link less between man and man than between man and animal. Apparently dolphins have been trained to reply with whistles to acoustic signals of great complexity and to imitate the "copying pitch contours very accurately." They can, in fact, reach the first human steps of echolalia, through which children first learn to use their organs of speech. The remarkable achievements of the creatures in *The Day of the Dolphin* are sheer science fiction. George C. Scott, in that film, proudly announces "First phonemes" and then "First morphemes." Impossible, apparently. The basis of any future language teaching for dolphins will be through sibilation. Birds in their whistling, as indeed in their talking, may imitate human beings, but we are not led thereby to a closer rapprochement with them. It is the mammals that count, especially the dolphins.

There is, you will see, still a great deal to learn about modes of oral communication. Now that we have completed our amateur study of phonetics, let us consider how a knowledge of what the mouth does when it produces speech may have an artistic and commercial purpose quite removed from disinterested scientific observation.

8.

SOUNDS THAT WE SEE

Early talking films were made the hard way. Microphones were insinuated onto the set, hidden in flower bowls, corsages, hats, or else placed frankly dangling from a boom, with the constant danger of boom shadow. If the camera was frightened of the microphone, the microphone was resentful of the camera, which made too much noise while it was being turned—and had, in consequence, to be muffled with blankets or sequestered in a soundproof chamber. All this is comically but accurately presented in the film *Singin' in the Rain*. The process of adding dialogue and sound effects after the shooting of the action, a convenient and time-saving technique, was fairly slow to be discovered. A whole constellation of terms is applied to the artifice whereby synchronic sound and action are achieved by diachronic means, but "dubbing" is the word best known.

Strictly speaking, dubbing implies not just the addition of sound to film shot silently. It presupposes an original sound track to be modified either partially or totally. In fact, "dub" can be given three definitions: (a) to make a new recording out of an original tape or record or track in order to accommodate changes, cuts, or additions; (b) to insert a totally new sound track, often a synchronized translation of the original dialogue; (c) to insert sound into a film or tape. A film can be entirely dubbed. Sounds can be dubbed in, too.

There are two ways of hearing a foreign film. The first and, these days, commonest—at least on the continent of Europe—is to suffer the illusion that the actors on the screen are actually speaking the language of the audience. The other, probably still the better of the two, is to hear the original dialogue and to have this translated on the screen in the form of subtitles. In multilingual communities like Malaysia, the second method is the only practicable one, though half the screen must be filled up with Bahasa (or Malay), Chinese, Tamil, and Hindi. In Scandinavia subtitling is the rule, and it is adduced as one explanation of the admirable English, usually with an American accent, spoken by young Danes, Norwegians, and Swedes. From an aesthetic point of view, it is very hard to defend dubbing, since the way an actor uses his voice is an important part of his artistic equipment. Humphrey Bogart not only had a distinctive vocal style but also slight labial paralysis that imparted a lisping quality to his lip consonants. This idiosyncrasy is never carried over into dubbed versions of his films, and there is a consequent loss of a highly individual flavor. Sometimes actors have foreign voices imposed on them that result in a mythic image quite at variance with the original. Thus, in Italy Stan Laurel and Oliver Hardy (called there Stanlio and Olio) are made to speak the kind of anglicized Tuscan a tin-eared British schoolboy might use, though, at the same time, a wholly Italian passion for *spaghetti alle vongole* is imposed on Stanlio. Occasionally, though, dubbing can be inspired. The alley cat of Walt Disney's *The Aristocats* (*Gli Aristogatti*) is turned into one of the nick-eared denizens of the cat colony of the Roman Colosseum. He speaks a very rich Roman dialect. Alberto Sordi does the dubbing.

Total dubbing is least applicable to musical films, where the original song lyrics, and sometimes recitativelike dialogue preceding, or contained in, "production numbers," are frequently permitted to intrude implausibly into the stream of translated speech. But dubbing has become a very fine art, especially in France and Italy, and an important musical film like *My Fair Lady* is deemed worthy of total translation. The ingenuity of the Italian version is worth remarking on. The basic *Pygmalion* situation has no applicability in Italy, where one dialect is as good as another, but there is a phonetic eccentricity in Bari—the raising of /a/ to /e/—which became the staple of Eliza Doolittle's idiolect. Though there is no aspirate in Italian, the process of teaching the girl to pronounce correctly phrases like "In Hertford, Hereford, and Hampshire hurricanes hardly ever happen" was justified by her need to look ahead and accommodate British patrons of her flower shop. Otherwise the aspirate was, following Italian custom, not taken seriously, and Eliza was not the only one to call her teacher 'Enry 'Iggins. "Bloody," the climactic expletive of the original play, is replaced by "arse" in the musical version. Italians use *culo* on all possible occasions, but the *culo* of Eliza's speech at Ascot had as devastating an effect on Italian audiences as the British equivalent on British. The situation of an idiomatic Italian comedy being played in a totally British environment is, when you come to think of it, bizarre, but the goodwill of an audience ready to be diverted can bridge the dizziest gaps. It is a kind of Elizabethan situation, with striking clocks and doublets in ancient Rome, but synchronically, not diachronically, so.

Culo may mean "arse," but it does not look like it. A disyllable opening with a back-stop consonant /k/ and containing two vowels that have lip-rounding (/u/ and /o/) is the translation of a monosyllable with an open spread vowel /ɑ:/. No amount of goodwill in an audience can bridge the gap between what the eye sees and what the ear hears. Very few people can lip-read, but most people are aware of the consonance between the movements of the mouth and the sounds those movements produce. The dubbers of *My Fair Lady* were lucky in that Eliza shouted at the horse she wanted to win ("Get off your arse, Dover!"), thus distorting her sounds, and was not shot in close-up. She was far enough away from the camera not to invite labial scrutiny. Still, luck cannot often be relied upon. My present concern is with the difficulties that have to be surmounted at the postsynchronizing stage in the making of a dubbed film. In other words, how can a mouth making one set of sounds be made to appear as if it were making another?

This is a rough-and-ready problem of rough-and-ready phonetic observation. It is mainly the lips that are involved, for the lips are visible, while the activity of the tongue is hidden away. With labiodentals like /f/ and /v/ there is visibility enough, as also with linguodentals—/θ/ as in "thin" and /ð/ as in "then." But the maximal visibility is accorded to the lip-rounding and lip spreading that are involved in the shaping of vowel sounds.

The problems do not arise only when a film in English is being dubbed into a foreign language. Excruciating gaffes are sometimes perpetrated by actors when recording on the set, unnoticed or uncorrected by the director—whose knowledge of English may be less than perfect. When run in the cutting room, these errors can often, with trickery, be put right. The actor will be available for sessions of postsynchronization or "looping"—so called because a loop of film is run and rerun to familiarize the actor with his own lip movements, enabling him to achieve an exact synchronization—but sometimes, for a variety of reasons, there has to be a drastic act of surgery on the body of the film itself. The error is most frequently discerned by the scriptwriter, and it can be a linguistic solecism or a serious deviation from the scenario. A good, or infuriating, example of the former occurred in the making of an "epic" film based on the life of Moses. Aaron, played by Sir Anthony Quayle, was permitted by the Italian director to say, "God has chosen people like you and I." A former director of the Royal Shakespeare Company should have known better. The offending "I" was uttered in close-up and could not easily be plucked out. The expense of reshooting the scene to accommodate the correction "me" would have been prohibitive. Looping to put right a single grammatical error would have been dear enough. A piece of film was taken from a different scene, in which Aaron presented his back to the camera, and this was cut in to cover the "me." The pronoun itself was uttered and recorded by a mere cutting-room technician, and nobody seemed any the wiser.

The elocutionary skill of actors often belies their limited mastery of the tongue they speak. Errors are common—"contemptuous" for "contemptible" seems the Anglo-American favorite—but confidence in knowing better than the scriptwriter can lead to expensive and time-consuming restorations of the lines originally written. Only an Orson Welles can, with his "cuckoo-clock" improvisation in *The Third Man*, improve on a Graham Greene. Burt Lancaster, playing Moses, made a radical alteration in the following passage: "You will not hear from me again, Pharaoh." "Why not, cousin Moses?" "I am slow of speed." This last utterance became "Because I am uncircumcised of lips," with an appropriate circular finger gesture around the mouth. There was no cover in the form of back views or reverse shots to accommodate a restoration of the original line. The lips had to remain uncircumcised. The scriptwriter is usually blamed, in such circumstances, for giving the actor poor material. The reader should now check the differences, in a mirror, or with probing fingers, between the two Mosaic statements: he will see, or feel, that the two lots of lipwork are incompatible.

Foreign actors without knowledge of the language of the film, who nevertheless have the professionalism to learn their unintelligible lines parrot-fashion to ease the eventual work of the dubber, are a great blessing to scriptwriters. Sessue Hayakawa, who played Colonel Saito in *The Bridge on the River Kwai*, did just that. He did not know what the words meant and hence did not try to improve them.

The coming of the day of the international film, with Cinecittà in Rome a Babel of monoglot actors, raised dubbing to a precise craft and a major cottage industry (domestic in the sense that dubbers form syndicates or families who become used to working together). It is interesting to visit a film set when an international film is being shot—like Fellini's *Casanova*, for instance—and hear an American actor and a German actress conducting a scene in their own languages, frequently a scene in which precision of verbal communication is essential to the narrative: the illusion of perfect mutual understanding is an aspect of histrionic skill. Bedroom scenes, of course, present no linguistic problems: sex is the one universal language. Since dubbing is a major part of the whole operation with such films, it may legitimately be asked why the films are shot, which they are, with sound. Why not return to the silent days of before 1928 and construct a mute artifact, regarding the adding of sound as a separate process under a separate director? There are various reasons why not. Since 1928 actors have expected to participate in a total acting process, being dually recorded by cameraman and sound engineer, even if dubbing has to occur later. The postsynchronization of speech is recognized, anyway, as a necessary evil, one submitted to because of difficulties in recording speech in the open air or in swift or violent action. But the scenes that can be shot with sound—indoor confrontations, for instance—should be so shot, exhibiting the total art of the performer. And whatever language the actor uses, it will be intelligible in one of the versions of the film.

Fellini shoots his films with sound, but is never greatly concerned about what is actually said. Indeed, he sometimes specifies that actors shall justify the use of their vocal organs by reciting sequences of cardinal numbers. Passionate performers prove to have been counting rigorously—*una, due, tre* or *jedan, puran, tri*—and it is possible to recognize the counting rhythm if one looks hard enough. Fellini is able to say, like an orchestral conductor, "Let us return to Number 94."

Awareness that dubbing is going to take place has influenced the director's approach to the visual aspects of his craft. Close-ups are dangerous, since they display a great deal of the anatomy of speech. In passages of dialogue, traditionally rendered by reverse shots, or cutting from speaker to speaker, increasingly we are shown the listener rather than the speaker, the words disembodied, the effect of the words on their receptor. The symbols VO (voice-over) and OS (out of shot) appear more and more frequently in shooting scripts. It is theoretically possible to make a film in which the lips of the speakers are never seen at all. Precision of lip synchronization is often decreed by the editors at the International Recording Studio in Rome or one of the workshops in Wardour Street, Soho, London. The scriptwriter is often called in to give plausible words to mouthing extras in the background: this is rather like Sarah Bernhardt's making up those parts of her body that would not be seen on the stage. When this vital business of equipping a film with a sound track is being conducted by nameless men in shirtsleeves among plastic coffee cups and half-eaten sandwiches, the director and the stars are basking in expensive sunshine.

The technicians responsible for preparing a script for dubbing have a fair knowledge of organic phonetics: at least they are aware of the relationship between sounds as acoustic entities and the oral athletics of their production. We never learn the names of the dubbers. I have dubbed a good deal myself from Italian into English, and do not expect my name to appear in the credits among the chief grips, the best boy, and the hairstylists. In practice a good deal of dubbing is worked out collectively and empirically. Men and women who edit films acquire a sensitivity to what is being silently mouthed on the editing tables, and they can at least suggest sequences of gibberish that fit exactly. Indeed, many lines of deathless script in its translated form begin as gibberish: take care of the sounds and let the sense come later.

The most difficult elements to render from one language to another when dubbing are, as might be expected, the commonest in both. "Yes" can easily become *ja*, especially when the speaker is a slack-mouthed American, but it is hard to turn it into *igen* or *kyllä* or *naam* or *ne* or *nevet*. A cowboy drawling *yah* or *yeah* might just about be saying *ouais*, if not *oui*, but Sir John Gielgud affirming with precise classical actor's diction in close-up was always excruciating to dub. Greek *ne* sounds like "no," and *o'chi*, which means "no," can never be made to fit a naying mouth. A common statement in films is "I love you." Actors with unathletic lips cause little trouble when the phrase is rendered into French. The vowels of *aime* and "love" are both open and unrounded, and the lip-rounding for "you" will serve for syllabic *-me* at the end of *aime*. *Ich liebe dich* will not fit loving anglophone lips, however. "To be or not to be" does not look like *Sein der nicht sein*, but *Essere o non essere* matches the original by having lip spreading for the key word and lip-rounding for the structural ones: "not to" -"*o non*."

A typical dubber's nightmare would occur if, say, one of the key episodes in a French film consisted of a hero's reciting the first stanza of Baudelaire's "L'Albatros" in a close shot:

> Souvent, pour s'amuser, les hommes d'équipage
> Prennent des albatros, vastes oiseaux des mers . . .

The script in straight translation would give: "Sometimes, to amuse themselves, the men of a ship's crew grab albatrosses, huge seabirds." Would any of these words fit the mouth of the reciter? Only "albatrosses," singularized to a vocable virtually identical with the original. What phrase could contain it—"grab a tame albatross"? The lip movement at the beginning of *prennent* is highly visible, as is the one at the end of "tame." Try "dazed albatross." Try, taking the last syllables of *équipage*, "play pranks on a dazed albatross." Complete the second line: "vast-winged hoverer." The 'i' and the second 'v' do not match the French lip positions. Try "vast white lord of the air." There is nothing in the English to explain the pout on *mers*. "Vast white-eyed dreamer" is eccentric but seems to fit. To put Baudelaire into a film is eccentric anyway. The whole thing might be rendered as:

> At sea, for pastime, see sailors who brutally play
> Pranks on a dazed albatross, vast white-eyed dreamer.

This is in accordance with nearly all the mouth positions of the French, but the problems of making the words sound like poetry and, when the next two lines come, finding rhymes, are as devastating as the reader will imagine—also time-consuming. It is not surprising that a lot of cinematic dubbing represents a mere approximation to matching exotic mouth positions with native sounds: speed of utterance, labial slackness (very common with American actors), and the listener-viewer's own ignorance are among the dubber's best friends. ("Play" will rhyme with "way" or "day," "dreamer" with "steamer": the thing becomes obsessive. And should not that "wide-eyed" be "wide-orbed" or "white-oared"?)

Probably subtitles are better than dubbing, if they are done well. A Hindi version of *Hamlet* (ten songs for Ophelia and a dance of gravediggers) did badly with "Shall I live or do myself in? I don't know," and only the other day I saw a televised American war film in which the question "Tanks?" was subtitled as *"Merci,"* but one accepts such hazards. Dubbing should be reserved for knights. On the other hand, from the point of view of the study of speech sounds, the existence of dubbing—a major craft in Europe, a lucrative trade for out-of-stagework actors—serves to remind us that the lips in action are the beginning of speech for all of us—"babba," "mama," and so on (even the head of the Catholic Church is only *papa* in Italian, the paternal name picked up in the cradle)—and that they are the most visible aspect of speech. What happens behind the lips is more important and of little concern to the film dubber. But the guesswork of the postlingual deaf (those not born deaf but afflicted after speech has been acquired) depends almost entirely on what the lips of an interlocutor are doing. There is too much slack lipwork around in English speech. This is not an aesthetic judgment but a social one.

9.

THE EAR BECOMES THE EYE

An alphabet seems the most natural thing in the world to children who play with ABC bricks, but all my life I have been ready to be betrayed into large enthusiasm about the "miracle" of its invention, placing it high above television, jet propulsion, and nuclear fission. It is clever enough to be able to record and reproduce by electronic means the sounds our mouths utter, but the conversion of speech into impulses and impulses back into speech cannot, I like to think, match the fundamental achievement of converting the temporal into the spatial—for speech works in time, but letters stand in space.

This enthusiasm, in the view of Professor Roy Harris, is misplaced. It is certainly old-fashioned—it goes back to scholars like W. F. Mavor, who, about 1785, said: "Writing is universally allowed to be the noblest invention that can possibly be conceived." By writing, Mavor means alphabetic writing. But the alphabet is only a stage in the development of systems of signs that stand for human utterances. If those of us who use English enthuse about our alphabet as an efficient means of recording sounds, properly phonemes, we had better look occasionally at its inefficiency and think again. And we had better note how unalphabetic the world of applied science is becoming. The remote control we use for changing television channels does not have alphabetic signs on its face, and in Europe our travel along highways or even through city streets is guided more by nonalphabetic signals than plain words. The 'H' signifying the way to a hospital may seem to bow to the alphabet, but not on Italian roads. The Italian for "hospital" is *ospedale:* there is no 'h' there.

I will try to damp my enthusiasm and look at the alphabet coolly. It is, shall we say, at least an interesting invention and a comparatively recent one. It is doubtful it is much more than three thousand years old, whereas speech is as old as man. Thus, the dawning of the principle of representing spoken sound by a written letter has come very late in human history, and it still has not come—or if come, been found acceptable—to a large proportion of mankind—the Chinese, for example. Unlike fire and agriculture, it did not come at various times to various races, widely separated in space but undergoing parallel developments. It came once, and once only, to a race of Semites trading in the lands of the Mediterranean, and like many large discoveries, it came almost in a fit of absentmindedness.

Before the alphabet, there were certain rough and cumbersome ways of granting permanence to words, but these had nothing to do with words as temporal events, successions of speech sounds. The Egyptians, the Mexicans, and the Indians of the Americas drew pictures that stood for words—they got behind the word itself and recorded what the word stood for. Picture writing is our oldest form of setting down signs for the *referents* of language—the things in the outside world that language refers to—and it has always been the least efficient.

The reason for this is that there are comparatively few aspects of language that lend themselves to adequate pictorialization. We can draw the sun, the moon, spears, jugs, leaves, loaves, stylized men and horses, but a statement of even so simple a type as "I lost my wife and five children in the last intervillage war" is hard to set down in pure pictures. The fact is that the *pictograms* (to use the technical term) of the prealphabetic civilizations were never really intended to provide a comprehensive writing system: we tend to impose our needs on societies quite happy without mailboxes, libraries, and daily newspapers. Pictograms probably arose only as reminders, signs of ownership, commemorative inscriptions. Consider how little urge there would be to make inscriptions at all when there were only stones and chisels as writing implements. If we had to leave the smooth ease of pen and ink and typewriter and word processor to go back to painful hammering, writing would die out quickly enough.

But the pictogram still retains its usefulness, even in sophisticated alphabetic societies. It is the most primitive and naive of all inscriptive techniques, but it can prevent—in international youth hostels—a male from using a female bathroom, and vice versa. The conventional symbol for a male is a two-legged stick man, that for a female the same, only with a skirt. Outside hotel and pub toilets these crudities have been refined into representations of people in eighteenth-century court dress, but the principle remains the same. Our English traffic signs show a fair variety of pictograms: a cross for a crossroads, a 'Z' for a bend, a 'T' for a road junction, a schoolboy and a schoolgirl for a school. (This last used to be an *ideogram* or *logogram*—terms we shall come to in a moment. There was a symbolic torch representing the *idea* of learning; this may have been too complex for many drivers, hence the reversion to a primitive pictogram.)

The development of writing is associated with a number of different social activities that, on close examination, are seen to be cognate. The growth of agriculture involves stargazing and moon watching—in other words, attempts to establish the limits of the seasons. Also, fertility rituals are performed and gods of fertility are worshiped. A priestly class emerges—elders who have no other work than to perform due ceremonies, predict drought or abundance, and intercede with the gods. It is difficult, in these early societies, to separate religion from agriculture: the priest is a magician is an astrologer is an astronomer is a scientist. He guards sacred mysteries, he needs to keep complex records, he compiles the tables of the law. By now simple pictograms are by no means enough. We are in the age of secret sophisticated writing, sacred carvings or hieroglyphics.

We are, in fact, in priest-ruled Egypt, with its holy men who learn how to predict the rise and fall of the Nile but are inevitably unwilling to share their secrets with others. Their kind of writing seems to use straightforward pictograms—which, theoretically, any plain man or woman can understand, just as any plain motorist can understand traffic signs—but in reality they use a priestly code, communication between the elect, holy and terrible symbols. An Egyptian priest would be a fool to make his system of writing common knowledge— he plays up the mystery of language to enhance his own power. He has a vested interest in codes and acrostics and other means of delimiting a system of communication to a chosen few.

There were various means of creating inscriptive symbols that should transcend the limitations of pictograms. One way was the way of metaphor. The Chinese, to this day, use a drawing of a man or a field to represent respectively those two words, bringing the symbols together to make the new word "farmer." This is plainly and admirably descriptive, but they have also to call on metaphor for abstract words—"not," for example. "Not" in Chinese shows a sort of plant with a line above it (see Figure 6). The plant is trying to grow, but the line is stopping it. This is a little poem of negativeness, a metaphor of notness. The Chinese symbol for "bright" brings together two symbols, that for the sun and that for the moon: two concrete images suggest a common property, abstracted into the word "brightness." The moon and sun symbols seem (see Figure 6) to have traveled some distance over the centuries from the time when they were simple circles, but that is the kind of thing that happens to pictograms. *Mu* and *lin* are highly representational, but look at *nyu* and *dze* and search for the elements that denote sonship and daughterliness.

When symbols are used to express ideas rather than to represent objects in the external world, we have *ideograms* ("idea drawings") or *logograms* ("word drawings"). With some of these (Chinese *pu* is a good example) it is possible to see vestiges of picture writing; with many the pictorial origins are obscure and the shapes seem quite arbitrary. Thus, the Arabic numerals that we use seem (except for the first) to relate to nothing pictorial: 2, 3, 4, 5, and the rest are arbitrary characters that, in all countries, carry the same arithmetical meaning. The Roman numerals seem to come closer to pictograms, especially as they appear on a clockface—I, II, III, IIII, V. They are drawings of fingers, except for V, which represents the space between index finger and thumb and thus stands for the whole hand. Signs like +, =, and % have clear meanings to the world, but they perform neither a pictorial nor a phonetic task. They are pure ideograms.

The modern Chinese language contrives to get on well enough with its ideograms: it produces books on Marxism and nuclear physics; the bulk of the literate are not noticeably clamoring for a Western alphabet. But occasionally, especially when introducing a foreign word or name, Chinese becomes suddenly aware of sounds and forgets about referents. It will transliterate a name like Churchill not by using the ideograms for a church and a hill but by choosing syllables that carry roughly the same sounds as the exotic form. This puzzles some readers of Chinese newspapers, for dialectic variations are ex-

MEN
door

K'OU
mouth opening

JEN
man

PU
no, not

MU
wood, timber

LIN
forest

RI
sun

YWE
moon

MING
bright

NYU
daughter

DZE
son

HAO
good

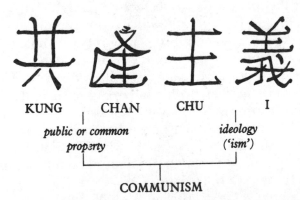

KUNG   CHAN   CHU   I

public or common   *ideology*
property   *('ism')*

COMMUNISM

FIGURE 6. SOME CHINESE CHARACTERS

treme and it's not possible for the ideograms chosen to convey the same phonetic information to everybody.

As soon as sound elements are introduced into nonalphabetic writing, as soon as a symbol represents a phonetic rather than a semantic notion, then we are on the way to learning our ABC's. The first glimmerings of phonetic writing among the Egyptian priests appear in puns, play upon words with the same sounds but with different meanings—what are termed *homophones*. It is easiest to understand this sort of trick if we think of the homophonic possibilities of English. Let us imagine that we are in the same situation as the Egyptian priests, possessing no alphabet, only pictograms. We have the word "sun," and the sun is easy enough to depict—a circle with a few wavy lines for rays. We have also the word "son," but a son is not so easy to draw. We can, after much trouble, achieve an acceptable likeness of a young man, but how can we convey relationship? The easiest thing to do is to use the pictogram for "sun," exploiting the homophonic. This will normally be enough, for the context should make all clear. "The father loves his /sʌn/" is not ambiguous. But to avoid confusion in statements like "The /sʌn/ sank into the sea," it might be useful to prefix the "sun" pictogram with a conventional sign denoting human maleness. The image of a man would do. Let us take another example—"see" and "sea." "Sea" is easily shown as wavy water; if we want the verb "to see," we can place the image of a human eye in front of it; if we want "see" in its episcopal sense, a simple drawing of a chess bishop ought to suffice. This way of defining by means of prefixes will give us a whole battery of little signs called *radicals*. The eye radical followed by a watch will indicate clearly what verb is meant. The man radical can give the pictogram of a buoy a wholly unambiguous meaning. Radicals exist in Chinese, and the learning of them eases recognition of certain words. When a radical is fused with a pictogram and, over centuries, simplified and conventionalized, it becomes difficult to pick out the representational element from the resultant ideogram.

This kind of punning—which, incidentally, must often have been contrived to confuse rather than enlighten—is still popular in children's-page competitions. The most elaborate type of pun is the multiple or syllabic—"horsefly" shown as a horse and a fly; "well-bred" as a well and a loaf; a chair, a man, and a ship to make up "chairmanship." One can go to excruciating lengths, as in charades, with "Socratic"—a sock, a rat, a "this-sum-is-right" tick, or—which deforms the word somewhat, but no matter—a paper clip, a toe, a horse's mane, and an ear for "kleptomania." These tricks and puzzles fossilize a stage of emergence toward the syllabic sense: one more step and we shall have an alphabet.

Everybody is able to recognize a syllable, even if some difficulty is experienced in defining what a syllable is. In the preceding chapter I noted that the old notion of a syllable's being recognizable by the presence of a vowel will not do. Words like "rhythm," "fission," and "nation" all end with a syllabic consonant—/m/ or /n/. Set a word to music, and you will know how many syllables there are. "Civility" has to be sung to four notes—four syllables. The number of sounds in the word will be guessed at from the number of letters, and for once the guess will be right. But how many sounds are there in the disyllables—"open," "fairground," "butcher"? How many in the trisyllables "possible," "photograph," "pertinent," "Westminster"? To the person with the minimum of phonological training, there should be no difficulty in giving the right answer; to the majority there will come an accession of doubt and head scratching.

It is no wonder, then, that with the scribes of a few thousand years ago there should be no urge to dissect words into phonemic units. Syllables, however, were a different matter, and the first breakthrough from a priestly or hieroglyphic script to a demotic or popular one was easy and natural enough: the old pictograms, in a conventionalized and simplified form, were turned into the materials of *syllabaries*. A syllabary thinks in terms of a single symbol standing for a consonant plus a vowel. It works best with a language like Japanese, where every word can be broken up into syllables, each following the easy formula C + V. Good examples are YO-KO-HA-MA; HI-RO-SHI-MA; MI-KA-DO.

Not that Japanese makes exclusive use of a syllabary. It is a language that early adopted the ideograms of Chinese but finds a syllabary useful when new or foreign words have to be presented. Chinese does not like borrowing from other languages; it prefers to reformulate a new concept in its own terms, so that "electricity" is rendered as "light spirit" and "gas" as "coal spirit." But Japanese will gladly accept English words like "gas," "page," "bus," "pound," "dress," and "typewriter" so long as it can adjust them to the native syllabic pattern as *gazu, peju, basu, pondo, doresu,* and *tuparita* respectively. To get these words on paper it will use a syllabary—either the Hiragana or the

Katakana. Written and printed Japanese makes use of both of these, together with about fifteen hundred Chinese characters.

The Katakana syllabary has five symbols corresponding to the five vowel letters A E I O U. It then has five corresponding to the syllables MA MI MU ME MO, five corresponding to NA NI NU NE NO, five for SA SI SU SE SO, and so on—the remaining consonants Z P B T D K G Y R H W each possessing five forms, according to which vowel is attached to it. This gives $14 \times 5 = 70$ symbols $+ 5$ (vowels on their own) $+$ the solitary closed form (that is, ending in a consonant) UN $= 76$. This is about the average number of signs required by a syllabary. Figure 7 shows the beginning of an article I wrote for a syndicate of Japanese newspapers. In it you will see the whole consort dancing together—Chinese ideograms, Hiragana, Katakana. My own name appears to the right—just left of the title in its hatched or shaded box. It is read from top to bottom as A-UN-SO-NI BA-ZI-YE-SU, which is, to the Japanese ear, near enough to "Anthony Burgess."

In the Far East, then, one may see all the prealphabetic sign systems in daily use: the pictogram, the ideogram, and the syllabary. There has, however, not been any sense of the need to take that extra step towards a true alphabet. Admittedly, it was a difficult extra step, and it was only achieved by the Semitic peoples of the Mediterranean because of an accident—that accident being the peculiar structure of Semitic languages.

All Semitic languages—Hebrew, Arabic, Phoenician, and the rest —possess in common a peculiar devotion to consonants. In fact, a Semite does not think of a Semitic word as being composed of syllables; he thinks of it as being made of the strong bones of consonants with the vowel sounds floating above like invisible spirits. Moreover, the vowels of a Hebrew or Arabic word have little to do with the determination of meaning. Meaning is firmly staked out by the consonants alone. Thus the three consonants 'k,' 't,' 'b' in Arabic possess a root meaning of "reading," so that *kitab* means a book, *khatib* means "mosque reader," the prefix 'm-' makes *maktaba*—"bookshop" or *mokhtab*—"college." I taught for some time in a *mokhtab*. The non-Muslim students irreverently called it a mucktub.

The consonants alone will establish meaning if the context is clear. In Hebrew the staking-out of three consonants to create a word gives characteristic flavor to proper names like Jacob, Rachel, David,

英作家のみたソ連の民衆生活

アンソニー・バージェス

のんびり

【本社特約OCS通信】英国の小説家アンソニー・バージェス氏はこのほどソ連のレニングラードを訪問し、帰英後BBC放送で旅行談を放送した。次に紹介するのはそのときの放送談話大要であるが、いわゆるソ連国民の非能率ぶりとか一枚舌についても作家らしい機知に富んだ解釈を示し多くの示唆をふくんだ観察を行なっている。

"能率"は上層部だけのもの?

私はソ連人の能率の悪い点が一番好きである。鉄のように冷たく厳しい社会生活を予想して、私はレニングラードを訪れたのだが、そこで見たのは最もヒューマンな人間、べつのことばでいえば最も非能率的な人間であった。

といっても非能率的な国民がスプートニクや宇宙飛行士を生み出

すはずはないのだが、おそらく能率というものはソ連社会では一番の上層部に浮いている薄いエキスのようなものなのだろう。学校にたとえてみると先生方はみな職員会議に集まっているか最高学級の物理実験に立ち合い、生徒たちは教室で自習をしているようなものる。また英字新聞を買おうら、英国共産党のデイリー・カー紙しかおいていないの開売子の少女は「ほかの新聞はもう売り切れましもしかしたらこれをウリのは間違いで、ソ連人が

FIGURE 7. A JAPANESE ARTICLE

Moloch, and Joseph. Spell the words as JCB, RCHL, DVD, MLCH, JSPH, and the meanings remain clear in Hebrew. English is a language that defines meaning as much with vowels as with consonants, and so DVD is ambiguous, even multiguous, as it stands. It could be, besides "David," "divide" or "dived." And MLCH could be, besides "Moloch," "milch" or "mulch." Only in the Semitic languages, rich in consonants but relatively poor in vowels, can a group of consonants stand for a whole word.

We believe that the Phoenician traders of the Mediterranean were the first to take over simplified Egyptian symbols and use them to represent consonants. They created a "betagam" rather than an alphabet, a BCD, not an ABC. They were not interested in finding vowel letters because vowel letters were not necessary to the writing of Phoenician, which shared that characteristic with the other Semitic languages. This meant that they were able to make do with twenty-odd symbols—a tremendous and epoch-making economy. Had they thought—as speakers of Western languages like English must think—in terms of consonant plus vowel, they would not have been able to leap beyond their simple syllabary, for Mediterranean man was not yet ready for the concept of vowels and consonants as independent partners in language. But the Phoenicians had the concept of *free consonants* in writing, though in speaking, those consonants would be attached to a vowel, and this made their discovery of a betagam possible.

What urged them to create this system of easily learned and easily handled letters? Not literature, not religion, but trade. They presumably needed to make out their bills and enter their books with some speed: a few quick strokes, and there was a memo or delivery note or invoice. Not for them the leisure of hieroglyphics or syllabaries. An Egyptian eye or head, bird or running water, must become abstract lines or circles—as with the letters of our own alphabet, which ultimately have the same derivation. Whether their letters would be curved or angular must depend on the materials used; our own 'R' and 'T' are essentially chiseled letters; the curved forms like 'S' and 'O' and 'U' suggest a softer ground, like paper, and the sinuous movements of a reed pen (see Figure 8).

In which direction did their letters travel—left to right, right to left, up, down? It varied; it did not seem to be of much consequence. Our own left-right habit is not based on any law of nature, any more than traffic rules are. When it comes to painting a name or a factory

FIGURE 8. ORIGIN AND DEVELOPMENT OF THE SYMBOLS FOUND IN *AMOR*

chimney, we are as ready as the Chinese or Japanese to start at the top and move down. The two great Semitic alphabets have settled for opening a book at the back and reading from right to left. When I first learned to use Arabic script, I feared I would get ink on my sleeve: it soon seemed to me the most natural and the cleanest—as well as the most sensuously satisfying—way of writing imaginable.

The earliest Semitic scripts have survived only fragmentarily, leaving no literature or tables of the law. The Hebrew and Arabic alphabets are very much with us today. The examples given (see Figures 9 and 10) show how important the consonantal letters are. Hebrew script has kept itself strictly to the Hebrew people and those few non-Semites who have been Judaized; Arabic script has traveled the world with the Arab traders and missionaries and been imposed on alien races along with Islam; wherever the flag of the star and crescent has been planted, the script of the Koran has been planted too—from the Indus to Spain and, farthest of all, to the East Indies. This has led to various modifications of the alphabet to fit the non-Semitic

ה ו ה י   ד ו ד

H { V H J   D V D
    W

JHVH = Jehovah   DVD = David

מ ה ר ב א   ל ב בּ

M H R B A   L BH B

ABRHM = Abraham   BBHL = Babyl(on)

ל א ו מ שׁ

L ' { V M S
    W

Samuel

FIGURE 9. SOME BIBLICAL NAMES IN HEBREW, UNPOINTED (I.E., WITH-OUT INDICATION OF VOWEL SOUNDS)

The letter 'aleph' is represented here as meaning either 'a' or ' '.' Actually it has no equivalent in English: it is a smooth breathing—not a vowel at all. In both Hebrew and Arabic script we must read from right to left.

structure of languages like Spanish and Malay. Malay, for instance, is allowed to use more vowel signs than would be thought proper in Mecca, though even then it keeps them down to a minimum. Persian or Iranian is an Indo-European language, like English, and it has not taken kindly to the imposition of an alphabet that is nearly all consonants. If the Arabs had conquered England in the Middle Ages, the works of Chaucer (if they would have been allowed to exist) would have had to submit to Arabesque curls and squiggles. This conquest could have taken place. As Edward Gibbon reminds us (*Decline and Fall of the Roman Empire* chapter 52), "The Rhine is not more impassable than the Nile or the Euphrates, and the Arabian fleet might have sailed without a naval combat into the mouth of the Thames. Perhaps the interpretation of the Koran would now be taught in the schools of Oxford, and her pulpits might demonstrate to a circumcised peo-

Read from right to left.

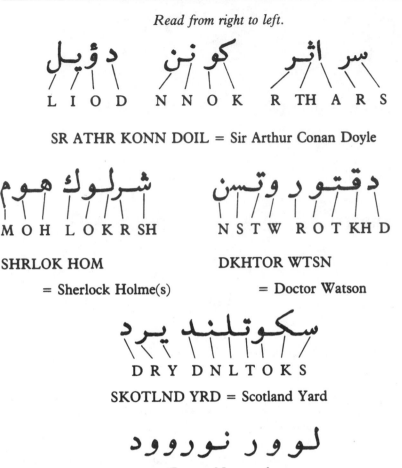

SR ATHR KONN DOIL = Sir Arthur Conan Doyle

SHRLOK HOM

= Sherlock Holme(s)

DKHTOR WTSN

= Doctor Watson

SKOTLND YRD = Scotland Yard

Lower Norwood

FIGURE 10. ENGLISH NAMES TAKEN FROM A TRANSLATION OF A SHERLOCK HOLMES STORY INTO MALAY

This is the Arabic alphabet in its *Jawi* (i.e., Eastern) form. Note that there are no capital letters, that fewer vowel signs are used than in the Roman alphabet (they are especially avoided before two consonants), and that what vowel letters there are perform two functions. **ﻭ** is /o/ or /u/ inside a word but /w/ at the beginning of a word; /i/ and /e/ are shown by two inferior dots that also serve initially for /j/. **ﺭ**, **ﻭ**, **ﺍ**, and **ﺩ** (road) are joined to a preceding letter but never to a following one. Most letters are given a calligraphic flourish at the end of the word.

ple the sanctity and truth of the revelation of Mahomet." English would have had to fit itself into the straitjacket of the Islamic BCD. How some English names take to this treatment is shown in Figure 10.

So far we have moved from pictograms to ideograms, then to syllabaries, then to a kind of demotic or popular writing that used only consonantal symbols. The final stage came when speakers of Indo-European tongues (more about what this means in a later chapter) wrestled with a Semitic alphabet and found it wanting. It was the Greeks who introduced vowel symbols and thus opened up the way to a fairly exact means of rendering spoken sounds. The vowel symbols had their origins, like the rest of the alphabet, in old pictograms (see Figure 6). Greek was content with seven: α ε η ι υ ω o.

These letters are so-called lowercase forms. The peoples of Italy took the capital or uppercase forms of five of these letters and thus equipped the Roman Empire and its tributaries with the tradition of the five vowels A E I O V.

This question of uppercase and lowercase letters (printers named them thus because of the relative positions of the flat wooden cases that held the type) is too big to go into here. Arabic, we may note, has never had the tradition of small letters and capitals; the IPA gets on well enough with lowercase symbols. The original Roman alphabet was all capitals; small letters are a later development associated with a running or "current" script, for capitals cannot easily be joined to each other. We would probably save much time and money if we followed the Arab example. German insists, as English used to, on a capital initial for every noun; we all insist on capital initials for proper names, the beginnings of sentences, and abbreviations like NATO, USSR, and EEC. Also, in English, we have the egomania of a capital for the first personal pronoun. Archy, the cockroach that wrote poems on Don Marquis's typewriter, could use only small letters but still, in his time, was a best-seller; the American poet e. e. cummings was able to use a shift key but produced an effect of flavorsome idiosyncrasy with his capitalless poems.

The Roman alphabet spread all over the West, undergoing only slight modifications in the various colonial territories where it was used to write down the local language; the Greek alphabet was introduced into the non-Greek territories of eastern Europe by more peaceful means than conquest. The present-day Russian alphabet (see Figure 12) closely resembles the Greek alphabet; indeed, some letters are identical—Saint Cyril, a missionary of the ninth century,

FIGURE 11. THE TITLE BOX OF THE RUSSIAN NEWSPAPER *PRAVDA* (*TRUTH*)

Above the name we read *Kommunisticheskaya Partiya Sovyetskovo Soyuza.* Note the palatalized vowels я (ya), е (ye), ю (yu). The г of the third word is normally pronounced like the 'g' in "gas," but in adjectival forms like this it becomes /v/. The phrase means "Communist Party of the Soviet Union." Below the title we read *Organ Tsyentral' Novo Komityeta Kommunisticheskol Partii Sovyetskovo Soyuza.* This seems fairly clear: "Organ of the Central Committee of the Communist Party of the Soviet Union." I have used an apostrophe to represent the ь in the second word. This symbol is a softener or palatalizer of the preceding vowel. The encircled hero is, of course, Lenin.

COCA-COLA	STRIPTEASE	FOOTBALL
Κoκa-κoλα	στριπτηζ	φυτμπoλ
Кока-кола	стриптиз	Футбол
كوكا كولا	ستريفتين	فوتبول

ASPIRIN	GUINNESS	JAZZ
ασπιριν	Γινις	διεζ
аспирин	Гиннисс	джаз
أسبيرين	كينيس	جيس

FIGURE 12. "INTERNATIONAL" WORDS IN ROMAN, GREEK, CYRILLIC, AND ARABIC (*JAWI* FORM) SCRIPT

took the Greek alphabet with him to the Slav territories he wished to convert to Christianity. Inevitably, it underwent modifications, owing to the particular needs of a Slav tongue, and it became virtually a new alphabet, and a very fine one, called to this day after the saint— the Cyrillic (in Russian, *Kirillitsa*) alphabet.

The world now has three great alphabets—the Roman, the Cyrillic, and the Arabic. The Roman and the Cyrillic, even to the least trained observer, must seem to possess a common origin, but the Arabic looks like neither, nor does it resemble the Hebrew alphabet or the syllabaries of non-Muslim India. Nevertheless, we can assert that all alphabets derive from the original Phoenician invention: the lack of consistency in writing or drawing the symbols, the tendency of each language group to develop its own quirks and create special letters to render its own idiosyncratic sounds—these are possible reasons for the eventual divergence of the forms. But if we look closely at, say, the 'L' symbol of Arabic, Greek, Russian, Hebrew, and the IPA alphabet, we find common elements—two lines at an angle. The Roman 'S' is a sort of snake; so is the corresponding Arabic sign. Even the Arabic 'T' symbol (*ta*, with its vertical line and two points at the top) bears a ghostly resemblance to our own. The conviction that alphabets are fundamentally one should ease our way into learning the great exotics. Whether or not we wish to learn the languages that these alphabets enshrine, sheer human curiosity must drive us to read the street signs that flash by in the television news. And to handle the Arabic alphabet is to be led into a little world of exquisite sensation.

The languages that have been most satisfied with the Roman alphabet as a set of phonemic signals are, inevitably, those that are derived from the Roman language. The Roman alphabet fitted Latin like a glove and it has fitted the dark-eyed daughters nearly as well, though French—language of dissent—has tended to chafe somewhat, introducing gussets of diacritical helpers (acute, grave, circumflex, and cedilla). The modern Latin tongues are so clearly agreed as to what the letters of the Roman alphabet signify that we are able to deduce by comparison what they stood for in Latin: we can almost reproduce the very phonemes that Vergil, Horace, and Catullus juggled with. Thus the letter 'i' means /i/ in Paris, Rome, Lisbon, Madrid, and Bucharest, 'e' means a half-closed or half-open front vowel (/e/ or /ɛ/), 'o' stands for a half-closed or half-open back vowel (/o/ or /ɔ/), 'a' can confidently be taken to stand for /a/, and 'u'—except in French—for /u/. It seems unlikely that they could have had any widely differing meaning in the parent language. This family sticking-together with the vowels, the loyalty to the imperial mother, is not exactly matched with the consonants. If 'c' means /k/ before 'a' or 'o'

or 'u,' it does not always mean /s/ before 'i' or 'e.' French opts for
the /s/, Italian for the affricate /tʃ/, Castilian Spanish (though not
provincial or South American) for /θ/. But, within the particular language, there is usually absolute consistency, so that French and Italian
'g' always means the palatal nasal /ɲ/, Spanish 'g' before 'e' or 'i' always
means /x/, Spanish "ll" and Portuguese "lh" always stand for /ʎ/.

But how about the Roman alphabet in England? What has gone
wrong here? Why is it that no foreigner can say with any confidence,
seeing a new English word in print, what the pronunciation is likely
to be? Why is the story of the Frenchman who drowned himself after
reading "AGATHA CHRISTIE'S 'THE MOUSETRAP' PRONOUNCED SUCCESS"
not really funny? How has it come about that we can spell "fish"
quite logically as "ghoti"? Why have we diverged so from common
Continental agreement about the significance of most of the Roman
letters? That in itself would be tolerable if English spelling were
consistent; but English not only fails to agree with French, Spanish,
Italian, and the rest—it fails to agree with itself. The only real problem of learning English is the problem of spelling. If only English
would say that "xy" stands for /i/ and "zfrgght" stands for /u/ and be
thoroughly consistent about it, then there would be no problem for
anyone—either native or foreign. It is the total lack of logic that is
infuriating. How did it come about? What can we do about it?

We may as well begin with a piece of Anglo-Saxon or Old English.
This ancestor of our present language was, roughly speaking, used
until after the Norman settlement in England and the fertilization of
the native language with French and the adoption of a French mode
of spelling. The following will be intelligible to the lay reader only if
he is told that it is a translation of the Lord's Prayer; it is very much
a foreign language to us now.

Fæder ūre,
Þū Þe eart on heofonum,
si Þīn nama gehālgod.
Tōbecume Þīn rīce.
Gewur Þe ðin willa on eorðan swā swā on heofonum . . .

This is recognizably written with the Roman alphabet, which, owing
to missionary activity from Rome, has superseded the Old Germanic
model of runic writing. The runic alphabet was called a *futhorc* after

the names of the first six letters in it—*feoh* ("wealth"), *ur* ("aurochs," an extinct form of bovine cattle), *th* ("thorn"), and so on. The runes were convenient for carving on hard surfaces, being all symbols made out of straight lines. Because the Germanic languages contained certain sounds that were not found in Latin and its descendants, certain of these runes had to be retained. The rune 'Þ' stood for 'th' in its unvoiced form (/θ/), and 'ð' for the voiced form (as in the IPA) but not with total consistency. The Frenchified 'th' took over for both, but 'Þ' still survives as the first letter of "Þe Olde Englisshe Tea Shoppe." It has been mistaken for 'Y,' but it is certainly not, and never was, pronounced /j/. Along with these two consonant letters, there was a coincidence of the Roman digraph 'æ' as in "Cæsar" (probably pronounced /ai/ in Latin) and the rune 'æ,' which, as in the IPA, stood for the vowel midway between /a/ and /ɛ/. Above certain vowel letters appears the diacritic ¯, a symbol of vowel length. Already the Roman alphabet is being strained to meet the requirements of a non-Latin language. Add the fact that some unvoiced consonants tend to be voiced in Old English between two vowels, and we find that the 'f' of *heofonum*—ancestor of modern "heaven"—represents /v/.

The vowels of Old and Middle English come close, both in sound and orthography, to Continental custom, but a large event took place in the fifteenth century and continued in the sixteenth (some say it is still going on). This was the Great Vowel Shift, in which the long vowels of English became diphthongized. I shall reserve an account of this to the section of this book that concentrates on English. For the moment one example of the shift will suffice. The Old English word for "mouse," was *mūs* (/mu:s/), as it still is in the dialects of Scottish English, but the length of the vowel led to instability and the gradual appearance of the diphthong /aʊ/, as in contemporary RP. The spelling "mouse," which imitates the French mode of representing /u/, gives no indication as to how the word should be pronounced. The German language does better with *Maus*. We can say, generally, that while the sound system of English changed rapidly, the alphabet stood still. With our eyes we see a variety of Middle English; with our ears we hear the language today.

The consonants have not undergone such violent changes as the vowel, and a consonant letter in Modern English can often be expected to give approximate guidance (in terms of the mother alphabet) to the sound it stands for. Digraphs like 'th' and 'sh' have had to be specially made for English and, while 'sh' is consistent, 'th' gives no indication as to whether a voiced or unvoiced sound is meant. Still, a consonant letter normally signals the presence of a consonantal sound, with certain exceptions. The digraph 'gh' is a memorial to a departed /x/—the unvoiced velar fricative as in "loch" or "Bach." "Light," "bright," "right," and the rest retain an unvoiced semivowel (/ç/) in their Scots pronunciation ("It's a braw bricht moonlicht nicht"), but for the rest of us the 'gh' is now merely an indicator of diphthongization in "light" and "bright" and of length in "taught" and "bought." In "laugh" and "cough" it means /f/, and in "hiccough," by a mistaken analogy with "cough," it disguises a /p/.

Certain consonants are silent in sound but still highly visible because of this inertia (essential to speech, Saussure said), which rubs off on the alphabetic representation of speech. But we have to distinguish between different kinds of validity. If 'r' is silent in the RP versions of "more," "there," "beer," and so on, having lapsed into schwa or /ə/, it is still lively in many English dialects and most of the versions of American speech. Consonants that are silent because they act only as visual pointers to the foreign derivation of a word are worth keeping because they both enshrine history (or etymology, if we are talking of the history of words) and assert kinship to Continental usage. We do not pronounce the 'ps' of "psychology" (though other languages do) nor the 'ch' in "yacht." Phonetic spellings look curiously neutral and homeless—"sikology," "yot." "Yacht" originally meant a hunting or chasing ship—the Dutch original being *jahtschip*, from *jagen*, "to chase." We can be, appropriately, doubtful about a form like "doubt," which has only the 'b' to show its Latin origin in *dubitare*. That, like "debt" (from *debitum*), is mere Renaissance pedantry. I carry another instance of that in my first name—"Anthony" derives from the Latin "Antonius," but there was once a false conviction that it came from the Greek *anthos*, meaning "flower."

During the English Renaissance, which was Shakespeare's time, there was no agreed-upon system of spelling, and this enabled the speaker of English to spell as he pronounced, or thought he pronounced. In the days of the new literacy this was a godsend to printers. To justify a line—that is, to fill it out to the right-hand margin—they would add unnecessary letters, turning "dog" to "dogg" or "dogge." "Not" could be expanded to "nott," "notte," even "noughtte." This practice ended during the seventeenth century, partly as a development of the newssheets of the Civil War, when compositors had no time to prettify their pages with neat margins, and tended to use the same spelling for any given word. Standardization of spelling was partly Dr. Johnson's achievement (one of so many), hammered home with the bulk of his remarkable *Dictionary*.

We all, if we are moderately literate, spell in the same way these days. We accept that there are such crimes as "spelling mistakes" and we are prepared to be penalized for them. Private letters, however, will sometimes break the rules and breathe the old Elizabethan freedom. I had an educated correspondent who spelled "Sealyham" as "Celium" and "coat of arms" as "court of arms." This latter showed that she pronounced "coat" as /kɔ:t/ and proclaimed that she was Welsh. "Phonetic" spelling of this kind would, if recorded sound did not exist, be a valuable guide to a posterity looking for the facts of twentieth-century pronunciation: we ourselves owe a vast amount of our knowledge of English sound changes to the letters of the past. Despite the existence of "official" spelling rules, however, and our general acceptance of standards, we are far from happy about English spelling and are always talking of doing something to change it.

Innumerable suggestions have been made, often by people untrained in linguistics, and George Bernard Shaw is but one of many who have sponsored—in life or from the grave—a "rational" spelling scheme for English. Shaw's *Androcles and the Lion* appeared in improved spelling, but it is now hard to find a copy. A modified teaching alphabet appeared in our schools, though not for long. British units of money and mensuration have bowed, up to a point, to Continental practice; would it be wise to take the plunge and give to the English alphabet something of the consistency possessed by the alphabets of Europe? There are various reasons for being cautious about the taking of so radical a step.

The rationalization of English spelling means to many people only one thing—spelling English "phonetically," making each symbol used stand for one sound and one sound only, achieving absolute consistency in our written or printed symbols. Is such consistency possible without losing the semantic identity of the word itself? For, to take a simple example, "the" is /ðə/ before a consonant and /ði/ before a vowel. Sometimes the indefinite article "a" is, in very deliberate American speech, pronounced not as schwa (/ə/) but as /eɪ/, as though it were merely the first letter of the alphabet. The pronunciation of a word will vary according to the emphasis it is given within a certain context. If the word is, to the eye, always to be the same word, an exact phonetic rendering is far from desirable.

Attempts to bring the spelling of English words in line with the values of the mother alphabet depend on which pronunciation is to be considered "standard" or "correct." The RP rendering of the diphthong in "rain" is /eɪ/, and to spell the word as "rein" seems reasonable. Eliza Doolittle's test piece could then be "The rein in Spein steiz meinly in the pleins." But is it fair to impose this rendering on Cockney flower sellers (if such still exist) who are content with their Middle English "rine in Spine"? What can be done about eliminating the 'l' in "talk" and "walk" and "chalk"? No dialect pronounces it, but the dumb consonant (which once was not dumb at all) cannot be excised to leave "tak" and "wak" and "chak." Substitutes for the combination 'al' would have to be of the order of 'au,' which is still not phonetic. One convention is as good as another; leave those words as they are.

Like Chinese, the written form of English has to serve for a great number of spoken forms, so that "father" means /fɑːðə/ or /faːðə/ or /fæːðr/ or /fɛːðər/ or /faːvə/, according to class or region. There is a lot to be said for regarding our existing English spelling as part phonetic and part ideographic: we get some idea of the sound of a word, but we chiefly regard the word as a visual shape suggesting a bundle of phonemes that carries an accepted meaning.

Any changes we wish to make, having digested the above arguments against change and found them wanting, ought, perhaps, to be limited to the consonants. To legislate for the vowels of the entire English-speaking world is presumptuous, for no standard form of the language can ever be universally imposed. But even if we eliminate 'gh' from "light" and "night," we are depriving the Scots of a consonantal point. And moreover, we shall have to create a new convention to show that 'i' is pronounced /aɪ/ and not /ɪ/. The allegedly vulgar American "nite" is sensible enough, but is it worthwhile taking all this trouble for a mere handful of words containing 'gh'? I would be glad to see a more consistent use of 'z,' creating unambiguous forms like "boyz," "birdz," and "scizzorz" (or "sizzorz"). The slangy title of the American film *Boyz in the Hood* is a step in this direction. I should like 'dh' to be used for the voiced form of 'th,' so that "thin" could be set against "dhen" and "thought" against "dhought." Incidentally, one would not object to the spelling "dho" for this latter; unfortunately, nearly all one's proposals for spelling reform are of this small and niggardly order—too insignificant to mean much in the great disorderly jungle of English orthography.

There is a very strong argument against a "phonetic" spelling for those words that derive from Greek and Latin—an argument that consults the foreign learner rather than the native schoolchild. "Education," "situation," "edifice," and other Romance words are near-identical in spelling to their Continental equivalents. The learner of English whose native word is *éducation* or *educación* or *educazione* will hardly see something like "edyukeishun" as familiar; the existing English spelling, though it may give no real clue to pronunciation, is at least intelligible as a visual symbol. And even when one considers the dropping of the 'k' in "knife" as reasonable, one is brought up short with the realization of how much this spelling helps a Frenchman with a *canif* in his pocket.

Should we leave well enough alone? On the whole, yes. Sort out a few minor irrationalities, but leave the great horrible bulk of our spelling untouched: much of it is a link with Europe (and Latin America), all of it is a link with our past. To understand how our spelling comes about is to forgive it. Let us make the fullest possible use of the International Phonetic Alphabet as an auxiliary, both in our schools and in our classes for foreigners; if we wish to show what the phonemes of English are, here at least is a scientific way of doing it. But let us not exaggerate the difficulties of English spelling; let us be merely tolerant of innocent transgressions, not always ready to bang a gong like a spelling-bee master. Nobody wants a "silent" correction of Jane Austen's *Love and Friendship*. A guage works as well as a gauge, and parallel lines still meet at infinity.

It remains to say that some people—including some teachers—have seriously proposed that we solve all our orthographical problems by letting the eye be the arbiter of pronunciation. I have heard a teacher trying to teach "cabbage" as "cab age" because of this mystic belief in the primacy of the visual form. Such a sin is the ultimate one of exalting the shadow above the substance, the appearance over the reality.

As we are concerned in this chapter with the appearance of language more than with the sonic reality, it might be as well to discuss the "pointing" or punctuation that is intended both to clarify meaning and provide what we may call breathing signals. Some of the devices used traditionally are in trouble today, chiefly because new modes of printing cannot incise them with any clarity. The full point or stop, or period to Americans, that closes a sentence is very dim on many computer printouts, and one becomes nostalgic for the diamond-shaped symbol that served William Caxton (1422?–1491), the father of English printing. Similarly, the colon (:) is not always easy to read, though the semicolon (;) and its lower component the comma (,) are clear enough. Caxton's use of the slash (/) for most punctuation signals is increasingly seen to be rational, as is the almost invariable dash (—), which serves to break up utterances in radio, television, and film scripts. We cannot do without the query (?) but might be happier to follow the Spanish custom of indicating a question both at the beginning and the end of the utterance, with the inverted question mark (¿) to start it off. This book has been, and will be, highly conservative in its use of punctuation marks, but there are indications that the inherited system is breaking down.

For instance, there is dubiety about the apostrophe that marks possession, as in "Jack's" or "Jill's." It was once assumed that "Jack's book" was a shortened form of "Jack his book," and that the feminine possessive "Jill's" was illogical, if not sexist, but convenient. We see from fruit barrows—"Ripe Tomato's"—and the total absence of one in "Lloyds Bank"—that the apostrophe's traditional function has ceased to be clear. George Bernard Shaw rid himself of it, and we might as well, however belatedly, follow him.

Pablo Picasso exaggeratedly called punctuation marks "the fig leaves that hide the private parts of literature." He said this at a time when he had temporarily abandoned painting for what he called poetry. He said it in Paris, where James Joyce had written the whole final section of his *Ulysses* without punctuation. Molly Bloom's monologue flows like a river without meeting the obstacles of stops: Joyce's own wife's letters had suggested this technique as useful for indicating women's disdain for the male form of rhetoric that punctuation reinforces. In the French version of *Ulysses*, Joyce proposed that Molly remove acute and grave accents and circumflexes like so many hairpins, but this was felt to be going too far: French accents are phonemic markers. One of the characteristics of literary modernism, especially in verse, was elimination of the traditional stops. The point was, I suppose, that a well-formed literary utterance contained its own clearly defined rhythm and did not need the mechanical aids of commas, brackets, and exclamation points.

Joyce also, following Continental usage, rid his dialogue of inverted commas (" "), substituting an opening dash, and Shaw, with similar Irish effrontery, eschewed emphasizing italics, as in "You are *not* to do it," spacing the letters of the emphatic word instead. So we have, on the highest literary level, sufficient encouragement to break with tradition. Publishers and printers, however, have their own house rules, and until (as may happen) the author becomes his own printer, both writers and readers must tolerate an inherited pedantry. Charles Dickens, whose Flora Finching anticipates Molly Bloom, had his own idiosyncratic modes of punctuation, which were consistent and logical, but he came up against house rules.

The point I would make is that "correct" punctuation has for too long been taken too seriously, and as there is room in personal letters for what teachers would call punctuation solecisms, there ought to be room in print for the idiosyncratic or even the eccentric. I would be happy to see slashes substituted for commas, semicolons, and full colons, and double slashes (//) for periods. As the study of language is ceasing to be "prescriptive," the same lack of dogmatism might as well rub off on to punctuation. But teachers with a vested interest in traditional "rules" are unlikely to agree with me.

10.

THE WORD

For the moment—but only for the moment—it will be safe to assume that we all know what is meant by the word "word." I may even consider that my typing fingers know it, defining a word—rather whimsically—as what comes between two spaces. The Greeks saw the word or *logos* as the minimal unit of speech; to them, too, the atom (*atomos* means "indivisible") was the minimal unit of matter.

Words as things uttered split up, as we have seen, into phonemes, but phonemes do not take meaning into account, except when they oppose one another to assert that they are genuinely phonemes and not mere allophones. We are not content, however, with mere phonemic fission; we need something of a higher order. Will division into syllables be acceptable? Obviously not, for syllables are mechanical and metrical, mere equal ticks of a clock or beats in a bar. If I divide, as for a children's reading primer, that word "metrical" into "met-ric-al," I have learned nothing new about the word: those three syllables are not functional as neutrons, protons, and electrons are functional. But if I divide the word as "metr-; ic; al" I have done something rather different. I have indicated that it is made of the root "metr-," which is found in "metronome" and, in a different disguise, in "metric," "kilometer," and other derivatives of the Greek *metron*, meaning "measure"; of "-ic," which is an adjectival ending found also in "toxic" and "physic" but which can sometimes indicate a noun, so that "metric" itself can be used in a prosodic examination of "John Milton's metric" with full noun status; finally of "-al," which is an unambiguous adjectival ending, as in "partial," "fatal," "martial," and "bestial." I have split "metrical" into three contributory forms, which, remembering that the Greek root *morph-* refers to shape or form, I can call morphemes. Let us now take a collocation of words—organized into a phrase or sentence—and attempt a more extended analysis. This will do: "Jack's father was eating his dinner very quickly." Here is a possible fission: (1) "Jack"; (2) "-s"; (3) "father"; (4) "was"; (5) "eat"; (6) "-ing"; (7) "hi-"; (8) "-s"; (9) "dinner"; (10) "very"; (11) "quick"; (12) "-ly", making a total of ten morphemes. It is clear that these morphemes are of two distinct types. "Jack" can exist on its own, but the addition of "-s"—a morpheme denoting possession—turns a proper noun into an adjective. "Father" cannot be reduced to smaller elements, for though "-er" is an ending common to our nouns of family relationship, "fath-" can no more exist on its own than "moth-" or "broth-" or "sist-." If you rush in and point to "moth" and "broth" as genuine nouns, I will be quick to ask you to look at the difference between the sounds. We are speaking of /mʌð/ and /brʌð/, not /mɒθ/ and /brɒθ/. "Eat" can be an infinitive or an imperative, but the suffix "-ing" turns it into a present participle. "Hi-" signals an aspect of the singular masculine personal pronoun, but it can have no real meaning until it is completed by the objective ending "-m" or, as here, the "-s" denoting possession. "Dinner" is indivisible, for "din" on its own belongs to a very different semantic region, and to use "din" for "dinner" (as some facetious people do) or to make a duplicated child's form "din-din" is merely to use a truncated form of a whole word, implying the prior existence of that word. Finally, "quick" is an adjective; the morpheme "-ly" turns it into an adverb.

Some morphemes, then, cannot stand on their own but require to be combined with another morpheme before they can convey a meaning—like "-s," "-ing," "hi-," "-ly." We can call these *bound forms* or *helper morphemes*. The other morphemes are those that can stand on their own and transmit a meaning, and these can be called *free forms* or *semantemes* ("meaning-forms"). "Jack," "father," "was," "eat," "dinner," and "quick" are of this order. They are simple free forms because they cannot be subdivided into smaller elements. But words like "Jack's," "his," and "quickly" *can* be subdivided, each into either

(a) a free form plus a bound form or (b) two bound forms—like "hi-" and "-s."

I have used the term "word" so far without attempting a definition, yet the fact that we have been able to analyze words into morphemes shows that we are capable of intuitively recognizing a word. But the time has come for definition, and the great Bloomfield suggested that a word was a "minimum free form," meaning a form unlimited as to the number of bound forms or helper morphemes but strictly limited to one free form only. This would make words of "John" (one free form), "John's" (one free form and one bound form), "its" (the same), and "his" (two bound forms adding up to one free form). It would not, however, make words of compounds like "penknife," "manhole cover," or German *Geheime Staatspolizei* ("Gestapo" or "Secret-state-police"). A term like "word compound" might vaguely serve to cover these and words like the following fantastic verb coined by Robert Browning:

> While treading down rose and ranunculus,
> You Tommy-make-room-for-your-uncle us,

that verb being the title of a popular Victorian music-hall song. But compounds frequently congeal into what seem like simple entities— "breakfast," not "break fast," "cupboard," not "cup board," "bos'n" or "bosun," not "boat swain." It is difficult to draw the line, and the need for Bloomfield's limited definition is not all that clear: a compound word is still a word, performing a word's function.

Bloomfield also said, more helpfully, that a free form could be recognized by its ability to stand as a complete utterance, granted a context of other words or of pure situation that would make the meaning of the isolated free form quite clear. Thus, we can take words from our sentence about Jack's father and his dinner and demonstrate the thesis in this manner:

> "Whose is that cap?" "*Jack's.*"
> "*Father!*" (The speaker is calling.)
> "She *is* pretty, isn't she?" "*Was.*"
> "What's he doing now?" "*Eating.*"
> "Whose money would you steal?" "*His.*"
> "What do you want?" "*Dinner.*"

"Ugly, isn't he?" "*Very.*"
"*Quickly!*" (The speaker gives an errand goer a shove.)

The trouble with this is that a breakdown occurs with the indefinite article—"a" or "an"—and the definite article "the." These can only make complete statements in a context of language, not of life: it is the words themselves that are referred to, not—as with the above examples—what the words stand for. Thus,

"What word did you use then?" "*The.*"
"Do you say 'a' or 'an' before 'hotel'?" "*An.*"

It seems that if Bloomfield's thesis is to hold so far, we must regard the articles as bound forms, forms incapable of individual action—in fact, not as words at all. Not all languages possess a definite article, but some that do seem unable to regard it as a distinct and separate word. Romania has a newspaper called *Timpul* ("The Times"); the original Latin was *Tempus Illud*, but now the remains of the *illud* act as an article glued to the end of the noun. The same final affixation is found in Aztec words that have been absorbed into our culture with their referents—*tomatl, chocolatl*. Arabic glues its article to the front, as in our own Arabic loanwords "alchemy," "algebra," "alcohol," and "apricot" (*al-precoq*). The article is separable in certain Arabic forms, though not in these loanwords, so that the name of Alexander the Great, Al-Iskander in Arabic, is assumed to have an article in front of it that can be detached to leave "Iskander," a personal name in certain territories of Islam. English itself has timidly dipped into the glue pot: "an adder" should be "a nadder," "an apron" "a napron," and "an orange," as in Spanish (*una naranja*), "a norange."

So, if the articles—"a," "an," "the"—are bound forms, they cannot properly be words; yet they are called words and have space before and behind them; they are defined in dictionaries. Evidently, something is wrong somewhere. For that matter, something seems to be wrong with the limitation of "single-word sentences" to bound forms. If a pupil says "I came quick," and the teacher utters the chiding correction "-ly," then an error of usage is being corrected: the referent of "-ly" is itself. But if a man says "It's been ages since I saw you. I'll just run upstairs and take a look at your son," the proud parents can correct him with "-s!" (/zzzzzz/), meaning "We've more than one son now." In other words, that bound form, the plural suffix, can refer not to mere accidence (the correct inflection of a word) but to something in the real, external world—"more than one son."

I suggest that we allow the morpheme in its two forms—the morpheme with a real-life referent, the morpheme that merely helps to modify meaning or create larger structures—to rest as our scientific unit. The term "word" cannot have any *significant* denotation; a word is what my typing fingers think it is—a cluster of symbols or even a single symbol separated by space from other clusters of single symbols. The words of connected speech do not even have the frame of silence around them: they are all epoxy-resined together in a single act of communication. But it is convenient to assume that words have real existence and even to create a science of word study called *lexicology* (not to be confused with *lexicography*, which is the harmless drudgery of dictionary making). Not delving too deeply into what a word is, we are able to embrace the single phoneme /ə/ (the indefinite article "a") or /o/ (French for "water"—*eau*) as easily as the word monsters of the so-called agglutinative languages. One of the Siberian tongues, Korya, has *nakomajn'ytamjun'n'ybolamyk*, which means "They're always telling lies to us." It appears to be a good language for telegrams.

Looking at words, we soon become aware that they fall into two rough categories—words that mean something in isolation, like "apple," "tulip," "sex," and "spindryer," and words that only possess meaning when combined with other words in phrases or sentences— such as "it" and "if," "and" and "or." These are clearly analogous to the two types of morpheme that can exist inside the word itself, like the free form "eat" and the bound form "-ing" in "eating." So in the statement "The orange is yellow" we can pick out "orange" and "yellow" as words that carry meaning if chalked up singly or written in the sky. These free forms, because they possess independent meaning, are called *autosemantemes*. "The" and "is," on the other hand, mean nothing outside the context of a sentence; they only develop meaning when we make a synthesis of them with words like "orange" and "yellow." We can call them *synsemantemes*.

But can a word really possess meaning outside a context? Are not perhaps all words really synsemantic? Having read the statement "The orange is yellow," you will have a clear enough image of a fruit that is juicy within and yellow (orange really) without. But if the word "orange" were suddenly to be written on the sky by an airplane, would we—without the assistance of other words—really be sure of its meaning? Certain contexts or associations might fix "orange" as a fruit (oranges are regularly advertised through various media), but the word might merely mean a color. In Ulster, "ORANGE" painted on a wall would certainly have unfruity and achromatic associations— William of Orange, the Orange Lodges, the Battle of the Boyne, the unending Catholic-Protestant enmity—and the element of inno- cence, citrus or onomastic, would be expunged by the political. Simi- larly, "yellow," without a context, hovers between the color and the slang adjective meaning "cowardly." Indeed, one can think of few words that are genuinely autosemantic, and these are not necessarily autosemantic in every language. "Milk" in English is unambiguous enough, but in Spanish *leche* is an insult, and *susu* in Malay can mean as much the source of the milk as the milk itself. This is as much as to say that no single thing in the nonlinguistic world is capable of preserving the word attached to it from vagueness, imprecision, or ambiguity.

One may, however, conceivably except proper names—words or word groups signifying some unique natural, human, or artificial referent. Examples would be: "the Taj Mahal"; "William Ewart Glad- stone"; "the English Channel"; "*La Bohème*"; "the late Elvis Presley"; "Lolita." Yet these names only strictly come within the field of the lexicologist when they start to shed their particular denotation. If a girl, in the 1960s, could be called a "proper little Lolita," then "Lolita" was turning into a common noun, a word expressive of a whole class instead of a single fictitious character. Indeed, proper names do not really possess a meaning at all: they are arbitrary signs, mere laundry marks. What does the name "Theodore" mean? Its etymology, or origin, is Greek, and the Greek words that make up the name mean "God's gift," but this tells us nothing about the person or persons to whom the name is attached. Etymology, one may say now, has nothing to do with the synchronic meaning of a word. "Silly" is derived from the Old English *saelig*—"happy, blessed, holy"—but this etymology does not help with a definition of present meaning. In poetry the situation may be different. Otherwise Theodore means all people called Theodore, and we ignore etymology just as we ignore the definition that does not exist.

The very imprecise science of meaning is termed *semantics*, and it deals with language at those points where it is closest to what we like to call the real world. The phonetician and grammarian can lock themselves into their laboratories, but the semantic specialist is close to the very roots of thought and action. George Orwell, in his novel *Nineteen Eighty-Four*, saw how it might be possible to change the whole structure of a society through semantic control. "Newspeak" is the official language of Ingsoc ("English Socialism"), and its limitation of the field of possible linguistic expression aims at making heterodox opinions impossible. Political rebellion cannot be conceived in the mind, for the semantic elements of dissidence do not exist. If "bad" means "opposed to the principles of Ingsoc," and Big Brother is the eternal personification of these principles, then a statement like "Big Brother is bad" is absurd; it is like saying "$x = $ not-x." In the totalitarian societies of our century we have seen how meaning can be delimited to serve the ends of the party; but even in free societies we are perpetually bombarded by semantic perversions—mainly from politicians and advertisers, whose interests are served by the distortion or delimiting of meaning. "The pacific uses of the hydrogen bomb" is as absurd but terrifying as the Orwellian "War is Peace." Terms like "peace offensive" or "anticipatory retaliation" (which presumably means dreaming up an enemy attack and striking before it happens) or "termination with extreme prejudice" (a CIA term that means plain killing) are used glibly and often. "X is a man's smoke" is a blatant exploitation of a limited area of connotation; "It's the ice-cream treat of the TV age" does not really admit of analysis.

Semantics is so large and important a subject that in the few decades of its acknowledged existence as a discipline, it has already built up a vast polyglot library. The book by C. K. Ogden (1889–1957) and I. A. Richards (1893–1979) called *The Meaning of Meaning* (1923) states in its title what the basic inquiry of semantics is. It is an inquiry that may well go on forever. We all use words; do we know how tentative, complex, and fundamentally perilous it is to commit even the simplest statement to the air? A friend says to me: "I like cats." I say that I understand his meaning. But once I start to analyze I find myself plunging into a world where things become unintelligible. What is "I"? What is "like"? (I like a grilled steak. Does my friend like cats in the same way?) What are "cats"—man-eating tigers as well as hearthrug purrers? I am drawn into ontology, psychology, physiology, zoology, and I end doubting the existence of everything, including the possibility of language's possessing any sense potentialities at all. I have to rely on matters where language does not necessarily intrude—knowledge of the world, particularly knowledge of my friend.

One thing we can be fairly certain about is that a word—a phonemic event—only exists at all because of some entity or some relationship that has prior existence in the nonlinguistic world. This nonlinguistic world may be seen as having two aspects: first, there are the things to which language ultimately refers—"real" events or objects, which we assume to have a life of their own; second, there is an area of the mind where the speaker and hearer (or writer and reader) meet to agree on some interpretation of the real event or object. Thus, at one end we have the *word*, at the other we have the *referent*, in the middle we have what may be termed the *sense*. The referent is a matter for the philosopher; the word is certainly the linguist's concern; the sense interests everybody, from the logician to the literary critic.

Whether the referent really—in the sense of "demonstrably"—exists is no concern of ours. We may talk about the attributes of God even though some would say that God's existence has not been satisfactorily proven. We may talk about the characters of a novel, knowing that these exist only in a very special sense—certainly not as the Albert Memorial or Red Square exists. A hypothesis may have a mental existence, and the white mouse running around on my table may have a physical one: to the user of words they inhabit the same area of reference. Ultimately, of course, even the most abstract idea must go back to something in the world of sense, so that the notion of God may derive from tree spirits, which themselves are an attempt to explain the outward manifestations of the life of a tree. I repeat this is no concern of our present study, though we cannot help being curious about referents. After all, as Dr. Johnson said in the preface to his *Dictionary*, "I am not yet so lost in lexicography, as to forget that words are the daughters of earth, and that things are the sons of Heaven."

A speaker speaks a word; a hearer hears it. If he understands the word he has stepped into the same area of sense as the speaker. The meaning of a word, then, may be thought of as this common area of meeting. But the sense, it goes without saying, depends on the referent, and the nature of the referent has to be defined by the context. Thus, the "cat" of "The cat sat on the mat" is different from the "cat" of "Bring back the cat for thugs and rapists." We cannot say that "cat" appears in these two statements as two homonyms—meaning words spelled and sounded alike but semantically different, as with "pick" in "pick of the bunch" and "pick" in "pick and shovel." The "cat" of the second sentence refers back etymologically—by the grim fancy of "cat-o'-nine-tails"—to the cat of the hearthrug, but context will expunge the etymology.

What makes words less precise than mathematical symbols is their tendency to suggest meanings other than the ones intended in particular limited contexts. The definition of context is often not enough: many words tremble at various frontiers of sense ambiguity, or even multiguity. Ambiguity comes about not merely through homonymity ("Well, then . . ."—"I am well"—"The well lacks water") or homophony ("I," "eye," "aye"), but also through metaphorical extension (the two "cats") and through the fact that words attempt two opposing functions—particularization and generalization. A cat can be a fully grown tiger or a newborn kitten, so that opposite notions (weakness:strength, tame:wild, tiny:huge) are contained in the same word. Shakespeare makes Henry V say that he loves France so well that he will not part with a single province of it, which is a legitimate use of "love" but hardly the one appropriate to the courtship of a French princess. It is, indeed, only with the poet or the imaginative prose writer that language functions smoothly. Ambiguity ceases to be a vice; its deliberate exploitation becomes a source of aesthetic excitement. There are layers of meaning, all relevant to the context. Homonyms and homophones become deliberate puns, not necessarily comic. Lady Macbeth will "gild" the faces of the grooms with blood, "for it must seem their guilt." "Die" in *Romeo and Juliet* means what it says, but also means the experience of sexual orgasm. "Reasons," to Falstaff, can be as plentiful as blackberries ("reasons" = /reːznz/ = "raisins"). A scientific age like our own tends to be disturbed by this aspect of language. Some readers of a novel of mine (banned for libel, eventually driven out of its reprint) were unhappy about the title *The Worm and the Ring*. What did it really mean? It meant sexual incapacity, the failure of a marriage because of the moral weakness of the husband, the lowliness of crawling things, and the golden round of heaven, the Wagnerian myth (*Wurm* = "dragon"). They were dissatisfied: meaning should be mathematical, unambiguous. But this plurality of reference is in the very nature of language, and its management and exploitation are what literature is about.

Words tend to be not merely ambiguous but emotional. "Mother" has a clear dictionary meaning—a *denotation*—but because of the filial status shared by all living beings, it is drenched in associations of strong feelings, and so has powerful *connotations*. Thus, "mother" may be attached to a country or a college ("motherland," "alma mater") so that appropriate attitudes of loyalty and love may be induced in citizens or alumni. But the connotations can be wiped out completely in a term like "mother-of-pearl," which is as coldly neutral as "matrix." This has much to do with the distribution of emphasis: "pearl" is the stressed element and the rest of the compound is pronounced weakly: /mʌðərəv'pɜːl/. The same process was at work when the BBC Home Service existed: the highly emotive "home" was given less stress than the word following. An ambiguity may be used by advertisers and demagogues to confuse or deceive, so that the emotional connotations of words like "England," "children," and "duty" can be exploited in wartime oratory or in bad poetry at any time. Words like these are assured of a "stock response" in the unwary reader; the bad poet lets emotive associations do his work for him.

It follows from what I have said, I think, that the learning of foreign languages involves more than the amassing of denotations. *Fille* and *baiser*, which seem to mean "girl" and "to kiss" respectively in French, are notoriously dangerous words to use. *Buang ayer* in Malaysia and Indonesia means literally "to throw water" but has taken on a particular gross meaning. *Bulan* in the same territories can mean primarily "moon" and "month" but also, by a natural extension, "menstruation." Danger lies not only in foreign languages when the learner is unwary, but also in international acronyms and trade names. A stupid manufacturer of potato crisps in England tried to sell them in Italy and Spain, where what was meant to be an onomatopoeic name—Cristo—was sheer blasphemy. The acronym AMGOT—Allied Military Government in Occupied Territories— had to be abandoned when it was discovered that *amgot* is obscene in Turkish.

I digress. One must keep one's eye on context. Meaning resides shadowily in the morpheme, less so in the word, less so again in the phrase or sentence or paragraph. But meaning only comes to its fullest flowering in the context of an entire way of life.

Everything flows—*panta rhei*—said Heracleitus, and language is no exception. One of the difficulties we meet with in the study of meaning is the fact that meanings change. There are various reasons for this—some essentially linguistic, others psychological or historical. *Pas* means "step" in French, as in *pas de deux*, and *ne . . . pas* means "not"—literally, "not a step." Because *pas* is associated with the negative *ne*, it has taken on a negative meaning of its own, as in *Pas moi*— "Not me." This, the effect of association, is entirely a linguistic cause of semantic change.

But most changes take place because society changes—either in its attitude to life or in its formal institutions. "Parliament" does not mean for us what it meant in the Middle Ages, because the institution that is the referent of the word has changed radically. Hamlet, talking about actors, refers to the "humorous man"—not the comedian but the emotional or passionate actor. The old theory of humors—the primary fluids of the body, which, according to the manner of their mixing, determined a man's temperament—has long gone, but it has left this word behind to take on a very limited meaning. Inertia and conservatism will ensure that a word remains in the vocabulary, but change of meaning will be enforced by the nonconservative elements in man himself.

We cannot examine all the types of semantic change here, but we can note the tendency of words to move from a wider to a narrower meaning. For instance, "fowl" once meant any kind of bird but now means only a chicken; "hound" signified any kind of dog, but its meaning, except in a jocular sense, is now confined to dogs that hunt; a deer was once a "beast in general." All these words retain the older Germanic meaning in their Modern German forms: *Vogel*; *Hund*; *Tier*. "Meat," once any kind of food, is now restricted to what comes from the butcher, though the older sense is fossilized in "sweetmeat." The opposite process—expansion instead of restriction of meaning—is rarer; perhaps the change in the meaning of "bird," which once meant merely a young bird, is due to the limiting of the meaning of "fowl."

Sometimes a limitation of meaning will be associated with a sort of value judgment, so that "smelly" refers only to a bad smell. We can call this a *pejorative change* and note some very peculiar examples. Italian, for instance, derives its word for "bad"—*cattivo*—from the Latin word for a prisoner—*captivus*. A cretin is, etymologically, a Christian (cretins were to be regarded as humans rather than bestial, and "Christian" was a synonym for "human being"). A knave was merely a boy (German *Knabe*). A villain once merely lived on a farm or *villa* in late Roman times; he was to become a serf and, finally, a bad man. This kind of social prejudice is matched by xenophobia or hatred or contempt of the foreign, making the Portuguese for "word"—*palavra*—stand for the empty gabble of "palaver." As the *hoc est corpus* of the Mass has become "hocus pocus," so Mary Magdalene's weeping has become "maudlin," and the fairings from Saint Audrey's fair "tawdry." Ameliorative changes—in which the worse becomes the better—are far rarer than pejorative ones: one should note "nice," though—*nescius* ("ignorant") in Latin, and always unfavorable (it could mean either "lascivious" or "trivial") in Shakespeare's time.

It is interesting to see what we do with foreign importations in our own time. The *Blitz* of *Blitzkrieg* lost its native meaning of "lightning" and now carries connotations of wanton aerial destruction and massive civic bravery. "Beatnik," now a virtually historical term, meant a member of a group devoted to pacifism and self-denial, but it quickly became as contemptuous a term as "teddy boy," itself an example of pejorative change. Conversely, "spiv"—which had a brief currency after World War II, with a meaning of "loudly dressed black marketeer" and a cluster of other bad meanings (a friend of mine was called a "spiv" by a policeman because he was looking for William Hazlitt's grave in Soho)—was taken over by the French as an epithet that, applied to a garment, meant "stylish." The label *très spiv* showed ameliorative change in action. The Malay word *pĕrang*, meaning "war," passed into RAF usage with the particularized meaning of an attack, usually a "wizard" one. "Lager," a once weak and harmless beer of Czech origin, is, as I write, developing evil connotations because it is drunk by delinquents who are called "lager louts." Words like *espresso* and *cappuccino* keep close to their referents. *Ombudsman*, like "science fiction," provided the name before the referent, but so, for a fair length of time, did "television."

All our major languages are quick to develop old words to serve new purposes. Often *apocope* is the way—cutting off the body but retaining the head, as in "pop" ("popular music") or the French *pub* for *publicité*. "Television" quickly became "telly" or (in French) *télé*— a half-contemptuous, half-affectionate shortening. An age that has worried about its approaching nuclear destruction was quick to coin "megadeath." Now it worries more about the annihilation of the environment and has spawned a crop of terms with an "eco-" (for "ecology") prefix. The making of words and the chopping and changing of their meanings goes on; no dictionary can keep pace.

11.

SHOULD WE LEARN
FOREIGN LANGUAGES?

The British, in their splendid isolation, used to regard foreigners as either a comic turn or a sexual menace. To learn a European language—apart from the dead ones from which English had kindly borrowed—was, at best, to seek to acquire a sort of girl's-finishing-school ornament, at worst, to capitulate feebly to the enemy. Things are slightly different now: an uneasy awareness is dawning that linguistic isolation is no longer possible, that the languages of these damned Europeans may have to be taken seriously if they persist in pretending not to understand English. Unfortunately, many educated Europeans do understand English, sometimes better than the British, and are very ready to speak it to British tourists and write it to British business firms, thus soothing that uneasy awareness back into insular complacency. But, in their soberest moments, most Anglophones will admit that the attitude of "Let them learn our language, blast them" will not really do.

What I say above is, of course, applicable to that bigger anglophone world that contains the former British colonies. Perhaps Americans get away with their monoglotism in Europe because there is a glamour, film-induced, about their way of life, energy, inventiveness, military and monetary power, and an exotic whimsicality about the emphatic nasality of their drawl. Many French television commercials exploit the American pronunciation of French: a sultry siren advertises *romans policiers* with "Dong toot lay bonn leebreree," meaning "*Dans toutes les bonnes librairies.*" Linguistic isolation is properly only a feature of those parts of the United States that are not New York, Miami, or San Francisco. Irish cops have to speak Spanish these days. But the American tourists in Europe do not know how to say "Good morning" in the vernacular that surrounds them or order a boiled egg for breakfast.

The ability to speak three or four foreign languages with moderate proficiency is regarded in Britain and America (not Canada) both as a property of headwaiters and hotel concièrges and a mark of genius. Yet many Welshmen of the north of the principality carry their bilingualism very lightly; Swiss citizens know French, German, Italian, and a dialect or two. A Port Said dragoman will know at least ten languages: I met one who spoke fifteen, as well as three English dialects. People like this are not towering intellectuals; they are often of very moderate intelligence. What makes them good at languages is the fact that social and economic circumstances force them to be good. So far, the anglophone world has never really been forced out of its monoglot complacency, and the legend that there is something in the Anglo-Saxon genes that forbids linguistic proficiency continues to be fostered.

And yet British colonial administrators, as well as planters and even liquor salesmen, have not merely mastered the tongues of Africa and the East but given them dictionaries, grammars, even literature. In any crowded London public bar it will not be hard to find at least one drinker who can understand demotic Arabic, Urdu, or Malay. If a sound enough motive can be adduced (soldier's hunger or loneliness, the colonial officer's proficiency bar), then a foreign language will be learned, and learned thoroughly. The death of the British Empire has, of course, locked the British who used to run it out of the rich linguistic world it represents: the Asians who used to be ruled as colonial subjects are now Bradford counselors and chain-store proprietors who have joined the expanding universe of Anglophonia. The British have become citizens of Europe, not the world, and to be European means also to be Indo-European, seeing French, Spanish, Italian, and German, possibly also Russian, as sister languages of English.

To find an urgent motive to approach another language is not always easy when the whole world is trying to learn English. The cozy tiredness of an after-work evening, when the daily paper or the television screen beckons, makes foreign text or tape look like hard labor. I have in mind, you will notice, the learning of a language as an adult undertaking, a matter of free choice. Let us look, however, at the reasons put forward for the learning of foreign languages in schools, where choice was not, till fairly recently, involved at all. Latin and Greek were imposed on my generation. As the tongues of two civilizations that have helped to make our own, they had to be accorded a peculiar reverence. Learning them, it was said, was an excellent mental discipline. They were logical and lucid and helped us to write English well. They enshrined important literatures. None of these justifications for slaving at aorists and principal parts was at all convincing, except the last. Ancient languages, with their batteries of irregularities, are far less "logical" than modern Chinese. Only the study of English can teach us to write English. On the other hand, there is a peculiar aesthetic thrill to be gained from reading Latin or Greek poets in the original, and this may well be the most cogent reason of all for learning to read (speaking does not come into it) the languages they so skillfully manipulated. Poetry, as Dr. Johnson said, is untranslatable and hence, if it is good, preserves the language it is written in. But to read Caesar's accounts of his conquests or Pliny on the habits of dolphins, one does not really need any Latin. A translation will suffice: it is the facts, not the language, that counts. Herodotus and Xenophon can be read with fair confidence in English, but the peculiar music of the poets, Greek and Latin, cannot be rendered into an alien tongue.

The suggestion that what will be called a smattering of Greek and Latin should be taught (both languages, not just one) at the secondary level, that Vergil and Homer should be tackled with a crib or pony, must horrify the conservative pedagogue. I make it seriously, however. The virtues of knowing how to write a good Latin or Greek composition are, surely, chimerical: unseen translation is of the same highbrow crossword order. If a "key" will help us to work out the meaning of a Latin or Greek passage, why should we not insert it in the lock. There will always be classical scholars who will go far beyond the minimal training I suggest—editors of texts and forgers of keys— but for the greater number it should be enough to be given a fairly painless entrée into the beauties of classical literature, the preservation of which is the only sound purpose behind preserving the languages it is written in.

We learn Latin not to juggle with subjunctive and gerunds but to understand the Roman mind. One aspect of its pre-Christian paganism was the sense of an approaching and eternal darkness (what Winston Churchill called "black velvet") that would wipe out the pleasures of life and love. Catullus expressed it perfectly:

Soles occidere et redire possunt:
Nobis cum semel occidit brevis lux,
Nox est perpetua una dormienda.
Da mihi basia mille, deinde centum,
Dein mille altera, dein secunda centum,
Deinde usque altera mille, deinde centum . . .

A literal translation and a minimum of linguistic exposition should enable a teacher to give a student with no Latin at all some notion of the poetry of the passage. Here, first, is a line-by-line translation:

Suns can (may) set and return:
For us, when once the brief light has set,
There is one perpetual night to-be-slept-through.
Give me a thousand kisses, then a hundred,
Then another thousand, then a second hundred,
Then yet another thousand, then a hundred . . .

Following traditional learning methods, no student of Latin could expect to approach a passage like this until the slow labor of learning paradigms and parts of irregular verbs had been completed. I see no reason why linguistic exposition should not follow a more empirical line—the breaking up of words into their constituent morphemes. Thus, sol- means "sun" (compare the English "solar" and "solstice," both of which derive from the Latin); -es is a pluralizing morpheme corresponding to the English "-s." Occide- means "set," and it is to be found in the word "occidental" ("western," "sun-sinking"); -re is an infinitive ending found also at the end of redire ("to return"). Poss- has the root meaning found in the English derivative "possible." Of verb endings found here, -t always stands for third person singular, while -nt signifies third person plural. Da means "give," the -a carrying an imperative force.

    Apart from the characteristic behavior of the morphemes of Latin that show what the words are doing, a good deal of the vocabulary of Catullus's poem is already possessed by the anglophone student who knows no Latin at all. Even *basia* ("kisses") will suggest some scrap of French or Latin or Italian that has attached itself to Anglo-Saxon culture (Italian chocolates called Baci, "kisses," the French *baiser*, Spanish songs like "Besame"—"Kiss Me"—or "Eso beso"—"That Kiss"). If *dein* and *deinde* ("then") seem to denote an inconsistency, we must remember that this is a poem and that a certain license is allowed. But even in nonpoetic English we use "till" and "until" indifferently.

A good way into Greek is by way of the New Testament, inferior to Homer and Aeschylus as literature (we are told that this is because the Greek that was the lingua franca of the Roman Empire is inferior as a language to the Attic—not a tenable judgment) but with its own powerful resonances even for the godless. Indeed, it would be useful to read the Gospels in a bilingual edition (Latin and Greek) with the New English Bible on the side. Take *Secundum Matthæum* or KATA MATAΘION ("according to Matthew") and you will find that it begins (in Latin) with *"Liber generationis Iesu Christi, filii David, filii Abraham."* The Greek goes: "Βίβλος γενέσεως Ἰησοῦ Χριστοῦ υἱοῦ Δαυὶδ υεοῦ Αβράμ." Both languages give us words associated with books—"library" from *liber*, "Bible" from *biblos*. "Generation" goes with "genetic" from *geneseos* ("genesis," for that matter). Greek *huiou* ("son" in the genitive or "of" case) provides no derivative, but *filii* does ("filial"). After reading a whole page about Jesus Christ's genetic background, you will at least know the Greek alphabet.

The point about selecting a passage of verse or prose that shall give aesthetic pleasure (or promote the awe proper to a sacred text), and then submitting it to linguistic analysis, is precisely that the end of learning a language can be presented along with the process of learning. In studying grammar, we swim miserably in a chill sea of abstractions, wondering at the point of it all. In reading—however haltingly—even a few lines out of the past, we do not wonder; the point is there before us.

The purpose of teaching modern foreign languages is usually presented as primarily utilitarian: we want to converse with Frenchmen or Germans, to read their newspapers, understand their films, write and receive letters in their languages. These aims are sound but rarely fulfilled. The tripper to Paris will find Parisians only too happy to sell everything in English; also he will find a minimum of pen pals. We have to admit that few Anglophones need foreign languages for the banal beaten holiday tracks. Only if they are prepared to recite Racine or Goethe in a café or *Bierstube*, thus astonishing the natives, will their linguistic studies seem to be justified.

For the final argument for learning the ancient languages is one of the most compelling for approaching the modern ones—namely, that certain literary pleasures are unavailable in translation. It is generally felt that the educated man or woman should be able to read Dante, Goethe, Baudelaire, Lorca, in the original—with, anyway, the crutch of a translation. To know certain authors in translation is not to know them at all. Edmund Wilson rightly warned us that we had better not deliver any literary judgment on Pasternak's *Doctor Zhivago* until we had come into contact with its wordplay and symbolism, which are confined to the Russian. One feels uneasy at reading Flaubert or Proust in translation, despite the excellent English versions that exist. The ultimate value of a translation lies in its power to ease our ways into the original.

What can be done about the kind of polyglotism I envisage in our state educational systems is not yet clear. This book is trying to hint at the possibility of extending the curricular slot traditionally devoted to what is called English into something vaguely termed Language. I would like to see examination papers on the following model:

1. Describe the organic processes involved in uttering the following words: (a) "thing," (b) "sister," (c) "futility."
2. Render your own pronunciation of the following into phonetic (IPA) script: "Time and the hour run through the roughest day."
3. Break the following down into its constituent morphemes, describing the function of each: "Jack's father was unwilling to provide him with any financial assistance."
4. Transcribe the following phonetically: (a) *fille*, (b) *figlia*, (c) *filha*, (d) *hija*. Describe the adventures that the Latin word *filia* has undergone in changing into these derivatives.
5. German *Zahn* and English *tooth* are cognate with the Gothic *tunthus*. What processes of historical change do you think the

German and English words have undergone since the time when they both resembled *tunthus*?

6. Write down the following names in (a) Arabic, (b) Cyrillic, (c) Greek script: Shakespeare, New York, Washington, Alfred Hitchcock.

7. Free translation of a passage from a French, Italian, Spanish, or German newspaper. Marks given for English style.

Our purpose in what follows is to ease the task of language learning for the average adult. It is sadly true that we begin to feel the urgent need to learn a foreign language when we have left school. The need may be commercial or social, or it may be an itch of sheer curiosity (it is often this last that produces the amateur student of Tibetan or Basque). Granted the need and the staying power, we can either enroll in part-time classes or—with the aid of books and cassettes— teach ourselves at home. Firmness of motive is of extreme importance; any teacher of evening classes will know that those of his students who have no real reason for learning Spanish but "thought it might be something useful to do in the winter evenings" will not last beyond the third lesson at most. The same thing can happen with the home learner; the books on French are not so immediately interesting as the James Bond rerun on television. One is tired. One has no gift for languages after all. Everybody in Lower Gambogia speaks English. The voices of these devils can be stilled only by a sense of the fundamental importance of what we are trying to do, and also by a technique that makes the process of learning interesting in itself.

Unfortunately, most of the primers on modern languages available to the home student are, where easy to follow, amateurish, and, where professional, discouraging. Some primers still inhabit a dreamworld where the words for "international cooperation" are available but the words for "yes" and "no" are hard to find. My own language library has a book on Finnish that gives neither "please" nor "thank you," a Russian primer that tells of a maggot in a cherry but not of the lack of a wash-basin plug in the bathroom, a work on colloquial Arabic that is a masterpiece of scholarship but a daunting guide to the simple mechanics of touristic need. When buying a foreign language primer, look first at the guide to pronunciation to see if the author has any real phonetic knowledge; then examine the range of vocabulary, see if the important things (drink, aspirin, bus stops, traveler's checks)

take precedence over the modern equivalent of lightning-struck pos-
tilions; finally, see whether grammar is rejoiced in as an end in itself
or treated as a minimal skeleton to the flesh of speech. You will, alas,
find very few books that are satisfactory. You will end, as I usually
end, by gutting the book you have bought and using its materials for
making a notebook primer of your own.

We will assume that you are going to visit the country where the
language of your choice is spoken. You will therefore require far
more than a reading knowledge. A writing knowledge will hardly
matter at all. But it is essential that you speak a little and understand
a lot. Learning to speak and learning to understand are two separate
disciplines. Men excel at the first and women, who have intuition on
their side, at the second. Many learners become discouraged because,
having attained a fair fluency in speech, they understand far less
than they think they ought when they listen to the radio or a café
altercation. They should not be discouraged. Anybody can speak if
he has in his own hands the control of structures and vocabulary; he
cannot control what the native speaker says. Some languages are
easier to understand than to speak: Dutch and German are two good
examples; German in particular does not slur its phonemes nor insist
on great speed. On the other hand, French—because of its tendency
to elision and nervous rapidity—is difficult to understand when spoken colloquially. That is why so many English speakers of French like
to keep talking all the time.

You are going to visit this foreign country in the summer. The
time to start work seriously is after the remnants of the Christmas
turkey have been turned into soup. First, if you have a new alphabet
to learn, as with Russian, learn the alphabet before you learn anything
else. It is not the body and soul of the language, only its dress. If the
Russians were to conquer Britain or America, we Anglophones might
have to write our own language in the Cyrillic alphabet. Try writing
"Selfridge's," "Bloomingdale's," and "7UP" as if they had already
been taken over but not yet nationalized. Do not trouble about learning Russian handwriting; it will be enough if you can manage a decent
print script. Use Cyrillic as a code for intimate entries in your new
diary.

Your next task gets closer to the heart of the language, the reality
under the alphabetic cover. I refer to pronunciation, and I would
emphasize that nothing is more important than to acquire a set of
foreign phonemes that shall be acceptable to your hosts. It is so

important that it is better to know twenty words with a perfect accent than twenty thousand with the sorry apology that contents most Anglophones. The Anglo-Saxon world has produced great playwrights and great actors: there is something in our culture that disposes us to the histrionic. Speaking a foreign language is acting: the mouth and body are both involved. And yet some English speakers of French overplay Jean Bull as if to show their unwillingness to be seduced. They will often have little difficulty in telling a funny and preferably obscene story in which foreigners are mocked, with a comic but passable pastiche of an exotic accent. They must carry this faculty over into the rather more serious world of discourse.

In the days when I taught foreign languages to evening classes, I noticed a phenomenon that is probably still alive and active—the tendency of students to spoil such phonetic advantages as they have by considering that a language class is a social occasion. I refer, of course, to those dialect speakers, or speakers of regionally accented RP, already equipped with fine Continental vowel sounds. These people decide to put on a refined or "hot potato" accent in the company of the strangers who are the other students of the class, and this is naturally transferred to the foreign sounds they are being asked to learn. It was a Lancashireman who noted, after his first visit to Paris, that "foreigners speak broad." He meant that there were a lot of vowels suitable less for Manchester than Irlam o'th' Heights. It was a fair notation. European vowels are English country vowels.

Let us be sure that we know precisely what the foreign phonemes we are learning are. With the minimal phonetic information given in this book, any student should be able to find his way about the human mouth. If his foreign language primer tells him that "the letter 'i' " in Middle Low Slobovian is like the sound in English "sea" or "we" or "three," he must not take this too literally. His own "sea" or "we" may be centralized, impure. He should know that what is meant is a high front forward vowel—/i/, not /ɨ/ or /əɨ/. If his Russian primer tells him that "the symbol ь softens the sound after which it appears," he should cry out for more information, write to the publisher, abuse the author. If his French book says that *thé* is very much like English "Tay," he should demand his money back. One has a right to an accurate description of the phonemic system one is trying to learn, and accuracy does not necessarily mean the use of scientific terms. To describe the "ll" of English "belly" as a singing sound and the "ll" of Welsh "Llanelly" as a blowing sound is good enough. To describe one of the Arabic gutturals as a "dry gargle" is excellent.

When one is familiar with the sounds of the foreign language and, as far as possible, the intonations (much listening is needed here), a start can be made on structures and vocabulary. Let us not be told what words we need to learn first; we ought to know. Remember, though, that we are not machines trying to communicate coldly with other machines: we are concerned with establishing contact with other human beings, convincing them that we (who have disconcertingly turned into foreigners) are human beings ourselves. Polite, smiling, friendly, deferential—even when the response is otherwise—we are also courting sympathy and help. We need the following utterances before we need any other:

> Excuse me, sir, madam, comrade, ladies, gentlemen. I'm a (British, Irish, American, Scottish, Welsh) tourist. I don't speak your beautiful language very well

With these we can practice pronunciation. We need to get them right. We shall have to use them often.

In expressing our particular need, we must learn a sentence frame:

> I'm looking for . . .
> Where is . . . ?
> Where, please, can I find . . . ?

—and, to fit in the frame, various words and expressions:

> a taxi, a doctor, a pharmacy, a tobacconist, a café, a porter, the Hotel Splendide, the Bureau de Change, the ladies' toilet.

After this we must learn "Thank you very much. You're most kind." Other frames follow:

> I would like . . .
> My wife would like . . .
> We would like . . .

And these are completed with terms like

> some tea, some coffee, some beer, some wine, some caviar, an omelette, a bottle of brandy.

Other words begin to suggest themselves now—demonstratives like "this" and "that"; the copula "is," "are" (if it exists in the language you are studying); adjectives like "hot," "cold," "red," "white," "good," "bad"; the numerals up to ten. Keep the phatic battery well charged with salutations, expressions of pleasure and of gratitude. In learning all of the above, do not rush, do not overload.

We have made a beginning. Our few simple frames can be completed with many nouns and phrases, and it is time now to say something about the learning of vocabulary. Let us, first, not subscribe to the curious fallacy that though we may not be able to think of the right word in our language, we must not indulge in the equivalent of "er" and "whatsit" in our acquired one. The French, for instance, have the useful *machin* (masc.) for "thingummy." Fumbling for a word is everybody's birthright.

Next, we have to devise techniques for learning vocabulary. In building up a Romance or Germanic lexis, we are helped by possessing a joint heritage: English is a Germanic language with a large Latin vocabulary. But what do we do when the language we are learning is utterly and completely foreign, totally outside the linguistic family to which English belongs? It is now that we have to use our most cunning and ingenious strategies. Let me draw on my experience when, in early middle age, I had to learn Malay with great speed.

I have no very special linguistic aptitude; moreover, I have an indifferent memory. So I had to resort to the most fantastic of mnemonics. The word for "if" in Malay is *kalau*. This is easy enough. Kipling wrote "If." "Kipling" rhymes with "stripling." A stripling is a callow person. "Callow" is close to *kalau*. The two other, more literary, words for "if" are *jikalau* and *jika*, easily remembered when one has planted the strong mnemonic root of the basic word. In time, the priming fantasy is forgotten, and neither Kipling nor his poem is associated with "if." Some mnemonics are essentially personal. *Kawan* is "friend." I had a friend named Cowan. Others are ultraingenious. *Bermastautin* is borrowed from Arabic and means "to settle in a country, be domiciled." I formed an image of a stout-drinking Scotsman lying in somebody else's bed, saying: "I'm settled here. Bear ma stout in." To remember *mualif*, another Arabic loanword meaning the editor of a newspaper, I had to make a tortuous rhyme:

If you've been drinking, chew a leaf
Of mint before seeing the *mualif*.

The fact that *mualif* is pronounced /mwalif/ and not /mualif/ did not matter. The image of the hard-drinking newspaper reporter has long departed, along with the imprecise rhyme, but the word remains. I pride myself upon being able to devise mnemonics—some of them so childish as to be shameful—on any foreign word in existence. Well, nearly any.

Russian is a language that, though it belongs to the Indo-European family, contains words hard to learn and remember. We can dispose of *brat*, meaning "brother" ("my brat of a brother") and *sad*, meaning "garden" ("a flowerless garden is a sad sight") but have to think hard with words like the following:

nozh—knife (try "Eat your nosh with a knife")
karandash—pencil (try "Get into the car and dash off that note with a pencil")
sobaka—dog (try "So bark a number of dogs")

I have had to work hard with "congratulate"—*pozdravlyaht'* (that final apostrophe stands for palatalization). "Congratulations—that trombone [German *Posaunen*] drave [old form of "drove"] Lee to go 'Ali—art!' " That clearly will not do for everyone. What will do is the old device of India hands who had to learn their Urdu or Hindi while busy with other things—a number of small cards carried in the pocket, with an English word on one side, the foreign word on the other, these to be drawn out arbitrarily throughout the day, and discarded when no longer needed. New cards may easily be substituted.

The learning of autosemantemes—nouns, verbs, adjectives—is, of course, a great deal easier than amassing a battery of synsemantemes like "with," "like," "when," especially as there is rarely any true correspondence between English and exotic forms (French *dans* is nothing like "in," nor can one invariably render the other). Moreover, such words seem to lack body, to be too frail and elusive to be memorable. Russian helper words are incredibly ghostlike—mere single phonemes like *i* ("and"), *v* ("in"), *s* ("with," "from," "since"). We need the skill to compose mnemonic rhymes for fixing these dabs of mortar in the memory. Like this—for the benefit of foreign students of English:

> *Out of* the station puffs the train,
> *Under* the bridge, then *up* the hill,
> *Down* the hill, *across* the plain,
> *Beside* a river, till once again
> It comes to a station and stands still.

Meanwhile, one must read, especially in books of verse with literal translations. The more poems we can learn by heart the better. When my French conversational powers lag, I start to recite Baudelaire's poem on the albatross (the one that would cause so many dubbing problems). Or the mysterious triolet the boy Rimbaud wrote when he was among coarse French soldiers:

> Ithyphalliques et pioupiesques,
> Leurs insultes l'ont dépravé.
> A la vesprée ils font des fresques
> Ithyphalliques et pioupiesques.
> O flots abracadabrantesques,
> Prenez mon coeur qu'il soit lavé.
> Ithyphalliques et pioupiesques,
> Leurs insultes l'ont dépravé.

That one, for some reason, always quietens my auditors.

12.

LANGUAGE AS

A FAMILY AFFAIR

You have met in these pages occasional allusions to the Indo-European family of languages. The time has come to say briefly what this is and how it affects us as students of language.

We have to imagine, in that prehistoric past that is really a past without written signs, a race—shadowy, dim, unknown, but undoubtedly real—that spread all over Europe and even farther east, taking its language with it, a language that, because of the inevitable processes of linguistic change and the fact of geographical isolation, gradually split itself up into the main languages of Europe and India. The pseudoscholars of Hitler's Germany tried to persuade the world to call this race "Aryan" (*Arya* is the Sanskrit for "noble" or "excellent") and even told the world what this race looked like—fair, tall, and muscular—and what its qualities were—athletic, powerful, and warlike. The image of the "Aryans" was very much the official Nazi image of the Germans themselves—blond and tall like Hitler and Goebbels, well-shaped like Goering, keen-eyed like Himmler. Because of the suspect nature of all Nazi scholarship, which was covertly or nakedly racist, nobody has cared to use the term "Aryan" anymore to describe the language of that remote people; even the disused term "Indo-Germanic" implies a nonexistent Teutonic bias in the mother language of most of Europe. "Indo-European" is accurate enough—though it leaves the Iranian languages out of the picture—and it is the term we shall use here.

Though the Indo-European language no longer exists (it divided into its constituent dialects before writing was invented), we cannot doubt the thesis that it was there, very solidly, in prehistory. It shows itself shadowily today through the kinship that exists—sometimes under a mask—between those dialects that are now termed languages. Just as English "milk" is like German *Milch*, "bread" like *Brot*, and "water" like *Wasser*, so "father" is like German *Vater*, Dutch *vader*, Gothic *fadar*, Old Norse *faðir*, Greek and Latin *pater*, and Sanskrit *pitar*; and so "brother" resembles Dutch *broeder*, German *Bruder*, Greek *phrater*, Latin *frater*, Sanskrit *bhratar*, Russian *brat*, and Irish *brathair*. The resemblances between English, Dutch, German, Gothic, and Old Norse words can be referred back to a common language called Old Germanic, but the similarities between Germanic, Greek, Latin, Indic, and Celtic forms push us into the arms of a more primitive mother. There is clearly a family face, and from it one may even learn to reconstruct probable forms in Indo-European. Thus the Indo-European word for "father" must have begun with a lip sound, the middle consonant must have been dental or alveolar, and there must have been a terminal r-sound. The ancient form for "brother" must have had an initial labial, then an r-sound, a back vowel, a dental or alveolar consonant, and a final 'r.'

Traditionally Indo-European has been divided into two main groups called *centum* and *satem*, from, respectively, the Latin and Avestan words for "hundred." Avestan is the oldest known language of the Persian or Iranian group. The /k/ of *centum* and the /s/ of *satem* do not refer solely to those two words: they refer to a shift that affected the old Indo-European /k/ in certain environments. The Celtic, Italic, Germanic, and Greek languages are on the *centum* side of the division; Armenian and Indo-Iranian are under the *satem* banner.

The words we can reconstruct in Indo-European are mere roots. We cannot doubt that like Latin, Greek, and Sanskrit, our mother language was rich in inflections, with special forms for "to a brother," "from a brother," "of brothers," and "with brothers." In the late eighteenth century European scholars began to look at Sanskrit—that ancient language of India—and, in the nineteenth century, a dim notion of Indo-European structure was gained from the examination of its conjugations and declensions. Here is the present tense of the verb "to be" in Sanskrit and some of its sister languages:

OLD ENGLISH	GOTHIC	LATIN	GREEK	SANSKRIT
eom (am)	*im*	*sum*	*eimi*	*asmi*
eart (art)	*is*	*es*	*ei*	*asi*
is (is)	*ist*	*est*	*esti*	*asti*
sindon (are)	*sijum*	*sumus*	*esmen*	*smas*
sindon (are)	*sijuth*	*estis*	*este*	*stha*
sindon (are)	*sind*	*sunt*	*eisi*	*santi*

We shrug our shoulders or else frown at the irregularities we find in our verbs today; it is interesting to note that the further back we go, the more irregularities tend to disappear. The present tense of the verb "to be" in Sanskrit is no different in its endings from other Sanskrit verbs. Compare "to give" (present tense) with "to be" above. Compare it also with the Greek:

SANSKRIT	GREEK
dadami (I give)	*didomi*
dadasi (thou givest)	*didos*
dadati (he gives)	*didosi*
dadmas (we give)	*didomen* (dialect *didomes*)
dattha (you give)	*didote*
dadati (they give)	*didoasi* (dialect *didonti*)

When the study of the Indo-European family was under way, early in the nineteenth century, a division was made between the "older" languages like Greek and Sanskrit (the family resemblance above is striking) and the "younger" Germanic ones. It was recognized—for, after all, this was a process that went on in recorded history—that Spanish, Italian, Portuguese, and French were derived from Latin; it was similarly recognized that German, Dutch, English, Gothic, and the Scandinavian languages had a common origin in a primitive Germanic tongue that was lost—like Indo-European itself—because of the lack of written records. But this primitive Germanic language could be guessed at as to its shape and content, and it seemed to have broken away from old patterns represented by the "classical" tongues, Latin, Greek, and Sanskrit.

Jacob Grimm formulated, in 1822, a law that accounted for the consonantal differences between Germanic and the older tongues. Really, he was trying to answer the question, Why, if the Germanic and the classical tongues have a common origin, is "brother" or *Bruder* so different from *frater*, "father," or *Vater* so different from *pater*, and so on? Why these considerable consonantal differences at the beginning and in the middle of words that are supposed to be fundamentally the same? Grimm's law could not explain, but it could formulate; it could show that the Germanic language, in separating itself from the "classical" phase of Indo-European, had at least followed a regular pattern of consonantal change.

This pattern can be summed up as follows. The area of articulation does not change. Labials in the classical tongues are labials in the Germanic ones; dentals and alveolars remain so; a velar is still a velar. The changes will be these: a labiodental will turn into a pure labial, or vice versa. A dental will become a linguodental (sounds formed with the tongue between the teeth). A fricative will become a stop, or the other way around. Voiced will be unvoiced, unvoiced voiced. If the following table represents the main consonants in these mouth areas, then the changes will be horizontal, never vertical:

	UNVOICED	VOICED	FRICATIVE
Labial	p	b	f or v
Dental	t	d	th or z
Velar	k (c)	g	ch (/x/) or h

Let us see how this works out in practice:

CLASSICAL	GERMANIC
Latin *pater*	father
Latin *frango*	break
Greek *odont-*, Latin *dent-*	tooth, *Zahn*
Latin *tenuis*	thin
Greek *kard-*, Latin *cord-*	heart, *Herz*
Latin *octo*	eight, *acht*
Latin *hortus*	garden, *Garten*
Greek *gonu*, Latin *genu*	knee
Greek *thugater*	daughter
Latin *fero*	bear (carry)

The rule seems to apply well enough: one kind of labial in the classical languages will correspond to a different kind of labial in the Germanic languages—here represented only by English and German. The same will apply to the other areas of articulation.

Grimm's law did not seem to give a totally satisfactory answer to many inquirers. For instance, why should the 't' in *pater* correspond to the 'th' in "father," but the 't' in Latin *centum* correspond to the 'd' in "hundred"? Surely, if the law is to apply consistently, the English word should be "hunthred." The Danish scholar Karl Verner (1846–1896) proposed, in 1875, a law of his own to explain seeming irregularities of that kind. It was all a matter of accentuation, he said. Indo-European 'k,' 't,' and 'p' became 'h,' 'th,' and 'f' respectively in Germanic if the original accent or stress was on the preceding syllable. But, if the accent was originally on a different syllable, the sounds became voiced—'g', 'd,' and 'b.' Granted that Latin *centum* is pronounced with the accent on the second syllable—/ken'tum/—then the correspondence of 't' with English 'd' in "hundred" is quite regular.

There is, of course, much more to these laws than can be presented here. Indeed, the modern student of language may be prepared to question the validity of linguistic laws that were formulated before phonetics existed as a science. But it is important to think in terms of regular principles of change when studying languages: the apparent caprice, the baffling irregularity, can always be explained. More, a knowledge of sound change helps us to ease our language-learning task, as we shall see later.

Let us now briefly see what languages make up the great Indo European group. The long-dead mother left behind nine tongues that have, in their turn, split up into a number of languages spoken today. The nine principal groups corresponding to the nine old daughter languages are Indian, Armenian, Hellenic, Albanian, Italic, Balto-Slavic, Celtic, and Germanic.

The Indian language Sanskrit is, as we have already noted, the oldest surviving language of the Indo-European group. Its sacred writings go back as far as 1500 B.C., and it is still read, chiefly by devout Hindus and students of Hinduism. An important Western poem, T. S. Eliot's *The Waste Land* (1922), bases its final section on three injunctions from the Upanishads (literally, this means "sitting down near something"—*upa* "near to," *ni* "down," *sidat* "he sits"— implying, one supposes, being at the feet of a master of Hindu ethics)—*Datta* ("give"), *Dayadhvam* ("sympathize"), *Damyata* ("control").

The whole poem ends with a triple Sanskrit blessing: *Shantih Shantih Shantih*. Sanskrit, like Latin, ceased to be a spoken language while it was still flourishing as a language of ritual and prayer. The local dialects that surrounded it have survived to become the living tongues of some hundreds of millions of Indians (one of them—Pali—has become also a literary and sacred language, the tongue of the Buddhists). The main ones are Hindi, Bengali, Punjabi, and Marathi. The Hindustani that, to old British India hands, was the lingua franca of the country (especially the North), is properly the dialect of Hindi spoken in Delhi—a mixture of pure Hindi, Persian, and Arabic. Terms like "chit," "pukka," "wallah," and "chota" have drifted into English from it. The tongues of the gypsies' Romany is a dialect of northwestern India, which, with the wanderers who speak it, has spread not only through Europe but into America as well. It is no mere "thieves' slang" but a genuine and ancient member of the Indian group of languages.

Iranian splits into two parts—the eastern language known as Avestan (or Zend, though this is not strictly accurate), which takes its name from the Avesta, the sacred book of the Zoroastrians—and the western language known as Old Persian, which is preserved only in the records of the achievements of Darius and Xerxes, some five hundred years before Christ. Out of Old Persian developed Pahlavi, which is the ancestor of the Persian, or Iranian, spoken today. There is a good deal of Arabic in it, and the alphabet itself is Arabic, but there is no doubt of the Indo-European roots of what must be the easiest Eastern language for a Westerner to learn. The following words disguise very recognizable forms (read from right to left):

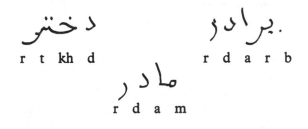

r t kh d   r d a r b

r d a m

—"brother," "daughter," and "mother," in fact.

Armenian is spoken around the Black Sea and the Caucasus, and it probably got there about seven centuries before Christ. It seems to have crossed the Hellespont in its migration, and there is evidence that the ancient languages Phrygian (spoken by the Homeric Trojans) and Macedonian have something in common with it. Modern Armenian, which has a large literature not much given to self-exportation, has been influenced by Iranian, Greek, and Turkish, and odd scraps of recognizably Semitic vocabulary season it. But under the mixed salad of the lexis the Indo-European structure shines clear. Like English and Iranian, Armenian has dropped grammatical gender.

The Hellenic group is large and complex. The Hellenes—or Greeks—entered the Aegean area about 2000 B.C. and spread into the mainland of Greece, as well as on to the Aegean islands and the coast of Asia Minor. The older languages—Lydian, Lycian, Carian, Hittite—went under, and the four Hellenic dialect groups—Ionic (of which Attic was a member), Aeolic, Arcadian-Cyprian, and Doric took control. Attic, being the dialect of the city-state of Athens, became the most important for obvious reasons—the commercial and political power of the Athenians, the great dramatists, philosophers, historians who wrote in Attic, and the great orators who exploited its rhetorical possibilities. The Attic dialect became the *koine* or popular Greek of Alexander's empire and, later, the eastern empire of Rome; it survives in the New Testament and in the Byzantine literature of Constantinople, which is now Turkish Istanbul. It split up, over the centuries, into the demotic Greek spoken by the Greek *demos* today, and the so-called pure Greek, with its nostalgia for the classical era, used in poetry, fiction, and even newspapers.

Albanian is spoken on the east coast of the Adriatic—the tongue of that Illyria that is the locale of Shakespeare's *Twelfth Night*. Its vocabulary is so bastardized a mélange of Latin, Greek, Turkish, and Slavonic that it is rather difficult to dig out the original elements.

Etruscan seems not to have been an Indo-European language. Latin, the tongue of the Romans who destroyed the Etruscan civilization D. H. Lawrence so adored, remains one of the major pillars of the Indo-European group. But it began as a mere Italic dialect, along with Umbrian and Oscan, confined at first to Latium, now Lazio, which contained and contains Rome. The tongue of Rome spread with conquest; its literature (whose practitioners knew it was inferior to the Greek) followed the legions and is still with us. The daughters of Latin are vigorous and need a chapter to themselves.

The Baltic and Slavic tongues are sufficiently like each other to justify our bundling them into a common group. The Baltic languages are, however, of more philological than literary, social, or political interest. German ousted what was once a lively Baltic language—Prussian—in the seventeenth century. Lettic is spoken by a couple of million people in Latvia. Lithuanian is of immense value to the language scholar because, of all living Indo-European tongues, it seems to conserve most of the structural elements of the ancient mother. A Sanskrit scholar of my acquaintance swore to me that he had made himself understood with that Indic tongue in a Lithuanian village.

The Slavic group contains the giant Russian. The language Saint Cyril gave a written form to in the ninth century is called Old Church Slavonic or Old Bulgarian—a South Slavic that is not too different from the old East Slavic that is the official mother of Great Russian. Great Russian (or just Russian) is obviously of immense and growing importance. Little Russian, or Ukrainian, is considered by the Ukrainians themselves to be an important branch of the Slavic original, and they emphasize its distinctness from the official tongue of the Kremlin, though with little justice. White Russian is found in western Russia and adjacent parts of Poland, and it is the mother tongue of some five million people.

Polish is the most important language of the West Slavic group, followed by Czecho-Slovakian. Sorbian or Wend is to be found in Germany, near Dresden, but it serves as the mother tongue of less than a million. In the South Slavic group we have Bulgarian, Serbo-Croat, and Slovenian—these last two spoken in Yugoslavia. All these Slavic tongues are very much like each other—far more like each other than English is like German, for instance—and to learn one is to half learn the others. The pan-Slav concert is very real, and language is its banner. Look at the following:

ENGLISH	POLISH	CZECH	SERBO-CROAT	RUSSIAN
bread	*chleb*	*chléb*	*hleb*	*khlep*
butter	*maslo*	*máslo*	*buter*	*maslo*
cabbage	*kapusta*	*kapusta*	*kupus*	*kapusta*
candle	*świeca*	*svička*	*sveća*	*svecha*
carrot	*marchew*	*mrkev*	*mrkva*	*markof*
cheese	*ser*	*syr*	*sir*	*sir*
cough	*kaszlec*	*kaslati*	*kasljati*	*kashlyat*
cow	*krowa*	*krava*	*krava*	*karova*
death	*smierc*	*smrt*	*smrt*	*smyert*

The Serbo-Croat *buter* is clearly a Germanic borrowing, and one wonders why it was necessary. If you can make pan-Slavic *sir* or *syr* or *ser* you should have no difficulty with *maslo*.

The Teutonic or Germanic group will require a chapter to itself. Its importance need not be emphasized here, as it contains both English and German, but we ought to note how the whole Teutonic family is divided. East Teutonic contained Gothic, the language of a powerful and aggressive people that survives in some fragments of biblical translation carried out in the fourth century by Bishop Ulfilas, who was a Greek. In the same group were Burgundian and Vandalic, but these have not survived at all. Despite the depredations of the Goths and the Vandals, the Latin language flourished. Conquerors need a literature if they are to eternize their language. North Teutonic contains the tongues of Scandinavia—Swedish and Danish to the east, Norwegian and Icelandic to the west. Literature keeps languages alive: we still think it important to learn Old Icelandic for the sake of the sagas. West Teutonic covers two branches—High and Low German, which came into being as separate subgroups about A.D. 600, when a sound shift rather like that ancient one described by Grimm started to operate. The terms "High" and "Low" are merely geographical appellations and have no whiff of value judgment. The old Low German tongues were Old Saxon, Old Low Franconian, Old Frisian, and Old English (or Anglo-Saxon). Out of Old Saxon came the modern *Plattdeutsch*, the homely day-to-day Low German (*Platt* means Low or Flat in this context) spoken in Germany but moving toward its borders in the west. Old Low Franconian turned into modern Dutch and Flemish. Frisian survives in Friesland and a few small islands. High German, which is divided into Old, Middle, and Modern, has become the official and literary language of Germany on both sides of the political divide; it is what we mean when we speak of "German." It gained its hold in the sixteenth century, when Luther translated the Bible into it.

The last of the Indo-European groups is the Celtic one, whose decline and fall make a curious and sad story. Two thousand years ago the Celts were everywhere—France, Spain, Britain, Germany, northern Italy; they had even, in the centuries before Christ, advanced into Greece and Asia Minor. But recorded history shows the Celtic languages receding—Gallic in France replaced by Latin, Cymric (or Brittanic Celtic) driven west by the Germanic invader, Welsh and Erse and Gaelic losing ground to English, Cornish dying out completely. Nationalistic movements in the "Celtic fringe" of Britain have succeeded in reviving dying tongues, but it would be unrealistic to pretend that such shots in the arm can do more than provide energy for waving a tattered banner.

There, briefly considered, are the languages of the Indo-European family. This, it will be noticed, by no means accounts for all the living tongues of Europe. Lappish, Finnish, Estonian, and Magyar (Hungarian) form a family of their own, called Finno-Ugrian. The language of Malta is a dialect of Arabic seasoned with the odd Italian, French, or English borrowing. Turkey takes its language from that Turco-Tartar family that gives Tartar and Kirghiz. But the motif of family prevails. Go east, and Chinese will be seen to be part of the Indo-Chinese group, along with Tibetan, Thai, and Burmese. Malay in all its forms belongs with Fijian, Tahitian, and Maori—the Malayo-Polynesian family. To know what family a language belongs to can be a help in learning it. To an Englishman, American, Frenchman, or Greek, the task of learning Russian will be eased once the fact of its Indo-European ancestry is made clear. There will be three genders, noun declensions, conjugations. Tackle Finnish, and we face new territory, exotic principles—agglutination, and noun cases we have not seen before. Turkish will give us agglutinative monsters like *Avrupalilastirilamiyanlardanmisiniz*? ("Are you one of those who cannot be Europeanized?" The answer is obvious.) The Semitic languages will follow their own ancient path, staking out three consonants before erecting the tent of a word. Chinese will behave most mysteriously of all, clinging to monosyllables and striking meaning as with strokes on a glockenspiel.

We are moving slowly in this book toward a survey of our own language through a kind of exotic jungle not lacking in blazed trails. I propose now to glance at some of the languages that are like English, and some that are not. You can take this as a kind of double approach—the comfort of similarity, and the shock of total difference.

13.

THE TONGUE

OF THE BRITISH

We can visit the Pentagon, and we can fill out a form in quintuplicate. The prefixes *pent-* and *quin-* both mean "five"; one is Greek and the other Latin. There is a difference there that enables us to call Greek a 'p-' language and Latin a 'q'-one. Within the Celtic group there is a similar division. The Welsh for "head" is *pen*; the Irish is *ceann*. *Pedwar* means "four" in Welsh; *ceathair* is the Irish equivalent. The 'q-' is properly a /k/ with a tendency to lip pursing at the close. In James Joyce's *Finnegans Wake*, the hero Earwicker is sometimes called Persse O'Reilley, a pun on the French *perce-oreille*, meaning "earwig." As Persse he is an Irish patriot, but in his endless dream that makes up the narrative, his name is changed to Kersse or kersey: he becomes cloth to be made into a suit or else to be torn. Joyce is making drama out of the 'p-'/'q-' situation.

The English call themselves British, but the true British are the Welsh, speakers of 'p-' Celtic. Those ancient Britons who fought the Romans and were at length subdued, who fought the invading Anglo-Saxons and were driven into the hills of Wales, are called "Welsh" by the English. The word means "foreign." It is the English who are the true foreigners. King Arthur is not an English hero, despite Purcell's opera and Tennyson's *Idylls of the King*. He was a Romanized Celt who fought to preserve British Christianity against the onslaughts of the pagan Anglo-Saxons. He spoke Cymric, or Welsh. That language, kept alive in schools and *eisteddfoda*, deserves our respect and our homage.

The great difficulty that presents itself to the learner of Welsh is the tendency of nouns to change their initial sounds in the phenomenon known as *mutation*. This means that a dictionary is quite useless until we have pierced the heart of the language. We cannot, as we can with almost any other Indo-European tongue, start reading, haltingly but triumphantly, right away. Look up *gadair* ("chair") or *bib* ("pipe") in a Welsh-English dictionary and you will find no entry. These, in fact, are mutations of the forms *cadair* and *pib* respectively.

Welsh has no indefinite article ("a" or "an") but it has a definite article—*y, yr,* or *'r*. This causes mutations of the so-called soft variety:

tref	a town	*y dref*	the town
basged	a basket	*y fasged*	the basket
desg	a desk	*y ddesg*	the desk
gardd	a garden	*yr ardd*	the garden

In the same way, soft mutation takes place with adjectives when these qualify a feminine noun (adjectives always come after):

llyfr bach	a little book	*fferm fach*	a little farm
hogyn drwg	a naughty boy	*geneth ddrwg*	a naughty girl
dwr poeth	hot water	*teisen boeth*	a hot cake

In addition, there are nasal mutations and spirant mutations, so that many words appear under four distinct forms (including the radical, or dictionary, form). Look up "horse" in the English-Welsh section of the dictionary, and you will find *ceffyl*. But "his horse" is *ei geffyl* (soft mutation), "my horse" is *fy ngheffyl* (nasal mutation), and "her horse" is *ei cheffyl* (spirant mutation). I use the traditional terms, but "spirant" could be modernized to "fricative." "Soft" means "voiced" and more. The 'd' of *desg* is already voiced; to mutate it to 'dd' is to change a dental consonant into a linguodental one ('dd' = /ð/). Here is the sequence of mutations for the radical *tad*, meaning "father": *ei dad* ("his father"); *ei thad* ("her father"; 'th' = /θ/); *fy nhad* ("my father").

Not even the numerals are free from this initial consonantal tinkering. *Un cant* is "one hundred" (there is a shining indication of the *centum* side of Indo-European to which Welsh belongs), but note the following:

200 = *dau gant*
300 = *tri chant* ('ch' as in German /x/)
400 = *pedwar cant*
500 = *pum cant*
600 = *chwe chant*

The 'g,' 'c' (/k/), and 'ch' (/x/) are all velar forms; hence the mutation (according to Grimm's law) is "horizontal." But the change from *mil* (1,000) to *dwy fil* (2,000) can be explained only in terms of a bilabial fricative (/β/) bridging the gap between 'm' and 'f' (pronounced /v/).

This sensitivity of initial consonants in Welsh may be regarded as the trademark of its morphology, just as the unvoiced 'l' ('ll' = /ł/) is the most idiosyncratic feature of its phonology. But to learners of Welsh there are attractive simplicities hardly to be found in other Indo-European languages. It is possible, for instance, to make any present tense form with the verb *bod* ("to be") and a present participle made out of an infinitive (*darllen*—"to read"; *yn darllen*—"reading"). The present tense of *bod* is as follows:

yr wyf i	I am	*yr ydym ni*	we are
yr wyf i	thou art	*yr ydych chwi*	you are
y mae ef	he is	*y maent hwy*	they are
y mae hi	she is		

The article *y* or *yr* has no real meaning. Note that the pronoun comes after the verb. This is characteristic of Welsh, which prefers the following word order: (1) verb, (2) subject, (3) object, and (4) the rest of the sentence. "I am reading" or "I read" is rendered as *Yr wyf i'n* (or *i yn*) *darllen*. "We are learning to read" is *Yr ydym ni'n dysgu darllen*. A special form of the third personal singular of *bod*—indifferently singular or plural—is used when a noun (not a pronoun) governs it as subject:

Y mae'r bachgen yn gwiethio.	The boy is working.
Y mae'r bechgyn yn chwarae.	The boys are playing.

The vocabulary of Welsh is naturally rich, but it absorbed, in its far past, a fair number of Latin loanwords:

llyfr	book (*liber*)	*pobl*	people (*populus*)
eglwys	church (*ecclesia*)	*pont*	bridge (*pont-*)
mur	wall (*murus*)	*gwin*	wine (*vinum*)
ffenstr	window (*fenestra*)	*coron*	crown (*corona*)

Inevitably there are plenty of appropriations from English:

bag		*desg*	(desk)
banc	(bank)	*ffatri*	(factory)
beisicl	(bicycle)	*ffilm*	
brecwast	(breakfast)	*inc*	
busnes	(business)	*lamp*	
bws	(bus)	*map*	
cwnstabl	(constable)	*papur*	
plismon	(policeman)		

But the Welsh language has left its mark on a number of place-names in England, as, indeed, the various forms of Old Celtic have survived in quite unexpected places in Europe. "Water" is *dwr* in Welsh (/dur/), and it wets place-names like these: Dour, Douro, Derwent, Dorchester, and Dordogne. An alternative word for "water" appears in the non-Cymric forms of Celtic as *uisge*; Welsh has *wysg*. The whole world has "whiskey" (Scottish Gaelic *uisge beatha*, "water of life"). But the nonintoxicant root is seen in Esk, Usk, Isis, Exe, Ouse, Ischia, Aisne, Ausonne, and Oise. The Welsh for "river" is *afon* (/avon/), and cognate forms are found in Aisne, Ain, and Vienne. "Avon," then, is no particular river. To call Shakespeare "sweet son of Avon" does not necessarily place him in Stratford.

Here, now, are some Welsh words that must look totally unfamiliar—that is, not cognate with anything outside the Celtic group in the whole Indo-European range:

anadl	breath	*eira*	snow
annwyd	cold	*gair*	word
arian	money	*haul*	sun
brenin	king	*ia*	ice
blodeuyn	flower	*llaeth*	milk

bwyd	food	*llong*	ship
coeden	tree	*plentyn*	child
chwaer	sister	*telyn*	harp
diolch	thanks	*wythnos*	week

Out of *haul* and *llaeth* seem to emerge the ghosts of *helios* (as in "heliograph") and *lact-* (as in "lactic"), but the other words are opaque. *Blodeuyn* and *brenin* appear as names—Blodwyn and Brennan—though the latter is more Irish than Cymric. There is a hard lesson to be learned here. The Welsh lexis ought, we like to think, to bear some signs of resemblance to that of its cousins, but it goes its own ways.

No one learns the Celtic languages in order to find his way about the Celtic countries. But the lure of Celtic literature, the poetry above all, is powerful. The term "bard" (*bardd* in Welsh) is rather romantically and imprecisely used in English. Shakespeare has been called the Bard, but bardic he was not. To be a bard is to exercise a traditional craft, to serve an apprenticeship to it and later to advance its technique. Gerard Manley Hopkins, an English poet who read Welsh and even wrote in it, is perhaps England's greatest practitioner of bardic verse. His themes are orthodox, but he is prepared to expand technique to the limit. Poets like Piaras Feiritéar, Daibhl O Bruadair, Aogan O Rathaille of Kerry, among the Irish, were great bards and are untranslatable, since they work with words, not ideas. We would like to read them but find the Irish alphabet too difficult—too many phonemes chasing too few letters: even the reformed Irish orthography of 1948, which simplified *claoidim* to *cloim* and *tosnughadh* to *tosnù*, is no real help. But Welsh spelling is highly phonetic. We ought to plunge into Cymric poetry as soon as we can. There is a wholly untranslatable charm in lyrics like the following, which it is worthwhile to learn by heart.

Ffarwel i blwyf Llangower,
   A'r Bala dirion deg;
Ffarwel fy annwyl gariad,
   Nid wyf yn enwi neb.

The pronunciation of the vowels follows the Continental pattern. 'W' is a vowel symbol, standing for /u/; 'y' after 'w' is /i/, otherwise it approaches /ə/. 'Ll,' of course, stands for the unvoiced lateral, while

/v/ is shown as 'f' and /f/ as 'ff.' The Welsh lilt, so different from the English or American monotone, may be picked up only from speakers of it. Now for the words and their meanings.

> *Ffarwel* (trilled 'r' and clear 'l') is a loanword—"farewell."
>
> *i* is a preposition—"to."
>
> *blwyf* is a mutated form of *plywf*—"parish"; the soft mutation has been brought about by the preceding *i*.
>
> *Llangower* is a place-name.
>
> *a'r* is a combination of *a* ("and") and *yr* ("the").
>
> *Bala* is another place-name.
>
> *dirion* is a soft mutation of *tirion* ("gentle").
>
> *deg* is a soft mutation of *teg* ("lovely"). Both adjectives qualify *Bala*.
>
> *fy* is "my."
>
> *annwyl* is "dear."
>
> *gariad* is a soft mutation of *cariad* ("sweetheart"). The preceding adjective has worked on it.
>
> *nid* is "not."
>
> *wyf* is the middle segment of *yr wyf i*—"I am."
>
> *yn enwi* is a combination of the untranslatable present participle marker *yn* and the infinitive *enwi* ("to name"). This then may be rendered as "naming," "giving the name of."
>
> *neb* is "nobody."

The whole quatrain therefore reads: "Farewell to the parish of Llangower/ and to gentle, lovely Bala;/ Farewell to my dear sweetheart/ (I won't mention her name)." The remaining stanza tells of going, with "heart like lead," to live in "the land of the Saxon." It is, for the English who call themselves British, the other side of the moon.

14.

THE TEUTONS

From even the flimsy survey of the Welsh or Cymric language we have just made, it will be clear that it is close to English only in a geographical sense. In comparison with Welsh, which came to Britain in prehistoric times, English is very much an imported language, and it has to leap back into Europe to find its nearest relatives. Though the Norman Conquest, and subsequent devotion to the languages of civilization—Latin and its daughter French—have given English the surface appearance of a Romance language, it is very much a Germanic dialect.

What is a dialect and what is a language? Many years ago I took a Londoner to visit my native Lancashire. In the village of Bamber Bridge, locally known as "t'Brigg" (there is a touch of Scandinavian there), we entered a pub on a rainy day, and my friend was asked: "Art witshert?" (/aˑt ˈwɪtʃət/). He did not understand. It was a way of saying "Are your feet wet?" ("Art thou wet-shod?"). Later the same dialect speaker said of his wife: "Oo's getten showder-wartsh" (/ɯːzˈgɛtn ˈʃaʊdə waˑtʃ/), meaning "She's got a pain in her shoulder." Again, my friend did not understand. What sounded to him like a foreign language was really good English, the dialect spoken in the Ribble Valley (later, in that same pub, he was to hear a sentimental song all too intelligibly—"Just a cot in Ribble Valley, with the roses round the door"). Native English, then, but to him as outlandish as Finnish or Lithuanian.

We like to clear an English dialect of the charge of being a foreign language by pointing to elements in it that seem foreign only because they are archaic. Thus, that "art" in dialectal "art tha" is a survival of what was good intimate English in Shakespeare's time. In "Oo's getten showder-wartsh" we can pick out the Old English "heo" that was replaced by "she." "Getten" is a form of the past participle cognate with "gotten," dead in British Standard English except in "forgotten" and "begotten" but still alive in America. "Showder" shows a development of Middle English "schulder" which, when one sees how "hūs" has become "house" and the dark 'l' of "talk" and "alms" has disappeared, has as good a claim to be called English as the standard form. "Wartsh" goes back to Old English "weorc," which, with a more generalized meaning than is found in this Lancashire form, is easily recognized as the ancestor of "work." All this, then, presents a paradox. Good honest native English can appear to an English speaker as a foreign language.

The process of historical analysis is no way of distinguishing "foreign language" from "dialect." For if I say *Mein Vater ist ein guter Mann* or *Der Winter ist kalt*, the meaning is clear enough to the Anglophone with no German: there are elements in both German and English that are fundamentally the same. Indeed, the two German sentences will be more intelligible to the Southern English speaker than the two Lancashire ones I have quoted. We must conclude, therefore, that the terms "dialect" and "language" have very indistinct boundaries, and that "foreign" has more social and ethnographical significance than linguistic. A language may be termed a dialect that waves a national flag.

It is a help when reading German to think in terms of the English of Shakespeare's day (or even earlier) rather than Modern English. This will help with forms like *fast* ("almost") and *oft*. Tricks of inversion in German—"That have I oft seen"—match earlier English usage. It is good training for thinking in German to play the harmless trick of inversion and verb shunting in our own language: it is not, after all, so very nonnative. We are sometimes surprised to find separation of verb and defining prefix—*anzeigen:* "to advertise"; "*Wir zeigen nicht an*": "We don't advertise"—but this is common enough in English: "Put your hat on"; "Kick the door to." We do not, of course, have the verbs "onput," (though we have the nouns "input" and "output") and "tokick."

Here is some Old English (or Anglo-Saxon) poetry:

Da waes on healle	heardecg togen,
sweord ofer setlum,	sidrand manig
hafen handa fæst:	helm ne gemunde,
byrnan side,	Þa hine se broga angeat . . .
. . . hra ðe heo æðelinga	anna hæfde
fæ ste befongen,	Þa heo to fenne gang . . .

That is a passage from our national epic *Beowulf*. It means "Then was in the hall the hard-edged (sword) seized, the sword over the benches, many a broad shield raised firmly in the hand: helmet did not remember the wide burnie, when him the monster seized . . . quickly she of the warriors one had securely seized, when she to the fen went . . ." The "she" ("heo") referred to is the mother of Grendel; both are foul murderous man-eating monsters. *Beowulf*, I have always maintained, would make a first-rate horror film. Here, for comparison, is a line or two from the German *Hildebrandslied* ("Song of Hildebrand"):

Ik gihorta ðat seggen,
ðat sih urhettun—aenon muotin,
Hiltibrant enti Haðubrant—untar heriun tuem,
sunu fatar ungo . . .

It can be translated freely as "I have heard it said that two chosen men, Hildebrand and Hathubrand, met in single combat between two armies, the son and the father . . ." If one wishes to learn an old Germanic language, is there much to choose between these two?

German vocabulary yearns to be "pure"; it hates to borrow from other languages. Where English, for instance, is only too ready to make its scientific terms out of Greek elements—"oxygen," "hydrogen," "nitrogen"—German produces homemade words like *Sauerstoff*, *Wasserstoff*, and *Stickstoff*. Even with new sciences like semantics German resists the international term and chooses *Bedeutungslehre* ("meaning-lore"), and phonetics is taught as *Lautlehre* ("sound-lore"). Much of this native Germanic vocabulary has ceased to be used in English—even "folklore" sounds quaint. German has *sehr* for "very"; English now prefers the Romance form to the Germanic "sore," as in "He was sore afraid." But a butcher is still a flesher (*Fleischer*) in the northern territories of Scotland and Ulster. "To dree" (*drehen*) is not "to turn," except in antique phrases like "Dree your own weird" ("Work out your own destiny").

When we look at older forms of the modern Germanic tongues, we tend to feel more at home the further back we go, chiefly because English has retained certain sounds once common to all the Germanic family but since—in all except English and Icelandic (an intensely conservative language)—shifted into sounds cognate but different. Take the two consonants /θ/ and /ð/, for instance, indifferently represented in English as 'th.' Icelandic clings to the old signs as well as the old sounds (this is from a newspaper: "Um 90 Þusand tunnur salta ðar alls á ollu landinu og i kvöld er buist við ad 200 Þusand . . ."), but see what has happened in German:

Dank	thanks	*Ding*	thing
dass	that	*Durst*	thirst
dann	then	*Distel*	thistle
dick	thick	*Dorn*	thorn
dünn	thin	*Dorf*	thorp (village)

The initial consonant 'th,' which, in the English words above, is sometimes a symbol for /θ/, sometimes for /ð/, has an invariable equivalent of 'd' in German. But in Swedish—belonging to that northern Germanic group that went a different way in many things—there is a clear differentiation: 't' for English /θ/ and 'd' for English /ð/.

tjock	thick	*det*	that
ting	thing	*dem*	them
tänka	think	*där*	there
tre	three	*fader*	father
tron	throne	*broder*	brother

Another shift that English resisted is that from /w/ to /v/. German spelling does not show the true pronunciation of *Wasser*, *Wurm*, *Wort*, and so on ("water," "worm," and "word"); we have to accept 'w' as a symbol for /v/. But in Swedish the spelling is honest:

vagn	wagon	*väder*	weather
vatten	water	*väl*	well

vild	wild	*vid*	wide
verk	work	*villig*	willing
varm	warm	*ved*	wood

My knowledge of Swedish is slight, mostly limited to what I can get out of Caj Lundgren's translations of my novels and newspaper articles. Here is a passage from *Any Old Iron*, first in English and then in his impeccable rendering:

He traveled to the borough of Brooklyn and at length found work in the Flatbush area. There was a restaurant there called the Nevsky Prospect, owned by a certain Pete or Piotr Likhutin. This man was a Russian atheist who had been a professional thief but was now reformed. He had fled St. Petersburg in 1907, not for reasons of political persecution or poverty but because he had been forced, in self-defense, to batter a pawnbroker near to death when entering her shop late at night. He had been seen by somebody who looked like an informer and so had to get away. He hopped a Finnish timber freighter with his wife and daughter and got to London by way of Tilbury.

Han for iväg till stadsdelen Brooklyn och hittade till slut ett arbete i Flatbushområdet. Det fanns en restaurang där som hette Nevskij Prospekt och ägdes av en viss Pete eller Piotr Lichutin. Denne var en rysk ateist som hade varit yrkestjuv men sedermera gjort bättring. Han hade flytt från Sankt Petersburg 1907, inte på grund av politisk förföljelse eller fattigdom utan därför att han nödgats att i självförsvar klubba en pantlånerska nästan till döds efter att ha stigit in i hennes butik sent en afton. Han hade blivit sedd av någon som tycktes vara polisspion och måste sålunda ge sig av. Han hoppade ombord på en finsk timmerskuta med sin fru ochs sin dotter och tog sig till London via Tilbury.

It is a crisp language, less heavy than German with its compound words like streams of not-yet-individualized sausage meat, and its economical relative pronouns like *som*. Its prepositions, close to English, like *till* and *från* (the tiny circle indicates rounding from /a/ to /o/) and *efter*, are unambiguous. English took *till* from the Danes but limited it to time, as in "till Thursday." "To and fro" should be "till and fro." "*Han hoppade ombord på en finsk timmerskuta med sin fru ochs sin dotter"* is identical in rhythm with the English. A characteristic of all the Scandinavian languages, and a very neat device, is the use of *en* for common nouns (masculine or feminine), and *et* for neuter nouns as the indefinite article ("a" or "an") when placed in front, but for the definite article ("the") when glued at the end: *en mann*—"a man"; *mannen*—"the man"; *et hus*—"a house"; *huset*—"the house." You see it above in *Flatbushområdet* as the definite article. Like Dutch, the Scandinavian tongues cling to a binary gender system; in this, they are more progressive than German. To German we now return.

The learning of German words is easier when we remember certain sound-shifts. First, English /t/ becomes the affricate /ts/, represented in German spelling as 'z':

tap	*Zapfen*
tongue	*Zunge*
to	*zu*

This is at the beginning of words; in the middle or at the end German goes the whole hog and has a full fricative—/s/ or 'ss':

better	*besser*
foot	*Fuss*
let	*lassen*
eat	*essen*
kettle	*Kessel*
water	*Wasser*

Voice the English /t/ to /d/, and this often comes out as German 't':

daughter	*Tochter*
day	*Tag*
drink	*trinken*

Two phenomena ought to be noted in the above first two examples. The English 'gh,' which used to stand for the velar /x/, is now a mere sign of vowel length. In trying to sort out the meaning of a German word, it is a good plan to substitute English 'gh' for German 'ch' and see if any sense comes out of it—as in *Licht*, *lach(en)*, or *Nacht*, for example. The 'g' of *Tag* (Old English *dæg*) has softened to 'y' in "day"; sometimes it appears in English as 'w' (both 'y' and 'w' are semivowels).

So, if the 'v' of *Vogel* is pronounced /f/, what does the whole word mean? How about *Pfennig, Bog(en)*, or *Weg*?

The German 'ch' stands for /x/ after a back vowel, /ç/ after a front one. It is sometimes equivalent to English 'k':

book	*Buch* /x/
make	*machen* /x/
week	*Woche* /x/
weak	*weich* /ç/
reek	*riechen* /ç/
rake	*Rechen* /x/

English 'p' either becomes the affricate 'pf' (/pf/) or else the full-blown fricative 'f' (/f/), according to position:

path	*Pfad*
pipe	*Pfeife*
pepper	*Pfeffer*
sleep	*schlafen*

This last example also reminds us that English 's' plus consonant appears in German as 'sch' (/ʃ/) plus consonant:

smut	*Schmutz*
swan	*Schwan*
snow	*Schnee*
sweat	*Schweiss*

Finally, English noninitial 'v' often appears as German 'b':

give	*geben*
have	*haben*
love	*lieben*

In addition to these disguised identities, there are several words that are patently the same in English and German, though German prefers that older pronunciation still retained in Lancashire English (e.g., *Butter, Mann, hier, Lamm*). And German sometimes gives a clearer indication of the English pronunciation of a word held in common than the English spelling itself—*Haus* and *Maus,* for instance.

It is not possible to work out tables of vowel equivalents for the two languages. English 'o-e' will sometimes appear as German 'ei' (/ai/), as in:

one	*ein*
bone	*Bein* (leg)
home	*Heim-*

But there is no invariable rule to be made out of it. As with the Semitic languages, German yields its secrets through the consonants. Remembering the Nazi racial philosophy, we may note a peculiar irony here.

The time has come to look at some literary German. I begin with a translation of a novel of mine entitled *The End of the World News,* made by Joachim Kalka. The German version is called *Erlöse Uns, Lynx*—"Redeem (or Free) Us, Lynx." Lynx is the name of a planet that approaches and then shatters the earth. The crew of a spaceship watches the preliminary destruction of the moon.

The moon had been circling its new host in a regular satellitic rhythm. But earth was eventually going to be in the way of one arc of its revolution. This had always been evident, and there had been distracted speculation as to what the moon would do—wobble out of its course, be hurled to the condition of a solar satellite? But what happened now, the obvious, the banal, had always been the prognosis of most of the *America* team. They saw the moon come gracefully wheeling, approach the earth and then, not brutally, not even rapidly, shatter to fragments against it. The point of impact, they adjudged, was the dead heart of Europe. The moon broke and went into gracefully sailing fragments that slowly changed to sunlit dust and, most beautifully, tried to become a dust-ring around Lynx. But earth was in the way. A ring spun, of most lovely pearly configuration, but, at the point of impact with earth, shattered to amorphous dust, only to re-form when free of that gross body.

Der Mond hatte seinen neuen Herrn in regelmässingem Satellitenrhythmus umkreist. Doch die Erde würde schliesslich einmal

in seine Kreisbahn geraten. Das war schon immer offensichtlich
gewesen, und man hatte umruhige Hypothesen aufgestellt, was
dann mit dem Mond geschehen würde: Würde er aus seiner Bahn
stolpern und, fortgeschleudert, zu einem Satelliten der Sohne wer-
den? Was nun geschah, das Einfache, Banale, war immer von den
meisten Mitgliedern des Amerika-Teams vorhergesagt worden. Sie
sahen den Mond sich in eleganter Kurve nähern, die Erde er-
reichen, und dann—nicht brutal, nicht einmal rasch—an ihr zu
kleinen Fragmenten zerschellen. Der Punkt des Auftreffens war,
schätzten sie, das tote Herz Europas ... Der Mond zersplitterte
in elegant davonsegelnde Teile und Teilchen, die sich langsam
in sonnen-bestrahlten Staub verwandelten und—wunderschön—
einen Staubring um Lynx zu bilden versuchten. Aber die Erde war
im Wege. Ein Ring kreiste, von herrlich perlendschimmernder
Zusammensetzung, aber als die Erde wieder auftraf, zerbarst er zu
amorphem Staub und rundete sich erst wieder, als er vom Sog
dieses dicken Körpers frei war.

I doubt if the translation could have taken quite this form had it
been attempted during the Nazi regime. There are a fair number of
Romance borrowings—*"eleganter Kurve,"* for example, and *"Fragmenten."* What will worry the non-German reader is the apparent perver-
sity of a masculine moon (*der Mond*) and a feminine sun (*die Sonne*).
For the rest, there is great elegance in such native forms as *Kreisbahn*—"revolution"—and *sonnen-bestrahlten*—"sunlit"—as well as *perlendschimmernder Zusammensetzung*, longer than "pearly configuration"
but rhythmically very satisfying. But I must beware of seeming to
attribute qualities to a language which are the property of the user
of the language. Let us turn now to a German poet, Friedrich Georg
Jünger (1898–1977), one of whose uncomplicated little works I
choose at random:

Mit dem Saft der Maulbeere haben die Kinder
Ihre kleinen Gesichter beschmiert.
Näscher sind sie, Koster der Süssigkeit.
Sie tanzen in ihren geflickten Kleidern,
Und mit ihren tanzt der Westwind,
Tanzt auf den Schnüren die Wasche.
Es ist, als ob ein Hauch des wunderbaren Lebens
Die leeren Hüllen des Menschen fülle.

After all that has been said about the ultimate identity of German and English, it will be a disappointment to find so many words here that have no equivalent form in Modern English. We have to remember that vocabulary is a capricious thing. Take a breath and look carefully. *Maulbeere* is surely "mulberry"; *beschmiert* is "besmeared"; "hulls" are, surely, strawberry calyxes—there they are, as a metaphor, in *Hüllen*. Here is a literal translation that retains the German word order:

> With the juice of the mulberry have the children their little faces besmeared. Fruit-stealers are they, tasters of sweetness. They dance in their patched clothing, and with them dances the west wind, dances on the lines the washing. It is as though a breath of wonderful life the empty hulls of men (people, humankind) fills.

And finally a passage from one of the great germanophone authors of the century, Franz Kafka (1883–1924). This is the opening of his story "Ein Landarzt." "Land" has taken on the specific meaning of "country" (as opposed to "town") in German; a *Landarzt* is a country doctor.

> Ich war in grosser Verlegenheit: eine dringende Reise stand mir bevor; ein Schwerkranker wartete auf mich in einem zehn Meilen entfernten Dorfe; starkes Schneegestöber füllte den weiten Raum zwischen mir und ihm; eines Wagen hatte ich, leicht, grossräderig, ganz wie er für unsere Landstrassen taugt; in den Pelz gepackt, die Instrumententasche in der Hand, stand ich reisefertig schon aud dem Hofe; aber das Pferde fehlte, das Pferd . . .

> Let us keep very close to the German: "I was in gross (great) embarrassment; an urgent ride (journey) stood me before (faced me); a sorely-sick-one waited on (for) me in a ten mile far thorp (village); stark (strong, heavy) snowstorm filled the wide room (large space) 'twixt (between) me and him; a wagon (carriage) had I, light, great-wheely, fully as it for our land-streets (country roads) is suitable; in the pelt (fur coat) i-packed (wrapped), the instrument-case in the hand, stood I ride-ready (ready for the journey), but the horse failed (was lacking), the horse . . ."

It will be evident from this how German and English have diverged from their common origins in respect of meanings or nuances.

"Stark" means less "strong" in English than "strongly plain"; "wagon" cannot mean a vehicle in general, as it still can in Hitler's gift to the folk, the *Volkswagen*. "I stand" in German is *ich stehe* ("I stay"); "I stood" is *ich stand*. *Strasse* is like "street" but means a road as well as a town thoroughfare (compare "Watling Street"). *Dorf* ("village") is a word in its own right as well as a suffix in place-names (Düsseldorf or Thistlethorpe is rather bigger than a village); it is only as a suffix that it survives in names like Scunthorpe, though I should have no objection to seeing "thorp" in a poem by, say, Thomas Hardy. *Pferd* has nothing to do with "horse." Still, the face of kinship cannot be gainsaid, and there is fascination in looking for the family face under the beard.

15.

Daughters of Latin

Despite the closeness (and ultimate identity) of English and German, most British and American language learners feel far more at home with the Romance sisters—French, Italian, Spanish, Portuguese, and Catalan (but perhaps not Romanian). This may be a tribute to the beauty and hospitality of the Mediterranean countries, to the fact that they, unlike Germany, have done no real harm to the Anglo-Saxon peoples, or, more likely, to the results of that Latinization of English that was encouraged by the Norman Conquest. There is hardly a semanteme in the Romance languages that does not find a cognate word in English. In starting to learn French, Italian, or Spanish we find ourselves already equipped with a vast number of words that, despite various phonetic disguises, bridge the distance between the lands of wine and the lands of gin and beer.

It is interesting to see how English has entered into the Latin stream: it has dived into it both naked and wearing the clothes of Old French. For instance, the word "count" (the verb, not the aristocratic title) comes from an early form of the French *compter*, which comes from Latin *computare*. But English also has the word "compute," taken directly from the Latin, whose meaning is perhaps a little more rarefied and intellectual than that of "count." With the instrument known as the computer there is a highly intellectual borrowing. The computer is an *ordinateur* in French, but Italian prefers to talk of the "computer" with a near-English pronunciation. Thus a Latin form gets back to a Latin language through a Germanic one. Here are some examples of twofold English borrowings:

STRAIGHT FROM FRENCH	STRAIGHT FROM LATIN	LATIN
conceit	concept	*conceptu*
constraint	constriction	*constrictione*
dainty	dignity	*dignitate*
esteem	estimate	*aestimare*
feat	fact	*facto*
loyal	legal	*legali*
poor	pauper	*pauperi*
royal	regal	*regali*
sure	secure	*securo*

Those interested in the inflections of Latin words will note that the Latin ablative singular is given here: it was mainly from that form of the Latin noun that the Romance languages derived their own invariable noun forms.

English, then, absorbed much of its vocabulary from the French; ever since, it has been taking words consciously and deliberately from classical Latin. It is not too much to say that any Latin semanteme is potentially an English word, and we are always at liberty to coin new Latinisms when we wish. Thus, if I want to talk of the farmer's wife of the "Three Blind Mice" round, I can—a little whimsically—refer to her as "muricidal" or "mouse-killing." The word may not be in the dictionary, but it is a true English word for all that. Whimsicality seems inseparable from such coinages, and even the accepted Latin equivalents for certain basic Germanic words must seem, when not pompous, to be humorous. "My son indulges in promiscuous osculation" is somewhat Edwardian and would not get a laugh now: sons go further than merely kissing around. "A nod is as good as a wink to a blind horse" was, in my youth, thought a great joke when Latinized to "A minimal inclination of the cranium is as adequate as a spasmodic movement of one optic to an equine quadruped devoid of visionary capacity." Speakers and writers of English are nowadays either less classically endowed than formerly or have moved on to sharper forms of humor. But we have in this Latinizing—and for that matter Hellenizing—

capacity of English a proof that a language is as much a body of potential words as an inventory of existing ones.

When I speak of "classical Latin," I am referring to a rather artificial, upper-class, literary kind of language, preserved in the works of Vergil, Horace, and Cicero, and not generally used by the common people of the Roman Empire. For instance, the patrician or literary word for "beautiful" was *pulcher*, and we find this in the learned or facetious "pulchritude." But the common people used instead *bello* (meaning, perhaps, "pretty"), and this survives in the French *bel, beau, belle*, and the Italian *bello* and *bella*. There seem to be no Romance derivatives of *pulcher*. *Formosus*, meaning perhaps "shapely" ("having form") has become the Spanish *hermoso*, though *bello*, too, is found, as in Lorca's "*La niña del bello rostro* . . ." The upper-class word for "horse" was *equus*, and this appears in various English words, such as "equine," "equestrian," and "equerry" (though in this last word there was mistaken etymology, *scutaria* probably being the Latin original). But the ordinary people called a horse *caballus*, from which has come a whole set of Romance words—French *cheval*, Spanish *caballo*, and Latin *cavallo*. A gentleman—cavalier or *caballero*—is a man who rides a horse; there are few gentlemen around these days. *Loqui* was the upper-class Latin word "to speak" (a whole host of English words have sprung out of this), but the word in common use was *fabulari*. This produced French *parler*, Italian *parlare*, and Spanish *hablar*.

The term "Romance" may well be buzzing in the rear of the reader's skull as a term overcommodious and hence ambiguous. It is a word of amatory associations—"A Fine Romance," sang Fred Astaire and Ginger Rogers; the late novelist Henry Green gave as his hobby in *Who's Who* "romancing over the bottle to a good band." It is a literary term meaning a novel of a contrived and emotional kind. Ultimately it is Latin *Romanicus*. It is used linguistically to distinguish the classical phase of Latin from its postimperial breakdown. The Romance languages all derive from Latin, but they show features more demotic or popular than patrician or upper-class. The erotic romance is still a demotic form.

"People's Latin," then, produced the Romance languages of today. Italian is, as it were, the domestic form that Latin took over the centuries; Spanish and Portuguese are the Latin that was taken to the Iberian peninsula; French is the kind of Latin that was spoken in Lutetia or Paris that eventually became the "official" tongue of the whole country. The essentially national terms now in use—we give the language the name of the people who speak it—took some time to come about. There was a time when the differentiation between the various kinds of spoken popular Latin was made in terms of the words used for "yes," a form slow to appear: the Latin response to the question "Have you done it?" would be "I have." Peter Abelard (1079?–1144) wrote a philosophical treatise in 1121 called *Sic et non* ("Thus and Not"), which shows an attempt to develop a simple affirmative in a language that did not possess it. Eventually three forms were distinguished in three different regions, and these were the badges of the major Romance tongues—*langue d'oc* in the French southern provinces; *langue d'oïl* (*oïl* = *oui*) in the north; *langue de si* in Italy. There is still a vast dialectal continuum that contradicts the formalities of the linguistic capitals: languages, or dialects, like Niçois and Monegasque, in Nice and Monaco respectively, are just two of the relics of *langue d'oc*. The tripartite linguistic division was recognized as late as the end of the thirteenth century, very much a part of historical time: we can watch French, Italian, and the Iberian tongues developing. Of these last, Catalan is important. Outlawed during the Franco regime, it is experiencing a literary renaissance as I write. It is the tongue of Catalonian dissent, unsubmissive to the centralizing influence of Madrid.

Let us eschew generalization and look first at a number of English words derived directly from Latin and compare them with their Romance equivalents. I have chosen words that all contain the consonant duo 'ct.' In Italian the Latin 'ct' changed to 'tt'; in Spanish it became 'ch'; in Portuguese and French it appears as '(i)t':

LATIN	ITALIAN	SPANISH	PORTUGUESE	FRENCH	ENGLISH
dicto (said)	*detto*	*dicho*	*dito*	*dit*	dictate
facto (done)	*fatto*	*hecho*	*feito*	*fait*	fact
lacte (milk)	*latte*	*leche*	*leite*	*lait*	lactic
nocte (night)	*notte*	*noche*	*noite*	*nuit*	night
octo (eight)	*otto*	*ocho*	*oito*	*huit*	October

(October was the eighth month in old Roman reckoning.) Note how the Latin ablative ending (the "by," "with," or "from" form) is retained in the first three of the Romance languages. French likes to be rid of its endings, and even what is retained in the spelling disappears in speech: none of the 't's here are pronounced.

Let us now take three Latin words that begin with consonant plus 'l':

pleno, "full" ("plenipotentiary" or "plenitude"); *clave,* "key" ("clavicle," "clavichord"); and *flamma,* "flame." In Italian the /l/ is vocalized to 'i': *pieno, chiave* (the 'ch' is pronounced /k/), *fiamma.* In Spanish the three forms—'pl,' 'cl,' and 'fl'—all become 'll' (the palatal /ʎ/ close to the 'lli' in "million"): *lleno, llave, llama.* Portuguese also uses the one sound for the three Latin consonant combinations: *chelo, chave, chama* (the 'ch' is pronounced /ʃ/). French, as if to compensate for dropping the Latin endings, retains the initial Latin consonant duo: *plein, clef, flamme.*

To attempt to explain these changes, seemingly as capricious as the retentions, would require a great deal of speculation, bringing in the possible influence of other, neighboring, tongues for instance. But the bilabial fricative /β/ (a recurring motif in this book) must have a lot to do with the following:

LATIN	ITALIAN	SPANISH	PORTUGUESE	FRENCH	ENGLISH
capillo	capello	cabello	cabelo	cheveu	hair
lepore	lepre	liebre	lebre	lièvre	hare
sapere	sapere	saber	saber	savoir	to know
bibere	be(ve)re	beber	beber	buvoir	to drink
habere	avere	haber	haver	avoir	to have

The intervocal 'p' of Latin must have been unsteady and wavering, and both the original and derived 'b' must have had a fricative quality; only thus can we explain the present-day forms shown above, the French 'v' a true /v/, the Iberian 'b' with a buzzed quality suggesting /v/.

Let us glance now at what has happened to some of the original Latin vowels:

LATIN	ITALIAN	SPANISH	PORTUGUESE	FRENCH	ENGLISH
pede	piede	pie	pé	pied	foot
petra	pietra	piedra	pedna	pierre	stone
decem	dieci	diez	dez	dix	ten
morit	muore	muere	morre	meurt	(he) dies
potet	puo	puede	pode	peut	(he) can
foco	fuoco	fuego	fogo	feu	fire

(The Latin *foco,* from *focus,* is properly a fireplace, the genuine focus of a room on a cold day.)

The front vowel 'e' is diphthongized in Italian, Spanish, and French to 'ie' (/ie/). This is not what Anglophones would regard as a true diphthong, since the first of the two vowels is raised to the palatal limit as /j/ (as in "yes"). The television-commercial ditty about a white Martini has "bee-anco," where /bjaŋko/ is correct. The back vowel 'o' has undergone three different kinds of pseudodiphthongization—*può* = /pwo/, *puede* = /pwede/, *peut* once was /peu/ but no longer. French now has in *peut* and *meurt* and *feu* the round front vowel /ø/. The Italian 'uo' merely seems to emphasize that we are uttering a very round sound; the Spanish 'ue' shows a pushing forward of the original Latin 'o' to the front of the mouth and a preceding 'u' to show that the changed vowel was once a round one.

The Latin double vowel 'au' has become a simple vowel /o/ in the Romance languages, though the spelling does not always show this. Thus, the *auro* ("gold") that we find in English "auriferous" ("gold-bearing") or even in the chemical symbol "Au," has become *oro* in both Italian and Spanish, *ouro* in Portuguese (all three words are pronounced /oro/), and *or* in French. *Causa*, which we find in English as "cause," has developed the meaning "thing" in the Romance languages, and appears as *cosa* in Italian and Spanish, *cousa* in Portuguese, and *chose* in French.

It will be evident from our examples so far that of all the daughters of Latin, French has strayed furthest from home. English words like "scripture," "slave," "space," "spice," and "scald" keep, in their initial sounds, very close to the original Latin, but see what they have become in French: *écriture*, *esclave*, *espace*, *épice*, and *échauffer*. In general the tendency of French is to discard an original Latin 's' where possible. Sometimes it feels guilty about this and erects a circumflex as a kind of funerary monument above the letter preceding the place where the 's' used to be. Compare the following:

MIDDLE FRENCH	MODERN FRENCH	ENGLISH
bastard	*bâtard*	bastard
beste	*bête*	beast
feste	*fête*	feast
oistre	*huître*	oyster

English is far truer to its Latin stepmother than French is to its flesh-and-blood progenetrix.

Another trick of French is to change the hard 'c' of Latin—retained in its sisters—to 'ch." This means that a /k/ has been pushed forward from the soft to the hard palate and turned into /ʃ/. English has, incidentally, done the same thing with a few Latin words, so that *episcopus* (from Greek *episkopos*—"overseer") appears as "bishop" and *casius* becomes "cheese." But French is fairly consistent:

LATIN	FRENCH	ENGLISH
caballo	*cheval*	horse
capra	*chèvre*	goat
caro	*cher*	dear
cantare	*chanter*	to sing
capitulo	*chapitre*	chapter

The voiced velar consonant of Latin—/g/—has been treated even more harshly than /k/ when it appears in the middle of a word. Augusto ("August") appears as *août* (pronounced, with desperate simplicity, as /u/); *lege* ("law") has become *loi*; *nigro* ("black") is Gallicized to *noir*. Elimination and shortening have been really drastic in French: consider that *eau* (/o/) comes from *aqua* ("water"), and that noël, which English has borrowed for its carols, derives ultimately from natalis—"natal," "relating to birth." The paring down is often more drastic than it looks, so that *front* ("forehead"), though its spelling shows a derivation from Latin *fronte*, no longer has an articulated 't,' and the 'n' has been diminished to a mere snorting of the preceding vowel. I can never become accustomed to the French truncation of Christ to /kri/.

Spanish and Portuguese show their own patterns of divergence—both singly and collectively. But both look more like Latin than does French. What gives Spanish its piquancy is its traces of the influence of non–Indo-European languages. The Basque tongue has no /f/, and this seems reflected in the following:

LATIN	SPANISH	ENGLISH
fabulari	*hablar*	to speak
facere	*hacer*	to make
filio	*hijo*	son
folia	*hoja*	leaf

The 'h' has no sound here, nor, indeed, in any of the Romance languages, though it seems to have had full aspirate value in Latin.

But if official Italian (Tuscan, really) merely acknowledges the dead phoneme /h/ with a silent memorial grapheme in *ho, hai, ha* ("I have," "thou hast," "he/she has") and *hanno* ("they have"), in the dialects of the north Adriatic the original Latin /h/ has become a /g/. This, as we shall see in the next chapter, has a parallel in Russian, so we may posit a Slavic influence. James Joyce's daughter, Lucia, brought up on the Italian of Trieste, wrote a postcard to her father beginning "*Caro babbo, go un bela bala*" ("Dear daddy, I have a lovely ball")—the *go* equivalent to Tuscan *ho* ("I have"). But back to Spanish.

Note that the middle 'li' of *filio* and *folia* in the table on page 200 has become a Spanish jota—'j,' pronounced /x/, suggesting a possible Arabic influence. That influence, however, is seen mostly in the vocabulary, giving words like *mezquino* ("poor"), *alguacil* ("constable"), *aljibe* ("cistern"), *laúd* ("lute"), *ataúd* ("coffin"), *zanahoria* ("carrot").

Portuguese resembles French in having eliminated some of the nasal consonants of original Latin and substituted nasalization of the preceding vowel or even (unlike French) the preceding diphthong. Spanish *lana* ("wool") appears in Portuguese as *lã*; Spanish *pan* ("bread") becomes *pão*. And Portuguese, somewhat like Italian, is not always concerned with retaining an original Latin 'l.' Latin *caelum* ("sky") appears in French as *ciel* and in Spanish as *cielo*; but Portuguese has *céu*. Latin and Italian *volare* ("to fly") is *volar* in Spanish but *voar* in Portuguese. The 'l' has disappeared even in the definite articles, so that *lo* and *la* have become *o* and *a*. Occasionally Portuguese has 'r' where other Romance tongues have 'l'. What is *blanc* in French, and *blanco* in Spanish, is *branco* in Portuguese. One is not "much obliged" in Portugal; one is *muito obrigado*.

When we have considered all the sound shifts, distortions, and disguises that make the modern Romance languages different from Latin—and from the Latin component of English—we are still left with a corpus of transparent identities. If English "experience" is *experiencia* in Spanish, *experiéncia* in Portuguese, and *esperienza* in Italian, we should have no difficulty in rendering other English words with the same termination, though we must not expect a total identity of meaning. *Expérience* in French carries a primal force of "experiment." English shares with French the ending '-ment' in words like "monument" and "element"; this meets '-mento' in the three other tongues. The suffix '-ty' in "identity" corresponds to French '-té,' Spanish '-dad,' Portuguese '-dade,' and Italian '-tà." And words like "education" appear as French *éducation*, Spanish *educación*, Portuguese *educação*, and Italian *educazione*. The recognition that our own language is, to some extent, as much a child of the Roman Empire as the true Latin languages should encourage us in our work on them. We may even take a breath and plunge into Romanian, which has developed out of the Latin spoken by Trajan's troops in the province of Dacia. There we shall find that the strange-looking *omul* is really *homo ille* ("the man") and *lupul* is *lupus ille* ("the wolf"). If there is a pleasure in this craft of language learning, it is chiefly to be found in the search for hidden identities.

Every schoolboy used to know that the Latin verb is a nightmare. The nightmare has partially dispersed in the descendants of Latin, which still, nevertheless, make heavier going of verbs than English or German. But the common people of the Empire were already at work on a simplification and rationalization unreflected in the high-bred literature and oratory. Where Cicero or Vergil would write *amavi* for "I have loved," the Roman plebs would prefer a form like our own: *habeo amatum* ("I have" - "loved"). In all the Romance languages you can make a past form, a future, and a conditional (the "should/would" tense) out of the verb "to have." Thus the French *j'ai* ("I have") gives us the conversational past tense of *j'ai aimé* ("I have loved") and the future *j'aimerai* (infinitive *aimer* + *ai*). The past tense (imperfect) *j'avais*—"I had"—will give not only the pluperfect "I had loved"—*j'avais aimé*—but the conditional "I would (might) love"—*j'aimerais* (infinitive *aimer* + *-ais*). The same process goes on in the sister languages.

Discussing verbs—not only here—I have said nothing of what are known as "moods" (or modes). Take the English sentence "If I were you, I'd get there early." We frequently hear (and read) "If I was you . . ." This signifies that what is called the subjunctive mood is giving way to the indicative—the mood that states what is happening, not what is merely imagined, supposed, feared, suspected, or, in brief, placed in a region of the mind where action belongs neither to the present nor the future nor the past but to the imagination. If the subjunctive mood is dying in English, with "I wish he was better" replacing "I wish he were better," it is still going strong in the Romance languages, where it is not a matter of stylistic choice but of stern syntactic necessity. "Although I am poor" has to be "*Quoique je sois pauvre*" in French (*sois*, not *suis*), and failure to observe the rule is a grave solecism. And yet, while this present tense subjunctive remains a lively aspect of the language, the past tense subjunctive is dying, if not already dead. There was, till recently, a word game on French television in which young people asked the past subjunctive of *parler, dire, finir,* and so on rarely came up with any answer at all. A year or so ago I was giving a lecture to some French students and gave away my age by saying something like "*Il fallait que vous parlassiez . . .*" I met a response of shock, bewilderment, and kindred emotions. This phasing out of the past subjunctive has not occurred in the other Romance languages. I find myself saying on the telephone in Italian: "*Sarebbe meglio si loro parlassero con mia moglie*" ("It would be better if they spoke to my wife") and seeing the point of a mood that refers to something that, so far, is lodged only in the room of the possible.

I am writing this book in Ticino, in southern Switzerland, a region where Italian is spoken, as well as a dialect known as Ticinese, and the German language, the property of Svizzera interna, meaning chiefly Zürich, is understood and used on the telephone or to tourists. The situation is interesting in this country, which has no single name—Suisse or Svizzera or Schweiz is a triune *patrie* or *patria* or *Vaterland*—although Confederatio Helvetica (CH) recalls unity under Rome. There are three major languages spoken and written in a manner acceptable to Paris, Milan, and Bonn respectively (this is not true of the French of Canada when heard in Paris), but there is a vast network of dialects, including Romansch (itself a network) and a brand of German called Schwyzertütsch. Romansch gets on to the banknotes—fifty francs is *cinquante francs, cincuanta franchi, fünfzig Franken,* and also *tschuncanta francs*—but most of the commodities one buys are content with trilingualism or even bilingualism. Milk is *Milch, lait,* and *latte* all at the same time, and the healthful substances that it *enthält* or *contient* or *contiene* shine through linguistic veils. The puzzled non-Germanophone may wonder at *Eiweiss* (eggwhite? in milk, for God's sake?) until it is revealed as *protéines.* The *éléments constitutifs* or *sostanze ricostituive* are building stuffs or *Baustoffe.* The Swiss are used to this polyglot situation. They also meet with no surprise dialects like this, from the Gruyère-producing region: "*Nouthra do-nadi maôr-tsè. Nouthra do-nadit maôr-tsè. Nojà nbin ein rè-jon dè no rè-siâô chu vo Po no j'a-po-yi lè crou-yo mo-min; pri dè vouthron fe, vo fô prè-yi por no, Pu no ti vouèrdâô dein le bon tse-min.*" Chinese? Vietnamese? No, a regional development of Latin. Surely "pray for us" is visible in that "*prè-yi por no.*"

This rich linguistic diversity does not noticeably worry the Swiss, though there have been demagogic cries for the verbal means of political unity. English is becoming, inevitably, an important force at commercial and banking levels, but it is unlikely to do anything for the national, as opposed to regional, unification of this dull and lovely land. I mention the Swiss situation only to indicate that polyglotism is neither unnatural nor conducive to neurosis. Swiss neurosis has nothing to do with language.

16.

THE RUSSIANS ARE COMING

Two new Russian words have recently been adopted not only into English but into (judging from what I hear on the international radio) most of the languages of the world. They are *glasnost* and *perestroika*. They are used by non-Russophones rather vaguely to connote, rather than denote, a new liberal openness in the Soviet Union, a softening of ideological rigidity. The dictionary definitions have no nimbus of political reform. *Glasnost'* (the final /t/ is spoken on the palate not the teeth, hence the conventional apostrophe) derives from *glas*, meaning "voice." *Glasit'* means "say" or "run" or "read," and *glasnost'* means no more than "publicity," which may well be delivered by the *glashatay* or town crier. *Perestroika* means "reconstruction" or "reorganization" and could as well refer to what was done during the revolutionary epoch as during the period of a market-oriented economy. I do not like this parroting of loanwords not seen in context. We had all better get down to learning some Russian.

The Cyrillic alphabet seems an obstacle, but it is altogether suitable for the language that it clothes, and it is easily learned. The following geographical names may be found useful.

Африка	Afrika	Africa
Брюссель	Briussel'	Brussels
Кембридж	Kyembridzh	Cambridge
Голландия	Gollandiya	Holland
Вальпарайзо	Val'paraizo	Valparaiso
Мельбурн	Myel'burn	Melbourne
Цейпон	Tsyeilon	Ceylon

Corresponding to the apostrophe in the second column above, you will notice the symbol ь, which indicates palatalization. The difference between л (/l/) and лъ (/ʎ/) is close to the difference between the 'l' of "mill" and the 'lli' of "million." Any consonant that has the "softening" symbol after it is, as it were, prevented from being articulated in the usual way: a /j/ (as in "yes") comes along and chokes it.

The difference between a plain consonant and a palatalized one is not (as is the difference between dark and clear 'l' in English) an allophonic matter. The addition of ь makes a new phoneme, as is shown by the difference in meaning between the following: угол ("corner"); уголъ ("coal"). Palatalization is dear to the heart of Russian, and there is a perfect opposition between plain and palatized vowels:

A, a, as in "h*a*rd"	Я, я, as in "*y*ard"
3, з, as in "d*e*n"	E, e, as in "*ye*s"
O, o, as in "*o*n"	Ё, ё, as in "*yo*nde"
Y, y, as in "bl*ue*"	ю, ю, as in "*you*"

One Russian vowel that has no equivalent in any other Western language is represented by ы. It is very much like the English /ɪ/ in "sit," but is more centralized (properly /ɨ/) and sometimes pronounced with lip-rounding. For the rest, the Russian sound system is straightforward enough, and Russian, like English, is willing to weaken a vowel if it is not in a stressed position. Thus, *Doctor Zhivago* does not, as would be the case in a Romance language, preserve perfectly the final rounded 'o.' The vowel is unstressed and approaches a centralized 'a.' The consonant 'Щ' is a cluster exactly like that found in the middle of the English phrase "smashed china." There is no aspirate /h/, but foreign words containing one are given the same treatment I have remarked in Adriatic versions of Italian. A homosexual is a "gomosexual," and Ernest Hemingway is "Yernyest Gemingvay." A voiced consonant at the end of a word—as in *kleb* ("bred") or the name Gorbachev—is unvoiced in the German manner.

The learning of stress in Russian is difficult: there are no stress marks or stress rules, and one is reminded again of English. But most Russian primers and dictionaries put a stress diacritic (´) above the stressed vowel of a word, and this helps. Stress is vigorous. The tone of Russian is virile, even bearish.

Russian has plenty of grammar, but to anyone who has studied a classical Indo-European language like Latin, there will not seem to be anything unfamiliar. There are three genders, words ending in a consonant or a semivowel и (/j/) tending to masculinity, feminine words being, as with Romance tongues, those with an '-a' or '-ya' ending, and the neuter nouns favoring a termination in '-o' or '-ye.' Adjectives—which come before the noun—have endings similar to those of the nouns, and both nouns and adjectives have full batteries of inflections.

The endings of the various parts of the verb have a Latin flavor. "I read" is *ya chitáyu*, "he reads" is *on chitáyet*, "we read" is *mi* (мы) *chitáyem*, and "they read" is *oni chitáyut*. There is only one past tense, but its endings reflect the gender of the subject, so that "I read" (/red/) or "I have read" will be *ya chitál*, *ya chitála*, or *ya chitálo* according to the gender of the speaker. The other persons of the singular ("thou," "he, she, it") take the same endings as does *ya*, and the plural— whether "we," "you," or "they"—has the invariable ending '-i': *mi chitáli*—"we read," *oni chitáli*—"they read," where "read" = /red/. English spelling can be a great nuisance.

The Russian verb has only three tenses, while English has twelve. To make up for this deficiency, Russian introduces what are called "aspects of the verb"—the *imperfective* and the *perfective*. If *chitál* means "I have read," the addition of a prefix will produce *prochitál*— "I have finished reading"; *budu chitat'* means "I shall read," but *prochitáyu* (a present-tense form used with a future meaning) will signify "I shall read (it) through." The simple form of the verb, then, implies no completion of action and hence is imperfective: the prefix changes it to a perfective form or aspect, and completion of the action is the very essence of its meaning. Here are other examples:

Ya rabótayu.	I work (continuously, habitually, or recurrently).
Ya porabótal.	I did some work (i.e., completed some).
Ya porabótayu.	I shall do some (a little) work (a present tense cannot indicate completion; so the present-tense form of perfective verbs has to convey a future meaning).

The bulk of the Russian vocabulary is pure Slavonic, but a vast number of loanwords (from German, French, even English) helps our learning task:

abort	abortion, miscarriage
abstraktniy	abstract
absurd	absurdity
ambitsiya	ambition
armiya	army
banknota	bank note
bryesh'	breach, gap
bufyet	sideboard, buffet
diplomaticheskiy	diplomatic
direktor	director, manager, chief
dyek	deck
evangelist	evangelist
geroy	hero
gimn	hymn
identichniy	identical
idyot	idiot
instruktsiya	instruction
karta	card, map, menu
konfyeta	sweetmeat
korpus	body, army corps
korrektniy	correct, proper
korryespondyentsya	correspondence
kortezh	procession, cortège
langust	lobster (cf. French *langouste*)
maskarad	fancy dress ball
planyeta	planet

plug	plough
tabak	tobacco
tambur	drum (cf. French *tambour*)
tramvay	tram, tramway
tsyellyulaniy	cellular
sharlatan	charlatan
shofyor	chauffeur
vokal'niy	vocal

It is time to look at some Russian in action, and we cannot do better than take a short poem by Alcksandr Sergeyevich Pushkin (1799–1837), the Byron of Russian literature. Here it is first in Cyrillic script:

Я вас пюби́п; пюбо́вь еще́, быть-мо́жет,
В душе́ мое́й уга́спа не совсе́м;
Но пусть она́ вас бо́пьше не трево́жит;
Я не хочу́ печа́пить ваc ниче́м.
Я вас пюби́п безмо́пвно, безнаде́жно,
То ра́достью, то ре́вностью томи́м;
Я вас пюби́п так и́скренно, так не́жно,
Как дай вам Бог пюби́мой быть други́м.

And here is an attempt at transliteration into the Roman alphabet:

Ya vas lyuhil; lyubov' yeshcho, bit'-mozhet,
V dushe moyey ugasla nye suvsyem;
No pust' ona vas bol'she nye tryevozhit;
Yu nye khochu pyechalit' vas nichem.
Ya vas lyubil byezmolvno, byeznadyozhno,
To radost'yu, to revnost'yu tomim;
Ya vas lyubil tak iskryenno, tak nyezhno,
Kak day vam Bog lyubimoy bit' drugim.

(Vowels have their "Continental" values; 'y' always stands for the 'y' in "yes"; 'g' is always velar, as in "got"; the apostrophe, as always, means the palatalizer ь.)

The key phrase is *Ya vas lyubil*—literally, "I you loved." Let us keep to the Russian word order for our literal translation: "I you loved: love still, perhaps/ In spirit my has-been-extinguished [*ugasla*] not entirely;/ But it you more let not trouble (let it trouble you no more)/ I not wish to sadden you with nothing./ I you loved without utterance [*byez*, silently], without hope (hopelessly),/ Now from joy, now from jealousy languishing;/ I you loved so sincerely, so tenderly,/ As grant you God be loved by another."

Learn the Russian by heart. It should melt to tears even a high official of the Komitet Gosudarstvennoi Bezopasnosti, KGB for short.

17.

Malay

We have taken brief tastes of Indo-European languages and seen what they have in common—inflections, conjugations, genders, and a stock of words that all spring from the same source. It will be salutary for us to move outside the great family and examine two languages that obey none of our rules—though, being products of that machine in the human brain that manufactures language, they may not be so outlandish as they look. Our first language of the East is Malay, which, in both Indonesia and Malaysia, is termed *Bahasa*, which means "the language." It is rich in dialects and is cognate with the tongues of the Dayaks and Ibans in Borneo, as well as (though more remotely) with Fijian and Maori. The Muslim invaders of Malacca gave Malay a form of the Arabic alphabet (called the *Jawi* or "Eastern" form), but Romanization has proved easy. Dutch Romanization, which used to prevail in Indonesia, differed from British, as it followed the spelling conventions of the Dutch language. Thus, the word for "grandchild" was spelled *tjoetjoe* in Indonesian Malay but *chuchu* in the Malay of British Malaya, now Malaysia. Since Malaysian independence, there have been somewhat irrational spelling reforms, so that 'ch' represents /k/ and 'c' /tʃ/. It is a pity, as Coca-Cola is much drunk under the tropical sun, and nobody feels inclined to call it Chocha-Chola.

Malay speakers, and more particularly the linguistic legislators, have never been sure of the difference between the phonemes /u/ and /o/—chiefly because the Arabic ‍9‍ has to be used for both. *Kampong* has been replaced by *kampung*. I will, for the sake of convenience and out of homage to memory, keep to the older spelling.

Malay has no frightening phonetic curiosities. Final plosives like /t/, /d/, /p/, and /b/ are initiated but not completed, and the letter /k/ stands for a glottal stop in words like *anak* ("child"), *sĕjuk* ("cold"), and *itek* ("duck"). Words can begin with /ŋ/, something not to be found in the West. The vowel symbols have roughly the same values as in Italian, but 'ĕ' stands for schwa. There is a tendency for the final 'a' in words like *ada* ("there is" or "there are") to take on the tense quality of the vowel of French *bleu*. Articulation is gentle but rapid. Vowels are sometimes lengthened for prosodic reasons, so that *jauh* ("far") can, in speech, be expanded to *jauuuuuh* if the distance indicated is great enough. The aspirate is pronounced, both fore and aft.

What strikes the learner of Malay is the complete lack of those typically Indo-European word changes necessary in the building of a sentence. In other words, morphology does not exist. Let us first look at the pronouns. *Saya* can be "I," "me," or, in post position, "my." "I hit him" is *saya pukul dia;* "he hits me" is *dia pukul saya*; "my wife" is *istĕri saya. Dia* is as invariable as *saya*, and it can stand for "he," "him," "she," "her," and "it," as well as the possessives of those pronouns; in speech it can also mean "they," the highbrow *mĕreka* being reserved for the written form of the language. "His wife" can be *istĕri dia*, but *istĕri-nya* is perhaps preferred. That nasalization of *di-* to *-ny* forms an interesting parallel (and not only here) to Welsh mutation. The Malay word for "you" is slippery and variable, showing the influence of old taboos and immemorial usages of courtesy. And so a Malay will choose carefully in asking the question "What do you want?" To a person of superior social status (particularly one who has made the trip to Mecca and become a *haji*) he will say, "*Apa tuan mahu?*" For a slightly lower social status *ĕnche* will replace *tuan*. There are other words that might be used: *lu* for a Chinese, *tuanku* ("my lord") to a ruler, *tĕngku* and *ĕngku* for rajas, *datok* for village chiefs, *'che gu'* (short for *guru*) for a schoolmaster (and for a cat, which, in Malay fables, figures as the teacher of the other beasts). The problem was always to find a general term that would offend nobody, and this has finally been imported from Indonesia—*anta*, a word that many profess not to understand, though they see it daily in advertisements like *Guinness* *baik untok anta* ("Guinness good for you"—there is no copula). Malay has one advantage over the Indo-European tongues in its words for "we": *kami* can exclude the person addressed, *kita* includes him. In Brunei *kita* is used for "you," so that there is a sort of governess flavor in statements like "We must not do that again, must we?"

The noun is invariable, and does not require change in the plural. *Rokok* is "cigarette," "a cigarette," "the cigarette," or "cigarettes," all being clarified by context. Pluralization can be shown by duplication, but *rokok-rokok* (written as *rokok2*) implies a variety, different kinds of cigarettes, rather than a simple plural. When number is specified— "two cigarettes"—or the nature of the pluralization is significant, as in "many cigarettes," a very Eastern device is used (it is also found in Chinese). This is the "numerical coefficient," which varies according to the semantic nature of the noun concerned. Human beings are preceded by the announcement "human being," so that "two clerks" is *dua orang kĕrani*, "four soldiers," is *ĕmpat orang soldadu* (note the Portuguese loanword *soldadu*, a relic of Portuguese Malacca), and "many women" is *banyak orang pĕrĕmpuan*. (Beware of calling the Borneo simian an *orangutan* [in Malaysia]. *Orang hutan* means "man of the jungle," and to attach the term to a beast is an insult. *Mawas* or *maias* is the word to use.) The coefficient for animals is *ekor*— "tail"—and "ten cats" is hence *sa-puloh ekor kuching*. Subtlety is required for inanimate objects. For anything big, round, or bulky, the coefficient *buah* ("fruit") is needed: "a car" is *sa buah kĕreta*, and "five hundred houses" is *lima ratus buah rumah*. For fruit, you use "egg" (*telor*) as a coefficient; for an egg you use *biji* ("seed").

If one immerses oneself deeply enough in Malay, one concludes that the Western concept of "parts of speech" is totally alien to it. A word is a word is a word, and it can fill any slot in a syntactical structure. Thus, *makan* expresses the notions of food and eating indifferently, so that *makan saya* can, logically, mean both "eat me" and "my food." *Tari* is either "dance" (the noun), "dancing," or the active verb "to dance." But, especially in written Malay, there is an interesting battery of affixes to call on that make more specific the function of the word in question. So *tarian* can mean only "a dance" or "the dance," while *mĕnari* (again the Welsh-type nasal mutation) has to be a verb. Much can be made out of little. The word *ada* can mean any of the following (I quote Wilkinson's Malay-English dictionary): "to be present, to exist, to be at home (to a visitor), to exist in connection with, to appertain to, to have." The root meaning is "existence." *Adakan* or *měngadakan* (the suffix *-kan* having a causative function) means "to call into existence, to appoint." *Běrada* is a polite way of saying "to be present," but *orang yang běrada* means "people of standing." *Kěadaan* (abstract-noun prefix *kě-*, noun suffix *-an*) means "state, existence, condition of life, position." One prefix, *těr-*, adds a remarkable nuance to a verb. If *kilat* has the primary meaning of "a flash (as of lightning)," and *běrkilat* means "to flash," *těrkilat* means "to flash suddenly, unawares," as of a darting fish. I have not heard *těrada* used, but it might be useful for describing intermittent being, as of a ghost. *Hantu těrada*—"The ghost was and then was not."

Malay has certain words that cannot be assigned to any Western category. A good example is *pun*, literally untranslatable. It is an emphasizing word, a word that "lights up" the semanteme that goes before. *Itu pun* means "that also," *sakali pun* is something like "yet" (*sakali* means literally "one time"), *dia pun pěrgi* means "He also went," the *pun* bestowing a past meaning on the invariable verb form *pěrgi*— "go." There is no single meaning for *pun*, and it is hard to get at its roots and origin; its correct use is incredibly difficult to learn. (When a Malay friend of mine said, in impeccable English, that he loved a pun, I was able to say, "*Saya pun juga*"—"I do too.") The enclitic *-lah* is again untranslatable. It lends force to what goes before, so that *Orang itu-lah yang pěrgi* means "It was *that* person who went." Words like these are perhaps essential to a language that does not use vocal stress for emphasis.

The vocabulary of Malay is, in its fundamentals, entirely fitted to the needs of a people concerned with the concrete facts of everyday living—fishing, gathering fruits and coconuts, planting rice, begetting children, and lying in the sun. This makes it poetical, metaphorical, happier with proverbs than with abstract constatations. But the Arabs brought Islam and the religious and philosophical terms that go with it. Loanwords from English and Portuguese are numerous. The need to cope—in schools, newspapers, and government directives—with the intellectual and technological notions of the modern world has forced Malay scholars, teachers, and editors to fashion neologisms, usually out of Arabic or Sanskrit (India has its influence). There have to be trade unions, strikes, parent-teacher associations, and cooperative societies. A new world of words, bewildering to the *padi* planter, is being forged. Terms like *měrdeka* came from the Sanskrit during the time of political independence to signify liberty, but to many it sounded like *muntega*—a Portuguese loanword for "butter."

Whether Malay could ever be democratized was an interesting question when *mĕrdeka* came in. The ancient feudal structure of Malay society has had a remarkable effect on the language. Words appropriate to the common man and woman cannot properly be used in connection with a ruler—sultan or raja. I walk (*jalan kaki*—"go with foot") but the sultan must *bĕrangkat*. I eat (*makan*) but the sultan *santap*. I sleep (*tidor*), while the sultan *bĕradu* (the root of the word has to do with a singing contest between the ladies of the seraglio: the one who won slept with the sultan). This may seem an unnecessary lot of luggage (there are many other specifically "royal" terms), and similarly, one grows impatient at the unwillingness of Malay to generalize (there is no single word for "brother" or "sister"; there is no one word for "rice"—*padi* in the field, *bĕras* in the shop, *nasi* on the table). But there is a fine economy and logic in the syntax of the language, just as there is in the numerical system. Malay starts its "teens" at eleven (*sabĕlas* = 11, *duabĕlas* = 12, *tigabĕlas* = 13, and so on) and wonders why the West counts as though it had twelve fingers.

We shall end with two specimens of Malay writing, the first a poem. A popular Malay verse form is the *pantun*, a quatrain that presents two contrasted ideas (two lines to each) that are made to show a kinship through symbolism and similarity of sound. It is a subtle form, in which expression—as in all true art—matters more than content. Every Malay has a great store of *pantuns* in his memory; some are adept at improvising them. Here is one of the finest: it is, of course, a possession of the folk and hence anonymous.

Kalau tuan mudek ka-hulu,
  Charikan saya bunga kĕmoja.
Kalau tuan mati dahulu,
  Nantikan saya di-pintu shurga.

This means literally: "If lord travel to riverhead/ Look for me for flower frangipani./ If lord die first before,/ Wait for me at gate heaven." A freer translation would be: "If you, my lover, go upriver, find me some frangipani. Should you be the first of us two to die, wait for me at the gates of heaven." Note the way in which the first and third lines, and the second and fourth, chime in assonance. Let us now look at the component words:

Kalau	if (met also as *jikalau* and *jika*).
tuan	literally "master," "lord," "lady." Used by a lover to his mistress and vice versa.
mudek	an invariable verb form whose meaning is "traveling upstream." Malay is particular about the right word, hating to generalize with some such colorless word as *pĕrgi*—"to go."
ka-	to, toward, into.
hulu	the root meaning is "head, upper portion." An ordinary person has a *kĕpala* under his hat, but a royal personage has a *hulu*. *Hulu* can be the halter of a weapon (*hulu kĕris*). With the addition of the noun prefix *pĕ-* and a linking nasal we get *pĕnghulu*—"headman of a village." Here *hulu* mean "head of the river."
Charikan	the root is *chari*—"searching"—and the addition of -*kan* confirms it as a verb with the active meaning of "search for."
saya	I, me, for me.
bunga	flower.
kĕmoja	frangipani (*kĕmboja* is another form). Like the cypress of the West, frangipani is associated with graveyards.
mati	death, dying, to die.
dahulu	before, in the past, ahead of time.
Nantikan	*nanti* means "waiting" or "wait." It sometimes means "shall," "will," and thus acts as a future auxiliary. Here the suffix -*kan* gives us the specific verb "to wait for."
di-	in, on, at.
pintu	door, gate.
shurga	heaven (a Sanskrit loanword).

Now let us examine a brief passage of modern Malay prose. It is taken from the introduction to *Pĕlita Beahasa Mĕlayu*—literally, *Lamp of the Malay Language*—by Za'ba, an illustrious pseudonym in Malaysia, but unknown in the West. Its theme is appropriate to this book on the phenomenon of language:

Tiap-tiap ["each, every"] bahasa ["language"] yang ["which"] hidup ["alive, living"] memang ["naturally, as a matter of course"] tabi'at ["character, nature"] dan ["and"] adat-nya ["behavior-its"] tumboh ["sprout, spring, erupt"] dan bĕrtambah ["increase, grow, develop"] sĕrta ["with, together with"] bĕrubah ["being altered"] pĕr-lahan-lahan ["slowly"]; dari ["from"] suatu ["one"] masa ["time"] ka- ["to"] suatu masa; jika ["if"] tiada ["there is not"] tumboh atau ["or"] bĕrtambah dan bĕrubah maka [an untranslatable "punctuation word"—not meant to be spoken—signifying the end of a subordinate clause] ĕrti-nya [literally, "the meaning of it = that is to say"] tiada bĕrgĕrak ["to move, stir"] dan tiada bĕrgĕrak itu ["that"] ĕrti-nya "mati" ["dead"] sa-bagaimana ["in the same way as"] bahasa Sanskrit dan Latin tĕlah ["have"] mati ["died"].

Here is a free translation:

The character and usage of any language that is living grows and develops—in a perfectly natural way—and changes slowly with the passage of time; if there were no growth and no development and no change, then the language would be static, and when a language is static that language has died, just as Sanskrit and Latin have died.

Look at the Malay once more, this time without interruptions:

Tiap-tiap bahasa yang hidup memang tabi'at dan adat-nya tumboh dan bĕrtambah sĕrta bĕrubah pĕrlahan-lahan dari suatu masa ka suatu masa; jika tiada tumboh atau bĕrtambah dan bĕrubah maka ĕrti-nya tiada bĕrgĕrak, dan tiada bĕrgĕrak itu ĕrti-nya "mati" sa-bagaimana bahasa Sanskrit dan Latin tĕlah mati.

Malay is evidently a supple, subtle language, musical with its chimes and duplications. It has admirable folk words for modern phenomena like the railway train (kĕreta api—"fire car"; kĕreta api sombong—"haughty fire car," meaning one that will not stop, hence an express), the phonograph (pĕti nyanyi—"singing box"), airplane (kapal tĕrbang or "flying ship"), but these are giving way to Western borrowings. When I praised, a few years ago, the hi-fi equipment of the sultan of Perak, he scorned my pĕti nyanyi: that second word sounded too much like the windup primitive instrument of Somerset Maugham's time. The sultan had traveled far beyond singing boxes.

JAPANESE

With the language of the ingenious people who dwell in what is sometimes called the Britain of the East (a reference to geographical position and certainly not to culture), we approach a disconcerting mixture of extreme simplicity and maddening complexity. There are aspects of the simplicity we have already met in Malay—a lack of concern with the tortuosities of verb, noun, and pronoun that plague us when we learn German or Russian. But all that Malay and Japanese have in common is the negative fact of not belonging to the Indo-European family. Japanese has borrowed richly from Chinese, but it is not related to it. It is not related to anything, except possibly Korean. It looks like Chinese, except for the two syllabaries that help out the ideograms, but it does not sound like it. It is not tonal, and it is not made out of single-syllable semantemes. There is a syllabic pattern of single vowels or of vowels preceded by single consonants, but these are the mere building blocks of words. If "I" or "me" in Chinese is *wo*, in Japanese it is *watakushi*. If Chinese "we" or "us" is *wo-men*, the Japanese equivalent is *watakushitachi* (or *watakushidomo*). The polysyllabic melody is recognizably the Japanese sound.

You are in the company of a learner of Japanese. In old age I decided that the language was too important for me to ignore, but I recognized that I would never get far with the reading of it. My concern is in holding a simple conversation with such Japanese businessmen as I meet in London or New York hotels. I have a desire at least to scratch the surface of the Japanese mentality. Japanese is, thank heaven, a language that lends itself easily to Romanization: there is even a quasiphonetic system authorized by the Japanese government in 1937 and termed *kunrei-siki*. Join me in my early lessons.

"How are you?" is *Ikaga desu ka?* That final questioning *ka* is, by sheer coincidence, equivalent to the question suffix -*kah* in Malay. The *ikaga* is a straightforward "how," and the *desu* is a genuine "is" or "are," a delightful verb form that is not to be conjugated. I do not need to use the pronoun "you." The reply to the polite inquiry is *Genki desu*, which means literally "Excellent-health is." When *watakushi* ("I" or "me") comes into the conversation, along with *anata* ("you" singular) or *anatachi* ("you" plural), the tone will be one of cautious politeness. When intimates show their teeth in greeting, "I" and "me" will be *boku*, and "you" will be *kimi*. For myself to use those forms would be a gross breach of courtesy.

When we come to less phatic statements, the grammatical difficulties begin. "My name is Kido," says my Japanese acquaintance, or rather *Watakushi no namae wa Kido desu*. The *desu* at the end is clear enough, but *watakushi* has been made into a possessive by the addition of *no*. The particle *wa* seems to be a sidling approach to the name Kido, not to be rendered, except as something like "as for." The camera on the table? "That is mine," says Kido, or *Sore ga watakushi no desu*. The *ga* is as good as announcing that *sore* ("that") is the subject of the statement. The rest is simple enough. He then asks: *"Anata wa sensei desu ka?"*—"Are you a teacher?" *Desu*—"is" or "are," *ka*—the questioning particle, *anata*—"you." *Sensei* is "teacher," but it must be approached with a certain indirectness, hence the *wa* before it. Old as I am, I reply: "No. I'm a student." No real problem here: *"Watakushi wa gakusei desu."* The temptation for a Westerner is to omit that *wa* as a bit of formalistic rubbish, but Japanese insists on it. Mr. Kido makes an obvious remark: "Today is Sunday"—*"Nichiyo desu,"* or "Sunday is." And I add, "It is raining." The patterns are different. *Desu* becomes *imasu*, and the whole phrase is *"Ame ga futte imasu"*—"Rain (*ga* to indicate that "rain" is the subject of the sentence) falling is."

We go further. I ask Kido if he speaks English. *"Anata wa eigo ga dekimasu ka?"* The form is correct, but I wonder when to use *wa* and when *ga*: they both seem to have the same function. It takes me time to discover that *ga* throws light on the subject of the sentence, *wa* on the predicate. "He is coming by airplane" is "*Kare wa hikoki de kimasu*" ("He is not coming by train"). "He (and not she or it) is coming by airplane?" "*Kare ga.*" I have had enough for one evening. I plead a headache and prepare to go to my room. "*Atama ga itaimasu*"—"Head (*ga* for subject) pains." Another Japanese gentleman approaches. Smiling with relief, Kido says: "*Yamazaki san ga kuru.*" ("Mr. Yamazaki comes").

Is life, or such life as is left to me, long enough for a longer journey into the Japanese labyrinth? Much depends on whether I can change my habits of syntactical thinking. "Can you eat with chopsticks?" Yes, I can, but can I say it? *Hashi de taberu koto ga dekimasu ka?* "Chopsticks with eat is-able ka?" But what is that *koto* doing? It seems to carry a vague force of "ever" or "never"—"Can you ever (or perhaps never) eat with chopsticks?" Try "I have never heard such a story"—*So iu hanashi o kiita koto ga arimasen*. That is, literally, "Such speak story heard fact is-not," with the *o* pointing to an object and the *ga* to a subject. "I am sorry that I did not speak to him." I cannot do it. Try. Very well—*Kare to hanasanakatta koto ga zannen desu*—"Him with did-not-speak (past negative of *hansu*, "to speak") fact disappointment is." *Koto* is coming clearer, though not clear enough. It has something to do with the fact of a thing being able to happen; it wobbles in a region of possibility.

Let us look at some solid things—numbers, for instance. Numbers turn out not to be so solid, since there is a native form and a Chinese form: (1) *hitotsu, ichi*; (2) *futatsu, ni*; (3) *mittsu, san* . . . The Chinese for (4)—*shi*—is not greatly liked, since the word coincides with the Japanese root meaning "death," and Japanese superstition—seen in the bewildering illogicality of the sequences of house numbers in Japanese towns—is notorious. I feel that I have come home to Malay when I meet the numerical coefficients, or classifiers, that slide in between numbers and nouns: *nin* for human beings, *hiki* for animals, *hon* for long thin things, *satsu* for books and magazines. *Hai* is used for "cupful" but gets mauled in a statement like *Kohii ippai ikaga desu ka?*—"How about a cup of coffee?" Telling the time is not easy: *Gogo shichiji gofun mae desu* means "P.M. seven o'clock five-minutes before is." It is perhaps better to show the inquirer one's watch.

As I have hinted elsewhere, it is the Japanese adjective that causes most trouble to the Western learner. The native adjectival forms are like verbs, and the pseudoadjectives, which are more like nouns, are usually of Chinese origin. We see the verbal nature of the true adjective in forms like *samui*—"cold"—and *samukaro*—"is probably cold"—so that "This room is probably cold in the winter" can be rendered as *Fuyu wa kono heya was samukaro*—"Winter as-for this room as-for probably-cold." We see the adjectival noun in forms like *Amerika no shofu*—"America of capital" and *Nihon no ocha*—"Japan of tea" ("Japanese tea"). The comparison of what we may as well call adjectives is tricky. There is nothing equivalent to "good, better, best," or "cheap, cheaper, cheapest." "Apples are cheaper than plums" is translated as *Ringo wa ume yori yasui desu*—"Apples as-for, plums than, cheap is." Translation becomes excruciating with "Which are cheaper, apples or plums?"—*Ringo tu ume to wa, dochira no ho ga yasui desu ka?* You will by now be greeting *desu ka?* as an old, and moderately intelligible friend. The literal rendering has to be something like "Apples with plums with as-for which of direction cheap is?" Eventually it all makes sense. In the meantime I must cling to the murmurs of polite if casual conversation—*Ohayo gozai-masu* ("Good morning"), *Gomen nasai* ("Excuse me," "I am sorry," "Forgive me"), and *Arigato* ("Thank you").

The trouble one has with Japanese increases one's yearning for a universal language. This is my next subject.

CAN BABEL BE UNBUILT?

The fact that the human race speaks many languages—most of them mutually unintelligible—has traditionally been regarded as a curse. The myth of Babel and the divine confusion of tongues converts an agelong process of change into a sudden and quite unexpected catastrophe. The Roman poet Giuseppe Gioacchino Belli (1791–1863), who wrote sonnets in the dialect of the Roman streets ("*E ttu, ccojjona, hai quer mazzato vizzio . . .*"—that hardly looks like Italian), saw what the myth was about in the following, which is my translation of one of his biblical sonnets:

> "We'd like to touch the stars," they cried, and, after,
>   "We've got to touch the stars. But how?" An able-
>   brained bastard told them: "Build the Tower of Babel.
> Start now, get moving. Dig holes, sink a shaft. A-
> Rise, arouse, raise rafter after rafter,
>   Get bricks, sand, limestone, scaffolding, and cable;
>   I'm clerk of works, fetch me a chair and table."
> God meanwhile well-nigh pissed himself with laughter.
>
> They'd just got level with the pope's top floor
>   When something in their mouths began to give.

They couldn't talk Italian anymore.
The project died in this linguistic slaughter.
Thus, if a man said: "Pass us that there sieve,"
His mate would hand him up a pail of water.

The point of the linguistic slaughter was the confusion of creative
action. Though man was no longer in Eden, he had better behave as
if he had never left.

The unscrambling of this chaos is celebrated at Pentecost, one of
the major feasts of the Christian calendar, which commemorates Saint
Peter's sensing himself able to address a polyglot crowd in Jerusalem
with no difficulty. This, of course, was a miracle. Quite outside the
realm of myth and divine intervention in men's affairs, is it possible
for man to redeem the curse, to create or select a common language
for the whole of the civilized world?

Certain men have thought so, and their thoughts have tended to
run on the same lines: let every man and woman be bilingual, with
his or her first language the national or regional mother tongue, the
second language a world auxiliary. Let this world auxiliary be an
artificial language, for only an artificial language can be truly supra-
national. One can see the point well enough: an existing language,
like English or French, is bound to have nationalistic associations
unpleasing to all but its native speakers. A national tongue is barred
from being its opposite. Hence—so the argument runs—the need
for a sort of plastic language, totally neutral and, one might expect,
totally flavorless.

Various artificial languages have, in fact, been painfully manufac-
tured, and some of them are in periodic use, not always on a world
scale. Volapük was probably the first (1880—the creation of the German cleric J. M. Schleyer), and it swiftly died out because it was too
complicated. A Malay or Chinese would have fainted at the needless
baggage of inflections. It was phonetically complicated, too—the very
name is meant to be a kind of English, with "ol" being a corruption
of "world" and "pük" Schleyer's interpretation of "speak." From Volapük we can learn how difficult it is for a language maker to shed
inborn prejudices: the messy grammar, the huge portmanteau words
of German seemed natural to Schleyer, and he incorporated them
accordingly in his brainchild. Volapük was logical—no irregular
verbs, no exceptions to rules of noun inflection—but it was not simple.
It took a long time for auxiliary forgers to learn how little grammar

is needed by languages like Malay, Chinese, and Iranian (and, for that matter, English). Why should one labor over creating grammar engines in the world auxiliary when one's own grammar was sleekly lacking in moving parts? Schleyer could not see this.

Eighteen eighty-seven saw the birth of Esperanto, perhaps still the most popular of the artificial auxiliaries. Its creator, Dr. Ludwik Lejzer Zamenhof (1859–1917), was an oculist of Warsaw. His language was first presented as Linguo Internacio de la Doktoro Esperanto, this latter pseudonym meaning "hopeful," and the name has stuck to his invention. The first journal in the language, *La Esperantisto*, was issued in 1889 from a press in Nuremberg. The Russian government, it is perhaps interesting to note, forbade its importation into the czar's territories because it contained a contribution by Tolstoy. But its westward spread, beginning in 1895 with its entry into France, ensured that Esperanto would become important enough to take on the status of a genuine language—not a mere toy or game—and the first international Esperanto congress, at Boulogne in 1905, worked on an assumption greatly desired by the inventor—that his invention be the world's property, untied to copyright.

Zamenhof saw that the great need was to have as little grammar as possible, and he realized, from his studies of English, how unfunctional much grammar was. But he insists on an accusative or objective case (*Ni lernas Esperanton*—"We're learning Esperanto") and the agreement of noun and adjective. His vocabulary is eclectic: he draws from all the European languages in fair proportion; what he does not do, however, is to remember how many international words already exist in those languages. Among the world linguistic lineup, the English "school" is represented as *école, escuela, scuola, escola, scoala, Schule, school* (Dutch), *skola* and *skole* (in Scandinavia), *szkola, skola, shkola* (Slav forms), *iskola* (Hungarian), *scholion* (Greek), *skuli* (Swahili), and *sekolah* (Bahasa). Zamenhof's word sticks out like a sore thumb—*lernejo*. His word for "sausage" discloses a Slav and Hungarian taste—*kolbaso*—but his scrambled eggs will do—*ovo batita*. Here is his Lord's Prayer: *Patro nia, kiu estas en la ciela: Sankta estu Via nomo: Venu regeco Via: Estu volo Via, kiel en la cielo, tiel ankau sur la tero: Panon nian ĉiutagan donu al ni hodiaĉu: Kaj pardonu . . .* and so on. It is a good language, but it has too many complications.

Attempts were made to simplify it: Ido and Esperantido cut out some of the grammatical excess. Then Interlingua tried to draw on the common roots of English and the Romance languages, producing a sort of Latin without Ciceronian grammar. Otto Jespersen (1860–1943), the great Danish philologist, created Novial, which never caught on. Lancelot Hogben (1895–1975) very sensibly created a language, Interglossa, out of Greek roots: Greek, after all, gives us our international scientific vocabulary. But we tend to return, in our search for a bomb for Babel, to existing tongues. French has long been an international language of diplomacy; ecumenical councils carry on in Church Latin. Now, more and more, it seems evident that English will provide the great world tongue for all kinds of communication—not purely ambassadorial or ecclesiastical.

Europeans are, at the moment, more concerned with finding a tongue for a united continent than considering the communication problems of the great world without. I have attended conferences at which the French had no doubt that their own flexible and elegant language, with its perfume of high literature and its history of colonial dissemination, should be the European auxiliary: to some extent, of course, it already is, or is presumed to be by the French organizers of literary or film festivals. The Germans, Italians, and Spaniards do not push the claims of their own languages. I have spoken up, eccentrically, for a modified form of Latin, my point being chiefly that there is no arbiter to condemn either accent or grammar. We do not have to feel embarrassed at our solecisms when trying to speak a dead tongue: Cicero is not there to rebuke us. But it looks as if, despite the rumbling of the French, English will prevail in Europe as in the rest of the world. Even French air pilots and control tower officers have to speak it.

There are extrinsic reasons for the spread of English, and these are sufficiently well known. The English have long been a maritime people, concerned not only with exporting goods in their ships but planting English-speaking communities in the wilder places of the earth. Of these communities, the United States of America has become the most powerful, leader of the so-called free world. Meanwhile, there exists a loosely linked commonwealth in which English is either the first language or the chief auxiliary. Advances in technology have been associated with English. English is, for Dutch, Indian, and Chinese children, a key to the whole of the outside world, not merely the American or British part of it.

But there are certain intrinsic elements in English that render it more suitable than, say, Finnish or Hungarian, Japanese or Hindi, for the world-auxiliary role. It has far less unnecessary grammar (though far more strategies) than any other Indo-European tongue; it has a considerable Graeco-Latin vocabulary, itself international; it can be polysyllabic, like German or Finnish, or monosyllabic, like Chinese. It has made its way, with no deliberate pushing, in the great world; it is felt that with certain adaptations and deliberate simplifications, it can go still further.

This was the view of C. K. Ogden and I. A. Richards, the devisors of Basic English. In their *The Meaning of Meaning*, they posed a fundamental question: what is the absolute minimum of English words required to define all the words in a dictionary? They concluded that it was something like 850. It seemed possible, then, to make out of English a very simple auxiliary, one that could be learned in two or three months. They proved, by a number of translations, that even the most monumental work of English literature could be rendered with a kind of denotative accuracy into Basic: the rich clusters of harmonics, the connotative magic would be missing, but the average reader would be unaware of anything strange, forced, or insufficient.

But knowing the basic words of a language may not be enough. One has to know the strategies. I have already demonstrated how much work can be done with the single verb "get": knowing how this work is done is rather more than knowing the word. The same may be said of "go" and "put." Meat can "go off"; when a woman nags, she "goes on and on and on." If we like something, we "go for it." One "puts up with" adversity; "puts up" somebody for the night or club membership; a vicious dog may be "put down" by the vet; you can "put in" a good word for somebody. French cannot say "go up" or "go down," only *monter* or *descendre;* but at least those two words are firmly fixed in slots of unambiguous meaning. One feels that certain forms in English show a virtuosity that is more dazzling than helpful. We do not hear so much of Basic English as we did.

We hear rather more of Nuclear English. Professor Randolph Quirk and colleagues have called for "a carpentered section of idiomatic English, with the more difficult features of the language set aside." Sentences of the "ditransitive" type like "We offered the girl a drink" would be replaced by "the prepositional alternative" "We offered a drink to the girl." Question tags in most languages are invariable—"It's cold, isn't it?" but also "She's pretty, isn't it?" in Welsh colloquial show what is almost a global rule. English varies the tag according to the statement—"You're an idiot, aren't you?" and "They're busy, aren't they?" Quirk suggests the elimination of the idiomatic tag and its replacement by some such formula as "isn't that right?" the aim being to develop a mode of compromise English inoffensive to native speakers and capable of being folded into "total English."

The problem with regard to the global spread of the language is the tendency of those who speak it on foreign territories to assimilate its sounds and idioms to those of their own mother tongue. This is certainly true of some of the communities of India. Tamils, who speak a Dravidian language, are adept at turning English into a Tamil dialect—the phonemes, idioms, and pace being so thoroughly Tamilized that it is difficult for a native Anglophone to understand what is being said. Writing and reading are, of course, a different matter. I could make no sense of *bu lokkar* until it was written down for me as "bullock cart."

There are problems, especially with a language so volatile and hospitable as English. Its maternal aspects make it willing to take any foreign lexis or idiom in; yet it can be as flighty as a young girl. It is time for us to look at it seriously, since it seems likely to be forced into responsibilities undreamed of by its first speakers.

PART TWO

English

20.

ENGLISH FROM

THE OUTSIDE

There are two ways of looking at the history of a language. There is
an internal history, whereby changes occur that owe nothing to the
big world outside: sounds shift, and grammar modifies its rules. This
process of structural change is, as it were, autonomous. A war may
be going on, cities may be burning, towers falling, enemy hordes
invading, but with the indifference of a child in its mother's womb, a
language goes its own way, obeying purely internal laws. The external
history is more closely connected with the history of the speakers of
the language. Invaders will modify the vocabulary, or words and
idioms will creep in, or even blaze in, through more peaceful foreign
contacts. Society will decree that one form of the language is better
than all the others; literature will exercise direct or subliminal influence (consider the impact of the Bible and the plays of Shakespeare
on English speech even at its most colloquial level). The history of
external change works, for the most part, in parallel to the deeper—
and mostly inexplicable—processes of phonic and structural change,
but the two levels occasionally meet. Thus, the diphthong we hear in
"boy" and "joy" did not exist in English until the Norman French
brought it over. Though the English we use today is deeply marked
by contact with French—and, through French or directly, Latin and
Greek—this contact is mainly limited to the lexis or word hoard (to

use an Anglo-Saxonism). It is easy to add new words to a language: English has always welcomed them. We can amplify the vocabulary both by borrowing and by fabrication ("harpworthy," "serviental," "toothachy"—I have just made those up), but such features of the language as the possessive 's' or the past termination '-ed' are inherited, holy, and untouchable.

Let us, then, first look at English as a substance that human history—as opposed to philological—may very well concern itself with, an attribute of the people who first spoke it. Let us go back to a time when it was slowly emerging out of the common stock of Germanic speech. The Roman historian Tacitus (A.D. 56?–120?) wrote, in A.D. 98, a book called *Germania*, in which he lists forty tribes all called "Germani." A Germanus or German is properly a "spearman": we still have the Germanic *gar* in "garlic." These Germani, obeying a nomadic urge summed up in the German term *Völkerwanderungen* (wanderings of the folk) had spread all over northern Europe and even ventured south. There were tribes named Frisii, Anglii, and Gotones—names that, from their continuity under changed forms, we can recognize—but also there were the Manimi, Lemorii, and Aestii, of whom we know little or nothing. Tacitus mentions a western group of Germani that we can call a tribal alliance. This consisted of the Ingvaeones, the Istvaeones, and the Erminones. The first lived on the shores of the North Sea, the second along the upper Rhine, and the others in the region that we now call Germany proper. There seems to be a correspondence here to the divisions of the West Germanic version of the original Germanic tongue—Old English, Old Saxon, and Old Frisian belonging to the Ingvaeones, Franconian to the Istvaeones, and Upper German to the Erminones. The northern division, of course, was to be found in Scandinavia.

We are speaking of the first century A.D. The ancestor of our own language has taken on a shape that we may call ancestral by the fifth century. This ancestor is sometimes named Anglo-Saxon after the people who spoke it, but Old English suggests a linguistic continuity that is, to some extent, illusory: we have to approach Old English as if it were a totally foreign language. Yet in that it was implanted in the country now called England and in that we are able to watch it changing into Modern English, the name Old English seems appropriate enough. It came to a Celtic-speaking country that had been colonized by the Romans.

Britannia was the farthest west of the Roman provinces. The Romans began to colonize it, against considerable native opposition, in A.D. 43, and they held it until 410. There was time enough to impose and sustain a distinctly Roman type of civilization, architectural remnants of which are still coming to light. If we have an image of a tranquil occupation, with Roman military power quieting enmity among the Celtic tribes of Britain and cowing invading Gaels from Ireland, as well as Pictic raiders from Scotland, we had better think again. The Ingvaeonic people, too, were an irritation to Roman order. The coastline from the Isle of Wight to the Wash was called the *Litus Saxonicum* or Saxon Shore, and there was a Roman official charged with its defense—the *Comes Litoris Saxonici, Comes* being translatable as "Count." The term "Saxon" was not, and still is not, an exact name for these hairy pagan marauders: it apparently meant to the Romans merely the Germans who had settled in the North Sea region.

By the time the fifth century had arrived, the British province was no longer an asset to the Roman power. The Roman Empire was being attacked on its home ground, and the Romanized British were left to look after their own territory. They had been taught the techniques of defense, but they lacked the resources of implementation. The Romans had regularly used foreign mercenaries to assist them in their campaigns; they had pitted tribe against tribe in their subjugation of the Celts, in Britain, Belgium, and Gaul. The British, abandoned by the Romans, unwisely invited the Germanic marauders to help them in their intertribal conflicts. The Venerable Bede (673?–735), belatedly canonized but still called by his lesser title, wrote a book called *Historia ecclesiastica gentis Anglorum* (about 731), in which he tells the story of Vortigern, a British tribal leader, who faced trouble with the Picts and Scots from the North—fellow Celts with no sense of racial or cultural unity. He invited the Saxons (as we, following the Romans, may call them) to help drive them back to their fastnesses, but this was interpreted as an invitation to stay. Bede says that this took place during the reign of the Emperor Marcian, who ruled from 450 to 457. The year usually assigned to the Germanic takeover is 449, and this will serve. Bede recounts the tale of three formidable Germanic races—the Saxons, Angles, and Jutes—setting out for the east coast of Britain in three long ships, landing, and at once being granted territory by Vortigern in exchange for military help. They defeated the enemy advancing from the North and then sent back word to the European homeland that the country was fertile and the Britons cowardly (Sellar and Yeatman, in their

1066 and All That, facetiously pun Caesar's *Veni, vidi, vici* into "weeny, weedy, and weaky"). The Romanized Celts had, in fact, yielded to the softness of imperial Christianity: they were not what they had been in the time of Boudicca (or Boadicea). A large fleet now came over with what Bede describes as an invincible army. The Britons again granted cash and territory in return for protection, but much of the land was no longer theirs to protect.

The Jutes were the ancestors of the people of Kent and the Isle of Wight; the Saxons were later distinguished as East, South, and West, giving their names to Essex, Sussex, and Wessex. The name "Wessex" survives only in the novels of Thomas Hardy. The Angles, according to Bede, made up the bulk of the rest of the island population, though their name now is commemorated only in East Anglia. This triple alliance is probably oversimple. There were probably Swabians around, if Swaffham in Norfolk (Old English *Swæfe*) is anything to go by, and some Franconians as well. But it is certain that three distinct dialects of Old English were established in a land to be named only for the Angles. The dialectal division still shows its traces today.

The Cymric people now became Welshmen, or "foreigners" (Old English *wealh*), and were driven to the edges of the island: they formed three groups—one in Wales, one in Devon and Cornwall, and one in southwest Scotland and northwest England. Welsh survives, but Cornish died out in the eighteenth century. The name Cumberland, through the Latin *Cumbri* derived from Celtic *cymry* (which means "fellow countryman"), commemorates a virtually vanished people. To call Cumberland and Westmorland together Cumbria serves the conveniences of administration but is historically false. Myth rather than history provides a misty picture of the Cymric kings fighting the Germanic barbarians with no success. King Arthur survives as a heroic Christian image: we have no documentary evidence that he actually existed.

The linguistic conquest of the island was near total: very few Celtic words were absorbed into the conquering tongue, except for place-names. We sometimes hear "brock" for "badger" and accept that a tor is a peak and a coombe or combe a valley. But Old English was as inclined to borrow a word from Ireland as from Celtic Britain—"ass" or "donkey" (ultimately Latin *asinus*) and "druid" (Old Irish *drui*) for a magician. The history of English is the history of a Germanic tongue—at least until 1066 and all that.

England is a small country; Britain is a small island. It is too easy to think of the Anglo-Saxon territory as a political unity. In fact, if we look at the land about a century and a half after the settlements, we see seven kingdoms east of Offa's Dyke, which marks off Wales, and the river Tamar, which is the Cornish boundary. These are the kingdoms of Northumbria, Mercia, East Anglia, Essex, Kent, Wessex, and Sussex. Each kingdom may be taken as possessing its own version of Old English: those ancient boundaries are shadowy now, but the questing dialectologist will still find distinguishing linguistic features marking the political boundaries. The seven kingdoms, or heptarchical aggregate, diminished, in time, to three. Northumbria, Mercia, and Wessex each swallowed contiguous kingdoms, and each assumed, at one time or another, political hegemony. Northumbria was the major kingdom of the seventh century, Mercia of the eighth, and Wessex of the ninth. King Alfred (849–899), the only English monarch to be termed "the Great," ruled over Wessex. His cultural as well as political influence was immense, and his dialect—the West Saxon or southwestern, with its standards set at Winchester—became something like a received form of the language.

A sense of racial, linguistic, and cultural unity undoubtedly came about with time. The Anglo-Saxons did not war among themselves. Unlike the Huns, they cultivated the land and the arts. They called their language *Englisc*, tongue of the Angles. "Saxon" was disappearing as an overall term, even in Latin. In 601 Pope Gregory called King Ethelbert of Kent *rex Anglorum*, and to the Venerable Bede, the *gens Anglorum* was the entire race from the Scottish border to maritime Sussex. The people were usually called, in *Englisc*, the "Anglekin" or *Angelcynn*. The name *Englaland* came late—not until the eleventh century. To the Celtic fringe the Anglekin are still the Saxons—Sassenachs or *Sais*. They did not, and do not, repine. They became tolerant and rather easygoing pagans, ripe for conversion to Christianity.

Our days of the week crystallize Anglo-Saxon theology. There was a pantheon of gods and goddesses—Tuisco, Woden, Thor, Freya— as well as the sun and the moon for rather casual veneration. There was none of the religious ferocity of the Celtic druidism, with its worship of the bloodthirsty goddess Brigantia, eventually to be Christianized into Saint Bridget. When the Christian missionaries arrived, they met a willingness to be converted, though no large fervor. The tepidity of today's Church of England has remote roots.

The missionaries came from two directions. The Irish, already

Christianized like their brother Celts on the English fringes, sent Columba, later canonized, to the island of Iona, off the west coast of Scotland, in 563. He set up a mission there and proceeded to convert the Picts. In Edinburgh and environs northern speakers of English came into contact with Irish-speaking Christians. The brand of Christianity taught was not quite that of Rome: until the reign of Henry II and the bull of *Laudabiliter* that brought, through an English king, the duty to pay Peter's pence to an English pope (the first and probably last—Adrian IV), Irish Christianity went its own way. The full rich cream of the Roman variety arrived in England in 597, when the Augustine who became Saint Augustine of Canterbury (not to be confused with the African Augustine of Hippo) arrived with a party of monks on the Isle of Thanet, which was part of the Kentish kingdom. King Ethelbert was not himself a Christian, but his wife, who was a Frank and had a Frankish bishop, had long practiced the faith. The language of initial propaganda employed by Augustine's assistants was undoubtedly Frankish; it may have been close enough to English to be understood by Ethelbert, or he may have learned Frankish from his queen. Bede, in his *Historia ecclesiastica*, has a rather moving passage about the spiritual loneliness of man that Christianity might do much to mitigate. His Latin is delightful, a timeless link with one who spoke an alien tongue that is nevertheless our own *in potentia*. Nevertheless, I quote him in the language of today:

> Such, O king, seems to me the present of life of men on earth, in comparison with that time which to us is uncertain, as if when on a winter's night you sit feasting with your ealdormen and thanes, a single sparrow should fly swiftly into the hall, and coming in at one door flies instantly out through another. In that time in which it is indoors it is not touched by the fury of the winter, but yet, this smallest space of calmness being passed almost in a flash, from winter going into winter again, it is lost to your eyes. Somewhat like that appears the life of man, but of what follows or what went before, we are utterly ignorant.

The speaker accepted conversion, but the king did not. He was not convinced of the validity of the new faith, but he cordially gave Augustine permission to spread the word wherever he wished. It was a very English kind of tolerance, the product of a mild climate and ample harvests. It was matched in other kingdoms of the English island. The East Saxons were converted in 604, their western brethren in 635, the Mercians in 655. Paulinus of Nola was made archbishop of Northumbria to no known English resentment, though he was an Italian, and from his episcopal seat he worked on King Edwin, who yielded in 627. Conversion was effected either directly on individual Anglekin or collectively through the monarch. Before the seventh century was over, England was as Christian as it was ever likely to be. Angus Wilson's novel *Anglo-Saxon Attitudes* deals with occasional reversions to paganism—fertility figures found in bishops' graves and so on—but history, which is not altogether fiction, records a remarkably smooth English yielding to the spiritual rule of Rome.

The contact with Rome and Roman Christianity is linguistically important. Previously, while the first English was being spoken in its native Europe, there had been infiltration into the language of words relating to Roman culture—words like *wīn*—"wine"—and *oele*—"oil." Vines had been planted in Britain by the Romans, but the olive tree could not flourish in that cold climate. *Oele* was attached to different kinds of oiliness, but wine remained, and remains, somewhat foreign. The Anglo-Saxons drank ale—*ealu*—and mead—*meadu*. The ale was not yet beer: hops did not come in till very much later. Words like *mynet*—"coin"—obviously came from Latin *moneta*, *pise*—"peas," a false plural, though not in "pease pudding"—was a Germanicizing of *pisum*, and *saeturnesdaeg*—"Saturday"—filled in a gap in the week with the Roman god of old age. These borrowings were nothing to those that came in with Christianity. Some of the religious Latinisms came, in the North, from their domestication in Irish—*ancor*, "hermit," and *cross*, but those from the South were more numerous. *Abbod* ("abbot"), *tempel* ("temple"), *mynster* ("minster"), have a directly religious reference, but there were secular terms, too, doubtless borrowed from exiled Roman clergy, such as *pīn*—"pine tree"—and *purpl* and *plante* and *fefor* ("fever") and, very secular and rather literary, *gigant*, which became "giant." English priests naturally learned Latin, the universal language of the Church until the fracturizing catastrophe of vernacularization in our own time. The point to be made is that Old English, like its successors, seemed ready to become a hybrid language once it had accepted the kiss of Rome. The Romance vocabulary of Modern English is immense, but we must not be deluded into thinking that English could not get along without it.

English, like its cousin High German, can express any idea out of its native resources. In the nineteenth century, the poet William Barnes

(1801–1886), a Dorset clergyman with a large knowledge of foreign languages, favored the coining of new words out of the native stock to replace foreign importations. "Omnibus," for instance, could be "folkwain" (rather close to Volkswagen). The telephone could be the "farspeaker"; in our own day, "television"—a Graeco-Latin hybrid— might be "farlooker," with "telescope," a totally Greek formation for the box or idiot's lantern, as "farseer." "To crucify" could be, as it was for a time with the Anglo-Saxons, "roodfasten" (or try "Christ was tree-nailed"). But such reliance on the homegrown looks eccentric today, as it must have increasingly looked to the English of the Dark and Middle Ages. There was a yearning of insular people in the cool North toward the fuller world of Mediterranean experience. This meant Latin and its derivatives, with the occasional touch of Greek.

Christianized England, like Christianized Britain before it, was not permitted to develop its fairly high culture in peace. In the eighth, ninth, and tenth centuries pagan marauders from the farther North raided the English east coast and even ventured farther inland. These were Scandinavians, indifferently called Danes, and they sought loot, finding it chiefly in the churches and monasteries, such as the magnificent complex at Lindisfarne in Northumbria, which they raided in 793, and Bede's own monastery at Jarrow the year after. They found sacred ornaments in precious metals and handmade books with gold and jeweled clasps. The priests and monks, guardians of Christian culture, grew discouraged. Alfred the Great, less concerned about the Danish filching than about the decline in learning, mourned the loss of Latin. He did not, however, do the logical thing and preside over a program of instruction in that language. Being English, he determined to do something about English. After all, he said, the sacred texts in Latin were no more than translations out of the Hebrew and Greek; why not expand the process and make translations into English equally holy? Under his aegis, and probably with his practical assistance, "all the young freemen of England" were encouraged to learn to read English; "then let those who want to learn more, and aspire to higher things, be taught Latin." There was first a trickle and then a flood of translations into English of not merely the Bible but also works of theology. Theology led to philosophy—like Boethius' *De consolatione philosophiae*. Secular poetry, like the national epic *Beowulf*, was given a fixed form in one Old English dialect or another by monkish scribes. A great deal of the literature of the Anglo-Saxons has thus been handed down to us. What we do not have is any precise record of ordinary speech: poetry as produced by the Anglo-Saxons was ornate and highly artificial, no true reflection of the way the language was handled daily in the field, byre, or marketplace.

Paradoxically, it was through the cultivation of Latin that what survives of ordinary speech—admittedly a somewhat stilted variety of it—is there to be read, as in Ælfric's *Colloquy*:

> Haefst Þu hafoc?
> > Habes accipitrem?
> > > [Do you have a hawk?]

> Ic haebbe.
> > Habeo.
> > > [I have.]

> Canst Þu temian hig?
> > Scis domitarc eos?
> > > [Do you know how to tame them?]

> Gea, ic cann. Hwaet sceolden hig me buton ic cuÞe temian hig?
> > Etiam, scio. Quid deberent mihi nisi domitare eos?
> > > [Yes, I do. What use would they be to me if I could not tame them?]

The Anglo-Saxon pupil learned Latin by way of his own tongue; we are helped to learn that tongue through Latin. Not that we should have much difficulty here. *Hafoc* is clearly "hawk": the 'f' was pronounced /v/ and probably something like /w/ before it was turned into a vowel. We still hear *Gea*, or "yeah," regarding it as coarse, while it is merely native. *Temian* is clearly "tame." When it comes to reading Old English of a higher, or liturgical, order, Latin is a great help. We can even compare a Northumbrian and Mercian (or North and Midlands) form of our ancestral language when they both attempt a translation of a verse from the Gospel According to Saint Matthew in its Vulgate version: "*Attendite a falsis prophetis qui veniunt ad vos in vestimenti ovium; intrinsecus autem sunt lupi rapaces*"—"Beware of false prophets, which come to you in sheep's clothing, but inwardly they are ravening wolves." In the North we have "*Behaldas ge from leasum witgum*," but in the Midlands "*Behaldeth eow with lease witgu*" (I have, for my typewriter's sake, replaced the old runes with the Frenchified 'th'). That *behaldeth* is an older form of the imperative—"beware"—while *behaldas* looks toward our own age, where the '-s' termination is a third-person-singular signal. *Wedum scipa* ("weeds of sheep"—compare "widow's weeds") in the North confronts *gewedum scepa* in the Midlands. Northern *cymes*—"(they) come"—opposes Mercian *cumath*. That third person '-s' is certainly coming, though here it suggests bad grammar—"they comes." For "wolves" Northumbria has *wulfes*, which looks as if it might become *wolves* (the 'f' is /v/), while Mercia has an older plural *wulfas*, with an 'a' apparently forbidding a rapid weakening to schwa.

Poetry is a tougher business. The eighth-century *Beowulf* has lines like the following:

hwaethre hē gemunde   maegenes strenge
ginfaeste gife,   the him God sealde,
and him tō Anwaldum   āre felyfde,
frōfre and fultum.

(Again, 'th' for Þ and ð). Only "and," "him," "he," and "to" in Modern English represent an unchanging continuity (the short vowels forbade change). We can translate as "Yet he remembered the power of his might,/ The ample gift that God had granted him,/ And trusted himself to the Lord for grace,/ Help and support." In the second line you can see more clearly than elsewhere the alliterative structure—properly "head rhyme"—that sustains the Old English poetic line. End rhyme was a Celtic invention, but English eventually received it from the Continent. W. H. Auden, and Ezra Pound in a remarkable translation of the Old English *Seafarer*, used the three-head-rhyming-words-to-a-line technique with great success, but nowadays it has the smell of a double archaism.

Schoolboys once composed Latin and Greek verses, though not for pleasure. Few have wished to attempt to get into the Anglo-Saxon mind by composing prose in the style of King Alfred or verse in the mode of Caedmon or the anonymous author or authors of *Beowulf*. I once conversed, ungrammatically, with Jorge Luis Borges in Old English at a Washington cocktail party, chiefly to frustrate listening Argentine spies. As a courting student of the language I used to say to my angry girlfriend "*Ic ēom særig for eallum mī num maenigfealdum misdædum*" ("I am sorry for all my manifold misdeeds"), but it never sounded sincere. We had better let Old English rest in the mists of the far past.

If Old English was, owing to the conversion to Christianity of its speakers, ready to absorb a number of Latinisms, it was, from the eighth century on, virtually forced into accepting an admittedly limited Scandinavian vocabulary from the invading and settling Danes. The *Anglo-Saxon Chronicle*, an invaluable monkish record, tells us of hit-and-run raids on the English coast from Viking marauders given to murder, robbery, and rape. These raids lasted from about 787 until about 850. But in that last year there was a massive invasion of Danes, who, in a fleet of some 350 ships, infested the Southeast of England, eventually taking London and Canterbury. Seventeen years later they were in York. When they turned their attention to King Alfred's territory, Wessex, probably in the early 870s, they met opposition they did not expect. Alfred defeated a huge Danish army at Ethandun in Wiltshire in 878. Rightly is he called "the Great." But the Danes did not leave England: by the Treaty of Wedmore the West of England was saved, but not the East. The Danes were permitted to rule in an area stretching from London to Chester: this was called the Danelaw, implying a legal right to possession and the application of whatever legal system they possessed. An important codicil to the treaty insisted that the Scandinavian pagans accept conversion to Christianity. There was, apparently, no problem there. Polytheism was on the way out.

The Danes settled, then, in an eastern segment of England divided from the Wessex area by a line jagging northeast from the Thames estuary. They settled also in the Northwest, though more thinly. In my native Lancashire the Norwegian element was stronger—those other Scandinavians had invaded from the Irish Sea—but neither in blood nor in language was there much to choose between them. The Danes fought for further territory, and one of the fiercest battles to drive them off took place at Maldon on the Essex coast in 991. Olaf Tryggvason, who was later to be king of Norway, met the East Saxon *eorl* or earl Byrhtnoth on that bloody field and won. The defeat is commemorated in the long poem "The Battle of Maldon," which is a triumph of literary art with a stoical-defiant conclusion: as might lessens, so will the will to fight on become the stronger. In 994 King

Sweyn I of Denmark joined Olaf in an assault on London. The Danes ceased to be an annex to an Anglo-Saxon country and became the dominant political force. As the first Christian millennium drew to a close, Bishop Wulfstan preached about the coming of Antichrist. Antichrist proved not to be too terrible. The son of Sweyn, Cnut or Knut or Canute, was crowned king of England in 1014. Cnut was turned into an English gentleman. England might officially be a Danish province, but there was no cultural or, more pertinently to our study, linguistic displacement. Danish did not prevail, though Old English, a West Germanic language, began to be infected by a tongue from the Northeast.

The Anglo-Saxons had driven the Welsh into the mountains; the Danes were content to let the English stay where they were and to live among them. Towns like York, Lincoln, and Derby were in the control of the Danes, but probably the bulk of the citizenry was English. The Danes would undoubtedly recognize the common Germanic ancestry of the invading and invaded tongues: the two languages could coexist and even casually interpenetrate. There was no language policy. An Englishman could address a Dane in English and expect to be, at least, partly understood. Also vice versa. There was, in other words, pacific bilingualism.

An inscription frequently quoted in histories of our language was found, inscribed in runes and not the Roman alphabet, in a church at Aldburgh in Yorkshire. It is an inscription made by a Dane, but it is in Old English: the conqueror had been conquered. It reads: "*Ulf let araeran cyrice for hanum and for Gunware saula*," which means literally, "Ulf caused church to be erected for him and for Gunwarer's soul." "Ulf" would be "Wulf" in English. The *hanum* is pure Danish, but all the rest is Old English. *Kirk* was available for *cyrice* or "church," as it still is in Scotland, but the anglicization of Ulf is, except for that *hanum*, which should be *him*, complete.

Whatever the Danes borrowed from the English language, the English language borrowed a good nine hundred words from the Danes. They are still with us today, words like "egg," "dirt," "fellow," "leg," "sky," "skull," "take," "window," and "ill." For "take," Old English preferred *niman*, still available in Yidglish in New York: "Nim a nosh a nickel" invited a Jewish delicatessen a year or so ago. A window is properly a *vind-auga* or "wind-eye," replacing Old English *eag-thyrel*; an eyehole as a nostril is a *nos-thyrel*. *Die* has taken over the general sense of *steorfan*, which in the South means to die of hunger but, in my territory, to die of cold. We have doublets like "skirt" and "shirt," which were once ways of describing the same garment. In the North we say "dike" instead of "ditch," preferring the imported to the homegrown.

There is no problem in absorbing foreign nonstructural forms—nouns, adjectives, and verbs. It is unusual, however, to find one language taking over from another such intimate and deep-rooted parts of speech as pronouns. But where pre-Danish Old English had *hie, hiera,* and *hem,* we now have "they," "their," and "them," found as *eirr, eirra,* and *eim* in Old Norse. When we say "Kick 'em," we are merely deaspirating the native form. The preposition *till* has become part of English with a purely temporal significance, as in "till Tuesday"; another preposition, *fro,* is petrified in the form "to and fro," which ought to be "till and fro." "Says the Tweed to the Till," goes the old Scottish rhyme, "What gars ye rin sae still?" That "gar," meaning "make," is a Viking borrowing. So is "lake," meaning "play" ("laking at taws up a ginnel" in Yorkshire means "playing marbles in a back alley"). And "bairns," for "children," is pure Scandinavian.

We can see where the Danes were by consulting place-names. Grimsby, Scunthorpe, and Lowestoft are all towns with North Germanic suffixes. Surnames ending in "-son" were a Danish importation. But, apart from those homely words that are merely alternatives for what we already have, the Viking tongue has left no traces. The Viking people were absorbed into an Anglo-Saxon culture. We fancy we see Scandinavian features and un-English blondness in England's eastern territories, but we may be deluded. Even physically the Danes were absorbed. As for the Danish monarchy, its line expired in 1042, and the Crown reverted to the English. By then, it was not important to think in terms of a continuity of racial bloodlines. Edward the Confessor became king, a pious man who might have been happier in the confession box. Of his sexual life we know nothing, except that he left no heir. No one of his family was available for the succession, but family succession, anyway, was not automatic. The vigorous Earl Godwin of Essex had a suitable son, named, in the Danish manner, Harold Godwinsson. He was unanimously elected.

But there was a duke of Normandy named Guillaume or William, and he claimed the English throne on two grounds—that of cousinship to the dead Edward, and that of a remembered promise from both Harold and Edward that he should have the throne. William's family stock was not impressive: he was an illegitimate son of the previous duke of Normandy; his mother was the daughter of a man who tanned hides for a living. He was, however, powerful, cunning, and persistent in his claim to the English crown, despite Harold's refusal to be dislodged. If a promise had ever been made to William, it had been made while Harold was a prisoner in Normandy: duress did not count. William was not the only foreign claimant. Harald Haardraade disembarked a Norwegian army in Lincolnshire to enforce his fancied right. Harold had to march there to fight and defeat him. Then he had to take the long road to the coast of Sussex, where William had just landed. The Battle of Hastings was a disaster for the English. Harold's death from an arrow in the eye demoralized his followers. He was a good soldier and might have been a good king—certainly, an English one. But now England had to submit to the rule of a foreigner who spoke no cognate language. William landed in September 1066 and was crowned at Westminster on Christmas Day in the same year. It was a swift confirmation of total mastership. The land was his, and Doomsday Book was to itemize in ruthless detail all he held.

What he did not do was to exercise a linguistic tyranny. The English language was left to itself. The notion of political control through control of language is a very modern, indeed Orwellian, idea. If English changed, moving from Old English to what is known as Middle English, a good deal of the transformation was internal or, if we wish, autonomous. The huge influx of French words was not the work of the French nobles and clergy who accompanied William to his new kingdom. There were, in fact, insufficient French speakers about to make much impact on the native population. Eighty percent of the total population consisted of small farmers and peasants. The French language in its Norman form did not touch them at all. In 1086, the year of Doomsday Book, 1 percent of the farming population was Norman: their task was to learn English in order to communicate with their laborers, not to force French on them. The lower clergy, of which perhaps 2 percent were francophone, could say mass in Latin but would meet little response if they preached in French. The aristocracy was, of course, French-speaking, but it formed a tightly closed social group that thrust out no tentacles to the lower orders. Like the colonial officers of the defunct British Empire, the ruling class, both clerical and lay, kept its heart in the homeland; unlike those brown-kneed exiles, it was not forced to converse with the natives. There would be a class of functionaries—English or

Norman—whose office was sustained by a kind of bilingualism. Where French got into English, as it did increasingly, was at the intellectual levels of law and literature.

The situation is not much different today. The bulk of the working-class vocabulary, in all anglophone territories, is Germanic; the Romance elements—French or Latin—creep in from journalism or the bureau of government. Even without the Norman Conquest, French would have asserted its cultural prestige on Anglo-Saxon intellectuals: it was smarter to write "despair" than *wanhope*. It is still smart, and still derided as snobbish, to use French expressions or long Latinate words. There are regular campaigns, usually in government departments, to reform the language of bureaucracy by reverting to the simple, meaning the Germanic, and eschewing the orotund, meaning the lexis of the Roman Empire. There persists a kind of conqueror-conquered dichotomy in English. What the English think of as hard or learned words, meaning Latin ones derived from the Norman Conquest, are the daily currency of French and Italian farm workers or factory operatives. It is only when a Greek word enters their Latin vocabulary that they respond with bafflement. In Naples the fish market is called the *Mercato Ittico* (from the Greek *ichthus*—"fish"), but the Neapolitans term it the *Mercato Ittico d[el] Pesci*—"fish of fish." This is analogous to the ailment we know as a "gastric stomach." But the Italians have no trouble with *gastrico*.

Old English in time became Middle English, and there is a school of linguistic thought that asserts that this language was a *creole*. A creole can be defined as a sophisticated *pidgin*, and a pidgin is a contact dialect of mixed vocabulary and elementary syntax with which foreign traders or soldiers can communicate crudely with the natives. British troops on duty at the Gibraltar-Spanish frontier used to point at the baskets of home-going Spanish workers and say "*Mungy?*" The workers would reply, "*Si, mungy.*" The British thought it was Spanish, and the Spanish thought it was English, which is sometimes the way with pidgins. To what language does "jigajig" belong? And where, for that matter, does "pidgin" come from? We are told that it is a Chinese attempt to say "business," but we cannot be sure.

We can be sure about "creole." It derives ultimately from the Portuguese *crioulo*, meaning a black brought up in a white master's home—*criar*, "bring up," from Latin *creare*, "create" or "beget." It came to connote mixed ancestry in the West Indies, white expatriation (the Empress Josephine was properly a Creole), eventually a white language adapted to the needs of a people of negroid stock. The terms "pidgin" and "creole" interpenetrate. The speakers of Tok Pisin or Neo-Melanesian call their language a pidgin, but it is a mother tongue with a fixed orthography, a dictionary, and a newspaper called *Wantok* ("one talk," or "united through language")—in other words, a full-fledged creole.

Nicole Z. Domingue published, in *The Journal of Creole Studies*, a scholarly article posing the question "Middle English: Another Creole?" The argument was briefly as follows. The English of medieval poems like *The Pearl* and *The Owl and the Nightingale* and even Chaucer is spectacularly different from the Old English of *Beowulf*. It does not look like a smooth development out of pre-Conquest English, as Tuscan looks like a painless transformation of Latin. The vocabularies are different. Professor Thomas Phyles says that 85 percent of the Middle English lexis is of French origin. But, as we know, there are Scandinavian elements as well—words like "they," "them," "their," and "are," the conjunction "though," the acceptance of the Scandinavian *father* over *faeder*. Middle English, it seems, could get on well enough without too much Old English vocabulary.

As for the revolution in structure, this was profound. Not long after the Norman Conquest, English was shedding noun classes, gender, personal verb endings, dual categories (*wit* for "we two"). It was trying to turn itself into an analytic language, very different from the heavily synthetic Germanic tongue that it seemed to be superseding. This resulted in, or was caused by, a loss of flexibility in word order—"a likely influence of French syntax, with its SVO and Aux-Main Verb orders in all classes." "SVO" means subject-verb-object. "Aux-Main Verb" means that in all clauses the auxiliary—like "have" or "will" or "would"—comes before the defining verb: "This is the girl whom I to the local mead hall taken have" sorts itself out into the verb order we know today. Why did genders disappear? Because Norman French was presenting a different gender system from the Germanic one spoken by the conquered natives, and "gender categories are notoriously difficult to learn in second-language-learning situations." The response is to get rid of genders altogether.

Middle English, then, according to this thesis, is a language whose sounds are Germanic but whose morphology is, though essentially Germanic, far simpler than the tongues of the grim North could at that time decently allow. But its lexicon is mainly non-Germanic, and it has a very large number of Norman French words. This, we are told, is typical of creoles—adoption of the invading vocabulary but not the invading structures—as are features that do not come from any of the original contributory languages: "While Old English, Scandinavian, and French were all heavily inflected languages, Middle English has no grammatical gender, only remnants of noun categories, case endings, and verbal inflections."

If a creole is an extended pidgin spoken as a mother tongue, we have to establish that a pidgin existed in English at the time of the Norman takeover. But there is no written evidence. There is no talk of the native tongue being corrupted by the foreigner, though there are some thirteenth-century denunciations of Anglo-Norman as "bad French." Yet the social situation presumes multilingualism, and that implies the necessary search for an area of very simple common understanding. There was also, so Dr. Domingue asserts, a situation of "unstable pre-pidgin continua," caused by two hundred years of Scandinavians and Anglo-Saxons communicating with each other "by reducing severely all features of language which were difficult to learn and along universal lines of reduction." The native speakers of English could have used the middle part of the continuum—the most pidginized part, the furthest away from both Old English and Scandinavian—to address the Norman invaders, accommodating, while they were about the simplifying process, the kind of simplification that the invaders wanted—such as the liquidation of gender categories. "Such a situation would have resulted in the formation of a *bona fide* pidgin or pidgins."

This thesis, though it has a certain fascination, is mainly of interest to those scholars who study creoles. Whatever we call post-Conquest English hardly affects the substance that it is. The evidence of literary texts gives no true clue to what was happening to the language of the people. If English changed after the Norman Conquest, the Normans had little to do with it. There was an influx of about ten thousand Norman-French words into the English vocabulary, but we are told that as many as 90 percent of these came in after 1250, when French was on the decline in England as a spoken language. As for the structure and phonology of English—that was purely a native concern, and an unwilled one at that.

It has to be conceded that the importation of French words did have some slight effect on the sound of English. I have already mentioned that the diphthong /oi/ came in along with the words that contained it—*joie* or "joy," for instance, which still keeps its old Norman-French sound, though French has transformed it into /wa/. But we have to note as well that certain sounds were not to be found in initial position in Old English words, though they appeared elsewhere. In *faran* ("to go"), *aefter*, and *wulf*, we hear /f/, but in *ofer* ("over") and *wulfas* ("wolves") we hear, as now, /v/. No /v/, in other words, at the beginning of a word. Similarly, you would hear /z/ in the middle, but not at the start. The Normans brought in words like the ancestors of "virgin," "vice," "victory," "zeal," and "zodiac," which necessitated a change of sonic habit. It was undoubtedly painless, like the lone introduction of /ʒ/ in *Doctor Zhivago*. Such innovations are trivial and do not affect the basic phonetic structure of a language.

Let us forget about the Norman Conquest and move on to the year 1285. It was then that King Henry III made the first proclamation in English since the coming of the Normans. Previously, as in the literature of the royal court, French or Latin had been preferred, but now the native tongue reasserted itself at the highest level. It would be tempting for us to suppose that Henry spoke "King's English," a model for the entire nation, a dialect of prestige. But this notion of a national tongue, as opposed to a bundle of regional dialects, had not yet emerged. It would come later, in the fourteenth century, with a totally English-speaking court in London, surrounded by, and even encouraging, a literature in the dialect that, for purely social reasons, possessed the greatest glamour. We have to keep in mind constantly that no one dialect or language has any intrinsic superiority over another. They prevail for nonlinguistic reasons.

There is a poem written in the early thirteenth century that has come down to us in two dialects—the one from the South-West Midlands and the other probably from the East Midlands. It is called "Three Sorrowful Things," and it still has a brisk poetic impact. We recognize it, especially when I substitute the new "th" for the old runes, as being certainly in our own language: it is not *Beowulf*. Here is the original, or South-West Midland, version: it must be the original, for the rhymes are genuine; it is not so in the other:

Wanne ich thenche thinges thre
ne mai neure blithe be:

that on is ich sal awe,
that other is ich ne wot wilk day.
That thridde is mi meste kare,
i ne woth nevre wuder i sal fare.

This has been near-copied in the other region as follows:

Wanne i thenke thinges thre
ne mai hi neure blithe ben:
the ton is dat I sal awei,
the tother is ne wot wilk dei.
The thridde is mi moste kare,
i ne wot wider I sal faren.

We may translate it as:

Whenever I think about things three
I can never happy be.
One is: I must go away,
Second: I know not which day.
The third one is my mostest care:
I know not where to I shall fare.

In the first version we have the modern infinitive "be," which rhymes with "thre." In the second the old, very Germanic infinitive ending forbids a rhyme, as it does in the last two lines. "Ich," for "I" as in Modern German, though pronounced like "itch," is giving place to the modern "I" (though without the egoism of a capital letter) more definitely in the second than in the first. The French "second" has not yet replaced "other" (or "tother," still facetiously with us) in either. "Thridde" is waiting to be metastasized to "third," just as "brid" in modern Lancashire dialect can turn into "bird" in the right company. "Biggest" will soon be preferred to "mostest," as in Irving Berlin's "the hostess with the mostest on the ball," and "meste." "Blithe" is still around, though only in the rhyme about the child, like myself, born on the Sabbath day—"bonny and blithe and good and gay." This medieval English is trying hard to turn into our own tongue. But it is not a unified medieval English: one dialect confronts another and neither wins.

As we look at later manuscripts—say from the fifteenth and sixteenth centuries—it seems that a national linguistic form is emerging, and that this is to be a Midland dialect. In the early fourteenth century it is recognized, in odd writings about the linguistic situation, that the North is too far north and the South too far south to grant a national norm, but, says Ranulph Higden in Latin, translated by John of Trevisa into South-West Midland, "men of myddel Engelond, as hyt were parteners of the endes, understondeth betre the syde longages, Northeron and Southeron, than Northeron and Southeron understondeth eyther other." The variety of Midland English that became what we now call Standard English was inevitably of the South-Eastern kind. This was preeminently the language of London. As was appropriate for a metropolitan tongue, in which representatives of all the regions met for commercial, legal, and cultural ends, it was somewhat synthetic. For instance, the third-person-singular ending of present tense verbs, as in "eats" and "drinks," was of Northern origin, though "eateth" and "drinketh," East Midland and Southern forms, persisted in translations of the Bible and highly formal utterances.

With Geoffrey Chaucer we see very clearly the immediate ancestor of the language we speak and write today. Writers survive through talent, or in Chaucer's instance genius, and the homage we pay to the author of *The Canterbury Tales* obscures the fact that he was preceded by and had as contemporaries writers, named and anonymous, who are now of more philological than literary interest. We may study *The Pearl* and *The Owl and the Nightingale* in college, but we read Chaucer for pleasure. *Sir Gawain and the Green Knight*, a brilliant narrative poem from the Wirral peninsula, is of such value that we brave its thickets of obscurity in order to get at the story, thumbing the glossary to make sense of "Your gryndellayk and your greme, and your grete words" (those two obscure great words are Scandinavian). This outstanding work of art, modestly put out anonymously, appeared about 1380. Go back to the *Ormulum* of 1200, and you may wonder, if you are not professionally concerned, whether the following is worth understanding:

& trigg & trowwe grithth & frithth
Reghghethth betwenenn lede.

(The digraphs that replace the old runes make it, unfairly, look comic.)

The old mystery plays, presented annually on Corpus Christi in the great provincial towns, show the linguistic situation outside the heart of centralized power and culture. They show also a kind of provincial chip-on-the-shoulder attitude to London English. The South still derides the speech of the North, and this is reciprocated. The following comes from the *Second Shepherd's Play*. The three *pastores* speak good Yorkshire, but Mak, the sheep stealer, assumes the authoritative tones of the South.

I PASTOR:	Why make ye it so qwaynt? Mak, ye do wrang.
II PASTOR:	Bot, Mak, lyst ye saynt? I trow that ye lang.
III PASTOR:	I trow the shrew can paynt, the dewyll myght him hang!
MAK:	Ich shall make comlaynt, and make you all to thwang At a Worde, And tell evyn how ye doth.
I PASTOR:	Bot, Mak, is that sothe? Now take outt that sothren tothe, And sett in a torde!

"Qwaynt" means "superior." It is Mak's "ich" that points to his putting on Southern airs: the others, in the Northern manner that has become standard, say "I." He is told to take out "that southern tooth and sit in a turd." Why "tooth"? Was there something toothy about his assumed speech? An aristocratic tooth-showing clarity as opposed to pastoral mumbling?

Chaucer could use Northern dialect when he wished. In "The Reeve's Tale" he has two characters from some unspecified northern district saying "ga" instead of "go" and "wagges" instead of "waggeth." But he was a Londoner, and his approach to the speech of the North is comically disdainful. Here is his Standard English:

Adam our fader, and his wyf also,
Fro Paradys to labor and to wo
Were driven for that vyce, it is no drede;
For whyl that Adam fasted, as I rede,
He was in Paradys; and whan that he
Eet of the fruyt defended on the tree,
Anon he was out-cast to wo and peyne . . .

This is the Pardoner in *The Canterbury Tales* attacking the sin of gluttony. The English seems not very far removed from our own, but the sound is totally different. The vowels are closer to Continental usage—French or Italian—and the final '-e' of "drede" and "rede" is pronounced. The Old English word endings have collapsed into schwa or something like it; later they will disappear altogether and "drede," "rede," and "peyne" turn into "dread," "read," and "pain." The vocabulary is recognizably our own, though that "defended" is clearly the French *défendu*, "forbidden." Let us look at the opening of the Prologue to *The Canterbury Tales*.

> Whan that Aprille with his shoures soote
> The droghte of Marche hath percéd to the roote,
> And bathed every veyne in swich licuor
> Of which vertu engendred is the flour;
> Whan Zephirus eek with his swete breeth
> Inspiréd hath in every holt and heeth
> The tendre croppes, and the yonge sonne
> Hath in the Ram his halfe cours y-ronne,
> And smale fowles maken melodye,
> That slepen al the night with open ye,
> (So priketh hem nature in hir corages);
> Than longen folk to goon on pilgrimages.

Here we seem to hear the language pulling two ways. The Germanic 'th' and 'gh' (still pronounced /x/ as in German *Bach*) and the decaying past participle prefix 'y-,' once the Old English and still the Modern German 'ge-,' as well as the infinitive ending '-en,' affirm the inherited structure of the language, while much of the vocabulary looks toward France—"licour," "vertu" (pronounced with a French /y/), "inspired," "tendre," "corages." The light or tripping quality of the rhythm is ensured by those sounded 'e's at the ends of words. Chaucer could write "As thikke as motes in the sonne-beem," while John Milton, in the seventeenth century, had to be content with "As the gay motes that people the sun-beam." Our English is thick and clotted in comparison with the Italianate quality of Chaucer's. This is an aesthetic judgment that properly has no place here, but it is hard to consider Chaucer merely as a bearer of a new linguistic standard. Too much eternal humanity comes across:

She wolde wepe if that she saw a mous
Caught in a trappe, if it were deed or bledde.
Of smale houndes had she; that she fedde
With rosted flesh, or milk and wastel-breed.
But sore weep she if oon of hem were deed.

That is the tenderhearted Prioress. Chaucer's own tenderness could be qualified with a hard eye for "the smyler with the knyf under the cloke," where that initial 'k' in "knyf" cuts like the smiler's own blade.

G. K. Chesterton, in his book on Chaucer, said, with journalistic exaggeration, that here was the creator of the English language. He was confusing the creation of great art in that medium with the medium itself. Chaucer was merely doing better what other men did well—John Gower, for instance (1330?–1408), Thomas Hoccleve (1370?–1450?), and John Lydgate (1370?–1451?). In Robert Henryson (1425?–1508?) we see the state of the language as a poetic medium after Chaucer's death (1400). Chaucer wrote *Troilus and Criseyde*, and Henryson continued the tale in *The Testament of Cresseid*, which ends with the moral:

Now, worthie wemen, in this ballet short
Made for your worship and instructioun,
Of cheritie, I monish and exhort—
Ming not your luve with false deceptioun.
Bear in your mind this short conclusioun
Of fair Cresseid, as I have said before,
Sen sho is deid, I speak of her no more.

This is solid uninspired English working its way towards modernity. Come to William Dunbar (1460?–1530) and we see how heavily it is possible to lean on the acquired French vocabulary:

Gemme of all joy, jasper of jocunditie,
    Most mighty carbuncle of vertue and valour:
Strong Troy in vigour and in strenuytie;
    Of royall cities rose and geraflour;
    Empress of townes, exalt in honour:
In beawtie berying the crowne imperiall;

Sweet paradys precelling in pleasure:
London, thou art the flower of Cities all.

Dunbar was a Scot who probably died at the Battle of Flodden. He is writing here in a style doubly foreign. With another Scot, Gavin or Gawin Douglas (1474–1522), we see that Old English has evolved, north of the border, into a dialect (or language, since it carries the Scottish flag) more conservative than Chaucer's but still willing to borrow from French:

The silly sheep and their litil herd-gromys
Lurkis under lee of bankis, woddis and bromys;
And other dantit grettar beastiall,
Within their stabilis sesyt into stall,
Sik as mulis, horssis, oxin and ky,
Fed tuskyt baris and far swine in sty,
Sustenyt were by mannys governance
On hervist and on simmeris purvyance.

In our next chapter, we shall consider what changes—chiefly phonetic—went on in English during its progress from the ancient form onward: these are internal and have little to do with what happened in the great world outside. For now, there are two things to think about—the amassing of a more exotic vocabulary than the Norman one, and the attempt to establish the notion of linguistic "correctness" that still obsesses us. Let us take the latter first.

The question of correctness arose in a large way with the introduction of printing into England. William Caxton (1422?–1491), who was in the printing business to make money, had to consider what form of the language would reach the biggest book-buying public. Naturally, it would be the East Midland dialect as spoken by the educated of London, and, of course, the two great universities, but there were problems of choice of vocabulary. Everyone, I think, knows the story of the man who asked for "egges" and was not understood by the London woman who was selling them. The man's companion asked for "eyren" (compare the German *Eier*), and that was understood very well. "Lo," says Caxton, "what shall a man say?" He recounts the story in the Vergil translation *Eneydos* (1490) before getting down to the task of rendering Latin into a kind of universal

English. Well, perhaps hardly universal, since Caxton had in mind as readers not "rude vplondysch" men but "clerkes" and "gentylmen." Book reading was for the elite; *Peg's Paper* and the *Sun* would be a long time coming.

What was and is known as "grammatical English" was to be decreed by pundits whose personal prejudices were erected into authoritarian regulations. William Shakespeare had no grammar books to consult—except Latin ones—and what dictionaries there were defined lists only of difficult and very unusual words. We now take the view that when in doubt, a writer of plays, novels, or even letters should consult an "authority"—someone who has received the word, or the way to use the word, on a kind of Mount Sinai. Shakespeare, without benefit of lexicographers and grammarians, did well enough, despite his double negatives, split infinitives, and singular verbs for plural subjects. His sense of what the language was was oceanic; the spume of solecism could be discounted, wiped away.

If he had lived in the eighteenth century, he might have joined the authors who, seeing their age as Augustan, wanted the language to be fixed and immutable like Latin, classical, immune to change, subject to the structures of an academy on the French model, capable of being put to sleep in a dictionary. Jonathan Swift raged against slang—like "mob," short for *mobile vulgus*—and Dr. Samuel Johnson worried about the "decay" of the language, "decay" merely being healthy change. We may be glad that Shakespeare had a limited notion of linguistic decorum, that he misused "weird" and introduced monsters like "orgulous." A talented barbarian to many of the Restoration and Augustan Age, he knew instinctively that language was sustained by rules too deep to probe, and that English was exceptionally hospitable to new words, daring usages, and creative errors.

If Swift and his contemporaries worried about the invasion of slang, they accepted the growth of vocabulary through the kinds of foreign contact proper to a seafaring people. The history of English since its pacific establishment as a language with a social and cultural center in the capital, the tongue of a people not further to be invaded after 1066, is the history of a vastly enlarged vocabulary. The Dutch, their maritime rivals, were allowed to give the naval lexis terms like "buoy," "deck," "splice," "smack," "cruiser," "jib" (extensible to the metaphor "I don't like the cut of his"), "schooner," and "keelhaul." The French, not the Norman French, enabled a British soldier to rise to colonel, command a brigade of dragoons, fire a barrage with carbons, examine terrain, and watch out for espionage. His lady wife, following Paris fashions, could choose between an indigo and a beige blouse, perhaps moiré, study what was the latest vogue, and if genteel enough, perhaps crochet in her spare time.

The Italians have not been slow to infiltrate into military terminology. Cavaliers may have disappeared, but there are still squadrons and salvos, attacks, barracks, and rockets. The main influence, however, has been pacific and creative. We can examine a building, appraising cupola and cornice, a stucco portico, filigree friezes on a corridor, skim over cartoons on the balcony of a villa, say of the landscape (Dutch *landskip*, really): "How picturesque." We can browse through a portfolio in a mezzanine arcade, visit a studio to admire a terra-cotta torso or a capolavoro of tempera, request the replica of a statue. We can go to the opera to hear recitatives and arias from a prima donna, or to a concert for fugues or madrigals, sonatas or soprano solos (or soli), observing how the allegro, largo, presto are managed, to say nothing of gradations from pianissimo to fortissimo. We can, in the home of Italian, meet a Papal Nuncio, see the work of artisans, avoid mountebanks and bandits, conduct intrigues at a gala carnival, read a manifesto in a gazette.

Spanish has not done badly either. We can tap sherry from a cask and take it with a rusk or even a banana, listening to a guitar in the plaza, or watching the parade of the matadors on their way to the corrida. Our nightmares can be oppressed during the siesta by renegades, tornadoes, and cannibals. A lady in chinchilla, eating her vanilla ice or smoking a cigarette, can scream at cockroaches. Those albino stevedores are dancing a quadrille. Let us go to a Hispanic former colony to see mustangs, stampedes, broncos, viewing the canyon from the patio of an adobe hacienda. If we tire of the Spanish, the Portuguese will serve us port and madeira or even yams. We can admire buffalos or flamingos and wonder how pagodas and mandarins, as well as palavers about assegais on a veranda, got into an Iberian language. But the traveling British have learned from other traveling peoples, and this is how languages are enriched.

I say "British" now and not "English." The indigenous Celts used to be the British, but the term came to be applied to the united-to-be nation and, indeed, commonwealth that speaks English. Great Britain opposes Little Britain or Brittany, where the Celtic Bretons are: it is not a boastful title. When James VI of Scotland became also James I of England in 1603, there had to be a new national term. Shakespeare picked it up quickly: "Fee fie foh fum, I smell the blood of a British man." Nowadays British English is just one of many kinds, of which the greatest may be American. But the important things that happened to English happened in England. Sound changes, for instance.

21

SOUNDS FROM THE PAST

Sometimes we wonder why the plurals of "foot," "mouse," and "tooth" should be "feet," "mice," and "teeth." It is legitimate wonder, for "foots," "mouses," and "tooths" are rational, intelligible, and even, perhaps, a portent for the future. But we are chained to phonological happenings not merely ancient but prehistoric.

There was once a phenomenon, very Germanic and very important, that philologists call i-mutation or i-umlaut. I have already used the term "assimilation" to explain colloquial pronunciations like "corm beef," "tim peaches," and "vogka." A consonant, in slack or rapid speech, will attract the consonant that comes before it toward its own position in the mouth. The /k/ in "vodka" draws the /d/ that ought to be pronounced away from the teethridge to the velum or back of the mouth, where a /g/ sounds—the voiced version of /k/. Assimilation occurred in i-mutation, but it was a matter of vowels, not consonants. We have to posit prehistoric plural endings for the Old English *mūs* (pronounced /mu:s/, as it still is in Scottish English) and *fōt* ("foot"—we still spell it as though it contained the Old English long 'o')—endings that contained either the vowel /i/ as in "machine" or the semivowel /j/ as in *Ja* or "yes." If we imagine that something like /mus/ ("mouse") was pluralized as /musi/, then it seems reasonable that the /u/ would have been fronted into /y/ (the vowel in French *lune*), remaining there even after the pluralizing -*i* had dropped off. The plural of Old English *mūs* was, in fact, *mys*; the /y:/ in the plural has become unrounded to /miˑs/ and, following diphthongization, settled into /maɪs/. A cartoon cat that spoke of "those miserable meeces" had evidently slept during the Great Vowel Shift. As for *fōt*, the back rounded vowel /o:/ was pulled toward the front of the mouth in the same way, becoming /ø:/, the sound we hear in French *bleu*. In time this rounded front vowel got itself spread to /e:/. Again, the modern spelling "feet" shows how the word used to be pronounced— the /e/ we hear in *café* lengthened.

Languages never stand still. Modern spelling crystallizes lost pronunciations: the visual never quite catches up with the aural. If our spelling is a chaos, Old English spelling was sweetness and light. If you were transported back to the England of, say, the ninth century and were able to view documents in a monastery or an Anglo-Saxon bureaucrat's office, you would see, in strong black ink, an accurate picture of the phonemic system. The 'll' of *full* would not be a mere spelling convention but an honest representation of a double sound. The 'tt' of our "settle," another convention that means nothing now, would indicate, in *settan* ("to set"), a genuine lengthened consonant. The Italians have these still, but we have lost them.

You would find Old English speech unintelligible, except for odd brief words—*for* and *him* and *and*. Carrying a phonetician's equipment with you, you would be able to make an inventory of the sounds the Anglo-Saxons used, but you might have difficulty in deciding what was phonemic and what was allophonic. For instance, there would be no /ŋ/ (as in "sing") as a full-fledged phoneme: it would be an allophone of /n/ before a velar consonant—/k/ or /g/. You would not hear /h/, except as an allophone of the /x/ of *Bach* and *loch*. You would hear the /æ/ of modern "man" (in RP) but not the /ɛ/ of "ten dead men." The /e/ of *café* would be doing the work now given to the more open, or less close, front short sound. You would hear only two diphthongs, both strange to modern ears—/æa/ and /eo/, both capable of being lengthened: the Anglo-Saxons were punctilious about length signals. *Bĕam*, with its superscript little line, is clearly the ancestor of "beam," but then meant "tree": there is the first of the two diphthongs. The second is in *hrēod* ("reed") and *hēorte* ("heart").

If you could prolong your stay in that vanished England till, say, the twelfth century, with the Normans in control but the language going its own Germanic way, you would find that Old English, ready to turn into Middle English, had kept all its consonants but shed a number of vowel sounds. There would be /i/, /e/, /o/, and /u/, along with their lengthened versions /i:/, /e:/, /o:/, and /u:/. There would be /ɑ:/ as in "father," in a long version only. The /a/ of Lancashire "man," in a short form only, and the /ɛ/ of "men," but only in the long form, would have arrived. The two diphthongs would have totally disappeared. No diphthongs at all. A very simple vowel system, in fact, ready to be transformed by time and change into today's complexities.

I have assumed, falsely, a unified language: there were, of course, a number of dialectal variations. When we come to that intermediate version of English whose emergence we can date, very roughly, from the twelfth century, it is necessary to make a clear distinction between what was spoken in the North and what was spoken elsewhere. This, again, is false, oversimplistic, but we cannot consider anything without grossly generalizing. But if I am asked the question, "What happened to Old English /ɑ:/ (as in "father") when it got to the Middle English stage?" I am not falsifying unduly when I reply, "In the North it turned into /a:/ and in the other regions to /ɔ:/ (as in 'jaw')." This may seem like dry-as-dust scholarship, but the two-way split (fronting in the North, rounding elsewhere) did produce a distinction we hear today. The Old English *bān*, meaning "bone," became /ba:n/ in the North and, in the South, /bɔ:n/. In other words, a round back vowel for the latter, for the former an unrounded front vowel—quite a difference. We end up with /bəʊn/ (listen to a BBC announcer) in London but /ben/ in Glasgow and /bɪən/ in Newcastle. To pronounce that second form say "beer" with an 'n' instead of a final 'r.'

You have met, briefly, the fearsome term "i-mutation." Meet now a new one not less dreadful—a vowel change called "Open Syllable Lengthening." If there was an Old English word with two syllables—the first stressed, the other not, as in *wicu*, "week"; *mete*, "meat"; *sama*, "same"; *duru*, "door"—and a vowel followed by a consonant in the first syllable, then the vowel became long. It also dropped from its old mouth position to a new one a stage lower. You know about these stages—/e/ is one stage lower than /i/; /o/ is one stage lower than /u/. So *wicu* had its vowel both lengthened and lowered to /e:/. The ending '-u' weakened to the central vowel schwa, a common fate for all of those once gender-announcing endings when they got into Middle English. Look at "week," where there is no vowel ending at all (what use was it?), where the "ee" is an image of the Middle English /e:/. The word *duru* had its ending weakened to /ə/ and its stressed vowel lengthened and lowered to /o:/, just as accurately rendered by /oo/ and still seen in the modern "door."

In the North and elsewhere, diphthongs—lost in late Old English—began to flourish. Two that we cannot do without emerged from the treatment of the Old English semivowels /j/ (*Ja*, "yes") and /w/. Old English *dæg*, meaning "day," was allowing its /g/ to become a voiced gargle when the plural appeared as *dagas*—those two back vowels were responsible. This, too, began to be vocalized like those two semivowels. The root *dæg*, pronounced /dæj/, became *dei* or *dai* in Middle English: that second diphthong, associated today with Cockney, has a respectable ancestry. Old English *boga*, "bow," became Middle English *bowe*, pronounced /bɔuə/. Old English *grōwan*— "grow"—became Middle English *growen*—/grɔuən/. The ancestor of "bought" was first *bōhte* (with the aspirate an allophone of /x/ as in *Bach*) and later *bouȝte*, the 'ȝ' or yogh being a more honest representation of /x/ than 'h.' The pronunciation of *bouȝte* was /bɔuxtə/. Old English *hēah*, which later became *hēh* /he:x/, changed into Middle English /heix/. Our immediate ancestor thus became a richly diphthongal language like our own, with /ai/, /ɔi/, /iu/, /ɛu/, /ɔu/, /ei/, and /au/. That /ɔi/ was, as I said earlier, a French borrowing.

French borrowing permitted /v/ and /z/ to begin words, a thing not known before. It became possible to have contrasts, or minimal pairs—"ferry" against "very," "seal" against "zeal." Initial 'th' had always been /θ/—as in "thick," "thin"—but it became voiced to /ð/ in a class of pronouns and determiners that are still with us—"the," "this," "that," "thou," "thee," and "then." By about 1400, the year of Chaucer's death, Middle English had all the consonants we have now, with the exception of the /ʒ/ in "vision" (though the /dʒ/ of "joy" and "judge" was around) and the /h/, which is still not to be found in a large number of British English dialects. Instead of /h/, whatever the spelling said, there was the harsh /x/ that now seems to us so foreign (even when we encounter it in Scottish). And /ŋ/ was still an allophone of /n/ before /k/ and /g/, as it continues to be in the dialect of my native Lancashire.

The vowel situation about 1400 can best be illustrated by taking certain modern words and showing what vowels they contained in their premodern forms. "Bit" had not /ɪ/, as today, but the short /i/

of French *lui*: Frenchmen who have not taken to /ɪ/ show us what the Middle English vowel used to be. In "bet" the 'e' was also French 'é.' Try "better bitter" with a French pronunciation, and you will come close to the vowels of King Henry V. The Old English vowel, which is also the Modern English vowel, in words like "man," "cat," and "cad," was not to be heard. The sound of "bat" would be very Lancashire or Yorkshire. In "but" the vowel was a genuine /u/: it would take time for it to become the /ʌ/ of today. "Pot," which today has a low round back sound in RP—though not in American English—had then a high round back sound—/o/. "Beet" was pronounced as it is spelled, with /e:/, while "beat" was altogether different—/bɛ:t/. This last persisted and still persists in dialect. The Lancashire boy who cried because his "mate" had fallen in the water ("t'watter") was asked, by a man who had fruitlessly dived in, where his mate had fallen from. He replied: "Off me bread." Middle English "mate" was pronounced as it is spelled—with an /a:/. "Out" has a French spelling that half disguises /u:/—"oot," if we are novelists trying to write down Scottish English. "Boot" was, rightly, pronounced /bo:t/, and "boat" was /bɔ:t/, like "bought." That 'a' after a vowel was a down signal—"drop your tongue toward /a/." As for the diphthongs, "day" contained a good Cockney /ai/, "boy" was what it is now, /au/ was the sound in "law," as it still is in parts of the American South, "knew" and "dew" contained /iu/, which has changed in RP into /ju/ and has thus ceased to be a diphthong. "Grow" began with the /ɔ/ of "for," though short, and glided toward /u/. Neither /ɪ/ nor /ʊ/, which are so much part of Modern English and have their origins as centralized and lowered versions of /i/ and /u/ respectively, had yet made an appearance.

Compare the situation of the vowels in 1400 and now, and we see huge changes. The last of our fearsome terms is the Great Vowel Shift, or GVS, which describes a radical transformation that seems to have begun in the fifteenth century and finished in the late sixteenth or early seventeenth, though some say it is still proceeding. To know precisely, or near precisely, what happened, we have to take another look at the mouth and the tongue positions appropriate to certain of the long vowels. At the front of the mouth /i:/ is close, /e:/ half-close, /ɛ:/ half-open, /a:/ fully open. You have enunciated the series before; do so again. Remember also the back rounded vowels /u:/ (fully close), /o:/ (half-close), and /ɔ:/ (half-open). Here is a diagram garnished with arrows that I shall explain:

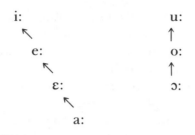

The GVS operated only with long vowels. Long vowels are, of their nature, unstable: the tongue is not a mechanical instrument programmed to hold the same position for too long: vowels waver when they are long: the time taken for the enunciation of short vowels—as in "it," "men," "man"—is too brief to admit wavering. The fully open vowel /ɑ/—unmodified by the tongue—does not concern us. What happened was that the half-close long vowels /e:/ and /o:/ pushed themselves out of place: they rose to occupy the next highest positions—those of /i:/ and /u:/. Where could /i:/ and /u:/ go when so pushed? They could not pierce the hard palate; they could only escape by turning themselves into something else—namely, diphthongs. So the /i:/ dropped out of the system of pure long vowels and eventually became the diphthong /ai/, though it had to be /ei/ or /ʌi/ or some other diphthong first. The same thing happened to /u:/, which opted out of the same system to turn into the diphthong /au/ by way of /ou/ and /ʌu/ and other forms. The fanciful impression given by these new diphthongs is of a low or lowish vowel trying to climb back to the original high position occupied by /i:/ or /u:/.

But those positions had been taken over by /e:/ and /o:/, in the sense that words that contained those sounds now contained them no longer. "Beet," once /be:t/, was now becoming /bi:t/, and "moon" was no longer /mo:n/ or /moon/ but /mu:n/. This is today's situation, the result of the GVS.

The raising of /e:/ to /i:/ and /o:/ to /u:/ meant that those two climbing vowels had left their old slots empty for the occupancy of the vowels just immediately below. Thus, /ɛ:/ took over the place of /e:/, and /ɔ:/ that of /o:/. There was only one long vowel left to rise, and this was /a:/, which rose to the slot where /ɛ:/ had been.

This systematic process of vowel change was a slow business, and it was not recognized while it was happening. The dates we give for the completion of the GVS, which was accomplished in two stages, have to be approximate. But this is the rough position in, say, 1564, the year of William Shakespeare's birth. "Bite" was pronounced /beit/—"bate" with a high second element, not the centralized /ɪ/ of today. But by about 1600, when the Globe playhouse was being built, it had become something like /bʌit/. That vowel /ʌ/ is the one we use in "love" and "shove" today if we are not from the British North. It is the /ɔ/ we already know—the vowel in "jaw"—but short and unrounded. It has yet to function as a free element. In 1564 "beet" was pronounced /bi:t/, as today, and "beat" was pronounced with /e:/, as in unselfconscious Dublin speech. This was also the position in 1600. In 1564 "mate" had /a:/, as though it were the Lancashire "mat" with the vowel prolonged. By 1600 it had arrived at /mɛ:t/— modern "met" with the same kind of unnatural-seeming prolongation. "Out" matched "bite" in 1600 by having /ʌ/ as its first element— /ʌut/, but in 1564 it had been /out/—near to "oat." "Boot" was recognizably the modern word in both years—/bu:t/, and "boat," which had been /bɔ:t/—like "bought"—in Middle English, became /bo:t/ by 1564 and stayed that way for the opening of the Globe.

There were other changes, less earthshaking than those produced by the GVS, and these were proceeding while Shakespeare was preparing for Stratford retirement. The Cockney-sounding /ai/ of "day" made way for the vowel (or monophthong) /a/, but /da:/ for "day" became /dɛ:/ and later /de:/. The /e:/, a long vowel never, like all long vowels, all that stable in an anglophone mouth, became diphthongized in time to /dei/, ending as our own /deɪ/, but Shakespeare probably pronounced "day" in what would sound to us a very rural manner. Words in the "beat" class, with their /e:/, rose to join the "beet" class, with /i:/. The situation today is one in which "beet" and "beat" are homophones. This is not true in Ireland, which fossilizes old features of Early Modern English. In the eighteenth century certain words resisted the change. Alexander Pope rhymed "obey" and "tea." We still pronounce "steak" and "break" with a long /e:/ converted into the diphthong /eɪ/. In parts of South Wales "steak" has joined the upward Wales shift, and is pronounced /sti:k/.

We get a hint of the situation before the GVS in the alternating vowels of "divine:divinity," "serene:serenity," and "profound:profundity." The adjectives, with their long vowels, have undergone change; the nouns, which all have short vowels, show the situation before the vocalic move upward. Wrench "divin-" free of its suffix, lengthen the vowels, and you get /divi:n/, which is how our pre-GVS ancestors said it. So with "seren-." Vowel lengthening gives /sere:n/.

And "profund-" will grant you the /u:/ that existed before that vowel was kicked upstairs and out of the sequence. Remember—short vowels were unaffected by the GVS; only the long ones suffered.

On the other hand, the short vowels underwent strange changes of their own, probably inexplicable. During Shakespeare's early manhood the short /a/, which is still a characteristic of Northern speech in "man," "cat," and "jannock," rose in the South to the /æ/ of today—a vowel that, to a Lancastrian, still seems to be both unnatural and unstable. It appears to be changing today in the speech of the young, becoming centralized and a little vague. The clear Italianate vowels /i/ and /u/ moved back and down a little to become, respectively, the vowel of "bit" and the vowel of "should." Words like "but" used to be pronounced as spelled—/but/—but in the seventeenth century, after the death of Shakespeare (1616), our vowel /ʌ/ began to appear as an independent son, not the mere onset of a diphthong, though it has still to seem natural in the North. A good number of words with the Middle English /u/ accommodated /ʌ/, but some did not. These are chiefly words with a labial in front—/p/ or /b/ or /w/—as we can hear in "pull" and "bull" and "wool." Some Middle English words with /u:/ in them underwent shortening in order to turn into /ʌ/, but words with /o:/ went two ways. If they shortened before /ʌ/ appeared in the vowel galaxy, they joined the class containing "blood," "flood," and "glove." If they shortened later, they appeared as /ʊ/ in words such as "good" and "book." None of this, of course, applies in Northern forms of English.

An important difference between British and American English—perhaps the one great definitive difference—was in preparation during the late seventeenth century while James, duke of York, was renaming New Amsterdam. The vowel /æ/ as in "man" was lengthening in certain contexts. In words like "laugh" and "path" and "pass," which end in unvoiced fricatives, in words like "dance" and "plant," which end in a nasal and an /s/ or /t/, and in words where the /æ/ was followed by /r/, that short vowel began to grow long. The older pronunciation of "dance" was /dæns/, wholly acceptable today to English speakers outside the cultural area dominated by London, but then it became /dæ:ns/. It was not until the nineteenth century, when John Keats was dying of tuberculosis, that this long /æ:/ decided to migrate to the back of the mouth and become the /ɑ/ that is characteristic of Southern English speech today. It is a source of mockery, or reluctant admiration, among provincials and ex-colonials. In his novel *Goodbye Mickey Mouse*, Len Deighton has a U.S. Air Force base in England during World War II. A dance is held, with a fine simulacrum of a "big band" on the Glenn Miller model and a singing group that acceptably renders "That Old Black Magic." The situation seems totally American until the singers enunciate "witchcraft"—not /wɪtʃkræft/ but /wɪtʃkrɑːft/. Then the exiled airmen become aware of their exile.

That whole back low region of the mouth seems not to have been in use in British English for a very long time. It is still not in use in the United States. In eighteenth-century England the returned nabobs drank what they had drunk in India—"brandy pani," or brandy with water, but they turned the "pani" into "pawnee." When Gibraltar was taken in 1704, its pronunciation had to be "Gibrawltar," since the Continental /ɑ/ was not available. If you wished to address your father, you had a choice between /fæðə/ and "fawther." The rounded version of that low back spread vowel, nowadays to be heard in "pot" and "not" as /ɒ/, is strange to Americans. Some older speakers of British English find it strange, too. They say "awf" for "off," but that usage is dying out.

What more has to be said about late-medieval or early-modern sound changes? When /ɔː/ rose to /oː/, obedient to the GVS, it left a slot that a monophthongized version of words like "law"—formerly /lau/ to rhyme with "cow"—was able to fill. Hence today's /lɔː/. In the seventeenth century, there was what might be termed a merger of some short vowels before /r/. "Bird" was once pronounced with an /i/, "hurt" with a /u/, and "fern" with an /e/—as the inherited spellings indicate. But they all became a centralized vowel, a long one, something like the /ɜː/ we hear today. What else? Up to the time when William Shakespeare was kicking in the womb of Mary Shakespeare, née Arden, /x/ was still to be heard in words like "night" and "bought," though it was either dying or turning into /f/ at the end of words— "though" as /ðoː/ but "tough" as /tuf/. At the beginnings of words the harsh /x/ was changing into our softer /h/—the guttural becoming a mere aspiration. Aspiration is pedantically observed in Ireland and the United States, but not so much in England. There is plenty of evidence to show that it was not taken with schoolroom seriousness in Tudor times. Falstaff talks of an "Ebrew Jew." An owlet was also an "howlet." If sounded at all in lower-class British speech, 'h' is traditionally used in positions of emphasis, and, even then, often wrongly. Thus, "the law is a hass." Consider "I told you to eat my dinner, not to heat it."

Literary scholars rarely take into account such linguistic situations as we have been discussing. What is sometimes called the lang-lit dichotomy persists. But the ways a poet sounded to himself or to his audience must, surely, be considered an aspect of his aesthetic impact. Let us now take one particular poet and relate him, in terms of the sounds of the words he dealt in, to the era in which he lived and wrote.

22.

HOW DID SHAKESPEARE SPEAK HIS LINES?

Born and brought up in Stratford-on-Avon, in the heart of the English Midlands, William Shakespeare undoubtedly spoke a kind of English somewhat different—though not all that different—from the polite language of London. When he became an actor, however, his English would have to accommodate itself to a kind of Received Thespian— a model dialect enunciated from the stage with professional sharpness and clarity. Probably the best exemplar of this theatrical English, also the English of the royal court, was Richard Burbage, chief actor in the Lord Chamberlain's Men, the troupe that, with the accession of James I, was elevated to the King's Men. Earlier in this book I suggested that a particular line spoken by Macbeth, a role that Burbage apparently excelled in, be, as an exercise, transcribed to show the manner in which it would be spoken today. The line is "Time and the hour runs through the roughest day" and the modern pronunciation would be something like /taɪm n̩ ði aʊə rʌnz θru ðə rʌfɪst deɪ/. (The subscript vertical line under /n/ indicates that the consonant is syllabic.) The Elizabethan, or Jacobean, rendering would sound to us very provincial. Let us take a good look at it: /tʌim n̩ ði aur runz θru ðə rufɪst dɛː/.

Shakespeare's English was rhotic: the 'r' in "hour" was pronounced; today it is, at least in RP, a mere vocalic murmur, the neutral vowel schwa. Our modern /ʊ/, as in "bull" and "could," might well have appeared in Burbage's pronunciation as an allophone of the short /u/, so that "runs" and "roughest" would be close to present-day Northern usage. "Day" has the pure vowel of "men" and "then," though lengthened. Try saying "den," then cut off the 'n,' ending with /dɛ/; then prolong the vowel. The pronunciation of "time," still heard in Dublin, would strike the modern ear as something like "toime," since we are used to the /ɔɪ/ diphthong, but the first element is the unrounded vowel of modern "run" and "blood," not yet established as an independent vowel. This single line from *Macbeth*, in the form in which Shakespeare and his audiences heard it, is worth learning by heart.

Let us now take one of Shakespeare's sonnets. He may have read this aloud to his patron the earl of Southampton, and his diction would not have been that of a glover's assistant from Stratford.

> The expense of spirit in a waste of shame
> Is lust in action; and till action lust
> Is perjur'd, murd'rous, bloody, full of blame,
> Savage, extreme, rude, cruel, not to trust.
> Enjoy'd no sooner but despiséd straight,
> Past reason hunted, and no sooner had
> Past reason hated, as a swallow'd bait
> On purpose laid to make the taker mad;
> Mad in pursuit and in possession so,
> Had, having, and in quest to have extreme;
> A bliss in proof and prov'd, a very woe;
> Before, a joy propos'd; behind, a dream.
> All this the world well knows, yet none knows well
> To shun the heaven that leads men to this hell.

This is in modern spelling, except for the apostrophes that appear in "perjur'd," "murd'rous," and so on. "Murd'rous" is a necessary injunction to cut out the syllable 'er,' but the apostrophes in the past participles are something of a convention that lasted well into the eighteenth century. Nobody was likely to say "perjuréd" or "proposéd," but as long as "despiséd" was to be pronounced in the older way, with three syllables, the convention was preserved. We pronounce "beloved" and "aged" (or some of us do) as if we were living in the Middle Ages.

The consonants are all as in Modern English, but we may have some dubiety about the aspirate, which was not, except in emphatic positions, observed. But it is evident here that in "Had, having, and in quest to have," the poet is evoking the panting of an animal. "Hunted" is contrasted with "hated," and "heaven" with "hell," so it is probable that these four words began with a fully enunciated aspirate. All the 'r' signals would have to be obeyed, so that "world" would sound Scottish, as would "purpose" also.

The vowels are, of course, a different matter. "Expense" would be as now, but "spirit" would have a short /i/, not the slack centralized vowel of today. "Waste" and "same" and other words now pronounced with /eɪ/ would have the /ɛ/ of "men," though lengthened. "Lust" and its rhyme would carry the short /u/, soon to become /ʊ/, as in Modern German Lust. "Bloody" would be very Lancastrian. "Extreme," rhyming with "dream," would have the vowel /e:/, in other words, the 'é' of café, though lengthened into 'ééé.' "Reason" would be identical in pronunciation with "raisin" (I have mentioned much earlier Falstaff's pun on the two words—now no longer intelligible). I suspect that "enjoy'd" and "despiséd" contained the same diphthong /ʌi/, confirmed in verses as late as Dryden and even Pope, where "join" and "line" usually rhyme. "So" contained a high /o:/ and was yet to be diphthongized. The same is true of all words now pronounced with /əʊ/ in RP—"do," "know," and so on. If we could be present at Shakespeare's reading aloud of this sonnet, we would find it wholly intelligible but would find it hard to contain our prejudices. We would deplore what we would think of as a provincial pronunciation, having the late Lord Olivier and Sir John Gielgud in mind.

It seems certain that Shakespeare played the part of the Ghost in Hamlet. Imagining the first performances of that tragedy, we can reconstruct for ourselves the authentic voice of the Bard himself.

> Sleeping within mine orchard,
> My custom always in the afternoon,
> Upon my secure hour thy uncle stole
> With juice of curséd hebenon in a vial,
> And in the porches of mine ears did pour
> The leperous distilment, whose effect
> Holds such an enmity with blood of man
> That swift as quicksilver it courses through
> The natural gates and alleys of the body,
> And with a sudden vigour it doth posset

And curd, like eager droppings into milk,
The thin and wholesome blood. So did it mine . . .

There are three words here that compel our attention—"body," "pos-set," and "droppings." The low back vowel /ɒ/ that we use today was not available to the Elizabethans, nor was its unrounded fellow /ɑ/, the sound the doctor makes us make when examining our throats. We can posit an "American" pronunciation for words like "body" in Elizabethan mouths, meaning various short vowels—front, middle, and not all that back—and even including /ʌ/ and /a/. When Hamlet puns on "mouse-trap" and "tropically" he seems to be giving an /æ/ value to "trop-", but the identity of the vowels in the two words is, to my mind or my historical ear, not certain. When, again, Hamlet wishes "this too too solid flesh" to melt, there may be an intended uncertainty about the vowel of "solid"—"sallied" and also "sullied"? We do not know enough about the ancestral short vowels. We know all we need to know about the long ones.

When we move on to the Restoration period and the Age of Reason that followed it, although Alexander Pope clearly pronounced "tea" in the Irish manner, for the most part we find the 'ee' -'ea' opposition disappearing, so that "meet" and "meat" become homophones. We know that /ʌ/ is well established in words like "love" (/luv/ for Shake-speare) by the time of Dr. Samuel Johnson (1709–1784), since his inviting his friends to drink "poonch" is gently mocked. The only real shock we would feel in time-traveling back to the eighteenth century would be in not yet hearing "dance" and "past" with the modern /ɑ:/ of Southern England. Americans at the time of the Revolutionary War would not be speaking a markedly different brand of English from that of the British enemy.

It is not necessary to take on trust everything that linguistic historians say about past English pronunciation. The secretary of the earl of Southampton, and probably Shakespeare's friend, was John Florio (1553?–1625?), an Italian Protestant who compiled a dictionary of English and Italian called A World of Words (1598). Florio gives instructions on the pronunciation of Italian (Tuscan really), which, having no long vowels, has not changed much between Shakespeare's time and our own. Florio says: "For so much as the Italians have two very different sounds for the two vowels E and O which for distinction's sake, they name the one close and the other open." (They still do.) "The close E . . . is pronounced as the English E or Ea, as in these words, Bell, Beane, Den, Deane, Fell, Flea, Meade, Quell, Sell, Tell &c and the open E . . . is ever pronounced as Ai in English, as in these words Baile, Baine, Daine, Faile, Maide, Quaile, Saile, Taile &c . . ." Florio, one thinks, was a close observer of sounds, as he was of meanings:

> Cazzo, *a man's privy member. Also as Cazzica.*
> Cazzolata, *a ladle-full. Also a musical instrument with strings.*
> Cazzo marino, *a Pintle-fish.*
> Cazzo ritto, *a stiffe standing pricke.*
> Cazzuto, *a man that hath a Pricke.*

Florio was not the only lexicographer of the time, though he was one of the best and his dictionary is still useful. We have little excuse for not having at least an elementary notion of how our Elizabethan ancestors spoke. Whether we must regard this as essential to the understanding and aesthetic appreciation of Shakespeare is something we must decide for ourselves. American actors seem pretty sure that their rendering of his plays should approach a modern British standard, as I know from working in the American theater. But the American language, especially in its Northeastern variety, comes closer to the way Shakespeare spoke than does the Thespian of Olivier, Gielgud, and Guinness. Combine a Boston with a Dublin accent and you have a dialect very apt for the man from Stratford. It is time to look at, or listen to, American English.

But, before leaving Shakespeare, let us fix in our minds a small reminder of how he spoke. A man's name is important to himself, and the way Shakespeare said "Shakespeare" (or however he preferred to spell it) can be attached, like a sound track, to his enigmatic image. The "William," with its short vowels, was close enough to our own version, but the surname, which now has the diphthongs /eɪ/ and /ɪə/, carried the two main varieties of 'e,' namely, the /ɛ/ of "met," only longer, and the /e/ of *café*, again prolonged. In other words, two long French sounds—'è' and 'é.' This ought to encourage the French in their belief that the original name was Jacques Père. It was not, of course. "Shakespeare" once meant what it said.

23.

TRANSATLANTIC

The Pilgrim Fathers, refugees from religious intolerance in their native England, sailed from Plymouth for America in 1620, taking their Puritanism with them. They also took their brand of Jacobean English. That English had already been transported to Jamestown, Virginia, in 1607, but the Massachusetts settlement, with Boston built in 1630, represents definitive colonization, stretching up to Maine and down to South Carolina, the irreversible establishment of English on a continent whose native Indian languages had nothing in common with the Indo-European family. The Indian lexis touched this imported English when it reacted to an exotic scene with exotic plants and animals, but the touch was feather-light. The tongues of the Iroquois and the Algonquians were, from the start, destined to be far more foreign than French or German. The Pilgrim Fathers and their successors had no doubt of the supremacy of their faith, culture, and language.

This was the language that Shakespeare had spoken. The new Americans had no poet of his stature, but they did have Mistress Anne Bradstreet (b. 1612? in Northampton, England, d. 1672 in Andover, Massachusetts). To her "dear and loving husband" Simon, for ten years governor of the colony, she wrote:

If ever two were one, then surely we.
If ever man were loved by wife, then thee.
If ever wife was happy in a man,
Compare with me ye women if you can.
I prize thy love more than whole mines of gold,
Of all the riches that the East doth hold.
My love is such that rivers cannot quench,
Nor aught but love from thee give recompense . . .

That bad rhyme cannot be blamed on American pronunciation; it is only fair to state that these verses were not meant for publication and were found after her death among her private papers. Feminist lovers of Mistress Bradstreet in modern America are entitled to recite the poem in modern American; the British will do it in their own way. But the true way is Shakespeare's way.

The English of the American seaboard changed over the centuries, as did the English of England, but we like to look for marks of archaism, or conservatism, in this exported version of the language. We are wrong to believe, as some do, that a kind of genuine Elizabethan language is spoken in places like the southern Appalachians, despite forms like "I'm a-thankin' ye" and the ancient aspirate in "it" ("We'll cook a possum and relish hit"); this was hardly much in evidence in the English of Elizabethan London. Archaisms are distributed everywhere in the United States, along with modernisms. Thus, American English is, for the most part, rhotic: the /r/ after vowels (which has disappeared in RP, though not in many dialects) is heard as it was in Shakespeare's time, although often reduced to a mere coloring. So, in words like "park" and "are," the tongue curls back while enunciating the vowel, producing the ghost of a retroflex 'r.' "Ass" for "arse" does not seem to represent a willingness, on British lines, to make the word arhotic; rather it is a puritanical substitution that forces a real ass to become a donkey or burro. *Each Actor on His Ass*, straight from *Hamlet* and suggested by me as the title for a projected Broadway musical about Shakespeare, was rejected with horror. And yet American speech and American novels are full of "a piece of ass" (a sexual object, not necessarily for sodomy) and "You'll lose your ass" and "Tell him to schlepp his ass round here" (we will come to the Yiddish element later).

The late changes in British English that produced a contrast between "cat" (/kæt/) and "cast" (/kæ:st/, later /kɑ:st/) never touched

America, except perhaps the upper-class reaches of Boston. Nor has the diphthong of "oh" and "old" turned, except in mockery of the British, to /əʊ/. A feature that British English is losing—a contrast between "whales" and "Wales," /ʍ/ versus /w/—is still to be heard in America. The insistence on aspiration, found in all social classes, has no parallel in any British dialect and is more forceful than in any of the most refined versions of RP. The British "Give it to 'im" must seem careless even to a New York taxi driver. On the other hand, American English has lost the aspirate in "herb" and its derivatives. *How to Plant an Herb Garden* must be the sole New York book title incapable of transfer across the Atlantic.

A general feature of most brands of United States English is a "dark" quality that does not apply solely to the lateral consonants in words like "lily" and "lull." It is as though the whole American phonetic system is pushed back farther in the mouth than is the case in Britain. "None" or "nun" is palatal rather than alveolar. If the American voice sounds darker, richer than the British, this may serve the national image of virility (women's voices do not sound, by European standards, all that feminine); Americans consider the British educated voice as higher pitched, when, in fact, the voice is placed farther forward and the phonemes seem to seek what we think of as a European "lightness." This, of course, may be pure fancy, partly anyway.

It is not fanciful to hear a slower rhythm in American speech than in British. The respectively "drawled" and "clipped" qualities can be objectively compared. The American vowel in "bit" takes 18.0 centiseconds to enunciate, the British vowel in the same word only 10.2. On the other hand, there is not much difference when it is a matter of saying "beet": 24.0 centiseconds for the United States, 22.3 for Britain. These are averages, of course, taken from a fairly small sector of speakers, but they correspond to a general judgment of comparison. The more deliberate measure of American speech is spectacularly evinced in its attitude to polysyllables. While the Brits give only one main stress to words like "laboratory" and "dictionary," banging out the first syllable and letting the rest fall away, the American way is to provide a secondary stress—"làboratòry," "dìctionàry." In the Crosby-Hope song in the film *The Road to Morocco* we hear "Like Webster's Diction Airy we're Morocco-bound." The U.S. mode is also the Elizabethan. Shakespeare's "customary" in Hamlet's speech about "customary suits of solemn black" fills up two full feet of the iambic pentameter.

If we take some specific examples of modes in which the Atlantic forms a sound barrier, we had better pay attention to the width and length of North America and note variations. In a swath covering western Pennsylvania, Ohio, Indiana, Illinois, Missouri, and Iowa, and also farther west, what are known as the Middle English /o/ and /au/ classes have merged: "cot" and "caught" are homophones. So are "collar"/"caller," "hock"/"hawk," and a number of other pairs. But in New York and New England the words differ in vowel length, as in Great Britain.

A more arresting phenomenon has affected words like "Mary," "merry," and "marry." The injunction "Marry merry Mary" in most British dialects contains two vowels—/æ/ and /ɛ/ and a diphthong—/ɛə/. In New England, or at least a western portion of it, upper New York State, and a number of territories farther west, you will hear the vowel of "mare" in "Mary" but the vowel of "bet" in both "merry" and "marry." Above the Great Lakes, but mostly with older speakers, the vowels of "merry" and "Mary" have merged into the vowel of "bet," while "marry" carries what RP speakers would consider an orthodox /æ/. But in a great part of the American West the three words sound alike—either /mɛrɪ/ or /mɛərɪ/. This applies, naturally, to other words of the same makeup, so that a fantastic statement like "The fair square staring hairy fairy is very merry when tearing a herring from a barrow" has, to British ears, a startling vocalic monotony.

Another highly noticeable difference between British and American usage is to be found in words like "do" and "dew." The semivowel /j/ makes one different from the other in most varieties of British English—/duː/ versus /djuː/. In America there has been a merger. The /j/ is retained after labials and velars, so that "music" and "cute" are pronounced in the British manner, but other initial consonants permit the loss of the semivowel—Americans sing toons and eat stoo while reading Toosday's noospapers with doo reserve. In Britain there is a certain dubiety about whether to wear a syuit or a soot, or string a lyute or a loot. America shows no dubiety.

This large country will not submit easily to the kind of generalizations I am forced to make about the speech sounds it uses, and the pragmatic split I propose—between the North, the Midlands, and the South—has to be a little impressionistic. Let me start with the varieties of low or lowish o-sound we hear in words like "horse" and "morning." Most British speakers would make a distinction between "horse" and "hoarse," and "morning" and "mourning," and so do most northern American speakers—/ɔ:/ for the first of the duo and /oʊ/ for the second—but things change when we move the tongue farther down. The British have a round short /ɒ/ for words like "wash," "wasp," "log," and "hog," but the American North will not have lip-rounding (any more than the Elizabethans would) and usually have /ɑ/ as in "calm." "Pot" and "cot," with their unvoiced terminal consonants, have a sound pushed somewhat forward, rather like the Lancashire /a/ of "that" but arrested in midchannel as /ä/ (the two dots signifying that the sound is central). So while RP has the same /ɒ/ in "pot" and "pod," a New Yorker, for example, would have /ä/ for the first and /ɑ/ or /ɑə/ for the second. He would also prefer this latter diphthong in a word like "calm," whereas RP would have merely a long /ɑ:/.

The /a/ of Middle English, and of the modern North of England, has gone two ways in RP, but the 'a' of "cat" and the 'a' of "dance" in northern American speech are the same, that is not /æ/ and /ɑ/ but /æ/ only. But the sound of "dance" in RP is long, while the American North is not sure about length. "Have" and "halve" are distinct—/æ/ versus /æ:/—but whether to say /dæns/ or /dæ:ns/ seems to depend on no rule. In popular songs "laugh" and "phonograph" can rhyme, but in speech "-graph" is never lengthened, while "laugh" may be. In some New York speech a difference is heard between "can" as an auxiliary verb and "can" as a receptacle for baked beans, the first being shorter than the second.

Get away from the coastal area and travel to towns like Buffalo, Chicago, and Detroit, and you will find a phenomenon called the Northern Cities Shift in operation. Words like "bat" contain not /æ/ but /ɛə/ as in "bear" or even /ɪə/ as in "beer," and words like "pot" have undergone vocalic fronting—/pat/ or even /pæt/. Apparently New Yorkers visiting Chicago do not know whether they are hearing "lack" or "lock," though they should, in time, realize that Chicago "lack" has a diphthongal quality—almost the sound in New York "fair."

New York City has undergone a great deal of speech study. Naturally, visitors, especially from Europe, hear what they think they ought to hear rather than what they actually do hear. They assume, for instance, that New York is rhotic—pronouncing 'r' where the British would not—but the tradition is, as with RP, arhotic. Pronouncing the 'r' after vowels—as in "park" and "hard"—has been gaining prestige only since World War II. In London this would sound like retrogression to provinciality, but New Yorkers think differently. Visitors think they hear, especially among lower-class speakers, "bird" pronounced like "boyd" (no *r*). But words of the "bird" class actually have the diphthong /əɪ/, which is very different from the /ɔɪ/ of "boyd." Try it. It is the indefinite article followed by the vowel of "it."

A quick glance at the Midlands. Here you will notice that "morning" and "mourning" are pronounced alike, and that "wash," "watch," "hod," and "log" sound British, except that the /ʃ/ of "wash" sometimes drags the vowel up to /ɔ/, often, inexplicably, with an intrusive 'r'—"worsh." Move somewhat south and you start hearing the diphthong of "I" or "bite" turning into a single vowel—/a:/.

In the South proper of magnolia and julep, that diphthong has become a full-blooded /ɑ:/, and "my prize mice" is "mah prahz mahs." On the coast the situation is arhotic, and there not even a linking 'r' in phrases like "far and near." Indeed, the pronunciation of 'r' after a vowel is associated with provincial backwardness (contrast New York), and you will even hear a blank between the vowels of "very." If words like "I" and "my" have been monophthongized, the short vowel /æ/ in "cat" has undergone the opposite process, so that "I can't pass" is /ɑ: kæɪnt pæɪs/. This turning of short vowels into diphthongs—the /ɪ/ of "it" and "his" becomes the diphthong of British "beer"—is associated, falsely of course, with the temperamental languor of the South. Northerners hear what folklore has led them to expect. The hero of Tom Wolfe's novel *The Bonfire of the Vanities* has a girlfriend named Maria. "Sherman? It came out Shuhhh-mun. Sherman was reassured. That was Maria, all right. She had the variety of Southern accent in which half the vowels are pronounced like 'u's, and the other half like short 'i's. Birds were *buds*, pens were *pins*, bombs were *bums*, and envelopes were *invilups*." This is amusing but not very accurate.

Canada speaks an English not so different from that of its sister below the forty-ninth parallel and the Great Lakes. This is because Canada is, linguistically, a transplanted United States in the sense that a great number of "United Empire Loyalists" fled, mostly from New York and New England, the consequences of the American Revolution in the 1780s and settled in the territory still loyal to the motherland.

Not all Americans wished to free themselves from the British yoke. True, Canada had its anglophone as well as francophone settlers from the sixteenth century on, but the linguistic character of the great dominion was determined by that influx from American independence.

There is no isogloss, or language boundary, corresponding to the political frontier. The phenomenon I am about to describe is called Canadian, but it is also to be found in United States territories abutting on Canada. It occurs in words like "bite" and "bide" on the one hand and words like "lout" and "loud" on the other. In RP the diphthong is always /aɪ/ in the first class and /aʊ/ in the second. But, with the so-called Canadian Diphthong Rule, diphthongs in both classes are affected by the sound that comes after. In the first class, an unvoiced consonant makes the diphthong into /əɪ/. We hear this clearly in the Canadian "knife." But the plural "knives" ends in the voiced /vz/, and this turns the diphthong into the regular RP /aɪ/. We can contrast "ripe" with "tribe," "white" with "wide," "ice" with "eyes." With the other class, which in RP has an invariable /aʊ/, "lout" has /ʌʊ/ because of the unvoiced /t/, but "loud," with its voiced /d/, has /aʊ/. That /ʌʊ/ may seem outlandish, but it is merely the 'u' of "but" gliding on to the 'u' of "bull." The /aʊ/ begins with the vowel of "cart" and moves to the "bull" vowel. A sentence like "White ice abides in his eyes" has two distinct diphthongs, and so does one like "His loutish mouth mouths loudly now." "Now" ends with the diphthong, but since this is voiced as much as /d/ is, the rule applies.

If visitors to Canada, and indeed long-settled Canadians, imagine that their English represents a strain totally distinct from what they hear below the border, this is because of a patriotic sentiment that ignores sonic reality. But ties with the homeland make for a tolerance of British modes of speech not always to be found in the United States, where their exoticism is either derided or treated as a piquant curiosity. The veteran Toronto author Robertson Davies speaks with what might be termed a silvery and wholly acceptable Oxford accent. Only a keen ear will detect that he obeys the Canadian Diphthong Rule.

There are items of American pronunciation that lie outside systematic phonemic structure. I mean that there are specific words pronounced in specific ways that do not conform to the usage of the motherland. Thus American "leisure" does not rhyme with "pleasure": it contains /i:/ and rhymes with "please ya." "Tomato" rhymes with "potato," useful in the song Fred Astaire sings: "We could be like a couple of hot tomaters/ But you're as cold as yesterday's mashed potaters." "Clerk" rhymes with "jerk" instead of "dark," though the name Clark or Clarke remembers what is properly an eighteenth-century pronunciation. "University" was once the full form of "varsity," which seems to have disappeared in Britain, although it is used in America in connection with interscholastic sports. The man who "starts" at "quarterback" plays on the "varsity squad." Henry Fielding the magistrate and novelist made a mocking distinction between "virtue" and "vartue"—the first a genuine moral property, the second hypocritical. Americans have been logical in making "clerk" join the shift to /ɜ:/. They are sensible in having /u:/ in the first syllable of lieutenant; the British /f/ is pointless. We may note again the presence of secondary stress in words like "secretary" and "laboratory" and American distaste at the British habit of using only a primary stress in such four-syllable words—"secrtry" and "laboratry." There is, to the carefully articulating Americans, a regrettable flavor of gabble in such usage. As for initial stressing in "margarine" and "research," as opposed to final stressing in British English, this neatly balances the American tendency to emphasize an original light final stress in words from the French, such as "attaché" and, indeed, names like Monet and Debussy.

Let us leave sounds and look at grammar. The difference between British mother and American daughter are not large, and a British reader of American expository prose feels totally at home until he comes to "fit" as a past tense ("This fits his theory") and the past participle "gotten," which has disappeared from Britain (except in dialectical forms, where it often appears as "getten"). American English has two forms of the verb "get" that only come clear in the past tense—"got" in the possessive sense and "gotten," meaning "obtained." British English has to use the one form "got" for both meanings. "He's got the bad habit of belching" is pure possessive, but the impossible form with "gotten" (used by British authors creating American characters) signifies that "he" has sought the habit and found it. British "I've got a pound of fresh liver from the butcher" takes "gotten" over the water.

A British reader of Raymond Chandler's sentence "The Indian smelled" may take it as an error for "smelt," but the '-ed' ending in past forms is regular in America and makes a difference to the sound ('-ed' = /d/ not /t/). I leant over in Britain, but I leaned over (the "leaned" with /i:/) in America. Still on verb forms, though Fred Astaire may ask "Shall we dance?" the 'sh-' forms ("shall" and "should") have given place to 'w-' forms ("will" and "would") in America, the Astaire invitation being regarded as a kind of fossil. "I should like that" becomes "I would like that." As in speech the auxiliary form is shortened to "I'd," (in Britain, too), the nice distinction between the forms is becoming academic in both countries. Of course, "should" expressing obligation is a different matter ("You should have paid him back"), but we are dealing here with the third person "you" and not the first persons "I" and "we."

The lexical differences between the two versions of English are probably too well known to itemize—"dinner jacket" versus "tuxedo," "chemist" versus "drugstore," and so on—and it may be said that the influence of American films on British viewers has made the vocabulary of the daughter country thoroughly familiar. British directors who hope to distribute their films in the United States take care to have Cockneys waiting on the sidewalk and threatening to see their attorneys. The traffic of borrowing seems almost completely one-way, and forms like "I'll take a rain check on that" and "Don't make a presidential issue out of it," common in Britain, have cut themselves loose from their original referents. Americans kindly reciprocate with "It's not cricket" and "Hardly my cup of tea," but not often. Some British speakers get into the habit of saying "elevator" for "lift," probably because a polysyllabic word seems more distinguished, and "faucet" sounds more technical than "tap." Difficulties arise only when a word held in common by both countries has branched into two distinct meanings. British hearers of the song "Walking My Baby Back Home" were uncomfortable with the line "I get her powder all over my vest," seeing this latter as an undershirt when it was merely a waistcoat. "Knickers" has a powerful erotic charge for the British, but the word, coming from the American "knickerbockers," is quite suitable for what one wears on a Florida golf course. "Pecker," as in "Keep your pecker up," is a dangerous expression for a British visitor to the United States to use, since there a pecker is a penis. And to "knock somebody up," meaning in Britain to awaken, means in

America to impregnate. Sex often makes language a minefield, as Anglophones visiting France who use *baiser*, meaning "to kiss," frequently discover.

A generalization—dangerous like all generalizations—that the British sometimes make about American discourse refers to an apparent inability to contrive a neutral mode that is neither pompous nor slangy. That the Americans use a great deal of slang has been regarded as endearing, expressive of the high spirits of a perennially youthful country, and their fondness for the language of technology (in all fields) has been interpreted as being somehow cognate—a love of the striking and unusual and unexpected. The two go together in California, according to Cyra McFadden's *The Serial: A Year in the Life of Marin County.* "Marin's this high-energy trip with all these happening people," as the Holroyds say, the central couple in *The Serial.* Those people are "into" crazes like "Gurdjieff, Silva Mind Control, actualism, analytical tracking, parapsychology, Human Life Styling, postural integration, the Fischer-Hoffman process, hatha and raja yoga, integral massage, orgonomy, palmistry, Neo-Reichian Bodywork and Feldenkreis functional integration"—indeed, one person alone has tried all these, or was into them. Cyra McFadden calls the Bay Area "the consciousness-raising capital of the western world," and the main preoccupation of the region was human relations, hence R. D. Rosen's term "psychobabble" for the dialect of the tribe. At a party in which the Holroyds, after a trial separation, renew their marriage vows and are pronounced "conjoined persons" by the Reverend Spike Thurston, statements like the following would be heard: "Harvey and I are going through the *dynamic* right now, and it's kinda where I'm at. I haven't got a lot of psychic energy left over for social interaction. So whatever it is, maybe you should just run it up by me right there. Off the walk." Note the conjoining of the imprecise with the apparently precise. As also in "She and Harry hadn't finalized the parameters of their own interface." The language has to be renewed and renewed again, and it does not matter whether the materials of the renewal are slang or the lexis of technology. What the mother country misses in the daughter countries—Australasia as well as North America—is a confident mode of middle-class speech that eschews two kinds of jargon—that of the school playground and that of the sophomoric lecture room. Any kind of discourse that has a flavor of the British ruling class, so powerful is ancestral memory, must be strenuously avoided.

The ideal politician, or even president, ought, when not saying "The confrontational parameters are at this time under congressional consideration, and I hope that answers your question, Jim," to be friendly and folksy. Sinclair Lewis's novel *It Can't Happen Here* (1935) has a president in the mode of the cowboy philosopher Will Rogers, Berzelius Windrip, popularly known as Buzz, whose ghosted autobiography *Zero Hour* makes statements like:

> When I was a kid, one time I had an old-maid teacher that used to tell me, "Buzz, you're the thickest-headed dunce in school." But I noticed that she told me this a whole lot oftener than she used to tell the other kids how smart they were, and I came to be the most talked-about scholar in the whole township. The United States isn't so different, and I want to thank a lot of stuffed shirts for their remarks about Yours Truly.

Buzz rules a totalitarian America in which "interlettles" and stuffed shirts are shot or put into concentration camps. But his pronouncements are comforting to the rest: "Like beef steak and potatoes stick to your ribs even if you're working your head off, so the words of the Good Book stick to you in perplexity and tribulation."

In his earlier masterpiece *Babbitt* (1922), Lewis presents the middle-class ethos of a boosting booming postwar America that has not yet taken on the burden of global responsibility and so learned guilt. The speech of George F. Babbitt, real estate broker or, as he would prefer, realtor, is loose, philistine, reactionary, but designed to assert no-nonsense pioneer values modified by urban ambitions—sometimes ruthless but always folksy:

> "How's the old horse-thief?"
> "All right, I guess. How're you, you poor shrimp?"
> "I'm first-rate, you second-hand hunk o' cheese."

He reads Chum Frink's syndicated verse (set as prose: lineation would smack of the highbrow):

> Then when I entered that hotel, I'd look around and say, "Well, well!" For there would be the same news-stand, same magazines

and candies grand, same smokes of famous standard brand, I'd find at home, I'll tell! And when I saw the jolly bunch come waltzing in for eats at lunch, and squaring up in natty duds to platters large of French fried spuds, why then I'd stand right up and bawl, "I've never left my home at all!" And all replete I'd sit me down beside some guy in derby brown upon a lobby chair of plush, and murmur to him in a rush, "Hello Bill, tell me, good old scout, how is your stock a-holdin' out?" Then we'd be off, two solid pals, a-chatterin' like giddy gals of flivvers, weather, home, and wives, lodge-brothers then for all our lives! So when Sam Satan makes you blue, good friend, that's what I'd up and do, for in these States where'er you roam, you never leave your home sweet home.

That sums up an American philosophy of decent material values in a slangy language that converts men, women, and children into guys, gals, and kids. Babbitt, in one of his after-dinner speeches, denies the virtues of skepticism and higher thought: "And when it comes to these blab-mouth, fault-finding, pessimistic, cynical University teachers, let me tell you that during this golden coming year it's just as much our duty to bring influence to have those cusses fired as it is to sell all the real estate and gather in all the good shekels we can." He concludes:

> Not till that is done will our sons and daughters see that the ideal of American manhood and culture isn't a lot of cranks sitting around chewing the rug about their Rights and Wrongs, but a God-fearing, hustling, successful, two-fisted Regular Guy, who belongs to some church with pep and piety to it, who belongs to the Boosters or the Rotarians or the Kiwanis, to the Elks or Moose or Red Men or Knights of Columbus, or to any one of a score of organizations of good, jolly, kidding, laughing, sweating, upstanding, lend-a-handing Royal Good Fellows, who plays hard and works hard, and whose answer to his critics is a square-toed boot that'll teach the grouches and smart alecks to respect the He-man and get out and root for Uncle Samuel, USA!

This mode of discourse is charmingly out of date and has been superseded by attempts at greater sophistication, though with more obscenity. Tom Wolfe's *The Bonfire of the Vanities* (1987), already cited for its inauthentic representation of Southern speech, is authentic

enough on the various levels of New York idiom. Kramer, who works
in the Bronx County district attorney's office, is subjected to abuse
from the wire-meshed wagon that brings in black and Hispanic criminals (they are "the chow," the food that the judicial system eats): "Yo!
Kramer! . . . You cocksucker! . . . Hey, Kramer, you piece a shit! . . .
Yo! Fuckhead! . . . Yo! Kramer! You Hymie asshole! . . . Yo! Kramer!
You faggot! Kiss my ass! . . . Aaaayyyy! Maaaan! Fokky you! Fokky
you!" and so on ("It was a chorus! A rain of garbage!" thinks Kramer.
"A *Rigoletto* from the sewer, from the rancid gullet of the Bronx!").
The judge Kovitsky (called "wormdick" and "you shriveled little
pecker") responds with a well-aimed gob of mucus but also says to
the van driver: "Are you fucking deaf? Your prisoners . . . *your* prisoners . . . You're a officer of the Department of Corrections . . . You
let your prisoners pull . . . this *shit* . . . on the citizens of this community and on the officers of *this court?*" Here the language of abuse is,
in the American manner, not found incongruous with terms of civic
dignity. The mayor of New York has an idiolect that can switch easily
from the legal and formal to the demotic: "We got this Wall Street
guy who runs over a black honor student and takes off. But now it
turns out there was a second black kid, and he's a crack dealer, and
maybe it was a robbery attempt. I guess I take the judicial approach.
I call for a full investigation and a careful weighing of the evidence.
Right?" Sherman, the Wall Street bond dealer, who makes a million
dollars a year, works in an atmosphere in which we hear: "This
Goldman order really fucked things up good!" . . . "—step up to the
fucking plate and" (there are a lot of baseball idioms) . . . "Jesus
Christ, what's going on?" . . . "I don't fucking believe this!" . . . "Holy
fucking shit! Ho-lee fuc-king shit." His wife, full of upward mobility,
speaks as an Englishwoman of her class might be expected to speak.
Mrs. Myra Babbitt, sixty years earlier, approaches Standard English
if not RP:

> "Shall we have the Gulches for our dinner, next week?"
> "Why, sure, you bet."
> "Now see here, George, I want you to put on your nice dinner
> jacket that evening."
> "Rats! The rest of 'em won't want to dress."
> "Of course they will. You remember when you didn't dress for
> the Littlefields' supper party, and all the rest did, and how embar-
> rassed you were."

"Embarrassed, hell! I wasn't embarrassed. Everybody knows I can put on as expensive a Tux as anyone else, and I should worry if I don't happen to have it on sometimes. All a darn nuisance, anyway . . ."

Two different dialects in the same marital bedroom.

English is the tongue of the American Founding Fathers—although H. L. Mencken considered, wrongly I think, that it had separated itself so thoroughly from the mother tongue that it deserved to be called the American Language—but, in some immigrant areas, it has to compete with other vernaculars, particularly Spanish. Only one of the imported languages of the post-revolutionary era seems to have made any impact on urban American English, and that is Yiddish. This is a Germanic dialect with Slavic and Hebrew loanwords. Leo Rosten, who has produced two best-selling books on the way Yiddish has affected the English chiefly of New York City, calls the resultant hybrid Yinglish. Yinglish could be Yankee English or English expressive of the yin as opposed to the yang; Yidglish might be more descriptive. Yidglish is not reserved to American Jews, any more than bagels are, and since show business is an American Jewish province, it was foreseeable that the language of the theater and cinema, even in Britain, should partake of Yidglish idioms, which include modes of emphasis and inversion as well as calques (or loanwords) and straight borrowings from Yiddish. One can hear a British stage producer say, "We need that like a *loch in kop*" (a hole in the head) or "Hamlet he wants to play" or (of a doubtful stage rural accent) "Mummerset yet." The production of plays and films places its participants in situations of stress and despair analogous to those of a whole long-suffering people, and Yidglish provides ironic tropes that contrast dramatically with the agonized cries and lavish curses of the Old Testament. You can rant prophetically in the Sinai desert or wail by the waters of Babylon; in the exile of cities, where nobody listens anyway, you can use Yidglish.

Some Yiddish words and expressions used in English defy translation. Take *Gevalt* (pronounced /gevolt/). The story is told of an obstetrician playing cards with Count Rothschild while his countess lay ready to deliver in her bedroom. She screamed, but he calmly went on playing. And again. And again. Only when she yelled "*Gevalt!*" did he leap to his feet and say, "Now!" Another story: the Nifkovitzes changed their name to Northridge and dined at a goy country club.

The waiter spilled soup on Mrs. Northridge's lap and she cried: "*Gevalt!*—whatever that means." Man, apparently, comes into the world with an *Oy!* and leaves it with a *Gevalt!*

Some idioms with a Yiddish origin have already been so long absorbed into standard American colloquial that it is difficult to establish provenance. "My son-in-law he wants to be" is clearly a Yiddish inversion, and so is the "nominal cancellation" of a curse (Rosten's expression) as in "May a fire burn his heart, God forbid." "Go fight city hall" is, in its rhythm and ellipsis as well as hopelessness, Yidglish, as is "Go talk to the wall," which must refer back to "*Red tsu der vant.*" In "Who paid you, Lefty? C'mon, *give*," the blunt intransitive imperative has a Yiddish flavor. "Enjoy" also is pure Yidglish. Another illustrative story. Nails (or Nate, or, to his momma, Nateleh) Koslovsky, a no-goodnick shot by the Callaghan mob, comes bleeding to death up the stairs. He groans: "Momma, I—" She replies: "Don't talk. First eat. Enjoy. Later you'll talk." Some tropes seem to be of Yiddish origin only by association—such as "Excuse the expression." Rosten tells the story of a lady in a crowded Tel Aviv bus groping for her purse. The man next to her says: "Lady, let me pay." She says: "No, I'll get my purse open." He says: "But till you get it open, you already unbuttoned three buttons on my—excuse the expression—fly." It was perhaps on the same bus that an immigrant Jewish lady talked Yiddish to her son and was rebuked by a fellow passenger for not speaking Hebrew. "I talk Yiddish to him," she said, "so he won't forget he's a Jew." There is some sense in this: to be a Jew, in her opinion, was to remember exile, of which Yiddish is the language (at least for the Ashkenazim). Hebrew is a proud settled national tongue.

A word like *kibitz* seems to be well established in American English because there is no homegrown alternative. To kibitz is to interfere or offer unwanted advice, especially as a spectator at a card game. An outsider who picks up the "box" of a game of cribbage and mutters or tut-tuts at it is a kibitzer. (In German a *Kiebitz* is a busybody.) *Shmaltz* is also a fine borrowing. It means literally the chicken fat used in cooking or for tempering the dryness of chopped liver, but it is a metaphor for richness or excess. "He delivers a line with enough *shmaltz* to fill a shovel" has the noun, while the verb is found in "She *shmaltzed* her speech like it was the Fourth of July." To marry rich is to fall in a *shmaltz-grub* and live in silk and *shmaltz*. The 'shm' cluster, not native to English, is perhaps more interesting than some of the words it initiates (*shmatte* and *shmegegge* and *shmei*, for example). The duplicate with 'shm' is used to denote contempt, as in "fancy-shmancy" and "Oedipus-shmedipus" ("What's it matter what's wrong with him so long as he loves his momma?") and (heard from a Harvard *goy* or gentile) "Data-shmata, I stick to my theory." It is unusual to see so much semantic weight attached to a mere bound morpheme. The response to that should be "Morpheme-shmorpheme."

With Yiddish around, a particular American solecism can probably be excused. If you can play the piano *gut*, you can also play it good. Ernest Hemingway was always talking of "writing good," which has a different flavor from "writing well." Of course, this may be a straight borrowing from German, like *Katzenjammer* for a hangover, but American English prefers the language of Isaac Bashevis Singer to that of Adolf Hitler. One may be a *goy* (*sheygets* if male, *shikse* if not) and still find Yiddish hospitable. In that respect it is close to English.

24.

THE DIALECT BUSINESS

The dialects of overseas English—American, Australasian, and South African—have their origins in the mother country. Just before the Second World War, speaking at the Second International Congress of Phonetic Sciences at University College, London, Professor Hans Kurath complained of the difficulty of studying the speech of New England without a greater knowledge of the speech of Old England:

> Unfortunately the lines leading back to the Mother Country, and to Northern Ireland, will remain vague and tentative until a linguistic atlas of the British Isles is made . . . for the great majority of colonists of the seventeenth century, whose descendants remained the most influential element in America during the eighteenth century and after, did not speak the cultivated speech of London, but various English dialects or provincial standards. These we know only very imperfectly through contemporary evidence. They must be reconstructed very largely on the basis of a linguistic atlas of English folk speech of the present day.

I will come to this question of a linguistic atlas in a moment. What Kurath said about American speech applies equally to Australian speech, except that the term "folk," with its rural associations, does not seem to apply to what was spoken by the convicts transported to Botany Bay. One associates crime with towns more than with fields and hedgerows, and the criminals who, with an admixture of free immigrants, made up the original English-speaking population of Australia, spoke a dialect that can roughly be identified with that of working-class London. The first migration of about 1500—half convicts and half military personnel and officials—landed at Sydney Cove in 1788 (in January; the more ignorant were surprised to find themselves sweltering in an antipodean summer), and transportation was abolished in 1851, so that Australian English may be thought of as a kind of fossilized Cockney of the Dickensian era. The point is that the great dominion has made its language out of a dialect that, to the cultivated who speak RP, has a debased flavor.

Before, following Hans Kurath's wish, we go into the English countryside, let us take a brief glance at this London English. What we note about its front vowels—in words like "bit" and "bet" and "bat"— is a tendency to raise them by one step. Modern London "bit" is close to the Australian version, imparting an /i/ quality to the vowel. Similarly, "bet" is closer to "bait"—a short /e/ as in *café* rather than the full diphthong /eɪ/—and "bat" is raised to something approaching "bet." Words of the "foot" class and the "pot" class have pretty much the same vowel as in RP, but that damnably unstable /ʌ/ as in RP "love" has become a kind of /a/. It is not the fully forward /a/ one hears in Lancashire "man": it is farther back in the mouth.

It is the long vowels and diphthongs of London English that cause most trouble to RP speakers who try to imitate them. A word like "beet" has, in cultivated Southern speech, a straightforward /i:/, but both Australia and London turn it into a diphthong—a centralized /ɪ/ as in "bit" gliding on to a short /i/. The /u:/ of RP "boot" is pushed into the middle of the mouth in London, but Australia, while retaining that ancestral sound, precedes it with a brief /ʊ/ as in "put." The most characteristic diphthong of both London and Australian speech is the one in "mate." This word is popularly supposed to be pronounced "mite," but this is not quite true. The first element of the diphthong is closer to the /æ/ of RP "man" than to /a/. This applies also to the first element in the diphthong of "out"; the /æ/ glides on to /ʊ/. What makes Australian speech archaic is the presence of /a/ in words like "fast"—a short version regarded as less posh than a long one; present-day London English is at one with RP in preferring /ɑ:/. Where Australia wholly parts company with London is in turning

/ɪ/ into schwa in forms like "eat it." Thus, "penis" rhymes with "Venus," which seems fitting.

What applies to Australia applies also to New Zealand, except for a few inevitable variants—New Zealand may be regarded as a linguistic colony of its large neighbor. The consciousness in both countries of the elevation of a substandard dialect into a national tongue has been responsible for a mixture of attitudes to citizens of the mother country—inferiority, defiance, and contempt. A blending of the first two may be responsible for the upward intonation pattern of answers, more appropriate to questions: "Where were you swimming?"—"On Bondi Beach," with a lift on the last word. I shall say something about antipodean slang later; for now it is enough to note that slang is of its nature defiant. It is also demotic—the colorful speech of the people who set themselves in opposition to the ruling class. But the ruling class of Australia is itself demotic. Lower-middle-class Australian speech has made itself widely known through popular television series and a flourishing film industry, but Australians who reverse the historical emigration pattern by returning to the mother country are rarely, except in deliberately comic exploitation, prepared to go the whole Australian hog. They compromise and sometimes assimilate.

In terms of its national and colonial spread, Standard English with Received Pronunciation is not as important as its speakers think. It remains, to Americans and Australians alike, the property of a disdainful ruling class that was never driven, by crime or economic necessity, into the agony of emigration. And in England itself it has not, despite the standard set by radio and television newscasters, prevailed as much as was once hoped or feared. The town dialects are still alive. It is clear, though, that the country dialects are dying. The plea made by Hans Kurath, for a "linguistic atlas of English folk speech" has been slow to be answered, but the necessity of the enterprise as seen by two scholars—one British, the late Harold Orton, and the other, Eugen Dieth, of the University of Zürich—in the prewar years.

Little could be done before 1945, when Dieth resumed a six-year-lapsed correspondence with Orton and spoke of the urgency of the need to start dialect mapping while there was still something to map. After the "ploughing up of a good deal of the linguistic ground" owing to the enforced wartime mixing of peoples, the stability of the English regional dialects had been impaired. The process was to be sped by new habits of social mobility and the influence of radio and television. By the end of the summer of 1947, Orton and Dieth had produced their first version of the questionnaire for field-workers.

These field-workers traveled mainly to English villages with small and stable populations, seeking chiefly men over sixty "with good mouths, teeth and hearing" who would answer questions like "What do you call the red-hot things that fall through the grate when the fire is burning?" or "What is the month before May?" The inquirers were after four things—phonology, lexis, morphology, and syntax, resolving into four kinds of map. Men were found to be more conservative and more honest than women—or rather women exhibited an interest in upward or outward mobility that militated against their giving the right answer. Lexically, there was never a wrong answer to give about that fruit on that tree over there, but the way to pronounce "apple" was the subject of the first phonological map. I am unable to reproduce it here, but the reader undoubtedly has a rough image of England in his mind. There is a huge swath of the country, from the Scottish border to the deep Midlands, where the "apple" vowel is /a/ as in French *patte* while the RP sound /æ/ is confined to a slender slice of the Southeast, part of the West Country, and, for some inexplicable reason, the Isle of Man. There are eccentric areas where the first vowel of "apple" is pushed back to the /ɒ/ of "hot" and up to the /ɛ/ of "get." There seems to be no pattern in all this: neither history nor geography grants an explanation.

Arrive at the word "Tuesday" and you face an immense phonological variety. The Northeast and nearly the whole of the East are loyal to the Middle English 'tiu-,' but there are pockets where "chu-' and 'tu-' can be heard, and there is a small slab near the Wash where the vowel approaches the schwa. This area of usage waves across at a central Midland region of identical usage, with a whole waste of regular 'tiu-' standing in the way. Just over a hundred years ago, when Prince Louis-Lucien Bonaparte made vicarious amends for his family's hatred of England by helping to pioneer English language studies, it was noted that isoglosses, or language frontiers, did not work out in terms of county and culture. The prince (a man, it was said, very interested in what a Suffolk farmer would say to his cow) found dialect features just where they ought not to be. There is nothing tidy about the distribution of English dialects. Why should Devon, in its pronunciation of "Tuesday," use a vowel that is a rounded version of the one in "fit"—/ʏ/ in the IPA? One expects to hear this only in German.

Speakers of RP tell the world that the word "worm" is pronounced /wɜːm/—a long schwa with no 'r' after it—but great tracts of the country opt for the historical 'r,' as much of America does, a fricative or a tap or, as in the far Northeast, something *grasséyé* as in French— the soft throaty growl. Almost the entire South and Midlands agree on "sheaf" (derived from the Middle English "scef" with a long /eː/ regularly raised to /iː/), but there are areas where the Middle Low German seems to be commemorated with something like "shoff" or "shoof" or even "shuff." The bewildering thing is the lack of grada- tion. In the far Northeast you will get as good a "sheaf" as in London, but the train runs south through "sheff" and "shaff" and "shofe" before you hit /iː/ again.

It is, inevitably, the vocabulary of rural occupations, which do not greatly interest the language courts of the capital or the older universities, that provide the richest variety of nomenclature. Take the decayed craft of thatching, for instance. The ropes used in the process are called billy-bands, binder-bands, coconut-bands, hay- bands, hazel-bands, pitch-bands, stack-bands, straw-bands, tar-bands, tarmarl-bands, thacking-bands, thumb-bonds, coir-rope (a borrowing from Malay *kayer*), over-ropes, reeden-ropes, thumb-ropes, and thumb-simes. The pegs are rick-pegs, thack-pegs, stack-prods, rick- spars, stack-pelks, rick-sprays, and stack-stobs. A donkey is called a cuddy, a dicky, a neddy, an ass, a fussock, a fussanock, a moke, a mokus, a nirrup, a jack nirrup, a bronkus, or a pronkus. "Cuddy" is not, on the appropriate map, given as a form used in my native Lancashire, but many pubs named for a horse, white or black or gray, are popularly The Cuddy, even in sophisticated Liverpool. The name is derived from "Cuthbert," which is given to the ass in medieval bestiaries. Most of England is content with "gosling," but the West prefers "gull," and "gib" is to be heard in Lincolnshire. The Northern "gesling" preserves the Middle English "geslying," itself from the Old Norse *gœslinger*.

Earth closets are necessaries or dikes or dunnekins (dunnies in Australia) or shithouses or petty holes. "Petty" is the term I remember as being regularly in use in my Lancashire childhood. A slice of meat is a slice of meat everywhere except in Norfolk, where it is a round, and on the Lancashire-Yorkshire border, where it is a slishe, and in my native region, where it is still a shive. "Dip," according to a map that deals with bacon fat, is mainly confined to Yorkshire, but it was the regular word in my boyhood in Manchester. It seems to be a version of "dripping," but it was always assumed that it was so called because one dipped one's bread in it.

As for morphology, there are many changes to be rung on basic forms like "I'm not" and "aren't" and "are you?" Standard English decrees a norm for the past tense of "come," but "came" is comparatively rare. You can travel from Penzance to Hadrian's Wall and hear "come" or "comed." Nor does the '-ing' present participle ending enjoy as much clout as printing would have us believe. "Laughing" as "laughin" or "laughen" or "laughn" (with a syllabic 'n') is widely preferred. But the verbal noun from "write" is everywhere curiously genteel—"writing." Perhaps because it is a genteel activity.

Devon and Cornwall prefer "We put on the light" to "We put the light on," which is standard usage nearly everywhere else. The "on Friday week" picture is like a harlequin quilt, with its "next Friday" and "next Friday week" and "a week on Friday" and "a week next Friday" and "a week come Friday" and "a week Friday." One finds all the varieties of the feminine pronoun—"she" and "sha" and "her" and "he" and "hoo" (I have yet to hear that 'h'). And muryans, pismires, pissy-beds, pissy-mices, pissy-motes, and pissy-mothers are as busy as emmets. Go to the pissy-mother, thou sluggard. Plenty of thouing and theeing, too. All this bewildering wealth of dialect is to be found in Harold Orton, Stewart Sanderson, and John Widdowson's *The Linguistic Atlas of England*. A great deal of it is dying, especially the lexis. The phonology, following Saussure's doctrine of linguistic inertia, keeps alive, but the sounds of regional English are best heard in the towns. They gain prestige only when they travel abroad and become the standard speech of independent nations. If convicts had been transported to Australia from the Liverpool or Hull area, the antipodean standard would be very different from what it is.

The prestige of Standard English with its Received Pronunciation had, as we have seen, its origin in a particular location, but that prestige transcended place and became attached to culture, political power, and, to some extent, wealth. It is still taken seriously, but not as seriously as it was. The "network English" of American newscasters, which eschews strongly regional features, has a powerful worldwide authority: there is an American news service available on television in international hotels. An international English, also artificially national, certainly not regional. But it may be said that whether in America or Australasia or, for that matter, South Africa, a particular region has prevailed, and that region is the Southeast of England. America may wince at /dɑ:ns/ and educated England at /dæns/, but both wince equally at "love" and "shove" pronounced with the vowel of "bull" and "full." The English North, which rejected the Great Vowel Shift, is accepted as the fount of tough industrialism and music-hall comedians, but its accent never pierced the heart of culture.

And yet it very occasionally happens that a particular cultural phenomenon grants a temporary prestige to a regional dialect—or, strictly, a regional accent. The prewar popularity of the Lancashire entertainer Gracie Fields, who took her accent to America with some success (university professors went to hear her and found remnants of Shakespeare's English in her vowels), and of George Formby, Jr., who never crossed the Atlantic but made immensely profitable "Manchester films," represented a slight boost for a formerly disregarded mode of speech, though mere entertainers do not make history. But with the emergence of the Beatles in the 1960s, and their huge international popularity, the type of Merseyside speech known as "Scouse" attained a prestige that was later enhanced by the "Liverpool poets." A subculture became not merely respectable but an aspect of serious art: one found John Lennon's lyrics in anthologies and structural analyses of Paul McCartney's melodies in musical textbooks. I am encouraged to examine the phonetics of Scouse. The term, by the way, comes from "lobscouse," a sailor's dish known widely in the maritime North (one can buy it in cans in Oslo). It consists of corned beef, onions, and diced potatoes (or sometimes hardtack), stewed. The "lob" is a dialect word for "boil," and "scouse," cognate with "souse" and "sauce," means a soup or a ragout.

Scouse is strictly a North Midland dialect with characteristic Western features. The final '-ing' of present participles has a Chaucerian added /g/. "One" and "won" are distinct forms, as is usual in the North; "one" rhymes with "gone." The "fair" and "hurt" classes have merged, "fair" sounding like "fur," though not always with the /ɜ:/ of RP. The preferred vowel seems to be a retracted /e/ or /ɛ/, with lengthening, so that both "fair" and "fur" can be transcribed as /fë:/ or /fë:/. Consonants seem to show Irish influence, inevitable when there is so large an Irish working-class population, so that voiceless stops like /p/ and /t/ and /k/ are affricated. This means that /t/ ends with an /s/ quality, "kill" has a "Bach" fricative, /x/; and "back" can end with a full /x/ as /bax/, though what may be written as /kx/ is commoner. The fricatives of "thin" and "then" sometimes change to /t/ and /d/ on the Irish pattern. For the rest, Scouse draws on the general Northern pool—/dans/ not /dɑ:ns/, and "love" with an unreformed /ʊ/. I once traveled on an airplane next to young New Yorkers and Californians visiting Liverpool as Muslims visit Mecca, all attempting the Scouse twang. But the Beatles fad is over, and the prestige of Liverpool speech nearly dead. Regional dialects have to become national tongues before they can attain lasting glory. As with America, as with Australia. Scottish is different because Scotland considers itself to be a nation. Its language deserves a chapter to itself.

25.

SCOTS, SCOTTIS, SCOTTISH, SCOTCH

*A **dialect that*** waves a flag may be called a language. The Scots dialect of English called itself Scottis as long ago as the end of the fifteenth century, asserting a difference from Inglis. It had literary status, a large prose and verse tradition, and a marked dissimilarity of sound, lexis, and, to some extent, morphology and syntax from its southern neighbor. Strictly, the Scots should not have been using it at all, being, until the seventeenth century, a Celtic nation speaking Gaelic, a language close enough to the Erse of Ireland to be identical with it. The English brought English, but their presence was explained by the fact that the territory between the Forth and the Tweed was originally part of the kingdom of Northumbria. They kept to the south, to the Lowlands that gave the term Lallans to the Scottis language. In 973 the Forth-Tweed area was ceded to King Kenneth II by King Edgar, and this placed a fair-sized English-speaking population under the Scottish Crown. Until about the fourteenth century, it was impossible to regard the Scottish border as an isogloss: the language of Northumbria was more or less the same as Scots, Scottis, Scottish, or Scotch—the true term has always been in doubt: "Scotch" is nowadays rejected except as the generic term for *uisge beatha* or *usquebaugh* or the water of life.

Before the Norman Conquest, there was a fair contact between this

Northern English and its Southern sister: Malcolm III MacDuncan, for instance, spent three years at the court of Edward the Confessor and married a princess of the English house. After the Conquest, there was a flood of Anglo-Saxon refugees from William's rule, and a number of Normans followed. There was no enforcement of English on the Scottish nation until the Jacobite risings of 1715 and 1745, which sadly failed (I speak as a member of a Jacobite family). The less decisive Anglo-Scottish wars of the Middle Ages affirmed the existence of two nations that were both, in their different ways, anglophone. Gaelic, which could have pointed Scottish separatism, was confined to the Highlands and the Isles, except for Orkney and Shetland, which used Icelandic. Where the extreme North now speaks English, it is in a Southern form that owes everything to the consequences of the failed risings of 1715 and 1745.

Although Scots has developed in its own manner, it could not easily evade the influence of London, especially as regards literary culture. It was a matter of the prestige that is associated with political power. Independence from England has for long been a Scottish dream that may, with the formation of the new Europe, be in some measure realized, but the cry for "fredome" from John Barbour (d. 1395) has a wistful rather than a defiant note:

A! Fredome is a noble thing!
Fredome mays man to haiff liking;
Fredome all solace to man giffis,
He levys at ese that frely levys!
A noble hart may haiff none ese,
Na ellys nocht that may him plese,
Gyff fredome fail; for fre liking
Is yarnyt our all othir thing . . .

This comes from his long poem *The Bruce*. Barbour, though a clergyman of Aberdeen, seems to have taught at the universities of both Oxford and Paris: the devotion to Scots or Scottis was no indication of an extreme provincialism. The term "provincialism," in fact, becomes applicable to Scots only with the appearance of an official translation of the Bible in 1560—the so-called Geneva version—which was used to teach Scottish children to read. It is only in our century that Scots has defied the imposition of the Southern biblical norm with a translation of the New Testament by William Lorimer (1983). It is vigorous and, it may be said, tendentious, since Standard English is spoken only by the Devil. Here is a specimen:

> As he gaed yont the gate frae there, he saw a man caa'd Matthew sittin at his dask i the Towbuid, an he said til him, "Fallow me"; an he rase an fallowt him.
>
> Efterhin he was i the house, lyin at the buird, an belyve a guid wheen taxuplifters an siclike outlans cam ben an lay doun aside Jesus an his disciples. Whan the Pharisees saw it, they said til his disciples, "What for taks your Maister his mait wi tax-uplifters an siclike outlans?"

Lorimer's translation may be taken as an aspect of a somewhat artificial renaissance of Scots as a serious language. With the hegemony of London English, the use of Scots in literature began to move below the salt, to become proper for low-life humor, rustic simplicity, and artless song. One thinks naturally of Robert Burns (1759–1796) with:

> Till a' the seas gang dry, my dear,
>   And the rocks melt wi' the sun:
> O I will love thee still, my dear,
>   While the sands o' life shall run.

But Burns could be inflammatory, too:

> Heard ye o' the Tree o' France,
>   And wat ye what's the name on't?
> Around it a' the patriots dance—
>   Well Europe kens the fame on't!
> It stands where ance the Bastille stood—
>   A prison built by kings, man,
> When Superstition's hellish brood
>   Kept France in leading-strings, man.

Here, though, the theme being of intense seriousness, Burns cannot easily avoid the literary idiom of England.

Christopher M. Grieve (1892–1978) determined to revive Lallans or Lowlands Scots as a literary language of European scope. His first experiments were produced under the pen name of Hugh MacDiar-mid—a pseudonym he could disavow if his experiments failed. They succeeded, and "MacDiarmid" supplanted his true name. Here is "The Watergaw" ("The Rainbow"):

> Ae wet forenicht i' the yow-trummle
> I saw yon antrin thing,
> A watergaw wi' its chitterin' licht
> Ayont the on-ding;
> An' I thocht o' the last wild look ye gied
> Afore ye deed!

> There was nae reek i' the laverock's hoose
> That nicht—an' nane i' mine;
> But I hae thocht o' that foolish licht
> Ever sin' syne;
> An' I think that mebbe at last I ken
> What your look meant then.

This, I think, requires translation:

> Before nightfall in the cold wind
> I saw that fleeting thing,
> A rainbow with its shivering light
> Beyond the storm;
> And I thought of the last wild look you gave
> Before you died!

> There was no smoke in the house of the lark
> That night—and none in mine;
> But I have thought of that foolish light
> Ever since;
> And I think that perhaps at last I know
> What your look meant then.

The following, which is about the sundering of Scotland from England, is clear enough, except for that "rax," meaning "reach."

> If there's a sword-like sang
> That can cut Scotland clear
> O' a' the warld beside

Rax me the hilt o't here.
For there's nae jewel till
Frae the rest o' earth it's free,
With the starry separateness
I'd fain to Scotland gie.

And here MacDiarmid mourns in pure English:

The rose of all the world is not for me.
I want for my part
Only the little white rose of Scotland
That smells sharp and sweet—and breaks the heart.

The languages of the North and South have traditionally been employed separately and together by Scottish writers, but one must hear the Standard English, whether in Burns or in MacDiarmid, dressed in a kilt and sporran. The sound system of Scots touches RP at several points, but there are significant differences. Scots does not use vowel length in the English manner. In what we may term Standard Scottish English, a word like "beet" has no long /iː/; SSE prefers /bit/. This gives Sassenach listeners the illusion that they are hearing something like /bɪt/ with a raised /ɪ/. A word like "bit" is much the same in SSE and RP, but there is a more demotic version with the /ɪ/ lowered almost to the /ɛ/ of "bet." The diphthong /eɪ/ in RP "mate" is a short /e/ in Scotland, but while "met" is the same in both types of English, words like "never," "ever," "seven," "leopard," "next," "bury," and "herd" sometimes have a centralized version of /ɛ/, represented phonetically as /ë/.

"Bat" and "palm" have two distinct vowels south of the border, the first short and the second long, but SSE prefers a short /a/ for both. The lack of vowel length enables a Scottish poet to rhyme "pot" with "bought" (/ɔ/ for both). Words of the "boat" class have a pure short /o/, lost in RP. "Boot" and "book," in the general Northern manner, have the same vowel /ü/—a centralized "blue" vowel, commoner in the whole of Great Britain than is sometimes believed. The Scot and the Southern Englishman will pronounce "but" in the same way— /bʌt/—but that /ʌ/ is used in SSE to begin the diphthong in "bite" and also "out." "Boy" begins with /ɔ/ in the Sassenach manner but ends in a tongue movement toward /e/.

There are certain subtleties to be noted in the Scots use of vowels.

If, for instance, we hear a short /i/ in "beet," "lea," and "east," we hear a longish one in "bee," "fear," "wreathe," and "breeze." Evidently the final /r/ and the voiced fricatives /vŏz/ are exerting an influence, as well as the zero ending (as in "bee"), which enables the vowel to float freely. The diphthong in "bite," "bide," and "life" is normally /ʌi/, but there is a total change of substance in words like "buy," "fire," "lithe," and "rise," where we hear /a·e/, the /a/ achieving a half-length appropriate, in RP, to a vowel coming before an unvoiced consonant—/bi·t/, for example. It is interesting to note also that grammatical form affects vowel length. "Greed" has a short /i/, giving us /grid/ as opposed to RP /gri:d/, but "agreed" has full vowel length in the RP manner. There are similar contrasts between "brood" and "brewed" (/ü/ versus /ü:/), "staid" and "stayed" (/sted/ versus /ste:d/), and "road" and "rowed" (/rod/ versus /ro:d/). That past ending, which should be purely a grammatical matter, intrudes into the field of phonology.

All varieties of Scots English are rhotic, retaining a full-bodied /r/ regarded as highly characteristic of the dialect (or language), and these seem to have kept in place a series of vowel distinctions lost in RP. I refer to the vowel in "first" and "heard," "herd" and "word," words pronounced in RP with an invariable /ɛ:/ and, of course, no /r/ after. But Scots pronounces "first" as /fɪrst/, "heard" as /hɛrd/, "herd" as /hёrd/ (the /ё/ being a centralized or tongue-thrust-back version of the vowel of "men"), and "word" as /wʌrd/.

Scots has one consonant made memorable by Harry Lauder songs ("If ye can say 'It's a braw bricht moonlicht nicht,' ye're a' richt, ye ken"), now totally lost to RP except when there is an attempt to pronounce Scots and Welsh place-names accurately. Even Sassenachs refer to the /lox nes/ Monster and can say "Och" (/ox/). There is a full contrast also between /w/ and /ʍ/, so that "whale" and "wail" are never homophones. The glottal stop /ʔ/, usually deplored when made to do duty for most of the unvoiced stops in Southeastern English, is acceptable in Scots. "Saturday" as /sæʔdɪ/ sounds slack when heard in the Home Counties, but Will Fyffe's /saʔrde/ is full-blooded.

A discussion of SSE leaves out of the question a great number of dialectal variations. An assertion that /a/ always does service for words like "gather" and "father" has to be humbled by the discovery of vigorous /a/-/ɑ/ opposition with some educated speakers. James Boswell was annoyed when one of his Edinburgh friends, referring to Dr. Samuel Johnson, asked "How is Sahmuel?" You will hear "gather" with an "ah" or /ɑ/, and also "salmon" pronounced as though it were a derivative of "psalm." Strictly, Boswell's friend should have remembered that he would say "Sam sings a psalm" with a contrast of /a/ and /ɑ/. He seems to have been eager to demonstrate that he had /ɑ/ in his inventory. Or it may have been a kind of mockery of English pretentiousness. The implications of speech are very subtle.

A spectacular instance of vocalic fantasy is to be found in the Angus approach to the vowels in "book," "bull," "foot," "boot," "lose," and "loose." RP shares /ʊ/ and /u:/ between them, and Standard Scots is satisfied with the centralized /u/ for the lot. But the speakers of the Angus dialect use /u/ for "book," /ʌ/ for "bull," /ɪ/ for "foot," /ø/ for "boot" (as though it were a hypothetical German *Böt*), /o/ for "lose," and /ʌu/ for "loose." The principle of upward or outward mobility is probably killing these variations. Indeed, the notion of status is inimical to prized Scots features like the ancient vowel in "house" and "mouse," especially in cities like Edinburgh and Glasgow.

The vocabulary of Scots fascinates Sassenachs, who usually fail to recognize that certain of its features were in common English use before the winds of change blew in from across the Channel or, without outside influence, events like the Great Vowel Shift decided to occur. Forms found in Robert Burns, like "mousie" and "beastie," seem whimsical, but probably record a fading awareness of a Middle English ending. "Wee"—properly, as the high vowel suggests, meaning extremely rather than merely small—is good Old English *wæg*. Words like "gar" and "bairn" are pure Scandinavian. "Gey" for "very," in both Scots and Northumbrian, appears to be a variant of "gay" that needs a good deal of semantic investigation. "Aye" for "yes" is, of course, generally Northern, as is "nay." Forms like "my ain hame" represent a vowel transformation from Old English /a:/, which preferred the spread-lipped high front of the mouth to the rounded high back. "Ane" and "one" are both originally Old English *ān*. In other words, the sound changes that Scots has undergone are as regular and authentic as anything that happened down south.

Scots may be said to have its own grammatical features, most notably in the expression of negatives. There is an avoidance of what is termed the cliticizing of "not" onto "will," so that English "I won't go" appears as "I'll not go," and "Will you not do it?" replaces "Won't you do it?" Cliticizing takes place, however, when the form '-na' or '-nae' is screwed on to the end of "can," as in "I canna(e) do it." We hear that reduced negative (the 't' has disappeared) in "I'll no do it" and "Can you no do it?" It becomes "ne" or "ny" or "nie" (pronounced

/ne/) after "does," and "does" itself becomes /dɪz/. To Professor Roger
Lass I owe the following Scots children's riddle: "What's the difference between Mickey Mouse and the man that invented him?" Answer: "Mickey Mouse got big ears and Walt Disney."

I must avoid saying that Scots is a fine language worthy of preservation, since no language admits nonlinguistic evaluation, and if a language dies, mortality must be accepted as the lot it shares with its
speakers. That it has produced a fine literature there is no doubt. It
is a literature we associate with terseness, honesty, and an incapacity
to deceive or tergiversate. I will end with another poem of Hugh
MacDiarmid entitled "Supper to God."

S'ud ye ha'e to gi'e
His supper to God
What like fare
'Ud ye set on the brod?

Lint-white linen
An siller-ware
And a tassie o' floo'ers
in the centre there?

Pot-luck 'ud be best,
I need ha'e nae fear
Gin God s'ud come
To's supper here.

Deal scrubbed like snaw
And blue-and-white delf
And let ilk ane
Rax oot for hisself.

A' that I'd ask
Is no' to ken whan,
Or gin it's Him
Or a trev'lin man.

Wi' powsoudie or drummock
Lapper-milk kebbuck and farle,
We can eye wecht the wame
Of anither puir carle.

The menu consists of sheepshead broth or oatmeal and water, butter-milk, cheese, and oatcake. "Wecht the wame" means "load (weight the belly (womb)." The artistic effect of this poem is strictly based on the resources of the language; this makes it untranslatable. Untrans-latability ought to ensure the survival of a literature. Burns has sur-vived and so will MacDiarmid. But not many Scots will read him.

26.

THEIR OWN THING

Languages can have evil associations—German with the Holocaust, Russian with the Stalinist terror, English (but also Spanish, Portuguese, and Dutch) with black slavery. It cannot be said too often that nothing capable of a moral assessment inheres in a language; it remains neutral and innocuous, though there are demagogues who do not find it in their interest to think so. Britain, and the United States after, gave English of a kind to its slave plantations; the concomitant decay of the African languages the slaves spoke must be regarded as a bad thing. When Britain abolished the slave trade at the beginning of the nineteenth century, manumission meant handing over the language of the former masters to free but often hapless black communities. Slavery was a deracinating device; black speech based on English is a language of deracination—what I have already referred to as a *creole*.

Krio, the language of the African West Coast, clearly gets its name from *creole*, but the oppressive associations have now vanished. Its center is Freetown, whither West Indian slaves were sent on the breaking of their chains, and there it flourishes as a mixture of English and Yoruba, an African tongue, with such other elements as Portuguese, which provides the preposition *na*, meaning "in," as well as some lexical items. There is a danger that uninformed or bigoted white people may see in Krio, as in other black forms of speech with an overwhelmingly English content, a debased attempt to speak "proper" English. This, as we shall see, is a prejudice that particularly applies to the ghetto speech of American blacks. It is monstrous to regard Krio as anything but a national tongue in its own right. Its grammatical structure is mainly African, as is its system of tones (as in Chinese), and its phonemes bear only an accidental relation to those of English. It has recently acquired a dictionary, compiled by Clifford N. Pyle and Eldred D. Jones, both native Krio speakers. Let us examine some items, taken necessarily at random from this massive work.

I select some entries under 'm.' *Manpus* for a tomcat and *man og* for a male pig may seem quaint or childishly poetic, but not to an ear attuned to African classificatory systems. *Manyuel labo* is manual labor and a *manyual ogan* is a church organ powered by hand-operated bellows. *Maogani* is mahogany. *Manzhe* is clearly a French borrowing, but it signifies eating only in a humorous sense. *Mao* is to steal, often brutally, but it is also to eat heartily or to be initiated into certain secret rituals. The word comes from Yoruba. *Mara*, from Mende, means to behave foolishly or coquettishly. If *marabu*, ultimately from Arabic, means a Muslim hermit or monk, then *marabu wachnet* (watch-night) means the eve of Ramadan, and a *marabu skul* is a school where you study the Koran. A *mangromonki*, or mango monkey, is a child fond of tree climbing. A child who can claim sailors as putative fathers is a *manawa pikin* or man-o'-war pickaninny.

The jargon of politics finds its way into the colloquial vocabulary. If *mandet* derives from "mandate" and means authority to act, then you can say: *U gi yu mandet fo go tok lek dat?*"—"Who gave you the right to talk in that manner?" There are plenty of idioms taken from the Christian missionaries—*mana from evin* and *mana indi wildanes; lov so amezin*—a jibe at persons who display overmuch affection (straight from Isaac Watts: "love so amazing, so divine"). *Jizos* is who we think it is—as in *Jizos avmasi* (have mercy), *Jizos awa fade, Jizyu frend of sina. God buk* is the Bible ("God" and "good" conjoined). If you say *God de wit* of a person, then that person is under divine protection. The great opposition is between *God en mamon.*

So far the language does not seem particularly foreign. But try this: *Ef uman drim bot snek, i go sun ge beleh*, which means "If a woman dreams of a snake, she will soon become pregnant." Or this: *Ef yu drim draifis, da min kowngowsa, oh pikin go dai*: "If you dream about dried fish, that means gossip, or else a child will die." I take these two dream interpretations from Professor Ian F. Hancock's compilation, made in Austin, Texas. Hancock collected his folklore from Krio speakers in Canada, Britain, and the United States. The language has certainly traveled.

There will be some too ready to shake their heads at the Krio-speaking blacks who have no wish to graduate, as it were, to the Standard English of West Coast bureaucrats. The same situation of contempt and wonder is to be found, rather more predictably, in the United States in connection with Black English, which is close enough to the white version ("the king's jive") to seem to be an eliminable aberration. "How will we eradicate Black English?" asked Dick Cavett, an American talk-show host. The answer from a linguist was: "You'll have to eradicate the black people." John Simon, the New York film critic who regards himself as a guardian of English pure and unde-filed, said, with some justice, that blacks should speak " 'standard English' in order to get ahead," and William Prashker, in *The New York Times*, wrote of the need for blacks to forget their ghetto culture when trying to "impress the man downtown." "The man" means, for American blacks, "Mister Charlie," the feared and despised white boss.

The response of Ishmael Reed, novelist, poet, essayist, and Na-tional Book Award nominee, was:

> You not gone make me give up Black English. When you ask me to give up my Black English you askin me to give up my soul. But for reasons of commerce, transportation hassleless mobility in everyday life, I will talk to 411 in a language both the operator and I can understand. I will answer the highway patrolman who stops me, for having a broken rear light, in words both he and I know. The highway patrolman, who grew up on Elvis Presley, might speak Black English at home, because Black English has influenced not only Blacks but whites too.

Sensible enough. But what, precisely or imprecisely, *is* Black English? The term came into current usage in the 1960s, along with Black Power and slogans like "Black is Beautiful." With the massive migra-tion of blacks to the big American cities, where ghettos were estab-lished and integration was resisted, there was pseudointellectual talk about the raising of "black consciousness," and this demanded a language. Universities were encouraged or bludgeoned into running black studies, and teachers of Swahili were sought (though usually rejected if they were white). Swahili, being an African East Coast language, was not the most appropriate medium for black consciousness, since nearly all black Americans are of West Coast provenance: Ibo would have been more fitting. Meanwhile, blacks were already speaking what had been considered a substandard version of ordinary American English, to be eradicated if possible in state schools, and this was elevated into a reputable language. Sociolinguists discounted the importance of regional variations, and government-sponsored materials and programs directed to the ennobling of Black English (as imprecise a term as White English) operated on a national basis. Reviewing the Urban Language Series published by the Center for Applied Linguistics in Washington, D.C., from 1966 to 1974, the linguist Lee Pederson remarked that "the Great Black English controversy" was "a pseudo-issue for linguistics, but a gut-issue for marketeering."

The work of scholarly dialectologists had to be ignored, and a simple genealogy for Black English was discovered in Gullah, an archaic dialect spoken on the coasts of South Carolina and Georgia. An unscholarly theory had it that this dialect owed nothing to importations from England, and that if it resembled White English at all this was because blacks had influenced whites, and not the other way around. As so often happens with racist demagoguery, a historical fantasy was concocted, in which white supremacists were trounced for having suppressed or despised a legitimate language, now recovered and rehabilitated, totally acceptable as the noble ancestor of the new speech (not really at all new) of black consciousness.

In Black English, so it is asserted, there are structures closer to ancestral African usages than to those of the enslavers. In the area of the verb, for instance, there is no need for tense, since the time element can be indicated adverbially—"He go yesterday" is clear enough. I am no expert in African languages, but I see a resemblance to Malay (and Chinese) here: *Saya pergi sekarang*—"I'm going now"; *Saya pergi kemarin*—"I went yesterday." "He ain' go" is either present or past. If a past form is used, it can be combined with an implied present form, as in "He stood there and he thinkin'." To say "He workin' when de boss come in" means something different from saying "He be workin' when de boss come in." The first states that the work and the boss's entry occur at the same time; the second has

the worker already at it before the arrival of the boss. "You makin'
sense, but you don't be makin' sense" is not as contradictory as it
seems—"You don't normally show intelligence, but now, unusually,
you have said something sensible." If a past action has definitely to
be specified, "done" and "been" and "is" are useful: "I done go, I
done went, I done been gone." "Have you seen him?" becomes "Is
you see(n) him?" There is a significant contrast between "be" and
zero as copula markers (a copula in Western languages is a form of
the verb "to be"; it does not exist in Russian and languages farther
east). Thus, "My brother sick" means that the sickness is happening
now but is unlikely to last long, while "My brother be sick" means
that the sickness is of some duration.

The main grammatical features of black speech are usually
summed up as follows. There is an uninflected plural, as in "five
girl" (the numeral is enough to indicate plurality), an uninflected
possessive, as in "the boy hat" (in Malay "the hat boy"), and an uninflected third person singular, as in "he think." Other uninflections
occur in "he play" (past as well as present tense) and "he has play"
and in the copula ("it be"). There is a compensatory overinflection in
"I knows." "It" is used in the so-called existential manner, giving "It
is a man there." There is question inversion—"I want to know can
he go." Phonetic differences from White English are well known and
frequently parodied. The fricatives in "this" and "that" are turned
into the alveolar /d/, but this is not peculiar to Black English, any
more than is the consonant reduction found in "firs" for "first."
Vowels are sometimes lengthened, in a very West Coast African manner, as an intensifying device—a "loooong waaaay." There are not
many diphthongs.

Two black linguists show respectively a conviction that Black English has a "proto-creole" deep structure unrelated to traditional
English dialects and a more tenable belief that Southern white speech
is "black" enough. Beryl Bailey, the Jamaican creolist, holds to the
view that Black English is all black; Juanita Williamson finds its features even in the speech of white "redneck" Ku Klux Klan terrorists
and bigots. But when a racial, social, or political issue infects language,
objective scholarship is not greatly wanted. Ten years ago Monroe K.
Spears, a professor of English at Rice University, wrote:

> My own opinion is that history interpreted in terms of affirmative
> action or radical chic is not going to help blacks; there is no black

history any more than there is black truth or black justice. For human beings, black or white, there is no escape from the constant struggle to keep in touch with reality; to abandon blacks to fantasies is to patronize and ultimately, to betray them.

In other words, Black English remains what it was—a deprived mode of communication that looks in at the ghetto rather than out at the big world. In the ten years since that statement, black activists in America, helped by white "radical chic" (a now outmoded term that smells of lavender), has given place to the more urgent struggle of black Africans not in enforced exile but *in* agonized *situ*. The linguistic issue is not all that important.

While the cult of black consciousness was proceeding, the rights of other oppressed minorities were being canvassed. They still are. The feminist movement known as "women's lib" saw the English language as a device of male domination. Presumably, by extension, all human language had to be seen as essentially a man's medium imposed on women, despite the probably accurate ancestral image of men silently hunting while women, washing clothes at the well, chattered away and thus created discourse. Human history, according to the feminists, is a male creation, and this is confirmed by the masculine possessive in the word itself. This is nonsense. *Histoire* and *storia* have no male flavor; the "his" of "history" is a mere accident. Nevertheless Anne Forfreedom (a real name?), writing in Sacramento in 1983, demanded that there be a new study called "herstory," to be defined as "the human story, as told by women about women (and, possibly, men): accounts of the human past and human activity that consider women as being at the center of society, not at the margins." Midge Lennert and Norma Willson, ten years earlier, were more succinct: "1. The past as seen through the eyes of women. 2. The removal of male self-glorification from history." Jo Haugerud, in 1982, suggested the spelling "hystery" in order to emphasize the part played by the creative organ (*hysteron*, Greek for "womb") that defines the downtrodden sex.

The new (or not so new) feminism is mainly an Anglo-Saxon movement, and Anglo-Saxon feminist rage with the English language is difficult to universalize. The English masculine pronouns—"he, him, his"—have no counterpoint in Oriental languages, and a sexed possessive is not to be found in the Romance languages. It is "he, him, his" that annoys when it appears as a so-called common gender form in statements like "The reader of this chapter, if he finds himself in disagreement with its content, may express his feelings to the author." These masculine particles must now be replaced with married or bonded ones—"he/she, him/her" and so on, but there are feminists who would reverse the order to "she/he" and "her/him," and yet others who would fabricate new forms like "hes," standing for "her/his." The dislike of the common-gender pronoun is cognate with the rejection of the '-man' suffix as a neutral form. Hence "chairperson," but not yet "chessperson" or, in furnishings, "highyoungperson."

Romance-speaking feminists, like their anglophone sisters, may think themselves entitled to be unhappy about the word "testimony" and its derivatives, since they see its root as *testis*, a testicle, which has, they think, come to mean a testimony of the reliable virility in a man, which makes his word in a court of law legally acceptable. Actually, however, *testis* meant "witness" before it meant "testicle," and there is no reason why women should feel offended at having to provide a testimony or even write a testament. Nevertheless, Rachel W. Evans, in 1978, coined the word "ovarimony" to serve for a female testimony—"The ovarimony of this witness is suspect." We have still to hear that in a court of law.

Cheris Kramarae and Paula A. Treichler are two American ladies who have compiled a *Feminist Dictionary*—one, naturally, limited to the English, or American, language. I am not sure whether it is in order to call them "ladies." In Old English, a lady was properly a *hlœfdige* or loaf-kneader, but she was eventually elevated, especially once the Virgin Mary began to be called Our Lady. Nowadays the term is rejected because it implies idleness, uselessness, and consumerism. The lady consumes while the woman works. The word "woman" is not much liked either, since it comes from the Old English *wifman* and joins *wif*, which itself means "woman," to "man," and seems to denote that she is part of him. The compilers of the *Feminist Dictionary* are clearly not happy about the word, to which they devote many pages, but there is little that they can do about it. Even the word "female" (which means belonging to the sex that produces offspring) has been corrupted. It comes from the Old French *femelle*, which in its turn comes from the Latin *femella*, a diminutive of *femina*, but "femal," which used to be the regular English form until the seventeenth century, was apparently meddled with by men as not being masculine enough, so they spelled it to look like a derivative of "male."

It is no wonder that the entry "male," and the derivative entries, make uncomfortable reading for men who break bounds to examine the *Feminist Dictionary*. Elizabeth Gould Davies said of the male in 1974:

> The first males were mutants, freaks produced by some damage to the genes caused perhaps [by] disease or a radiation bombardment from the sun. Maleness remains a recessive genetic trait like colour-blindedness and haemophilia, with which it is linked. The suspicion that maleness is abnormal and that the Y chromosome is an accidental mutation boding no good for the race is strongly supported by the recent discovery by geneticists that congenital killers and criminals are possessed of not one but *two* Y chromosomes, bearing a double dose, as it were, of genetically undesirable maleness. If the Y chromosome is a degeneration and a deformity of the female X chromosome, then the male sex represents a degeneration and deformity of the female.

As for the "male mind," according to the late Mary Ellmann in 1968, this is "assumed to function primarily like a penis. Its fundamental character is seen to be aggression, and this quality is held to be essential (by men) to the highest or best working of the intellect."

If man is to be mistrusted or written off, his language must go, too, and it was perhaps inevitable that the women's liberationists should produce a few ingenious individuals prepared to introduce a wholly artificial language designed to be spoken by women to women—a kind of feminist Esperanto. Suzette Haden Elgin, in June 1982, published a science-fiction novel entitled *Native Tongue*, which contains the language Làadan. This contains words descriptive of women's feelings and functions not included in "natural" languages. Ms. Elgin kindly advertises: "If there are words which you would like to have to express female meanings, the Làadan Group will be happy to supply you with a Làadan word for the purpose. Write to Suzette Haden Elgin, Route 4, Box 192-E, Huntsville, AR 72740, USA, sending the information you need and a stamped addressed envelope." If you want words for menstruation, here they are. The generic term is *oshàana*; to menstruate for the first time is *elashàana*; late—*weshàana*;

painfully—*hushàana*; joyfully—*àashàana*. To undergo menopause uneventfully is *zhàadin*. The male menopause seems to be considered a myth.

Such a prospectus is depressing to male eavesdroppers. The depression derives not from the sense that women dislike and despise men, nor even from the linguistic frontier they wish to erect between the sexes, but from the suspicion that men are totally useless in the great world, mere genetic monsters, and that the Ninth Symphony, the *Pietà*, the *Divine Comedy*, and *King Lear*, to say nothing of the moon landing, the Brooklyn Bridge, penicillin, and computers, are mere toys to fill up empty time, since the important work is all done by women. Biologically this is probably true, but values like beauty, truth, and goodness cannot be ignored, and men have worked hard at these. One thing that men have done better than women, despite feminist dictionaries, is lexicography, but here I anticipate.

More compelling than grumbles about male-dominated language is the literary evidence that language is neutral but can be feminized very satisfactorily, as in the writings of Erica Jong. In her novel *Fear of Flying* (1973), she rejects the constraints of traditional womanly, or ladylike, decorum: "The zipless fuck was more than a fuck. It was a platonic ideal. Zipless because when you came together zippers fell away like rose petals, underwear blew off in one breath like dandelion fluff. Tongues intertwined and turned liquid. Your whole soul flowed out through your tongue and into the mouth of your lover. For the true, ultimate zipless fuck, it was necessary that you never get to know the man very well." And so on. It would be an insult to regard her style of writing as bawdily masculine. The Wife of Bath in Chaucer sets a precedent. Language is what we want it to be. Women may do what they wish with it, but to castigate it as a male-dominated construct is unworthy.

Homosexuals, demanding liberty of action, have associated themselves with both the black and feminist movements. The slogan "Gay Power" seems to have emerged in June 1969, when a group of male homosexuals and lesbians resisted a routine police raid on the Stonewall, a dance bar in Greenwich Village in New York. The voicing of the slogan was humorous, since homosexuals had traditionally been defensive rather than aggressive. However purists may resent it, "gay" has become the regular group term for homosexuals. Lesbians are designated by a word nobly associated with the poetess Sappho and her island of Lesbos; males with a taste for each other have languished under a term that sounds clinical. It is a pity that the traditional associations of "gay," as in the rhyme that makes me, a Sabbath child, bonny, blithe, and good, and the other thing, have to yield to the net limitation of meaning. The film *The Gay Divorcée*, the dance the Gay Gordons, the whole concept of innocent gaiety— these have to assume a quaint historicity when faced with books like Jonathan Katz's *Gay American History*, a record of some grimness.

In the nineteenth century, "gay" had underground meanings that were totally heterosexual. A brothel could be a "gay house." If a woman was "gay," she was loose or immoral. The connotations are of freshness, spiciness, even ribaldry. The special meaning and the general, traditional one conjoin in their connotation of irresponsible liberty. At the beginning of the present century, the American slang term "gay cat" was applied to the young male companion of a hobo or vagrant, and the wholly homosexual denotation has to be accepted as American. It is short and convenient and has been readily adopted into other languages. I have just read an article in an Italian women's magazine entitled "Mio figlio è Gay." Women themselves have not been ready to accept the term as a synonym for "lesbian," feeling that their own cult has more to do with the general issue of female liberation rather than the rights of what the frowning "straight" world calls sexual deviants.

Gay men (most of whom are unhappy with "gay" as a noun, as in "I am one of the gays") have developed their own vocabulary, and they have even, though this is dying, employed a pronominal usage known as gender substitution. "She" and "her," applied to a gay man, had a flavor of contempt, though W. H. Auden used the application of femininity to himself, and even to God, with ironic affection— "Miss Me" and "Miss God." Gay speech still uses feminine attributions, brutally or facetiously, though less than before—"Don't be such a cunt" (this is wholly American, since "cunt" has always had in Britain an asexual denotation of "fool" or "idiot"); "Look, bitch, don't cross me"; "Go, girl, shake that money-maker." The feminization of gay men— making them "Nelly"—belongs to a period when not to be heterosexually male was necessarily to belong to the only other traditional category available. Nowadays, gay males pose as cowboys, truck drivers, and boxers, and it is not always a pose. The camp queen who screams and "dishes" (jocularly insults) is now rare. "Camp," incidentally, seems to have as much a nineteenth-century provenance as "gay." It seems to refer to a period of military or railroad camps, all male inevitably, where an exaggerated pose of femininity in those who had the histrionic talent relieved the brutish monotony: also, of course, homosexual practices were a welcome substitute among the heterosexually deprived, and the preferred mode for others. Men about town in Victorian London who slipped into the Hyde Park tents of the Guards were after "a bit of camp," and this was no playacting.

In gay publications one may read advertisements for lovers, or love-less sexual partners, which specify "macho" or "butch" and add "no femmes need apply." "Beautiful" in gay language signifies the well-formed face, but the well-formed body is "hot." Sometimes this thermal quality is applied to mere style or presence. An attractive man earns the comment "That's hot." The use of the demonstrative is significant: it depersonalizes, turns a human being into a mere sex object, and refers back to a time when "it" was in order for a casual partner: "The trick was fine in bed, but I had to throw it out in the morning."

There used to be an element of the theatrical in gay usage, with "slave" and "master" to describe the receptive and active roles in the sexual act. Nowadays, the potential "slave" is asked, "Are you into a bottom scene?" Euphemism of this kind turns "sadomasochism" into "S and M" or "rough stuff," and chains and whips are hidden in "B and D"—bondage and discipline. The "bird circuit" is the predatory hunt of gay bars; "playing checkers" is seeking a partner by shifting seats in a cinema; a "meat rack" is a gay pickup place. "What number and what color?" means "Which sexual practices do you prefer?" "Payola" means, or meant, police payoff by gay men. None of these terms represent more than an inside slang. No homosexual activist wishes to go as far as Ms. Elgin, with a gay equivalent of Làadan.

There is no pretension in gay talk, but sociolinguists have tried to find in the language of youth a phenomenon of large significance. The so-called youth revolution was partially a product of full employment for teenagers—already a thing of the past—which meant a specialized consumer market in which the cunning old provided, at a price, the materials of a life-style for the innocent young. But those of the young who scorned to consume, except the produce of ill-run communes, made a countercontribution and, indeed, founded what was known as a counterculture. It is convenient to think in terms of a youthful semiotic system that rejects the language of the adult world. This system has, I think, to be defined negatively: it is based on rejection more than acceptance.

It is impossible to make a dictionary of what may be termed "teenspeak." Ever since Dr. Johnson, a dictionary has been a tool of the cultivated, meaning the literary. A major characteristic of the young is their rejection of literature. Their vocabulary is not fed by the past, which belongs to the old. We can record lexical terms used in teenspeak, but by the time the record is made, the items are no longer in use. It is impossible to convey in print the ironical nuance that makes "charming" mean unacceptable and "chum" denote the opposite of a friend. The teenspeak of my native Manchester taught me, a year or so ago, such examples of rhyming slang as "Whalley Range" for "strange," and metonymies like "neck"—to eat, swallow—and "naughty neck," to pop pills. These are highly ephemeral. Once the enemy—the not so young—has learned the secret password, that chunk of lexis is abandoned.

I tried, back in 1960, to write a novel about violent teenagers, and with inexcusable innocence, I amassed a suitable real-life glossary. Then I realized that all this would be demoded by the time the book appeared, so I had to invent a lexis, setting my story in an imagined future that is already historic. The irony is that in the United States, a number of teenagers appropriated items from the lexis—words of Russian origin like "droog" and "groodies" and "nadsat"—and this shoved my future into the discardable past.

There is no acceptable term for those elements of language that belong to closed groups or are mere fiery spurts of instant poetry doomed to die as soon as they are born—the elements, in fact, that waver on the borders of the corpus of the standard language. The word "slang" is vague and its etymology obscure. It suggests the slinging of odd stones or dollops of mud at the windows of the stately home of linguistic decorum. The *Collins Dictionary* proffers this definition: "Vocabulary, idiom, etc., that is not appropriate to the standard form of a language or to formal contexts, may be restricted as to social status or distribution, and is characteristically more metaphorical and transitory than standard language." It is hard to fault this, though terms like "appropriate" and "formal contexts" and "social status" draw us to a sphere where linguistic considerations defer to the rules of society. Whatever slang is, we had better now take a look at it.

LOW-LIFE LANGUAGE

Eric Partridge, the late, great master of slang lexicography, entitled his massive work *A Dictionary of Slang and Unconventional English,* adding the explanatory subtitle *Colloquialisms and Catch Phrases, Fossilised Jokes and Puns, General Nicknames, Vulgarisms and Such Americanisms as Have Been Naturalised.* In his preface to the first edition (1937), he gave approximate proportions of contents which, he recognized, were heterogeneous: slang and cant, 50 percent; colloquialisms, 35 percent; solecisms and catachreses, 6.5 percent; catchphrases, 6.5 percent; nicknames, 1.5 percent; vulgarisms, 0.5 percent. Slang has already been defined for us. Cant is a group vocabulary such as belongs to thieves, journalists, or lawyers; it is sometimes termed jargon. Colloquialisms are informal expressions—not to be used in elevated discourse. Catachreses are hard to distinguish from solecisms—errors in vocabulary (whereas solecisms can be grammatically erroneous), including malapropisms (Mrs. Malaprop in R. B. Sheridan's *The Rivals* talks of "a nice derangement of epitaphs" when she means "a nice arrangement of epithets"). Catchphrases, of which Partridge compiled a separate dictionary, are on the order of "Roll on, Death, and let's have a go at the angels." Nicknames we know. Vulgarisms are harder to define, and Partridge gives few.

The original *Dictionary of Slang* was expanded with a volume of addenda over half the size of the original. After Partridge's death, Paul Beale conflated the two volumes into one, but expansion necessarily must go on forever. Beale, movingly, ends his preface to what became the eighth edition of the work with these words: "The preparation of this volume . . . has . . . given me a renewed and even greater respect for all those anonymous and otherwise unremembered ancestors of ours who were able to laugh in the blackest of hells, be it in the stews of Alsatia, in the condemned cell awaiting execution at Tyburn, or in all the horror of the trenches, and to cheer their fellow victim with a word or phrase that sparkled so brightly as to be treasured and repeated over and over—for what is this Dictionary, really, but a pile of fossilised jokes and puns and ironies, tinselly gems dulled eventually by overmuch handling, but gleaming still when held up to the light." This places what we must vaguely term slang into the right perspective—the homemade language of the ruled, not the rulers, the acted upon, the used, the used up. It is demotic poetry emerging in flashes of ironic insight.

When Partridge compiled his *Dictionary*, certain words that have now entered the compendia of conventional English were taboo. In the rough and ready taxonomy that digging round the edges of language imposed, they got themselves mixed up with slang. These are words like "fuck," "cunt," "shit," and "piss." They are not slang; they are ancient words long buried by a social decorum not so mindlessly repressive as our permissive age seems to think. Some seem to believe that there was once a sort of golden age in which no fig leaf was imposed on language, but squeamishness about those four words, and others with sexual or excretory referents, goes back a long way. Florio's fine English-Italian dictionary defined *follere* as "to jape, to sarde, to fucke, to swive, to occupy." His friend Shakespeare undoubtedly knew "fuck" and probably used it in everyday speech, but the word is not to be found in his plays or poems. Samuel Johnson once said that the two most important activities in life were "fucking and drinking," but never in print. The earl of Rochester, known for extreme dissoluteness, in privately distributed verses such as his "A Ramble in St. James's Park," did not shrink from using words such as the following:

> Had she picked out, to rub her arse on,
> Some stiff-pricked clown or well-hung parson,
> Each job of whose spermatic sluice

Had filled her cunt with wholesome juice,
I the proceeding should have raised
In hope sh' had quenched a fire I raised.

But this was not a poem he himself prepared (or possibly intended) for publication; when published, most early editions deleted the body of his obscenities, relying on the reader to supply the missing letters in "c—t" and "f—k." To call these good old Anglo-Saxon words that later propriety has expunged from the language is to ignore the total lack of documentary evidence.

"Fuck" seems to be cognate with the German *ficken*, to strike, but Partridge doubted if this could be demonstrated, though he was not against connecting it with the Latin *pungere*, also "to strike." There might be a semantic tie-up with "prick," an instrument of sharp assault that God tells Saul not to kick against. The word "fuck" was openly used in a BBC television program in the 1960s by the drama critic Kenneth Tynan, who innocently affirmed that it described too common and legitimate an action to be censored: "A man fucks his wife." If man does, or, by extension, his wife does, the associations are a little too brutal and violent for the marriage bed. With the lifting of the ban on D. H. Lawrence's *Lady Chatterley's Lover* in 1960, the word was admissible in print, but the Laurentian use of the word— in the context of sexual tenderness, totally inappropriate—tended to prevail. The novels of Ms. Jackie Collins are rich in invitations like "Baby, let's fuck," but the term refers solely to the act of penetration: "Let's make love," though apparently evasive and vague, is probably more fitting for the total activity of arousal, penetration, orgasm, and affectionate convalescence.

"Cunt" remains the most problematic of the so-called obscenities. Since the fifteenth century it has been avoided in speech and writing, and from about 1700 to the present day—when the use of the word is commoner in women's writing than in men's—it was a legal offense to employ it in print. Partridge's history of the word begins with the Old English *cwithe*, "the womb," and concentrates on the meaning of the 'cu-' element, finding the 'nt' hard to explain. In 'cu-' he finds a radical descriptive of "quintessential physical femineity," as clear in "cow" (Old English *cu*) as in "queen" (*cwen*). "Quim," a synonym for "cunt," found also as "queme," "quim-box," "quimsby," and "quin," reinforces the latter, regional, connection. Partridge thinks that the original is Celtic *cwm*, a valley or cleft. The extensions of the word are not now much found—"quim-bush" or "quim-whiskers" or "quim-wig" for the female pubic hair, "quim-wedge" for the penis, "quim-sticking" for sexual intercourse. "Twat," usually pronounced /twɒt/, cleansed through rhyming slang into "pratt," which gives the alternative pronunciation of the vowel, may come from dialect "twitchel," a passage, or "twatch," to mend a gap in a hedge. It is another synonym for "cunt," though not much used by the feminist writers. Robert Browning, in *Pippa Passes*, seems to have thought that a twat was a nun's headgear—"a hair-raising misapprehension," says Partridge, "the literary world's worst 'brick.'"

The excretory words, considered as offensive as the sexual ones, have, of course, an anatomical association with them, and man's being born between urine and feces reinforced, for the Church Fathers, his sordid unregeneracy. "Piss," initialized to "pee," has, as has the French *pisser*, always hovered on the edge of near-respectability, since the sibilant /s/, poetically extensible to /sssss/, has an onomatopoeic aptness lacking in the staider "urinate" or "micturate." As for "shit," C. T. Onions's *Oxford Dictionary of English Etymology* provides a very venerable history: "Superseding (dial.) *shite*, OE *scitan*, p[ast] p[articiple] *sciten* = M[iddle] L[ow] G[erman] *schiten* Du[tch] *schijten* O[ld] H[igh] G[erman] *skizan* (G[erman] *scheissen*), O[ld] N[orse] *skita*; f[rom] Germ[anic] **skit* [the * indicates a hypothetical form, no actual form surviving] (whence OE. *scitol* purgative, *scitte* diarrhœa)." Onions posits a probable Indo-European root—**skheid*, split, divide—showing a connection with schism and schizophrenia. The action of excreting induces the sensation of a forcible division of the fundament. The literal use of half those once taboo terms is now in the province of the general lexicographers. Once they are used metaphorically, slang dictionaries take over.

It is understandable that the excretory terms should be used in contexts of contempt, dislike, pain—"Shit weighs heavy" (a Canadian catchphrase directed at a boaster); "Shit Street"—a situation of extreme difficulty; "shit-sack"—a Nonconformist (recorded in 1769); "feel like a shitehawk's breakfast"—possess a profound hangover. If "shit a brick" is a mixture of the literal and the metaphorical—to defecate after prolonged constipation—"shit a top-block" is shipyard worker's slang for "to become excited or angry or both," pure metaphor. In the catchphrase " 'Shit!' said the king, and all his loyal subjects strained in unison," the joke, if any, lies in the descent from the figurative to the literal. Slang is nearly all metaphor, and if terms of excretion are separated from the actual to be used as rough poetry, excretion itself must be poeticized. Thus, "to piss" becomes "to bleed the liver, drain the dragon, get rid of the bladder matter, have a gypsy's kiss (rhyming slang; the 'kiss' may be omitted), point percy at the porcelain, shake hands with the wife's best friend, shake the dew off the lily, splash the boots, strain the spuds, siphon the python, visit Miss Murphy," and so on. Diarrhea becomes "the Aztec two step, Cairo crud, Delhi belly, Gyppy tummy, Hong Kong dog, Montezuma's revenge, Rangoon runs." These are all exotic, while the home-based variety is "the toms" (Australia rhyming slang—"tomtits" = "shits") or "the scoots" or "the trots."

Why the most pleasurable activity known to mankind, and the organs by which it is procured, should be debased through the use of the basic, or quadriliteral, terms as expressions of opprobrium has never been adquately explained. "Fucking," it is true, can be used as a neutral intensifier in "fucking good" and "fucking stupid," but to be "fucked" or participate in a "fuckup" or a "snafu" ("situation normal: all fucked up") is to be in a state of distress. I once heard an army motor mechanic complain of his recalcitrant engine by crying "Fuck it, the fucking fucker's fucking fucked." There you have the word used as five distinct parts of speech. To be called "a prick" (though never "a penis"), "a cunt," or "a twat" is not pleasant. There is perhaps a fundamental puritanism in such usages, a denial of the holiness of sexual pleasure, which, of course, explains the taboo.

Slang metaphors for "cunt" are uncountable—"apple, bacon sandwich, barge, beaver, bite, boat, booty, box, butcher's window, canyon, catty-cat, central cut, chasm, chopped liver, chuff, cock (U.S. South), cono, cooch, coot, cooze, crack, cranny, crevice, damp, Dead End Street, fanny (UK; the USA uses the term for 'fundament'), finger pie, front bum, furburger, fuzzburger, G (for 'goodies'), Garden of Eden (U.S. black), golden doughnut (Australian), PEEP (perfect elegant eating pussy), sharp and blunt (rhyming slang)"—one could go on. The penis is anything from "acorn, almond (rhyming slang: almond rock = cock), baldheaded hermit, beef (U.S. black), beef bayonet, big foot Joe, blue-veined piccolo, candy stick, cherry splitter" to (when it is erect) "Bethlehem steel (U.S. black), Marquis of Lorne (rhyming slang = horn), prong, scope." None of these terms is the answer to a taboo, since the taboo terms—in literal or figurative use—have never caused *pudeur*. Slang fulfills a desire to make poetry.

I take most of the above poeticisms from Jonathon Green's *Slang*

Thesaurus. There are other kinds of slang that, while poetic enough, have the primary function of speaking a language proper to a closed circle. The late David Maurer, professor emeritus of linguistics at the University of Louisville, collected less generalized slang than criminal argots, though, as he confined himself to the United States, land of individualism, he found it difficult to decide sometimes precisely what criminality was. He started his collecting career with North Atlantic fishermen, who used terms like "gurry" for fish entrails, "dong" for penis, "put a face on" for "spoil someone's looks" but also had peculiarities of verb morphology—"I has seed" but "he have seed," "I does" (/duːz/) but "he do." Then he touched the socially irregular with circuses and carnivals, finding "cheaters" (spectacles), "saw-buck" (ten-dollar bill), "century" (hundred-dollar bill, hence "C-note"), "hustler" (prostitute), "mitt" (palmist), and "lucky-boy" (lazy young man who lives off a circus girl). If prostitution is a crime, then its argot is criminal, though Maurer did not find much of it. He said:

> Argots originate in tightly closed cliques, in groups where there is a strong sense of camaraderie and highly developed group solidarity based primarily on community of occupation. Since prostitution, by its very low position in the hierarchy of the crime world and by virtue of its internal organization, denies the prostitute all claim to true professional status, it is obvious that professional pride is lacking as a motive for argot.

It is probable also that there is in prostitution a desire for conformity and respectability, as is evident from the fantasies of prostitutes willing to talk over a drink. Dr. Johnson had a prostitute friend named Bet Flint, who tried to eternize her ladylike ambitions in verse:

> When first I had my mortal birth
> A little minikin I stepped upon earth
> And then I came from a dark abode
> Into this bad and bawdy world.

Bet wished Johnson to write a preface for this poem, but he gave her half a crown instead, "which she liked as well." The language of the game may be a poor thing, but it has phrases like "public enemy" for a client's wife, "Oom Paul," a customer, not necessarily a Boer, who likes cunnilingus. This must be the only trade that calls on a classic play to designate one of its specialties: "She stoops to conquer" describes fellatio, which, by the less cultivated, may be called "Way down South in Dixie." As for sodomy, the collecting of terms was left to two American ladies, Judith S. Neaman and Carole G. Silver, who found "go Hollywood," "kiss or kiss off," "kneel at the altar," and "ride the deck." Maurer has coition "up the dirt road" as "a turquoise," which must be a deformation of "Turkish."

Is the moonshiner a true criminal? Only in the sense that the Volstead Act, which forbade Americans to drink liquor, was a piece of just legislation. History has decided that it was not. Therefore the distillers of whiskey in the Kentucky hills and elsewhere were performing a reputable act. Here we have examples of argot that require a great deal of explaining. It is not enough to define "kerosene liquor" as "liquor contaminated by kerosene." We have to know that a teaspoon of kerosene in a thousand-gallon vat of beer will cause all the liquor to taste of it. "Horse-blanket whiskey" describes a crude liquor made by covering a boiling kettle of beer with a heavily folded horse blanket that is periodically wrung of its condensed moisture. "This technique is not approved by first-class moonshiners," says Maurer. To "bulldog" is "to heat used barrels by setting them against a large oil drum in which a fire is built in order to sweat out the whisky that has soaked into the barrel staves." All this is a means of cheating the "revenooers."

The cream of the criminal world are probably the confidence men, whose techniques involve a mastery of conventional language but who have a considerable inner argot. The victim is "the mark," but he is also the "apple, fink, savage, winchell, chump, and Mr. John Bates." On him is played the "big con" or the "short con." The biggest of the big con games is the "payoff," and the term is shorthand for a whole scenario. A wealthy mark is led to believe that he has been taken into a deal by which a big racing syndicate is to be swindled. "At first," says Maurer, "he plays with money furnished by the confidence men, then is put on the send for all the cash he can raise, fleeced and blown off." There is also the "wire," in which a bogus Western Union official convinces the mark that he can delay the transmission of race results to the bookmakers long enough for the mark to place a bet after the race is run, as in the movie *The Sting*. I see that I have been led away from mere words to the totality of the acts that they signify. This is to remember Dr. Johnson's fine statement about words being the daughters of men while things—which include criminal activities—are the sons of heaven.

The etymology of slang is often a problem. Eric Partridge, believing that it was important to know where words came from, was often tentative and fanciful on the assumption that anything was better than nothing. Does "posh" really derive from "Port Outward Starboard Homeward" (the cooler cabins on the P and O's eastern run)? In the absence of more plausible etymology it will serve. How about "O.K." or "okay"? "Orl kerrect" will not do. H. L. Mencken, the great separatist who believed in the American Language, rightly said that "O.K." is the "most successful of Americanisms," but he could not give a convincing account of its origin. Woodrow Wilson thought it was Choctaw Indian—okeh—and persuaded a record company of the 1920s (the one that first pressed Louis Armstrong) to adopt it as a trade name. Charles Berlitz believed it was really Aux Cayes in Haiti, a port where sailors found the rum good. Andrew Jackson, who is often credited with the illiterate origin above, was an attorney and not very facetious. Nobody knows about "O.K." but everybody knows where "O.K.D." comes from. It is a Philadelphia expression "used in conversation by two Main Line women about a third who is not"—"she's nice enough but not quite O.K.D.," or "our kind, dear."

I take this information from William and Mary Morris's *Morris Dictionary of Word and Phrase Origins*, in which American slang mingles with conventional English in the quest for provenance. Is "dogie" a slang term for "a calf that has lost its mammy and whose daddy has run off with another cow" or a necessary technicality? Orphan calves had to subsist on grass and water, too heavy for their young bellies, which came to resemble a "batch of sourdough carried in a sack," hence "dough-guts," hence "dogie." A ten-gallon hat, or John B. (after John B. Stetson) has what is termed a folk-etymological name, a domesticizing of the Mexican *sombrero galon*—the braided hat of the *vaqueros*. A "thank you ma'am" is a small bump in the road. When a young couple went driving, the man was entitled to kiss the girl when they met one of these bumps. "Snollygoster" means "shyster," and not, as the late President Truman thought, a man born out of wedlock, and a shyster (I follow Partridge here) is "an unprofessional, dishonest or rapacious lawyer," properly (thieves' slang) "shicer" (German *Scheisse*), hence bemerded, dirty, shitten. But one cannot be sure of that history; one rarely can.

Post-Maurer circus argot presents etymological mysteries. "Zebra" is fitting for an American convict, and a "gopher" is clearly a lad who is circus-struck and will respond to "Hey, kid, go for some coffee." We think we know why an acrobat is a "kinker" (he ties himself into knots or kinks), but the word "shill"—for a "sucker enticer" or confidence trickster's confederate or decoy (most particularly) in the three-card trick—does not easily yield its origins even when expanded to "shillaber." The grinder is the spieler who delivers his bally in front of his pitch or concession. "Bally" probably comes from "ballyhoo" and hence from "ballyhooly" in the phrase "the ballyhooly truth" (the whole bloody truth), a music-hall tag from the 1880s. "Spiel" has a German origin—a *Spieler* is a player, often a cardplayer, frequently a crafty gamester, hence a glib fellow: the rest seems to follow. The spiel is ground out like so much sausage meat.

Some of our terms are held to be Gypsy or Romany in origin, but there is an ancient confusion—which goes back to Shakespeare's day—between genuine Gypsy speech and the cant of thieves and vagrants. Some of the words are long dead—"apple-squire" for a pimp or brothel servant, "autem" for a church, "autem mort" for a female vagrant married in a church, "bene faker of gibes" for a first-class forger of certificates ("faker" is still with us), "dell" for a virgin, soon to be a "doxy." "Cheats" were things in general—a pig in a field was "a grunting cheat in greenmans," a tongue a "prattling cheat," teeth were "crashing cheats." London is no longer "Romeville," but "booze" is still liquor ("Romeville booze" was wine), and the "beak" was, then as now, a magistrate.

Why some items of cant, argot, or slang remain with us, others not, is a mystery. Of its nature, a slang dictionary dates, sometimes very rapidly. As terms go out of use, their origin slides into darkness. Harold Wentworth and Stuart Berg Flexner produced an American slang dictionary in 1960 after ten years' work, and their revision of the compendium in 1971 grants us only a means of understanding tough American fiction and punchy American journalism up to that date. They do not help with origins. I still do not know what "twenty-three skidoo" really means, and, for that matter, most of America's numerical slang is a profound enigma. In the 1930s, "two and a half" was a lunch-counter term meaning a small glass of milk, and a "twenty-one" was a glass of limeade or orangeade. "Thirty-three" was an order for ground beefsteak but also a customer who would not buy from one salesman and so was handed over to another. "Thirty-four," meaning "Go away," was used by one salesman to another who was interfering with a sale. "O.K.—thirty for now," from a Shirley Temple film, means good-bye, and it derives from the triple X at the end of a telegraphic message or newspaper correspondent's dispatch. The third, electrically charged and hence untouchable rail of a railroad gives rise to the phrase "third rail," which can signify either a person not to be bribed, or a strong drink. A patron who has had too many third rails might well be "eighty-sixed" by the bartender, or thrown out; "deep-sixed," a term for someone who has been murdered, has perhaps a more obvious derivation. A "three-letter" man is a homosexual or fag, whose queerness is reinforced by the "three-dollar bill," which is the epitome of phoniness.

"Fag" is still, as I write, in use. It became a term for a homosexual in the United States about 1920, but its adoption into British usage has been repelled by the inveterate use of the word to mean a cigarette. Wentworth and Flexner try to find a connection between cigarette smoking, considered effeminate by pipe and cigar men, and homosexuality, but without success. Nor does the British public school practice of "fagging" really help. If "fag" comes from "faggot," a loose bundle, it has to contend with the mainly feminine meaning of the word, as in "old faggot."

The so-called drug culture has spawned a vast lexis which melts like snow—"A-bomb"—marijuana and opium rolled into a cigarette; "Acapulco gold"—high-grade Mexican marijuana; "bam"—a mixture of a depressant and a stimulant; "big Harry"—heroin; "campfire boy"—an opium addict, and so on. These expressions already smell of lavender. As, probably, do "ecofreak"—a supporter of ecological programs, "faunlet"—a juvenile homosexual object, "Afro-Saxon"—a black who "Toms" or apes the Man, "bad nigger"—a black that takes no shit from nobody, "Barbie doll," named for a plastic blonde gynomorph for children but also a WASP (White Anglo-Saxon Protestant) conformist.

To my surprise, I find myself in Wentworth and Flexner's *Dictionary of American Slang* as the inventor of the euphemism "corksacking." I seem to have written the following for *The New York Times Magazine* on October 29, 1972: "I have already had several abusive phone calls, telling me to eff off back to effing Russia, you effing corksacking limey effer." Under, in the same dictionary, "eff," another euphemism, I give the reason, which I had forgotten, along with the abuse, for the abuse: "This is because I suggested some time ago . . . that America would be better off for a bit of socialized medicine." Despite the linguistic permissiveness of American novels, some newspapers remain shy of obscene explicitness, hence my coinages. "Corksacking" is, of course, "cocksucking." Americans, judging from their contemporary literature (John Updike, in *Couples*, has "To fuck is human but to be blown divine"), are given to oral sex, but there is a tradition that this is a filthy British habit (also Continental). Hence the form taken by that anglophone abuse.

Let us leave words and phrases and examine whole slang statements. Australians who wish to boast that they have many sexual partners say that they must "climb trees to get away from it" or "get more arse than a toilet seat" or "have more pricks than a secondhand dartboard" or "have to swim underwater to get away from it" or are "so busy I've had to put a man on to help." There are no outlandish words here; the slang element resides in witty exaggeration; the flamboyant impulse that creates a slang term has expanded to encompass an idea. These statements are properly catchphrases, but a catchphrase is hard to define. Partridge, putting together a dictionary of them, charmingly declines the duty of definition, merely conjugating "catch" and suggesting that if a phrase has caught on it is catchy enough. But "phrase" is a misnomer: we are dealing here with complete sentences that take on the quality of a proverbial saying or a famous quotation. But they are mostly phatic, mere social gestures with little or no meaning, like "Put another pea in the pot and hang the expense," and "Never mind, lads, it'll soon be Christmas," and "Ah well, as one door shuts another door closes"—pointless, feeble, downright silly, but, as any serviceman knows or ex-serviceman remembers, the warm and comfortable stuff of human companionship. They frequently fill in gaps at army drinking sessions.

Stephen Potter, in his *The Sense of Humour*, recalls a pub landlord whose entire conversation consisted of unmotivated and unrelated catchphrases. These were taken mostly from BBC radio programs of comic content, particularly the wartime series *ITMA* (an acronym for "It's That Man Again"). Acronyms and strings of initials were part of the bureaucratic experience of wartime, and the *ITMA* catchphrases were of the order of "TTFN" ("tata for now"), and (a virtuoso effort) "NCAWWASBE" ("Never clean a window with a soft-boiled egg"). Such phrases were surrealistically free from context; they had a floating quality. "White whitey kay" provoked the question "What does that mean?" and got the answer "You're too young to know" (YTYTK). IITYWIMWYBMAD can be found painted over many an American bar; the unsuspecting patron who asks about it is told, "If I tell you what it means will you buy me a drink?"

It has been mostly the armed forces that have spawned the most memorable catchphrases, which, it may be suggested, are often the product of oppression—and boredom. The groans of waking at reveille are not soothed by "Come on out, the sun's scorching your eyeballs" or "Rise and shine, rise and shine. Hands off your cocks, pull on your socks, orderly rooms at nine" or "Out of them bloody wanking pits" or "Shit, shave, shampoo, and piss buckets out of the window" or (sinister enough for T. S. Eliot's *The Waste Land*) "You've had your time, I'll have mine." Tropical service, military or civilian, made catchphrases out of the native languages, like "Apa changkul dua malam" (Malay)—literally "What hoe two night" (Australian "What-ho to-night?")—and "*Shufti cush, shufti zubrick*" (bazaar Arabic—"show cunt, show prick").

Some catchphrases breed ripostes, which in their turn breed others, and it is hard to know where to stop. "Are you a man or a mouse?" is easily answered with "A man. My wife's scared of mice." "Sister Anna shall carry the banner" is followed by "But I carried it last week"—"You'll carry it this week"—"But I'm in the family way"— "You're in every fucker's way." Ribald prose recitations, which must be learned by heart with absolute verbal fidelity (but who imposes this, and who invented them?), are monster catchphrases. Typical is the description of the Hula-Hula Bird, which "flies round in ever-decreasing concentric circles, finally disappearing up its own arsehole, from which safe but insalubrious refuge it pours forth a mixture of shite and smoke upon its baffled foe."

I have already alluded to the euphemism (from Greek *eu*—well, good, pleasant—and *pheme*—speech). It is a device for hiding the harsh or offensive through circumlocution or gentle falsification, and it used to operate in those areas—sex and excrement—where taboos were most rigidly enforced. As race is one of the most sensitive themes of our age, with racism subject to state laws, it might be expected that terms like "nigger," "wop," "kike," "limey," and so on would disappear, with either new euphemisms or neutral "dictionary" terms replacing what we must call cacophemisms (Greek *kako*, as in "cacophony"). But no race has ever really liked other races. There is always the prospect of war between them, and this explains the large number of euphemisms that has appeared in the period following World War II, accepting the principle of national aggression but hypocritically trying to disguise it.

Thus, the people who make a fortune out of the instruments of death are to be called the Armament Community, which replaces the Munitions Interests. Total nuclear war has become an All Out Strategic Exchange. The strategy planners are Defense Intellectuals. A nuclear explosion is an Energetic Disassembly and even a fire may be called a Rapid Oxidation. Troops not competent in killing are put on to BEST, or Behavioral Skills Training (as, in the civilian field, slow learners are named Exceptional Children). One man's guerrilla is another man's freedom fighter. Hiring mercenaries is Greenbacking (an allusion to the American dollar). Grave registration is in the hands of the U.S. Memorial Services. If you crash in a military plane, Old Newton takes you. Termination with Extreme Prejudice is a CIA term for assassination.

The United States Central Intelligence Agency (whose special assassination unit is called the Health Alteration Committee) seems to have the best euphemisms. It invented the term Overflight for illegal aerial investigation of neutral territory considered potentially hostile, calling them also National Technical Means of Verification, which sounds almost friendly. The Company, as the CIA is called, has assets (listening posts and monitoring stations), and when it sends out a military operative under civilian cover, it terms this Sheepdipping. Protected by the Intelligence Identity enactment of House Bill 5615, he traps Targets who are either Ill (arrested on suspicion) or in The Hospital (jail). He can perform a Technical Trespass or break-in, and all his investigative Covert Operations feed a huge official network called the Backchannel.

Even when governments are not concerned with the discomfiture of a putative enemy, they are apt at hiding realities under the euphemisms long known as gobbledygook. The Nixon administration produced the term Biosphere Overload for overpopulation. Benign Neglect (coined by the earl of Durham in 1839 to describe Britain's treatment of Canada) is now used to mean allowing the underprivileged to fight their own way up. Personnel Ceiling Reductions are employment cutbacks. To do a Uey (U-turn) sounds, and is, Australian, and it means to change your political point of view. We still await a euphemism for unemployment, but that is surely on its way. State-paid Temporary Leisure? REST (Right to Earn Statutorily Terminated)? GARDENING (Guaranteed Absence of Reemployment Due to Economic Nonrecovery Indicated by National Geostatistics)? There is no limit to the modes in which language can be used to lie, obfuscate, worry, even kill.

28

THE DICTIONARY
MAKERS

I have, in a desultory fashion, made reference to specialist dictionaries in the preceding chapters. Now we must look at the great dictionaries that encompass the whole of the English language and that no reader or writer of any seriousness can properly do without. This, anyway, is the modern view. With some awe we have to remind ourselves that writers like Chaucer, Shakespeare, and Milton had no access to what we would call dictionaries. Spelling did not much worry them, as it worries a modern author who runs to his dictionary to check on difficult words like "hemorrhage" (my personal blind spot). Milton spelled in his own creative manner, preferring "mee" to "me" when he wished to be emphatic; Shakespeare went the free and easy Elizabethan way, leaving his own name to be juggled with in a variety of orthographical fantasies; with Chaucer the encoding of speech sounds was logical and required no checking. As for meaning, an empirical consensus prevailed, with no tablet of the law to lay down definitions. The question as to whether a word existed—that is, was authorized by some remote linguistic authority—never arose. If Shakespeare required a word and had not met it in civilized discourse, he unhesitatingly made it up. There was a fund of Latin and Greek (not that Shakespeare knew much of the latter) to be drawn on for what is called neologizing, as indeed there still is.

During the English Renaissance, attempts were admittedly made to line up the English vocabulary. Bilingual dictionaries—Latin-English, French-English, Italian-English—at least ranged it in alphabetical order. But the emphasis in the first English-English dictionaries was on very difficult words, as in John Bullokar's *English Expositor* (1616— just too late for Shakespeare to use) and Henry Cockeram's *The English Dictionarie* (1623). These were what could be called "inkhorn terms"—"commotrix" ("a maid that makes ready and vnready her Mistris"), "parentate" ("to celebrate ones parents funerals"), and "gargarize" ("to wash or scowre the mouth with any Physicall liquor")—far too learned for everyday discourse. It was assumed that the consultant of the dictionary already knew the simple words.

We are, of course, waiting for Dr. Samuel Johnson's magisterial work to appear (1750 onward), but it is unwise to neglect the now-forgotten pioneer work in serious dictionary making upon which Johnson was able to build. Edward Phillips has eleven thousand items in his *New World in Words* (1658), but he was not sure whether to be a lexicographer or an encyclopedist. Till recently, it was not proper for a dictionary to deal in proper names, but Phillips has, for instance, "California—a very large part of Northern America, uncertain whether Continent or island." In 1702 J. Kersey's *A New English Dictionary*—"chiefly designed for the benefit of young Scholars, Tradesmen, Artificers, and the Female Sex, who would learn to spell truely"—brought the word count up to twenty-eight thousand, and in 1721 Nathan Bailey's *Universal Etymological English Dictionary* raised it to about forty thousand. The question of word origin was, as the title indicates, now becoming important. Bailey's dictionary was the most popular before Johnson's: William Pitt the Elder is said to have read through it twice, as if it were a novel. This is a legitimate way to approaching a dictionary: if it is not too bulky, it makes a suitable bed companion for insomniacs. It may also cure insomnia.

In 1747 Samuel Johnson published *The Plan of a Dictionary of the English Language*, in which he declared his intent "to preserve the purity and ascertain the meaning of the English idiom." He implies profound prescriptivism—a dogmatic assertion of what is acceptable in speech and writing—and this is in keeping with the nature of the man himself: bulky, formidable, a convinced Tory and Anglican, and also immensely learned. Johnson, it was said, knew more books than any man alive. As the value of his *Dictionary* lies as much in its literal illustrations of usage as in its (occasionally quirky) definitions, the bookishness is the most important of Johnson's qualifications after those he shares with other lexicographers—energy, doggedness, and a clear brain. The astonishing thing about the making of the *Dictionary* is that it was a one-man effort. Jonathan Swift and others had cried out for an academy on the French model that could fix English forever in a pure mold. French academicians (forty of them) had been working for forty years on the first definitive French dictionary. Johnson saw that committees meant dissensions and delays, that a dictionary, even one of twenty-three hundred pages, was only a book, and a book was a thing that a writer wrote.

Johnson signed his contract for the enterprise in June 1746. The bookseller Robert Dodsley was to take charge of the printing and selling (there were no real publishers in those days), and undertook to pay Johnson £1,575 in installments. Out of this he had to pay assistants—six in number, five of them Scottish—and set up a workroom, apart from buying books. The work was completed in 1755, having been printed at intervals from 1750 onward, a compendium of more than 40,000 words, their usage illustrated by more than 114,000 quotations from the Elizabethan Age to his own time. If Johnson could not go earlier than the Elizabethans, this was because so few of the old texts were available to the inquiring scholar, being shut up in the libraries of the mansions of the nobility. Limited in time, he was self-limited in space, paying little attention to the development of English in the American Colonies. He imposed no limitation on his prejudices, as is well known from definitions like that of "Oats—A grain, which in England is generally given to horses, but in Scotland supports the people" and "Patron—One who countenances, supports or protects. Commonly a wretch who supports with insolence, and is paid with flattery." Hating Bolingbroke, he could not keep him out of his definition of "Irony—A mode of speech in which the meaning is contrary to the words: as, *Bolingbroke was a holy man.*" He made inexcusable errors, like giving "leeward" and "windward" the same meaning. Berated by a lady for defining "pastern" as "the knee of a horse," he offered no elaborate defense, merely saying: "Ignorance, madam, pure ignorance." (One might add to that an anecdotal snippet that Johnson had just beaten a young lady in a race over a lawn in Devonshire. The victory made him complaisant.) In defining "pension" he wrote: ". . . in England it is generally understood to mean pay given to a state hireling for treason to his country," and though himself granted the modest affluence of a state pension, he never changed that definition.

Johnson's *Dictionary* remains a great work, but it had no hope of fixing the language and decreeing linguistic decorum. In Thackeray's novel *Vanity Fair*, Becky Sharp, a sort of new woman of the Napoleonic Era, leaves Miss Pinkerton's academy for young ladies and throws away the copy of Johnson's *Dictionary*—an invariable gift to departing students—she has just received. It is not the least of her gestures in the direction of modernity. That great book now seemed to be a dog walking on its hind legs and, moreover, walking backward. It was not a dictionary for the scientific age that would start to bloom after Waterloo. Noah Webster in America (starting in 1828), Charles Richardson in England (1775–1865), and Joseph Worcester (1846 and 1860), again in America—were all to learn from Johnson what not to be—namely, subjective and eccentric—but they were to learn too that no scholarly dictionary—as opposed to the pocket word list you bought for a penny—could do its work without ample citation. That had been Johnson's real achievement. Richardson was so taken by this aspect of the *Dictionary* that he relied totally on citation, dispensing with definition. It is doubtful whether this can really be called lexicography. Moreover, Richardson's notion of etymology was derived from Horne Tooke's *Diversions of Purley* (1786). This was a dangerous book that went in for philosophical conjecture about the origins of words and was quite capable of deriving "hash" from the Persian *ash*, meaning stew.

Eighteen seventy-six was a momentous year for British lexicography, though the impulse that made it so came from America. All that the English-speaking world then had in the way of dictionaries (apart from Johnson's doorstopper) was Webster, Worcester, and Richardson, and none of them was suitable for the age that had already seen Darwin's *On the Origin of Species* (1859) and Karl Marx's *Das Kapital* (1867), to say nothing of the publications of the British Philological Society. Harper, the American publisher, wished to cooperate with Macmillan in London in the production of a new dictionary "like Webster, in bulk, and as far superior in quality as possible." Webster's dictionary, intended for the American people and establishing spellings that the Americans have used ever since, was no small achievement in 1828, but in the huge and authoritative edition of 1864 it was a great masterpiece. So Harper's conception was bold enough.

The fulfillment of the proposal depended on the finding of an editor (not a single polymath like Dr. Johnson) who could lash a team of lexicographers (subdefined by Johnson as harmless drudges) into doing the work not merely efficiently but expeditiously. There was only one possible man for the task, and he was James Murray.

Murray was the consummate example of the self-made scholar. Born near Hawick in Roxburghshire, his father a small tailor of Covenanter stock (a Covenanter was a person who upheld the National Covenant of 1638 or the Solemn League and Covenant of 1643 between England and Scotland, with the end of establishing and defending the Presbyterian faith), himself a God-fearing teetotaling nonsmoking family-begetting bizarrely learned teacher ("dominie" is a more fitting word for a Scot), he was at that time a master at Mill Hill School near London. This was a dissenting academy, that is to say an establishment set up for pupils who were not baptized members of the Church of England. Great public schools like Rugby, Winchester, Eton, and Harrow admitted Anglicans but no others. Murray was suffused by a passion for learning that, if it ever needed justification, could find it in the duty to serve God through useful action and honor him by trying to understand his creation. But his temperament was naturally that of a man infinitely curious, especially about language. He seems to have had at least a theoretical knowledge of literally every language, living and dead. When the exiled Hungarian patriot Kossuth visited Hawick—a town passionate about national liberties—he was met not only by the town band but by a banner inscribed in Magyar—*Jöjjön-el a' te orszagod*, meaning "Thy kingdom come." James Murray had been at work. He always learned his modern languages from the Bible. He tackled a Chinese Book of Genesis as a boy, and he could still cite its characters in whitebearded old age. He was a man intended for whitebeardedness; he had a lot of the Old Testament prophet about him.

Brought up as he was on the English-Scottish border, he was struck while still a very young child by the failure of a political boundary to coincide with an isogloss. The Sassenachs down there spoke his kind of language. Language was a continuum, in time as well as space. Old English still existed, though Alfred the Great was long dead. Dialects were not "incorrect" speech but survivals of earlier forms of the language. He became—passionately, as with everything he did—a member of that movement dedicated to the study of the English language as a totality—diachronic and synchronic, as we say today.

There were great men in the movement, and they joined together to form the Philological Society. One of them, Henry Sweet, was transformed by George Bernard Shaw and, later, by the makers of *My Fair Lady*, into a world figure of romantic myth. Shaw admired him as a phonetician, and was determined to make phonetics a subject suitable for popular drama. Sweet's nature belied his name. He had a right to be sour and prickly, especially in his attitude to the scholarly establishment of Great Britain. Oxford and Cambridge despised the study of English. The new linguistic scholars were in a catch-22 situation, for they could not propagate the new learning without a degree in it, and they could not get a degree in what they themselves were bringing to birth. Frederick James Furnivall, founder of the Early English Text Society, had started off as a mathematician. One always had to start off as something else. James Murray never went to a university, though. Edinburgh was eventually to award him an honorary doctor's degree. He found the doctor's cap kept his bald head warm, and he wore it even at meals. The philologists were a mixed and eccentric company and very quarrelsome. Probably their discipline, *philology*, meaning "word love," would be called linguistics today—philology is a suitable hobby for amateurs; there was nothing amateurish about this gang of text devourers and arguers about 'i'-mutation.

As good commercial drama could be made out of Murray's life as out of Sweet's. Indeed, there is hardly a personage in the whole mad history of nineteenth-century philology who does not demand Shavian treatment (or more detailed Shavian treatment than some of the philologists get in the preface to *Pygmalion*). Frederick James Furnivall, whose doctor father had attended Mary Shelley, author of *Frankenstein*, in her confinement of 1817, seems to have lent some of his characteristics to Henry Higgins:

> He never understood, or attempted to understand, the quality of tact. It was a species of dishonesty. What he held to be true was to be enounced in the face of all opposition, with unfaltering directness and clarity; what he held to be false was to be denounced with Athanasian intensity and resolution.

Furnivall had learned to hate religion and cared nothing for convention. He married a lady's maid and later left her: this was so scandalous that Murray stuck stamp paper over the signature of the correspondent who gave him the news. Furnivall would have married Eliza Doolittle, dirty and unreformed, as readily. Professor Freeman called him the Early English Text Society's madman and said he ought to be chained up or gagged. Then there was Alexander Ellis, who wanted spelling reform, but only according to his own system. A rival proposal was "bad from every conceivable point of view . . . a disgrace to the committee . . . all bosh." Such men would willingly fight with fists over the pronunciation of the Middle English letter yogh. Furnivall accused Murray of spending five pounds of the society's money to get a yogh specially made for a printing of *The Complaynte of Scotland*. "A beastly big ȝ," yelled Furnivall. But it was really the printer's fault.

Murray was very modern in his approach to language, and the proponents of language laboratories would be unwise to find fault with his tackling new tongues through biblical texts. Where Dr. Johnson would speak French with an English accent, Murray saw that the essence of language was its sound system, and that there was no point in transcribing a piece of, say, Border English in the amateur orthography of a Robert Burns. (He had a lot against Burns, who compromised in his treatment of Scots grammar for the benefit of an English audience: "Scots wha hae" should have been "Scots 'at hae.") Phonetics was the key to accurate transcription, and he went to the lectures of Alexander Melville Bell, the inventor of Bell's Visible Speech. If you run a videocassette of the film of *Pygmalion* (with Leslie Howard and Wendy Hiller), you will catch a glimpse of this. It is a system that uses stylized depictions of tongue and lip positions and looks very fearsome, somewhat like Sanskrit, but being rational and consistent, it works. There was also Broad Romic, based on conventional orthography, the ancestor of the International Phonetic Alphabet in which we have already dabbled together. While Murray sat at the feet of Alexander Melville Bell, Alexander Graham Bell, his teenage son, sought lessons in electricity from the man who knew everything (except, so far, phonetics). Murray gave him lessons; Graham invented the telephone. The grandfather of the telephone, as Graham later insisted on calling him, was, in a distracted way, preparing himself for a task both thrilling and appalling. He had a Scots engineer's patience and integrity toward every aspect of linguistic research. He was an etymologist temperamentally incapable of tolerating false etymology (like "marmalade" from "*Marie est malade*" or "bloody" from "by Our Lady"). His knowledge of early English texts—gained through Furnivall's bullying him into doing most of the work—was formidable. He was destined to become the century's greatest lexicographer.

Murray saw that the Harper-Macmillan proposal could bring Anglo-American lexicography into the modern mainstream of philology running strong in Germany, where Henry Sweet had studied. He knew also that the Philological Society had been for twenty years gathering materials for a new dictionary of its own. What he did not expect was that the society, in the bullying and ebullient person of Furnivall, should decide to force its own concept on Macmillan. Harper had thought of a book of some two thousand pages; the society thought of more than six thousand. Soon Macmillan and Harper grew frightened as the prospect of a dictionary, unmanageable and unprofitable, possibly even ruinous, presented itself. The delegates of the Oxford University Press took over the project, though not even they had any conception of how large the work was ultimately to be. We know, because we have the book, all twenty volumes of it in the 1989 edition, but nobody knew then, though Murray began to have his suspicions. *The Oxford English Dictionary*, though Murray did not live to edit all of it, and though it must be said to be always in the making and remaking, is as great a product of Victorian enterprise as the engineering of Brunel or the Disraelian Empire. And, of course, far more enduring.

It seems incredible to us that this gigantic undertaking was conducted at first as a spare-time activity. Murray was still teaching at Mill Hill. Admittedly he was given time off from the classroom, with a corresponding reduction in salary, but the emoluments from the delegates were, by our standards, derisory. There was more scholarly, or patriotic, martyrdom in the enterprise than profit. Not that Murray disliked the martyr's role, since it had honorable precedents and brought him closer to God. It also brought him, at the last, honorary doctorates and a worrying knighthood (he feared, rightly, that the tradesmen would put up their prices), but it never brought him what he most wished—acceptance by the Oxford dons as one of themselves, the university's confirmation of a scholarly ability to which few of its members could pretend. Sweet had always warned him about Oxford:

You must be prepared for a good deal of vexatious interference & dictation hereafter, liable to be enforced any moment by summary dismissal. You will then see your materials & the assistants trained by you utilized by some Oxford swell, who will draw a good salary for doing nothing. I know something of Oxford, & of its low state of morality as regards jobbery & personal interest.

In the garden of his house at Mill Hill Murray set up an iron shed that gained the name of the Scriptorium and lined it with pigeon-holes. The idea of pigeonholes had come from Herbert Coleridge, first editor of the Philological Society's project, who had fifty-four of these, adjudging them sufficient for the hundred thousand word slips the dictionary would need. Coleridge had died at thirty-one. Warned that he would not recover from the consumption brought on by sitting in damp clothes at a society lecture, he spoke heroic words: "I must begin Sanskrit tomorrow." Murray, who trusted God not to take him too soon, had a thousand pigeonholes, but these were soon crammed. Words resisted the carpenter's taxonomy. The two tons of paper slips that Murray got from Furnivall were a mere Continental breakfast. Inedible, mostly. These, the contributions of volunteer workers over the years, consisted of headwords with quotations. They came in sacks (a dead rat in one, a live mouse with family in another), parcels, and a baby's perambulator. A hamper of words beginning with 'I,' the bottom broken, had been left behind in an empty vicarage at Harrow. 'H' was found with the American consul in Florence, though it had started life fifteen years earlier with Horace Moule, Thomas Hardy's teacher and friend. Fragments of 'Fa' were found in a stable in county Cavan, Ireland, but most of the slips had been used for lighting fires.

So little of the material inherited from the enthusiastic but slapdash Furnivall was of value that Murray had to start all over again, appealing for volunteer readers all over the English-speaking world, laying down rules of admirable clarity for the making of slips, playing the dominie in letters of inordinate length to his colexicographers. Murray's children, who had fine old Anglo-Saxon names like Wilfrid, Hilda, Oswyn, Ethelwyn, Elsie, Harold, Ethelbert, Aelfric, and Rosfrith (there was a bow to Wales with Gwyneth), got their pocket money from slip sorting and, inevitably, acquired precocious vocabularies. In the Scriptorium the editor sat a foot higher than his fistful of assistants, doing with skill and delicacy the work he alone could do— contriving definitions of wonderful terseness, indicating pronunciation through a system that has only now, in the second edition, been replaced by the IPA, and demonstrating, by means of a brief historical procession of quotations, the semantic complex that we call a word. Despite his uprightness of life, reflected in a great chasteness of speech, Murray did not believe in omitting words because they were substandard or taboo. His approach to language was totally scientific: one could not apply moral judgments to words. But he yielded to the prejudices of the middle class, and nothing in the *OED* could bring a blush to the cheek of innocence. The second edition is, of course, a different matter. One can imagine Murray in heaven nodding his beard in approval at the scholarly treatment of "fuck" and "cunt."

One excellent feature of the *OED* is typographical. Murray learned early in his schoolmaster's career the pedagogic value of a variety of types in a textbook. One of the set texts at Mill Hill, imposed by the examiners of the Cambridge Locals, was William Paley's *Horae Paulinae*, a worthy exposition of theological utilitarianism that Murray's pupils found baffling. Paley's analogy of human greed—a flock of pigeons fighting for crumbs—earned him the nickname Pigeon Paley. He argued the existence of God somewhat mechanistically, likening the universe to a clock that somebody had first to make and then keep winding. He was considered important, and he had to be studied at a very early age. Murray was a great maker of easy primers, though the only one he published was his *Synopsis of Paley's Horae Paulinae* (1872). This used different kinds of print to make Paley's arguments, as Murray put it, "eloquent to the eye." The *OED* is not only a triumph of linguistic engineering; it is satisfying to handle because of Murray's appreciation of the semiology of type—something that the Oxford swells, who had never taught children, were slow to see.

The story of the setbacks, scholarly blindness, tyrannous demands, spurts of official indifference, and unworthy commercialism that beset the road from 'A' to 'T' (as far as Murray got) makes painful and infuriating reading, and it is best read in Elisabeth Murray's book on her grandfather, *Caught in the Web of Words*. Murray's transfer of home and Scriptorium from Mill Hill to Oxford, as much in the hope of a university appointment as out of a fancied need that Oxford would be more lexicographically nourishing than Mill Hill, is an episode in life wholly pathetic. But no less self-pitying character than Murray ever strode the new terrain of philology. Complaining to the cook that his porridge was (or were: "parritch" is a plural) "too waesh" or "too brose," shouting for his wife Ada (a heroine of the age) with

"Where's my lovey?," stern but loving with the children, a great man to be with on holiday (he knew all about marine biology and could make a life-size Grendel out of sand), he is a supreme example of the virtues of the poor ambitious dissenting class. Samuel Johnson, poor, ambitious, but also Anglican and Tory, besides a hater of the Scots, would have entertained very mixed attitudes toward him.

The study of language may beget madness. The rogue god Mercury presides over philology, as well as thievery. It is true that Murray's preoccupation with the *OED* begot a kind of monomania, but it must be regarded as a beneficent or at least an innocuous one. It became hard for him to make aesthetic judgments on literature: words kept getting in the way. Murray got into correspondence with Robert Browning, but only to ask about the meaning of "apparitional" in Elizabeth Barrett Browning's *Aurora Leigh*. When his son Oswyn later said how much he admired Browning's poetry, Murray's grave response was, "Browning constantly used words without regard to their proper meaning. He has added greatly to the difficulties of the Dictionary." He was conceivably thinking of that misuse of "twat" in *Pippa Passes*.

Murray died in 1915 at seventy-eight. It took another thirteen years—under first Henry Bradley, later William Craigie and Charles Onions (who helped us some pages back with the etymology of "shit" and to whom the Murray children would derisively sing "Charlie Is My Darling") to bring out the final volume. The work continues to be Murray's monument, a thing he never sought and did not want: "It is extremely annoying to me to see the Dictionary referred to as Murray's English Dictionary." He wanted anonymity:

> I wish we knew nothing of Carlyle but his writings. I am thankful we know so little of Chaucer & Shakespeare. I have persistently refused to answer the whole buzzing swarm of biographers, saying simply "I am a nobody—if you have anything to say about the Dictionary, there it is at your will—but treat me as a solar myth, or an irrational quantity, or ignore me altogether."

I have deliberately allowed a great lexicographer to enter our company as a human being—though humanity is hardly the primary concern of this book—in order that my readers may see the making of a dictionary as at least as heroic as the building of a bridge. Since the death of Murray a great number of new technical resources have eased dictionary making—above all the computer—but the heroism remains, the sheer dedication and slog. *The Oxford English Dictionary* was, in its first form, a remarkable engineering feat, but unlike the works of Brunel, it was seen from the start that it could never be finished. A dictionary is obsolete as soon as it appears, in the sense that it cannot keep up with the influx of new words into the language. It requires periodic supplementation, and the *OED* has had four massive volumes added to it, under the editorship of R. W. Burchfield. Thanks to the computer, it has been possible with immense speed to incorporate these many additions into the existing body of the original work. In 1989 the second edition of the *OED* comprised twenty large volumes, but it by no means represents the totality of the English language, since about four hundred new words come into it every year. Murray was selective in a way that the new lexicographers may not be, but the principle of selection remains. Some words—"nonce words" (neologisms coined for a particular occasion but destined to die soon), trade names, cant, and terms heavily technological—present problems and require long discussion. The new *OED* is a liberal triumph—there are no taboo terms anymore. You will find definitions of all the slang and argot that formerly were reserved to specialist dictionaries like Partridge's.

I take, at random, some of the newer entries. A "Rubik's cube" is defined as "a puzzle consisting of a cube seemingly formed by 27 small cubes, uniform in size but of various colours, each layer of nine or eight smaller cubes being capable of rotation in its own plane; the task is to restore each face of the cube to a single colour after the uniformity has been destroyed by rotation of the various layers." "Quark," a term in physics taken from James Joyce's *Finnegans Wake* ("Three quarks for Muster Mark"—the jeers of seagulls), has its pronunciation "kwork" justified in the reproduction of a letter sent to the editor by Murray Gell-Mann on June 27, 1978, Gell-Mann being the professor who adapted the Joyceism to physics: "I needed an excuse for retaining the pronunciation quork despite the occurrence of 'Mark,' 'bark,' 'mark' and so forth in *Finnegans Wake*. I found that excuse by supposing that one ingredient of the line 'Three quarks for Muster Mark' was a cry of 'Three quarts for Muster . . .' heard in H. C. Earwicker's pub." We do not normally expect so much information in a dictionary.

Some words that once seemed too fragile or nonceish to endure have found their way into the eternal canon. The queen may be called "queenie," since it is not, as it appeared to be in the 1960s, a term of good-humored contempt but one of affection, like "Queen Mum," a usage ratified by the *Times* (August 4, 1980): "The dear old Queen Mum is . . . the best loved lady in the land." "Pseud," "pseudery," "pseudish," and "Pseuds' Corner," all taken from the satirical magazine *Private Eye*, are part of the accepted vocabulary, like "Philly"— a U.S. slang abbreviation for "Philadelphia," but not given (since trade names are not yet wholeheartedly acceptable) as a British shortening for the name of a brand of processed cheese. "Queerie" is acceptable for one who is queer. "Pakis" are around, being duly assaulted; "paki-bashing" is defined as "wanton physical assault on or other violence directed against Pakistani immigrants." The phrase "in petto" (properly "in the breast or heart—not disclosed, used of the names of cardinals designate") is falsely used to mean "on a small scale" (confusion with French *petit*) but false usage has to be included, since language is nothing if it is not usage.

What words, anyway, ought to go in? When does a nonce word become a genuine neologism, and when is a neologism accepted as a fully paid-up part of the lexis? I invented some years ago the term "amation," for the art of making love, and still think it useful. But I have to persuade others to use it in print before it is eligible for lexicographizing. T. S. Eliot's considerable authority got the word "juvescence" in without the corroboration of other bad Latinists. It comes from the lines in the poem "Gerontion": "In the juvescence of the year/Came Christ the tiger . . ." It should be "juvenescence," but Eliot never corrected it. Terms made up for one occasion only— like "apothaneintheloish"—stand little chance. The sibyl in Petronius' novel *Satyricon* says "Apathanein thelo"—I want to die. Scholars would see the value of the nonce word but would never subscribe to its becoming a part of the English lexis.

Sometimes a writer will employ an unlikely word in a playful or sincere attempt to revive its currency. The *OED* defines "defenestration" as "the action of throwing out a window." The word was apparently coined after some Bohemian radicals threw several imperial commissioners out a window in Prague; their act was a "prelude to the Thirty Years' War." In his novel *V.*, Thomas Pynchon reclaims the word: "Winsome came awake from a dream of defenestration, wondering why he hadn't thought of it before. From Rachel's bedroom window it was seven stories to a courtyard used for mean purposes only: drunk's evacuation, a dump for old beer cans and mop dust, the pleasures of nighttime cats." Years later, in *Vineland*, Pynchon returns to the word in an adjectival variant, pointing out a useful contrast between the "defenestrative personality, which prefers jumping out of windows, and the transfenestrative, which tends to jump through, each reflecting an entirely different psychic subtext . . ." At least one of Pynchon's admirers, T. Coraghessan Boyle, has used the word (in *Water Music*), but one feels the word is unlikely to be seen in print much more than this.

The Oxford English Dictionary is perhaps too great a work, as well as too bulky, for the casual consultation of someone reading a book and finding a word he does not know, or wishing to be put right on a spelling or pronunciation. When one takes down a volume of the *OED* it is for a deeper and wider instruction than quick sharp definition represents. That is why the shorter versions of the *OED* exist, such as the *Concise Oxford*. This does not give "paki-bashing" and it limits "queenie" to homosexuals. It is a compendium that has to stand comparison with the *Collins Dictionary of the English Language*—an original work that owes nothing to Oxford—which does better in most areas than its older counterpart or rival. Its definitions are more elegant. The *Concise Oxford* gives, for "cunnilingus," "stimulation of the vulva or clitoris by licking," while the *Collins* has "a sexual activity in which the female genitalia are stimulated by the partner's lips and tongue." Both dictionaries are vague on "fugue," but *Collins* does at least specify the repetition of the fugal theme a fifth above or a fourth below, while the definition in the *Concise Oxford* could refer to a canon.

Collins, too, is more exact in its science. It suffices the *Concise Oxford* to define "entropy" as "measure of the unavailability of a system's thermal energy for conversion into mechanical work; measure of the degradation or disorganization of the universe." In *Collins* we end with a formula: "$S = k\text{-log } P + c$ where P is the probability that a particular state of the system exists, k is the Boltzmann constant, and c is another constant." For "phoneme" the *Concise Oxford* is content merely with "unit of significant sound in a specified language." We need more than this, and *Collins* gives it: "/p/ and /b/ are separate phonemes in English because they distinguish such words as *pet* and *bet*, whereas the light and dark /l/ sounds in *little* are not separate phonemes since they may be transposed without changing meaning." "Phrygian" is merely, to the *Concise*, "an ancient Greek mode, reputed warlike in character," and the third of the "church modes (with E as final and C as dominant)." That "C" should be "B." *Collins* spells it out: "the natural diatonic scale from E to E."

The *Collins* probably represents the modern ideal in dictionaries of one volume that do not encumber the desk or tire the lifting hand. It also takes on, which is what we are coming to expect from dictionaries, the function of a small encyclopedia. It is probably as reasonable to want the meaning of "Quant" as of "quant," the latter meaning a punt pole and the other (Mary) the dress designer and mother of the miniskirt. Look up "Rolling Stones" and you will find

> English rock group (formed 1962): comprising Mick Jagger (born 1943; lead vocals), Keith Richards (born 1943; guitar, vocals), Brian Jones (1942–69; guitar), Charles Watts (born 1941; drums), Bill Wyman (born 1936; bass guitar), and subsequently Mick Taylor (born 1941; guitar; with the group 1969–74), and Ron Wood (born 1947; guitar; with the group from 1975). Their classic recordings include many hit singles.

The entry goes on to exemplify these and add that many of them were written by Jagger and Richards. The length of the article is an indication of the importance that the age (especially its young) accords to this rock group. The Beatles (1962–1970) are here, but not so much as the Rolling Stones. Presley, Elvis, has outlasted Dean, James. Monroe, Marilyn, follows Monroe, James, and is herself followed by the Monroe Doctrine.

Dr. Johnson, in his insular way, ignored what was happening to the English language in the American Colonies. Modern dictionaries, which consult commercial prospects as well as an ever-increasing inclusiveness, straddle the Atlantic but cannot easily disguise which foot stayed home while the other moved. *Collins* gives the parts of the verb "fit" as "fits, fitting, fitted," but it forgets that the American preterite is "fit." "Hopefully" in the sense of the German *hoffentlich* is an Americanism that had to get in, as had "ass" in the sense of "arse." An American dictionary is likely to give "arse" in the sense of "ass." *The American Heritage Dictionary* is chiefly American in its devotion to excessive scholarship, which America can afford better than Britain. For instance, it gives a supplement of Indo-European roots. And it tells one more about "chopsticks" than anyone needs to know, unless he wishes to show off in a Chinese restaurant:

Pidgin English *chop*, fast, probably from Cantonese *kap*, corresponding to Mandarin Chinese chi^2, fast, hurried.—STICK(S). A loose translation of Cantonese *fai chi* and Mandarin $kwai^4$ *tse*, 'fast ones' (originally a boatman's substitute for chu^4, chopsticks, which is a homonym of chu^4, to stop, stand still, an unlucky word for boatmen.

The numerals refer to the Chinese tones. Not even the *OED* has those.

With the growth of English as a world language, there is clearly a necessity for a kind of dictionary that consults the needs of nonnative speakers. Professor Barbara Strang, in her *A History of English*, distinguishes between three kinds of English users. The A-speakers have English as a mother tongue; B-speakers, found mostly in the former British colonial territories, learn it in childhood and accord it a special status as the tongue of law and culture; the C-speakers are the others, foreigners who study English at school and university and recognize its importance as a medium of world communication. This means that there are a lot of English users: the A group alone probably comprises four hundred million. *The Longman Dictionary of Contemporary English* is a good example of a work for the C-speakers. It posits for the user an initial maximum vocabulary of two thousand words, and computers were employed to stop that vocabulary getting above itself. The nudity of some of the definitions would have shocked Dr. Johnson. "Net," which he was able to define only by calling up such words as "decussated" and "reticulated" (the literary artist instinctively making his definition an image of the thing itself) is here "a material of strings, wires, threads, etc. twisted, tied or woven together with regular equal spaces between them." This is lucid. Let us go back to that word "entropy" and look at definition 1 of *The American Heritage Dictionary*:

A measure of the capacity of a system to undergo spontaneous change thermodynamically specified by the relationship $dS = dQ/T$, where dS is an infinitesimal change in the measure of a system absorbing an infinitesimal quantity of heat dQ at absolute temperature.

Longman gives: "a measure of the difference between the temperatures of something which heats and something which is being heated."

That is definition 1. Definition 2 is: "the state which the universe will reach when all the heat is spread out evenly." The *American Heritage*, though for A-users, is not helpful to the reader of an A-book that contains a statement like "American literature from *The Education of Henry Adams* to Thomas Pynchon's *Gravity's Rainbow* is a pessimistic forecast of human entropy." The *Longman*, whose users will be a long time getting to Henry Adams, is nakedly clear and concise.

We are so accustomed to the blurring of definition in sexual areas that we are a little shocked to find "fuck: (esp. of a man) to have sex with (someone, esp. a woman)" and "cunt: VAGINA (you + N) a foolish or nasty person." A dildo is "an object shaped like the male sex organ (PENIS) that can be placed inside the female sex organ (VAGINA) for sexual pleasure." Some aspects of religion are, it seems, too naively presented. An angel in *Longman* is "a messenger and servant of God, usu. represented as a person with large wings and dressed in white clothes." Join the A-train of the *American Heritage* and you will arrive at "an immortal, spiritual being attendant upon God. In medieval angelology, one of nine orders of spiritual beings (listed from the highest to the lowest in rank): seraphim, cherubim, thrones, dominations or dominions, virtues, powers, principalities, archangels, and angels." No wings, no white garments. C-English, of its nature, cannot penetrate far below surfaces. But, with the non-cradle speaker, it is the only way to A. A means Henry James and Joseph Conrad and the historical approach to the language that will lead back to Shakespeare, Chaucer, eventually *Beowulf* and Alfred the Great. A very tiny percentage of the English speakers of the world want English literature.

All dictionaries now indicate pronunciation with the International Phonetic Alphabet. The great Murray devised his own phonetic system, excellent in its way and retained until the second edition of the *OED*: its main drawback was its inability to represent foreign sounds. Knowing English means knowing a large number of exotic expressions—*tête-à-tête, table d'hôte, con amore,* and so on—which are further proof of the hospitable nature of the language. *Le Mot Juste: The Penguin Dictionary of Foreign Terms and Phrases* has four hundred pages of items that appear in one's general reading, sometimes even at the journalistic level. Ability to give *Weltanschauung* and *perestroika* the right pronunciation is regarded as a mark of culture. One needs the IPA.

Dictionaries that once timidly flirted with it used what is known as the broad variety. This is dangerous and not now much found. It presents "feet" as /fiːt/ and "fit" as /fit/, implying that the vowel is the same in both instances, length being the only differentiator. The same thing happens with "suit" (/suːt/) and "soot" (/sut/). The narrow form—the one I have employed in this book—is the only one to be used, and it should be as narrow as possible. The pronunciation that all British dictionaries give is RP, which not all English speakers— especially in Britain—wish to follow. I, as a Mancunian, am not always happy with the dictionary representations of RP myself. The diphthong in "know" is invariably given as /əʊ/. It used to be /ou/, which signified lip-rounding on both elements of the diphthong, but the initial schwa has taken over. To me, this makes the pronunciation of "oboe" affected in the manner of J. Arthur Rank starlets in British films of the 1950s. I am not too happy either with the pronunciation of my own name as given in the *Collins Dictionary of the English Language*—/bɜːdʒɪs/. In the second syllable I have, till this quiet correction, used the schwa. After a month or so of docile obedience to *Collins*—and, for that matter, to the Duke of Edinburgh, who announced a discourse of mine at a language conference with what is apparently the orthodox rendering of my name, merely recorded by *Collins*—I reverted to the schwa—/bɜːdʒəs/. There is nobody who dare say that I am wrong. We all have our pet pronunciations of names and words: I, for instance, stress "masturbatory" on the second syllable and not on the first (secondary stress) and the third (primary stress). All dictionaries beg to differ with me. We are permitted our small eccentricities, but in the main, we must cling to what the dictionaries say. They speak not with the authority of their editors, but with that of the language community. My idiolect, or personal manner of using English, must finally bend to the consensus of the tribe.

29.

GIVING IT STRAIGHT

In our age, anything we say may be taken down and used in evidence against us. When our speech is taken down electronically—by tape or cassette—we are given evidence of our own linguistic incompetence. Our conversation is full of unnecessary stabilizers like "you see" and "you know" and "actually," the right word is groped for and not always found, we fill in with the schwa spelled as "er," our grammar is faulty, sentences begin but do not end. This is the nature of informal speech, as also of informal speeches. To improvise at length is to court great linguistic danger. Though language is essentially what the mouth utters, the discourse that fills up so much of our lives is recognized by us all as lacking in such qualities as elegance and conciseness, to say nothing of what the pundits would call correctness. When we write, not speak, we have an opportunity to consult these, er, desiderata.

Language is a slippery medium, and it is not really suited to exactness. In the "Memories" sections of his *Myths and Memories* (1986), Gilbert Adair gives us the following:

I remember, on television, the credit title sequence of the Harry Worth show: the camera (though, of course, invisible) was positioned, manifestly on the pavement itself, at one end of a street coextensively flanked by a shop window; at the far end of the street, precisely where it formed a right-angle-intersection with another, stood Worth, the right side of his body obscured by the transversal section of the same shop window, with the result that the visible (left) side of his body was "completed" by its own full-length reflection in that section of the window running parallel to the spectator's viewpoint. When he (Worth) raised his left leg in the air, one therefore had the illusion of both his legs leaving the ground simultaneously (and the prolixity of that description impresses upon me just how difficult it is to convey in words alone the sort of trivial memory which has no need of them).

Precisely. Language is far better fitted to the description of the emotional impact of a sunset than to that of a precise visual experience that depends more on line than on color. When language attempts the lexicographer's task, that of defining, it is often in difficulties.

Here, for example, is the *Collins* definition of "wood": "the hard fibrous substance consisting of xylem tissue that occurs beneath the bark in trees, shrubs, and similar plants." If we look up, as most of us must, "xylem," we find: "a plant tissue that conducts water and mineral salts from the roots to all other parts, provides mechanical support, and forms the wood of trees and shrubs." "Wood" gets into that definition, and there is a sensation of circularity, especially since xylem derives from the Greek *xulon,* meaning "wood." Words can be defined only by using other words, and words represent a closed system in which we are trapped. If "man" means "an adult male human being, as distinguished from a woman," "male" has to mean "of, relating to, or characteristic of a man, masculine," unless we prefer "of, relating to, or designating the sex producing gametes (spermatozoa) that can fertilise female gametes (ova)." One kind of exactness is achieved only by rigorous technical description, daunting to those inquirers who seek a quick, straight, simple answer. Imagine the reader of a novel who has just met "He banged out a dominant seventh chord on the organ." He already knows, he thinks, "chord." What is a dominant seventh? "A chord consisting of the dominant and the major third, perfect fifth, and minor seventh above it. Its most natural resolution is to a chord on the tonic." And what is the dominant? "The fifth of the scale." A scale? "A group of notes taken in ascending or descending order, esp. within the compass of one octave." All he really wants is something like "He

banged out a chord that said, in effect, that the next chord would be
the last one."

The majority of the words in a dictionary we already know. The
defining of them, which with words like "man" and "wood" we do
not really need, is really a kind of exercise of a strongly intellectual
nature—understanding by verbal reduction, though the reduction is
often a trick. A dictionary appeals to the brain, not to the sense or
the emotion. A good deal of the reading we do addresses the brain.
This, for example, put out in the owner's manual of the A-007 auto
reverse double cassette deck and printed in Tokyo:

CONNECTING THE BUS LINE JACKS

By connecting the BUS LINE jacks, the power on/off of this unit
can be operated on the amplifier.
Connect the BUS LINE jack to the BUS LINE jack of the A-007 ampli-
fier with the supplied control cord.
The BUS LINE jacks can be used as either input or output.
Make connection to either jack.
When connecting the BUS LINE jacks, be sure to turn off the power
of this unit and the A-007 amplifier.
Refer to the owner's manual of the A-007 amplifier for using this
unit in the L component system.

It is as well to know what a jack is. It is as well to have the instrument,
the physical entity that words feebly describe, in front of one. This
language of instruction is filling part of our lives. Another part is
broached by information we think we need, though we are not sure
what to do with it. We get a great deal of it from our newspapers.

Here is some journalistic information:

Startling new research suggests that adding chlorine to drinking
water may increase the risk of children contracting leukemia.

A paper to be presented to the annual conference of the Institute
of British Geographers in Glasgow this week shows that children
drinking water with low levels of chlorine tend to be less likely to
contract acute lymphatic leukemia than those subjected to higher
levels of the chemical.

If confirmed, the findings could confront Britain's beleaguered
water industry with its biggest health crisis to date. Most drinking
water is treated with chlorine to kill bacteria.

Some scientists have already warned that the treatment could cause cancer, but firm evidence has been scarce. If the results of this new research are confirmed, the water industry is likely to face demands to switch to different ways of purifying drinking water, an expensive exercise which would pose problems for the newly privatised water companies.

This does not seem, like the technical instructions emanating from Tokyo, to be the product of a kind of writing machine, except in the secondary senses of word processing (or typing) and printing. There is a person who has put the information together (and much more). He is Geoffrey Lean, the environment correspondent of the *Observer*, the British Sunday newspaper. He hardly intrudes here, except with the words "startling" and "beleaguered," which imply a minimal judgment on his part. The information is all that really counts. We may have an emotional response to it—fear, indignation—but this response is not engineered by the words used, only by the facts delivered by the words. The information Mr. Lean received from his sources has been arranged by him to instruct the reader aimlessly, if that is the right word, and with as much impersonality as a person can contrive. If, forsaking journalism and assuming the demagogue's role, he had wished to fire the public to anger and action, he might have made the following statement:

Every child in Britain is likely to die, and die soon, painfully, agonisingly, horribly. Make no mistake about it—the ghastly scourge of leukemia is going to strike, to strike deeply, to strike widely. And why? Because of the criminal stupidity of a government that blithely, thoughtlessly, and yet murderously infects our drinking water with the deadly pollutant chlorine.

And so on. This is a kind of political rhetoric that seeks to make its impact through exaggeration, repetition, cliché ("ghastly scourge," "criminal stupidity," and so on), and lies. The facts are less important than the attitude.

It is probably easier to make language appeal to the emotions—which usually means the prejudices—than to the understanding. The mere act of constructing statements intended to give objective information draws, often unconsciously, on rhetorical devices—metaphors, melodious repetitions, the strategic placing of key words—

which move as much as they instruct. In his *Axel's Castle* (1931) the late Edmund Wilson cites a passage from the *United States Court Martial Manual*:

> The Army is an emergent arm of the public service which the Nation holds ready for a time of great peril. Military service is an obligation which every citizen owes to the government. It is settled law that such service may be compelled, if necessary, by draft. Nor is the obligation of the soldier who volunteers for a fixed period different from that of the drafted soldier. By his act of volunteering he consecrates himself to the military service. His engagement, supported by an oath of allegiance, is that the nation may depend on him for such service during the fixed period, whatever may be the emergency. When this engagement is breached a high obligation to the nation is disregarded, a solemn oath of allegiance is violated, and the Government is defrauded in the amount of its outlay incident to inducting the soldier into the military service, training, clothing and caring for him, and transporting him to the station from which he deserts. Desertion is thus seen to be, not simply a breach of contract for personal service, but a grave crime against the Government; in time of war perhaps the gravest that a soldier can commit, and at such times punishable with death.

Wilson points at the "cumulative rhythms" and particularly the resounding drum thump of the final "death." But the whole extract is full of emotive expressions like "compelled" and "obligation" and "consecrates," the last word bringing a dim religious light to the theme of secular duty. "A solemn oath of allegiance is violated": one expects "death" at the end. The government is turned, by association, into a mother who clothes and cares for her son, whose betrayal is the ultimate wickedness. The few dollars it costs to transport him "to the station from which he deserts" are the grimly saved and ruthlessly squandered pennies of a poor old woman, and it seems that he is transported to a station from which, from the start, the wretched soldier intends to desert. In the reading, as opposed to the far more rhetorical hearing, of the passage, stock responses are engendered by uppercase letters—"Army," "Nation," "Government"—as though these were God. Yet this passage was intended to give objective information. It is evidently the work of a jurist (defined as a "writer of legal subjects"), but one suspects also an advocate skilled in prosecution briefs.

The writing of the late nineteenth century, in both Britain and the United States, was the work of men and women schooled in Latin, who tried to bring the orotundity of Cicero to English, a language that does not naturally behave like the grammar-bound tongue of the Roman Empire. Here is John Ruskin (1819–1900) in his Preface to the first edition of *Modern Painters*:

> Perhaps there is no more impressive scene on earth than the solitary extent of the Campagna of Rome under evening light. Let the reader imagine himself for a moment withdrawn from the sounds and motion of the living world, and sent forth alone into this wild and wasted plain. The earth yields and crumbles beneath his foot, tread he never so lightly, for its substance is white, hollow, and carious, like the dusty wreck of the bones of men. The long knotted grass waves and tosses feebly in the evening wind, and the shadows of its motion shake feverishly along the banks of ruin that lift themselves to the sunlight. Hillocks of mouldering earth heave around him, as if the dead beneath were struggling in their sleep; scattered blocks of black stone, four-square, remnants of mighty edifices, not one left upon another, lie upon them to keep them down . . .

And here is Cardinal John Henry Newman (1801–1890), writing, in his *Grammar of Assent*, of the importance of the classical authors:

> Passages which to a boy are but rhetorical commonplaces, neither better nor worse than a hundred others which any clever writer might supply, which he gets by heart and thinks very fine, and imitates, as he thinks, successfully, in his own flowing versification; at length come home to him when long years have passed, and he has had experience of life, and pierce him, as if he had never before known them, with their sad earnestness and vivid exactness. Then he comes to understand how it is that lines, the birth of some chance morning or evening at an Ionian festival, or among the Sabine hills, have lasted generation after generation, for thousands of years, with a power over the mind and a charm which the current

literature of his own day, with all its obvious advantages, is utterly unable to rival . . .

Ruskin and Newman are excellent writers, and very persuasive. Describing the Roman Campagna, Ruskin is not merely giving topographical information: he is using words to instill an attitude in the reader, to convey to him a personal sense of desolation in that particular landscape. "White, hollow, and carious" is especially telling, since it seems to refer to a tooth, locating external decay in the very person of the reader. The sheer length of the sentences in the Newman passage connote earnestness, a desire to persuade through making the sentence structures seem the product of long, slow, preliminary lucubration—no tentativeness, no hesitation. We are persuaded that what he writes is generally true, though it must be demonstrably true only of himself.

In the twentieth century, and especially after the Great War, some authors associated this manner of writing with the mode of thought of an outmoded culture, a rhetoric that may in itself have been responsible for the complacency that slaughtered, unthinkingly, a whole generation. There was probably no logic in this attitude, but certainly there was, with writers like Ernest Hemingway (1899–1961), a desire to be restricted to very plain statements, "simple declarative sentences," as Hemingway put it, which should expunge the dangerously rhetorical, even the intellectual, and seem to present humanity as driven by physical impulses, not by thought or even emotion. So, in his *The Old Man and the Sea*, a fairly late production, Hemingway presents his old Cuban fisherman, who has been battling with sharks, like this:

> He started to climb again and at the top he fell and lay for some time with the mast across his shoulder. He tried to get up. But it was too difficult and he sat there with the mast on his shoulder and looked at the road. A cat passed on the far side going about its business and the old man watched it. Then he just watched the road.
>
> Finally he put the mast down and stood up. He picked the mast up and put it on his shoulder and started up the road. He had to sit down five times before he reached his shack.
>
> Inside the shack he leaned the mast against the wall. In the dark he found a water bottle and took a drink. Then he lay down on

the bed. He pulled the blanket over his shoulders and then over his back and legs and he slept face down on the newspapers with his arms out straight and the palms of his hands up.

The Hemingway style can all too easily be parodied. Louis MacNeice (1907–1963) imagined a Hemingway character entering a Hebridean hovel:

A man knocked at the door of the Black House. Nobody answered. The man opened the door and went into the byre. He went through the byre into the living-room. There were four men in the living-room and a woman. The room was full of smoke.

"May I sit down?" he asked them.

The men and the woman said nothing.

He took a box that was lying on its side. He turned the box up on end and sat on the end of the box.

"I would like a drink," he said.

"Aye," one of the men said.

"I would like a drink," he said.

The woman looked at him and got up. She took a broken cup down from the dresser. She took a jug off the dresser and poured water from the jug into the cup. She gave him the cup and sat down again in her chair. The chair had a castor missing.

He tasted the water and put the cup down on the floor.

"I would like a drink," he said.

The woman shrugged her shoulders.

"I would like a drink," he said.

This way of writing, obviously more suitable for narrative than the exposition of ideas, has a respectable ancestry. Hemingway, working as a cub reporter on the *Kansas City Star*, had been told to keep things plain and simple, and he transferred the journalistic technique to literature. But the true ancestor is to be found in the Bible. Because of the tendency in the Hebrew language to avoid what are known as subordinating conjunctions—"when," "since," "although"—and to join sentences with the coordinating conjunctions "and" and "but," the style of the Authorized Version (1611) seems, to readers of Ruskin and Newman, telling but primitive—the written record of a prehistoric society struggling into history. Hemingway was reverting from a stage of high sophistication to one in which men and women, like the early Hebrews, were concerned with survival, not the delicacies of civilization. He was also producing literature, which we are not yet ready to define. Are the Ruskin and Newman extracts also literature? In the sense that both are didactic, concerned with employing a number of verbal devices to make up the reader's mind for him, they are not quite literature. Pornography uses verbal devices also to induce a state of sexual excitement, but however efficiently the end is achieved (the reader panting, eventually masturbating) we do not consider it to be literature either. Literature clearly has something to do with not forcing the reader into a state of mind (or physicality) that places the writer in a position of advantage over him. How about that newspaper item about leukemia and chlorine—is that literature? No, because it makes no appeal to the imagination: it presents bald facts, as does my A-007 manual. Literature, then, is both static (in that it neither teaches nor inflames) and imaginative. And—this is important from the angle of our present study—it does not quite obey the regular laws of language.

In the higher journalism, not the tabloids, we often seem to be on the verge of literature. I do not refer to news items, though these may be presented by a special correspondent in a manner that consults elegance and the need for imaginative appeal. But, however much the journalist renders his own opinions or experience, he is tied to a medium whose main function is to inform. Here is Katharine Whitehorn (again the *Observer*):

> Our vet leads a varied life. He de-worms pussy cats, he spays bitches, he helps when the erotic snakes used by Soho strippers go limp. But he won't go to quite a few guard dogs at all: he says they have been made deliberately uncontrollable. They are a good cheap way to guard unoccupied premises: yet the dog can't know the difference between a gang come to steal the plant, and an adventurous eight-year-old who has managed to climb the fence. In the last century they outlawed man-traps, on the grounds that they were punishment without trial; all the same arguments apply to dogs expected to savage and maim intruders.

This is not news, but it is information, although it may be said to be information on which we have already been long informed. The informality is appropriate to a weekly column that, catering to the same readership for years, has to be relaxed and friendly while nevertheless doing a job for which that readership pays. Thus, "vet," not "veterinary surgeon," "pussy cats," a touch of naughtiness in the reference to striptease artistes, and enough colorless language or cliché to reinforce the relaxed attitude. Journalism may not dare too much. It can be gently humorous and ironic, very lightly touched by idiosyncrasy, but it must not repel readers by digging too deeply. This is especially true of its approach to language: the conventions are not questioned. The questioning of linguistic conventions is one of the main duties of what we call literature.

30.

WHAT WE CALL LITERATURE

It has always been accepted that literature does not use the language of everyday life. This is especially true of poetry, which, even when its lexis draws on the stock of ordinary speech, uses elements that seem artificial, though artistic (and no seeming about it) would be an apter term.

> Let us go then, you and I,
> When the evening is spread out against the sky
> Like a patient etherised upon a table;

That is the opening of T. S. Eliot's "The Love Song of J. Alfred Prufrock," a modern or modernist poem first published in 1915. It upset lovers of Keats, Shelley, Tennyson, and the Georgian poets precisely because its language was colloquial, not high-flown, and its images startled, as those of traditional poetry did not. The experience of a surgical operation was not considered proper material for a simile. There is not one word in those three lines, except perhaps for "etherised," that we would not use in everyday life, and yet the arrangement of the words is somewhat remote from ordinary usage. We do not rhyme when we speak, and we do not fabricate surprising images: few of us would naturally liken evening to a patient awaiting an operation. The modernist movement in poetry was distinguished by a desire to get away from this kind of thing:

> When do I see thee most, beloved one?
>   When in the light the spirits of mine eyes
>   Before thy face, their altar, solemnise
> The worship of that Love through thee made known
> Or when, in the dusk hours, (we two alone),
>   Close-kissed and eloquent of still replies
>   Thy twilight-hidden glimmering visage lies,
> And my soul only sees thy soul its own?

That is the octave of a sonnet by Dante Gabriel Rossetti (1828–1882). Victorians did not speak like that—"thee" and "thou" and "thy" had long disappeared, except in dialect, and "close-kissed" and "twilight-hidden" and "glimmering visage" were not items in ordinary discourse. Yet Eliot (1888–1965), even as he reformed the language of poetry, was committed, as Rossetti had been, to manipulating words in the service of a kind of communication remote from that of the street and the marketplace. This is in the nature of poetry.

The remoteness goes back a long way. We have, as I said much earlier, little notion of how Old English was used in the banal but necessary exchanges of ordinary living, but we have the high-flown work of the Anglo-Saxon *scops* or poets. They did not use rhyme, which was probably a Celtic invention, but they fastened the elements of their lines together with alliteration:

> Wæs se grimma gæst   Grendel haten,
> mære mearc-stapa,   se Þe moras heold,
> fen ond fæsten.

("That grim spirit was called Grendel,/the renowned wanderer of the marshes,/who held the moors, the fen and the fastness.") The need to find words beginning with the same sound (properly head rhyme, since alliteration is concerned with the same letters) meant frequently avoiding common terms and devising uncommon ones. *Wiga* meant "warrior," but it had to be ornamented with a prefix for the sake of the sound—*æsc-wiga* ("spear-warrior"), *beado-wiga* ("battle-warrior"), *byrn-wiga* ("warrior in his corselet"), *gar-wiga* ("spear-warrior"), and so on. The tradition of what is called poetic diction started early.

Petrified forms that had pushed themselves away from daily usage
are typical of eighteenth-century poetry. Here is Dr. Johnson, as poet
or merely versifier, in his Prologue to *Cato*, a play by Joseph Addison
(1672–1719):

> The drama's laws, the drama's patrons give,
> For we that live to please, must please to live.
> Then prompt no more the follies you decry,
> As tyrants doom their tools of guilt to die;
> 'Tis Yours, this night, to bid the reign commence
> Of rescued Nature and reviving Sense;
> To chase the charms of Sound, the pomp of Show
> For useful Mirth and salutary Woe;
> Bid scenic Virtue form the rising age,
> And Truth diffuse her radiance from the stage.

That opening couplet shows in an exemplary manner the power
of verse to sum up briefly in an epigram and, in effect, to create a
piece of proverbial wisdom, but the rest of this sample is so abstract
that it conveys no images and, indeed, very little meaning. An eighteenth-century versifier was expected to parade generalities of this
kind ("Nature," "Sense," "Sound," "Mirth," "Woe," "Virtue") and
sustain, with this special language, a distinction between the way men
speak and poets write. Here is Oliver Goldsmith (1730–1774) with
his *The Deserted Village*:

> But times are alter'd: trade's unfeeling train
> Usurp the land and dispossess the swain;
> Along the lawn, where scatter'd hamlets rose,
> Unwieldy wealth: and cumbrous pomp repose;
> And every want to opulence allied,
> And every pang that folly pays to pride . . .

"Swain," from Old English *swān*, meaning "swineherd," has no longer
any vitality; it is a purely conventional term that hides the image of
a genuine sweating peasant. It is an abstraction, like "wealth" and
"pomp." It was the aim of William Wordsworth (1770–1850) to bring
to poetry the speech of ordinary men and women, but not even he
could divest himself of old poetic habits, such as the inversion of
words:

A slumber did my spirit seal;
  I had no human fears:
She seem'd a thing that could not feel
  The touch of earthly years . . .

Nobody speaks, or spoke, in the manner of that first line. With the
Romantic movement, which Wordsworth, with Samuel Taylor Coleridge (1772–1834), may be said to have initiated in England, there
is, true, an eschewal of the old Johnsonian and Goldsmithian diction,
a return to the actual and particular, as in Shakespeare ("Daffodils,
that come before the swallow dares"), but we are no nearer to the
language we use in the street and the home. John Keats (1795–1821)
writes, in his exquisite "Ode on Melancholy":

Ay, in the very temple of delight
  Veil'd Melancholy has her sovran shrine,
Though seen of none save him whose strenuous tongue
  Can burst Joy's grape against his palate fine;
His soul shall taste the sadness of her might,
  And be among her cloudy trophies hung.

He was not a Lancastrian but a Cockney and would not naturally say
"Ay." He would say "sovereign," not "sovran." He would speak of a
"fine palate," admitting that the inversion was "poetical." He would
not, as in that last line, normally follow the Germanic usage of a past
participle shunted to the end of the clause. Keats was great enough
to transcend the limitations of the new poetic diction, but as the
nineteenth century advanced, there was the danger with lesser poets
that the language of their verse would take off into the air, becoming
a kind of mindless music not anchored to sense as we think we know
it. Algernon Charles Swinburne (1837–1909) has, in his *Atalanta in
Calydon*:

The ivy falls with the Bacchanal's hair
  Over her eyebrows hiding her eyes;
The wild vine slipping down leaves bare
  Her bright breast shortening into sighs;
The wild vine slips with the weight of its leaves,
But the berried ivy catches and cleaves

To the limbs that glitter, the feet that scare
  The wolf that follows, the fawn that flies.

The vocabulary here, except for "Bacchanal," has, in fact, no items
that we would disdain to use in ordinary speech, but the rhythm
seems more important than the meaning, to say nothing of the head
rhyme that does not have, as in Old English poetry, a structural
function but is purely decorative. There would be no loss of general
effect if the stanza were rewritten like this:

The Bacchanal falls with the ivy's hair
  Hiding her eyebrows over her eyes;
The slipping vine leaves leave it bare—
  Her breast short brightening into sighs;
The vine waits wild with the lisp of its leaves,
But the ivy catches the buried sheaves
To the feet that flitter, the limbs that snare
  The fawn that follows, the fox that flies.

T. S. Eliot and Ezra Pound (1885–1972) tried to bring the language
of verse and of common discourse (though mostly the common discourse of the highly educated) closer together. This sometimes entailed the liquidation of properties once thought indispensable to
poetry—regular meters and often, though not always, rhyme. Vers
libre, or free verse, brought poetry closer to prose and demonstrated
that the distinction between prose and poetry had never been a valid
one. Poetry lay in the compression of language, the deployment of
connotation, the telling image.

There died a myriad,
And of the best, among them,
For an old bitch gone in the teeth,
For a botched civilisation.
Charm, smiling at the good mouth,
Quick eyes gone under earth's lid.

For two gross of broken statues,
For a few thousand battered books.

That comes from the poem sequence *Hugh Selwyn Mauberley* and is Pound's epitaph on the fallen of the Great War. There are some remnants of regular verse in it—the chime of "bitch" and "botched" and the slant rhyme of "teeth" and "mouth." The first line employs an inversion in the old style, but it was probably essential to shunt the key word "myriad" to the end. Words carry a heavier weight than they would in normal speech. The "quick" eyes are live (as in "the quick and the dead") as well as lively, and they go under the earth quickly. The eyes have lids, and the earth has a lid whose closure forbids the resumption of quickness. The "two gross" of statues are, arithmetically, 288, an insufficient number to represent the art which, with the 3,000 or 4,000 books (3,000 would be more than "a few"), stand for Western civilization, but the numerology of poetry bears little relation to that of the nonpoetic world. The "gross" is there for its adjectival connotation. The "old bitch gone in the teeth" is a fusion of Queen Victoria and the aged and impotent British lion. The kind of linguistic study we have been conducting is not really competent to explicate the poem. Orthodox grammar must frown on the sixth and seventh lines, which do not make a "well-formed sentence" and do not seem to stand in apposition to the "myriad" of the opening.

The verse will not accommodate the kind of scansion appropriate to "I wandered lonely as a cloud," but the lineation is necessary, and the passage would produce a different effect on the reader if set as prose. The unit of verse is the line, but the unit of prose is the sentence. To sum up, the language is, except for that "myriad" (which means too large a number to compute, though in Greek—*murios*—it means ten thousand), that of ordinary speech; its organization, however, is in conformity with the assumption that literature does not work in the same way as ordinary discourse.

The modernists' use of free verse did not, except with inferior practitioners, blur the prose-verse dichotomy. The opening of T. S. Eliot's *The Waste Land* makes a prosodic pattern out of present participle endings that are not quite rhyme:

April is the cruelest month, breeding
Lilacs out of the dead land, mixing
Memory and desire, stirring
Dull roots with spring rain.

Winter kept us warm, covering
Earth in forgetful snow, feeding
A little life with dried tubers.

But what immediately follows seems to be only ostensibly verse. It must retain the appearance of verse to obviate a kind of shock to the reading eye, but it is genuine prose:

Summer surprised us, coming over the Starnbergersee
With a shower of rain; we stopped in the colonnade,
And went on in sunlight, into the Hofgarten,
And drank coffee, and talked for an hour.
Bin gar keine Russin, stamm' aus Litauen, echt deutsch.
And when we were children, staying at the archduke's
My cousin's, he took me out on a sled,
And I was frightened . . .

Genuine prose in its movement, but not in its organization. The sudden shift of scene, the intrusion of a voice without introduction, the continuation ("And") of a conversation rather than its commencement, all point to a technique closer to cinema than to prose narrative. But cinema is visual poetry: poetry came first. Poetry is compression.

Gerard Manley Hopkins (1844–1889) was a modernist ahead of his time, and his poetry was first published in book form in 1918, when the Pound-Eliot movement had already begun. Hopkins's innovations sought to introduce into verse the rhythm of speech without dissolving the existing verse forms, particularly the sonnet. He was very far from being a writer of free verse: freedom was to consist in obeying the traditional rules of prosody in all respects save one—the number of syllables in a line was to be highly variable. Alfred Lord Tennyson (1809–1892) could write:

Myriads of rivulets hurrying thro' the lawn,
The moan of doves in immemorial elms,
And murmuring of innumerable bees,

maintaining a pattern of five beats to a line and more or less ten syllables. This Hopkins called "running rhythm." His own technique he called "sprung rhythm," implying that the syllabic patterns sprung out of the stress element. The following is the opening of the sonnet "Duns Scotus's Oxford":

> Towery city and branchy between towers;
> Cuckoo-echoing, bell-swarmèd, lark-charmèd, rook-racked,
>   river-rounded;
> The dapple-eared a lily below thee; that country and town did
> Once encounter in, here coped and poisèd powers . . .

The first line is as orthodox as any of Tennyson's, but the second has seventeen syllables—unthinkable under the old dispensation but acceptable if one accommodates speed of utterance to the steady beat of live stresses. This is sprung rhythm. It is only in the invocation of speech, which is rhythmically variable and impatient of the tum-ti tum-ti tum beat of the older poetry, that Hopkins seems to be breaking away from the past. He has a "thee" there and will soon have a "thou"; his composite words ("cuckoo-echoing," "lark-charmèd," and so on) follow the Romantic tradition and even, as with "charmèd," resurrect a lost pronunciation. But, if we look more closely at those epithets, we shall see a compression not associated with Romantic poetry. "Lark-charmèd" is perhaps vague, but "bell-swarmèd" is not. "Cuckoo-echoing" is a small marvel of evocation.

Hopkins worked in packed lines, with every word loaded to the limit with meaning and (here he is a very eccentric subject for language students) with an impatient elimination of colorless morphemes. In "The Loss of the Eurydice" he has:

> But to Christ lord of thunder
> Crouch; lay knee by earth low under:
>   "Holiest, loveliest, bravest,
> Save my hero, O Hero savest,
>
> And the prayer thou hearst me making
> Have, at the awful overtaking,
>   Heard; have heard and granted
> Grace that day grace was wanted."

The imperative "have heard" is rare enough, and made somewhat grotesque, though telling, by the interposition of "at the awful overtaking." But the omission of the relative pronoun in "O Hero savest"

is inexcusable, though justified by Hopkins on the grounds of analogy
with forms like "the girl I love" (no relative pronoun there). In "The
Bugler's First Communion" we have the following:

Recorded only, I have put my lips on please
Would brandle adamantine heaven with ride and jar, did
        Prayer go disregarded;
Forward-like, but however, and like favourable heaven heard
    these.

The second line is semantically startling. "Brandle" is an obsolete
word for "shake"; "adamantine" is both "unyielding, inflexible" and
"lustrous, like a diamond"; "ride and jar"—a brusque pair of monosyllables in contrast to that learned polysyllable—make physical sense
without translation. But that final line has to be rendered somewhat
in this manner: "Perhaps I have been too eager, but that is the way
things are, and it is probable that Heaven was favorable and heard
my prayers." That is less a translation than a reading between the
words. The statement could not possibly yield to orthodox grammatical analysis.

The interchanging of parts of speech is common in colloquial English. "All systems go"—an astronaut's signal—uses a verb as a kind
of adjective. Some black New Yorkers guilty of rape in Central Park
said they were "wilding"—adjective as verb. But Hopkins follows
Shakespeare in much bolder transpositions. To "selve" is to be oneself, to express unequivocally one's inner essence. But when a forest
falls to the ax it is "unselved." The word "sake" in "for God's sake" is
a very shadowy noun that only achieves bright nounhood in Hopkins.
Of Henry Purcell he says:

Let him oh! with his air of angels then lift me, lay me! only I'll
Have an eye to the sakes of him, quaint moonmarks, to his
    pelted
                plumage under
Wings . . .

He explains what he means in a letter to his friend Robert Bridges:

It is the *sake* of "for the sake of," *forsake, namesake, keepsake.* I mean
by it the being a thing has outside itself, as a voice by its echo, a

face by its reflection, a body by its shadow, a man by his name, fame, or memory, *and also* that in the thing by virtue of which especially it has this being abroad, and that is something distinctive, marked, specifically or individually speaking, as for a voice and echo clearness; for a reflected image light, brightness; for a shadow-casting body bulk; for a man of genius, great achievements, amiability and so on. In this case it is, as the sonnet says, distinctive quality in genius.

Words work hard in Hopkins, so hard that they may contain not only a large number of connotations in addition to the denotation, or bald dictionary definition, but even a direct contradiction. We occasionally meet, in everyday life, a word that can have two opposed meanings, such as "let." To let is to allow, but it is also to prevent or, as a noun, the act of preventing. In British passports foreign governments are asked to allow the traveler to move "without let or hindrance," and Hamlet, saying "By heaven, I'll make a ghost of him that lets me," is using the verb in the sense of "stops." We have no problem in keeping the two meanings distinct, but in a poem the opposition could be exploited to the end of deliberate ambiguity. This happens with the word "buckle" in Hopkins's sonnet "The Windhover." Hopkins, a Jesuit priest of great devoutness, sees a kestrel or windhover flying and finds in it something of the beauty of Christ. He says: "Brute beauty and valour and act, oh, air, pride, plume, here/Buckle! . . ." "Buckle" can be used to describe the collapse of a bicycle wheel but also the fastening of a belt. This latter meaning has very positive associations: it suggests, for instance, preparing for military acts. Hopkins seems to be describing (especially as he addresses the kestrel Christ as "my chevalier") the properties of proud flight as being fastened together like a suit of armor. At the same time they collate in his own mind as a complex of action, beauty, and nobility that he is unworthy to attain and in whose presence he feels humble. This use of language (not necessarily a conscious use) has been dealt with at some length in the late William Empson's *Seven Types of Ambiguity* (1930). Ambiguity is dangerous in utilitarian language, but it provides the harmonics of the complicated music of literature. A poet will be more strongly aware of the history of a word than its mere casual user. Inside that history changes of meaning leading to eventual ambiguity will be set forth. W. H. Auden (1907–1973) was, for instance, fascinated by the word "buxom," which is applied to a woman of healthy proportions. He could not forget that the Old English word *būgan*, to bend, was behind it (be pliant? Be yielding?). It is hard for a poet not to notice that "violin" is close to "violence," even though there is no etymological connection.

If Hopkins, among the poets, is the least tractable of artists from the viewpoint of linguistic science, James Joyce (1882–1941) is his counterpart in the field of the novel. *Ulysses* (1922—the same year as Eliot's *The Waste Land*) upset, among other things, old notions of literary decorum, such as the assumption that a writer should always try to write well (elegantly, intelligently, with a measure of originality). Joyce deliberately writes badly:

> Prepatory to anything else Mr. Bloom brushed off the greater bulk of the shavings and handed Stephen the hat and ashplant and bucked him up generally in orthodox Samaritan fashion which he very badly needed. His (Stephen's) mind was not exactly what you would call wandering but a bit unsteady and on his expressed desire for some beverage to drink Mr. Bloom in view of the hour it was and there being no pump of Vartry water available for their ablutions let alone drinking purposes hit upon an expedient by suggesting, off the reel, the propriety of the cabman's shelter, as it was called, hardly a stonesthrow away near Butt bridge where they might hit upon some drinkables in the shape of a milk and soda or a mineral. But how to get there was the rub. For the nonce he was rather nonplussed but inasmuch as the duty plainly devolved upon him to take some measures on the subject he pondered suitable ways and means during which Stephen repeatedly yawned . . .

This may be called brilliant bad writing. It is, like the whole long chapter it begins, an exercise in the use of cliché. A cliché may be defined as a word or expression that has lost its original force through overuse. The origin of the term is instructive: in French it imitates the sound made by a printing matrix when it is dropped into hot metal, and it means in that language a stereotype, a printing plate. As printing plates can be reused and reused, the application of "cliché" to well-worn phraseology is reasonable. The kind of language study we have been indulging in does not make literary judgments, and a cliché like "It never rains but it pours" is as acceptable as Shakespeare's "When sorrows come, they come not single spies but in battalions." But, wandering into the linguistics of literature, I cannot help also touching its aesthetics. What Joyce is doing here is describing two very tired people in the language appropriate to tiredness.

Where, in *Ulysses*, Joyce breaks rules of language rather than of literary decorum, he is attempting to reach that area of the mind in which language is not yet ready to become "well-formed." His characters do not speak, they think and feel, and Joyce has to find a verbal technique for representing what may be a preverbal process. Here is Mr. Leopold Bloom on Sandymount shore:

> Short snooze now if I had. Must be near nine. Liverpool boat long gone. Not even the smoke. And she can do the other. Did too. And Belfast. I won't go. Race there, race back to Ennis. Let him. Just close my eyes a moment. Won't sleep though. Half dream. It never comes the same. But again. No harm in him. Just a few.
>
> O sweety all your little girlwhite up I saw dirty bracegirdle made me do love sticky we two naughty Grace darling she him half past the bed met him pike hoses frillies for Raoul to perfume your wife black hair heave under embon señorita young eyes Mulvey plump years dreams return tail Agendath swoony lovey shoed me her next year in drawers return next in her next her next.

This will make perfect sense to the reader who has attended closely to the thought and action of *Ulysses* up to this point (the end of the first half of the book). That "met him pike hoses," for instance, refers back to Mrs. Molly Bloom's seeing "metempsychosis" in a book and mispronouncing it. There is a strong sexual content in that second paragraph, all the more seductive for jettisoning syntax. Here Bloom is dozing off. In his next and last big book, *Finnegans Wake*, Joyce goes beyond the dozing stage. The entire action takes place in the sleep of the hero. The work is oneiric, or concerned with a dream. Here is the opening:

> riverrun past Eve and Adam's, from swerve of shore to bend of bay, brings us by a commodius vicus of recirculation back to Howth Castle and Environs. Sir Tristram, violer d'amores, fr'over the short sea, had passencore rearrived from North Armorica on this side the scraggy isthmus of Europe Minor to wielderfight his penisolate war: nor had topsawyer's rocks by the stream Oconee exaggerated themselse to Laurens County's gorgios while they went doublin their mumper all the time: nor avoice from afire bellowsed

mishe mishe to tauftauf thupartpeatrick: not yet, though venissoon after, had a kidscad buttended a bland old isaac: not yet, though all's fair in vanessy, were sosie sesthers wroth with twone nathandjoe. Rot a peck of pa's malt had Jhem or Shen brewed by arclight and rory end to the regginbrow was to be seen ringsome on the acuaface.

I refuse to let this go as a piece of eccentricity auguring the collapse of English. It is intelligible if we examine it closely enough, and it is entirely appropriate for the expression of the quality of a dream. Moreover, unlike that passage from *Ulysses* quoted on page 371, it is syntactically coherent: each sentence is "well-formed." We have the impression of the dream voice of a historical guide who holds on to traditional structure but has allowed his lexis to become deranged. The first sentence looks complete, but the lowercase opening is an indication that it is not. The beginning is to be found on the last page of the book, which hence does not end with a full stop: "A way a lone a last a loved a long the." The book is circular, as is history: every event in human life is repeated. This is not just circulation but recirculation. Joyce borrowed the thesis of the cycle of history from Giambattista Vico (1668–1744), whose *Scienza Nuova* (1725) postulates that civilizations rise and fall in cycles: myths, poetry, and language provide the evidence for this. Vico's name, in its Latin form, appears in the first sentence.

The scene is Dublin. The river is the Liffey. There is a church in Dublin known as Adam and Eve's. Howth Castle stands on the hill above Dublin. We see the initials of the hero of the book—Humphrey Chimpden Earwicker—in "Howth Castle and Environs." He is always present in some form or other: his initials are sewn into the fabric like a monogram. He is mankind in general: Here Comes Everybody. The story of mankind starts with the beginning of the world and the founding of the first city, which might as well be Dublin.

The events described in the second sentence have happened, but they have not yet happened again. Tristram, the lover of Isolde or Iseult, is also the lover of the only young woman in the story— Earwicker's daughter Isobel. Isobel is also Iseult la Belle. There were two Iseults in the Tristram legend—the Iseult whose love potion compelled Tristram's passion; the gentler Iseult of the White Hands, whose shrine was at Chapelizod, where Earwicker keeps a pub. Isobel is always a schizoid girl, like Joyce's own daughter, Lucia, in love with her own reflection in a mirror. Tristram violated his oath to his uncle King Mark, for whom he brought Iseult as a bride, by falling in love with her. He is thus a "violer d'amores" (he has done it more than once, hence the plural). But he also plays on the viola d'amore, an instrument with seven strings. "Passencore" (*pas encore*) means "not yet." North Armorica is North America but also North Brittany: what happens in the Old World must also happen in the New. "Wielder-fight" is to wield weapons in a fight, but also to fight again (German *wieder*). Tristram is one of the forms of one of the twin sons of Earwicker, usually known as Shaun. Like Cain and Abel, the brothers fight. Also like Napoleon and Wellington, who fought the Peninsular War. The other brother, normally seen as Shem (Irish for James, so that he contains aspects of Joyce himself), is an artist who fights with the pen in isolation. Shaun wields his penis. Both notions are contained in "penisolate."

As there are two Iseults, there are two Tristrams. Sir Almeric Tristram founded the great Lawrence family of Dublin and built Howth Castle. If North Armorica and North America are both contained in the story, we shall find a King Mark in both. There is in fact a Mark II or Mark Twain in America, complete with two sons— Tom Sawyer and Huckleberry Finn. Finn, the name of the legendary giant who is superseded by Earwicker but also identifiable with him, is a huge body stretched in sleep, under the city of Dublin. The dream that is the book is really his dream. In Laurens County in Georgia in America there is a river called the Oconee, and on it a town called Dublin stands. "Fr'over" is an archaism for "from over," but it also adds the color of "rover," free adventurer, to Tristram's passionate passage. "Doublin their mumper" contains not only the name of the city, but also the idea of reduplication. A mumper is an impostor, and both sons pretend to be as good as their father, which they are not. "Gorgios" contains "Georgia," "gorges," and the gypsy word for "sons" (it also contains the name of Joyce's own son, Giorgio).

A voice from afar, also from a fire, said to Saint Bridget, Ireland's female protective saint, "Mishe, mishe," the Erse for "I am, I am." This was the voice of God. Saint Patrick brought Christianity to Ireland. "Thou art Patrick" (which echoes "Thou art Peter, and upon this rock I will build my church") is also "Thou art a peat rick," intended for peaty Ireland herself. Patrick was a pupil of Saint Germanicus; hence it is appropriate to hear the German word *taufen* in "tauftauf"—"baptize, baptize." "Venissoon" (also "very soon") and "vanessy" both suggest Inverness, where Macbeth met the witches or weird "sesthers." There is a faint whiff of venison, suggesting an Old Testament sacrifice. Jacob, who is also James or Shem, showed artist's cunning in disguising himself as his hairy brother Esau (who is Shaun), thus deceiving his blind old father Isaac. But Isaac is also Isaac Butt, who was removed from the Irish leadership by Parnell. The ousters were cadets, younger members of the family but also cads. Susanna, Esther, and Ruth in the Old Testament ("sosie sesthers roth") were all loved by older men, as—and this is the driving force of the narrative—young Isobel is loved by her own father HCE. Nathan and Joseph—the wise prophet and the hero who would not yield to Potiphar's wife Zuleika—are combined into "nathandjoe"— two in one or "twone." "Nathandjoe" can be remade as "Jonathan," first name of Dean Swift, of Saint Patrick's, Dublin, who here incurs the wrath of two women with the same name—Esther Johnson, better known as Stella, and Esther Vanhomrigh, whose pet name was Vanessa (back to "vanessy")—for his inadequacy in love. The two Esthers appear as "sosies"—French for twins. This relates them to Isobel, who is twinned by her mirror.

We end with a reference to Noah and his sons. As there are only two young boys in the dream—Earwicker's sons—they have to take on three roles between them—Ham, Shem, and Japheth—hence the strange new names Jhem and Shen. The "arclight" is the light of the *arc en ciel*, or rainbow, and "regginbrow" is close to the German *Regenbogen*, also a rainbow, though it cannot accommodate an ark. The rainbow has seven colors, just as the viola d'amore has seven strings. Need I go on? The pun, a mere joke, has been elevated to a lofty literary device, which nevertheless cannot forget its *Alice in Wonderland* origin. We are meant to smile with pleasure, not frown in puzzlement. The title of the book encapsulates Joyce's method, but only if left unapostrophized. "Finnegan's Wake" is the name of a New York Irish ballad in which a bricklayer falls drunk from his ladder, dies, but is resuscitated with whiskey. *Finnegans Wake* refers to the song but also to the dead giant Finn waking again, an end (*fin*) denying (*negans*) a resurrection (*wake*), and our all being Finnegans who arise to resume the cycle of life.

I have spent some time on this attempt to explain, inadequately enough, what, ever since publication in 1939, has been regarded as a willful assassination of English, as well as the ultimate attestation of its possibilities. Apparently it has to enter Europe, as Joyce did, to fulfill itself. He has had no followers in such massive experimentation, but he has encouraged later writers to change our orthodox assumptions of the nature of English. Russell Hoban, in his *Riddley Walker* (1980), invents a dialect altogether appropriate to an imaginary England that, after a nuclear war, is trying to organize tribal culture after the total destruction of a centralized industrial civilization. The past has been forgotten, and even the art of making fire has to be relearned. This is the way the eponymous hero writes:

> Wen Mr Clevver wuz Big Man uv Inland they had evere thing clevver. They had boats in the ayr & picters on the win & evere thing lyk that. Eusa was a noing man were quik he cud tern his han tu enne thing. He wuz werkin for Mr Clevver wen thayr cum enemes aul roun & maykin Warr. Eusa sed tu Mr Clevver, Now wewl nead masheans uv Warr. Wewl nead boats that go on the water & boats that go in the ayr as wel wewl nead Berstin Fyr.

Finally they make use of "the Littl Shynin Man the Addom he runs in the wud."

This lingo, of course, runs counter to the Joycean technique of cramming words with meaning, but it shows that semantic reduction can be as telling and shocking as augmentation. Hemingway, whom I glanced at briefly in the previous chapter, was perhaps as important as Joyce in compelling a new look at the language. To sum up the two paths available to the modernist, let us take a normal sentence and then change it according to the opposed literary techniques. "The fat ginger cat lay before the hot fire on a rug, on which lay also a saucer of milk untouched as yet by the cat, which was not thirsty." Hemingway would break this down into: "The cat lay on the rug. It was fat. It was ginger. The rug was before the fire. The fire was hot. On the rug there was also a saucer. It contained milk. It had been placed there by the cat's mistress. The cat had not yet touched it. It was not thirsty." That is better than the original, in that like the cat, it is primitive, a succession of sensuous impressions unprocessed by a brain capable of constructing subordinate clauses. Joyce might turn the cat into a day of the week as well as a bank, and suggest, through cheese, Alice's Cheshire variety; the cat could also have been in a rooftop fight: "The fatterday ginjured catterday grindlay and barclay afour in mourning afore fire excausted on a red rag rug where whitelay auchooch a saucer (zausted) of not yet batter not yet scream not yet Wednesdaydale (not thursday) put by's mastress."

Experiments with English may lead to nonsense. Gertrude Stein (1874–1946), in her desire to cleanse the language, very sensibly said "A rose is a rose is a rose" to emphasize that that flower is not a multifoliate marvel meet for an exalted symbol but merely the thing that it is. The following makes sense in a Picasso-like way (Edmund Wilson said analogous to a Cubist canvas), but it will strike many as nonsensical:

A Sound.   Elephant beaten with candy and little pops and chews all bolts and reckless rats, this is this.
Custard.   Custard is this. It has aches, aches when. Not to be narrowly. This makes a whole little hill.
          It is better than a little thing that has mellow real mellow. It is better than lakes whole lakes, it is better than seeing.
Chicken.   Alas a dirty word, alas a dirty bird, alas a dirty third.

This being so obviously meaningless, one is forced to search for a meaning, and that meaning may be precisely the ease with which language can be disrupted. Danger comes when the meaningless sounds meaningful because of the acceptability of the structure. Syntax can, through its coherence, suggest that its semantic burden is coherent too. Hence political gobbledygook: "The nuclear capability of the national entity under consideration has not at this time been rendered susceptible of any viable clarification in reference to its notional belligerent capacity." The trouble with even sincere and sensible statements is that they can deal only in either tautology or lies. "Chinese women have exquisite legs." That cannot be true since there have to be exceptions. "Some Chinese women have exquisite legs." That is true but it is not worth saying.

Literary artists, who take words seriously, despise the language of politicians. They also avoid tautology by telling lies that are termed figurative statements. April is not really the cruelest month, despite the huge authority of T. S. Eliot, Nobelist and Order of Merit, and when, in the same author's unfinished play *Sweeney Agonistes*, the antihero Sweeney says, "Life is death," he is uttering nonsense. But there is a sense in which we can be forced to take a fresh look at reality only by accepting its contradictions. For, as *Finnegans Wake* propounds at great length, life is circular, and the beginning of a circle is also its end; life is not a linear continuum. Thus the season of renewal is cruel because renewal entails the death of the old, and we may have committed ourselves to the old. Life is death because it moves toward death from its very beginning. The discourse of ordinary life avoids this kind of truth, and hence avoids statements of a poetic nature.

The poet's awareness of the circularity of life, in which things can be expressed in terms of their opposites, sometimes leads him to an aesthetic in which anything can be expressed as anything. If life can be death, it can also, and perhaps more reasonably, be a bowl of cherries, an automobile, a force 9 wind, or a black dog. Take it further: life is a unity, and hence all aspects of life are relevant to each other. Draw from the unconscious an arbitrary string of words, and they can all be made to stand in a tenable relation. Perspex, keyboard, cognac, magenta, spider, yogurt, eyes, forge, epilogue— these images, expressed as words, can be forced into a coherent pattern: "The spider forges its Perspex keyboard, eyes the magenta yogurt and its cognac epilogue." That can easily be dismissed as nonsense, but the cautious will prefer to speak of surrealism. Since everything relates to everything else, it is not easy to write nonsense. A runcible spoon and a runcible hat have in common the attribute of runcibility. If they did not possess it they would be unruncible or, more likely, irruncible. If it means nothing else, "runcible" means belonging to the world of the rhymes of Edward Lear.

The impossibility of nonsense may strike a certain kind of writer with despair. I mean, perhaps, the writer who envies music its self-referring components (musical notes and patterns mean only themselves). Aware of the unity of the outside world as mirrored in the unity of his own mind, and of the difficulty of making words, aspects of the unity, transcend the unity, he may be driven to destroy syntax. For syntax expresses the relationship between entities, and a "well-formed" sentence confirms external reality. It is because my sentence about the spider and its Perspex keyboard is well-formed that it seems to make sense, even though the sense is dreamlike. To make an ill-formed sentence like "Boy out now Wellington transfuse coop" is to write true nonsense, but we are so structured that we will find a meaning in it if we can. We will take it that the printer has erred, and that a boy just out of prison in the town of Wellington is willing to cooperate in giving blood or a transfusion. Or perhaps the writer is reproducing the effect on the reader's eye of the rapid skimming of a page of newsprint. The American writer William Burroughs (b. 1914) employs a "fold-in" technique that is intended to have just this effect. No writer, however, will deliberately choose syntactical nonsense in order to free language (hence himself) from the external world. Such nonsense, he knows, is a symptom of dementia, and art should be the sole sanity in a mad world. Nonsense is cognate with glossolalia, in which phonemes are reduced to phones, and that, too, is a disease.

Whatever the literary experimentalist tries to do, he will not deliberately, except for satirical purposes, employ the language of the politician, which he will consider too evasive, or even mendacious, to serve the reality (sometimes called truth) that literature attempts to show. It is a satirical irony that George Orwell, in his novel *Nineteen Eighty-Four*, should present an imaginary government of the future (already past) endeavoring to impose a version of English so clear and unambiguous that it defies literary exploitation. "Newspeak," designed to make heterodox political expression impossible through sheer lack of a dissident vocabulary, is, in some ways, a rather attractive dialect, with its "doubleplusungood" replacing "very bad," "love" turned to "sexcrime," "duckspeak" to designate discourse that uses the organs of speech but not the brain. It is essentially a literary fantasy, for language cannot be so frozen, being autonomous and highly changeable of its nature.

As a kind of Orwellian joke, I once suggested that what could be called Worker's English (WE) might be imposed on the public by a Trades Union Congress that had taken over every aspect of government. It would stand in opposition to Bourgeois English, or BE, and be recommended for its simplicity and rationality. Thus, all BE verbs could be replaced by a verbal phrase governed by "get":

drink	=	get some drink down
eat	=	get grub in your guts
eliminate	=	get rid of
fuck off	=	get the fuck out of here
sleep	=	get your head (swede, loaf) down

The use of "ain't" as negation of both "to be" and "to have" represents an economy:

He ain't there   = he isn't there
He ain't been there   = he hasn't been there

And so does the identification of preterite and past participle:

I seen it;   I've seen it
I done it;   I've done it
I ate it;   I've ate it
I swum;   I've swum
I forgot;   I've forgot

And so on. This is not quite fantasy, coming closely as it does to proletarian usage: it is the imposition of the dialect by governmental fiat that demands suspension of disbelief.

Literature plays games with language, but these games are in the service of the truth about its nature, for language is not just what is in the dictionaries and the grammar books. Literature (which we have still not defined) deals with language as painting deals with pigment and sculpture with stone, and its artistic use is regarded as subsisting in parallel with its use in the street, marketplace, or bedroom. But the speech and writing of the educated is suffused with the literary, sometimes without conscious knowledge, and a language cannot easily develop without the aid of the makers of literature. There is, or used to be, one outstanding example of a book that affected the language of the entire anglophone world. Let us consider it now.

Literature, by the way, may be defined as the aesthetic exploitation of language.

31.

BIBLICAL MATTERS

What we call the Bible, or the Holy Bible, pretends to be a book when in fact it is a number of books. The medieval Latin *biblia* is really Greek, a plural of *biblion*, which means a book and is a diminutive of *biblos*, papyrus, named after the Phoenician port Biblos, where the Greeks obtained their supplies of Egyptian papyrus. The two languages of the Bible, Hebrew and Greek, are not even related, and the messianic fulfillment of the New Testament is foretold in the Old only to Christians. As court witnesses we are asked to swear on the Bible, a procedure that imparts a magical rather than religious quality to the black-bound heavyweight. In *Under Milk Wood*, Dylan Thomas speaks of the "bible-black" night: the connotations go further than the mere color of the binding, implying something elemental and possibly dangerous. It has always been difficult for believers to accept that the Bible is a kind of literary anthology, capable of being assessed in an aesthetic or critical spirit and not as the indubitable Word of the Lord. In the 1930s an edition of the book appeared called *The Bible Designed to Be Read as Literature*, artily bound, with large type and, where appropriate, poetic lineation. This aesthetic approach was considered blasphemous to some: the Bible ought to be a black churchy untouchable respository of the ultimate truth, holiest when least intelligible. I devote a chapter to it not because of its intrinsic theological significance but because it has had a profound influence on the way Anglophones use English, an influence very much on the wane.

Increasingly the Bible has become a work of interest to secular literary scholars concerned with showing that the authors of its various components were literary artists, and that, so far as the Old Testament is concerned, we can have no notion of how their art functions if we do not go back to the original Hebrew. Fundamentalists in the American South consider the 1611 translation into Jacobean English as the final authenticity, and one pious woman was heard to say that if the English language was good enough for God it was good enough for her. But English cannot render the rhetoric and wordplay of Hebrew. Professor G. D. Caird, who teaches the exegesis of Holy Scripture at Oxford University, asks us, for instance, to look at the Book of Amos, chapter 8, verse 2, where "a basket of summer fruit becomes a portent of Israel's end" because the basket is *qais* and the end is *qes*. An almond tree (*shaqed*) is "a reminder that God is keeping watch (*shoqed*) over his word" (Jer. 1:11). When, in Matt. 3:9, John the Baptist tells his mockers that God could make children for Abraham out of the stones lying around, he is drawing on the Hebrew pun *'ebnayya—benayya*, even though his words are recorded in Greek. In Isa. 5:7, justice (*mishpat*) is sought but oppression (*mishpah*) is found. Professor Caird also warns of the danger of taking literally Oriental rhetoric, which goes in greatly for forceful exaggeration. Saint Paul did not mean by "resurrection of the body" the calling together of sundered bones on the Day of Judgment: the Day of Judgment may be here and now, in God's time, which is not time at all, not at some remote calendar date. The Kingdom of God is not up there but in here. It began when Christ started his mission. We are used to taking English as plain statement, not as metaphor. We need to read more poetry, of which there is plenty in the Bible.

Professor Robert Alter, of the University of California at Berkeley, looks more closely, in his *The Art of Biblical Narrative*, at the employment of Hebrew wordplay to a storytelling end. Let us look briefly at Jacob and Esau. Esau is all red hair, thick-pelted, something of an animal. In Hebrew "red" is *'adom*, and this explains "Thus is his name called Edom." Jacob is *tam*—mild, retiring, capable of cunning. "The heart is treacherous," cries Jeremiah—*'aqov ha-lev*—and Esau is aware of the meaning of Jacob's name—*Ya 'aqov*: "He will deceive." Esau, famished after a day's hunting, asks for a mouthful of the "red stuff"

Jacob is cooking. The stress is on brutish hunger; Esau cannot, in his famished state, perform the human office of naming a lentil stew directly. The verb he uses—*hil'it*—is more appropriate for beasts than for men: "let me cram my belly." Esau's character is shown in the animalistic rush of the verbs: "he ate, drank, rose, went off." But he is polite enough to use the particle of entreaty—*na*—when crying for food, while Jacob is in the strong position of not having to use it when demanding in return Esau's birthright—sold for a mess of pottage.

We do not have to know Hebrew to appreciate the Old Testament's use of what are known as narrative formulae. There is, for instance, what Professor Alter calls the "betrothal-type scene." The future bridegroom journeys to a foreign land, meets a *na'arah* (maiden) or a number of them at a well, draws water for them, accepts the invitation to a meal from the girl's or girls' father, makes acquaintance with the family, eventually is betrothed. In this manner Abraham's servant meets Rebekah, Jacob meets Rachel, and Moses meets Zipporah. When the narrative artist sets up this same situation for Saul, Saul breaks all storytelling expectations. He does not draw water; he asks instead: "Is there a seer near here?" There is, and Saul meets the man who will launch him on his disastrous destiny. Bible study can, with American evangelists and American murderers, work as magic or prophecy. Billy Graham finds in its texts predictions of the destruction of a drug-taking fornicating world. Convicted killer Charles Manson saw the Beatles as the archangels of Revelation, with their breastplates changed to guitars. The end was coming, a time for murder. Safer Bible study is wholly secular.

English translations of the Bible form a chain binding successive stages of the language. Starting at the present, with the New English Bible in its revised form (1989), we can pursue a text back for a thousand years. Thus, today's version of the first and second verses of the eighth chapter of the Gospel According to Saint Matthew runs: "After he had come down from the hill he was followed by a great crowd. And now a leper approached him, bowed low, and said, 'Sir, if only you will, you can cleanse me.' " The King James or Authorized Version of 1611 gives: "When he was come down from the mountain, great multitudes followed him./And behold, there came a leper and worshipped him, saying, Lord, if thou wilt, thou canst make me clean." Tyndale in 1525 has "When Jesus came down from the mountayne, much people followe him./And lo! there cam a lepre and worsheped him, sayinge, Master, if thou wylt, thou canst make me clene." The Wycliffe Bible, in 1389, gives this rendering: "Forsothe when Jhesus hadde comen doun fro the hill, many cumpanyes folewiden hym./And loo! a leprouse man cummynge worshipide hym, sayinge, Lord, yif thou wilt, thou maist make me clene." Back in 995, the effect of confronting the foreign language that is Old English is softened by our already knowing what it means: "*Sothlice tha se Hælend of tham munte nyther astah, tha fyligdon hym mycle mænio./Tha genealæthe an hreofla to him and hine to him geathmedde, and thus cwæth, Drihten, gyf thu wylt, thu miht me geclænsian.*" The Bible provides a comforting talisman to protect us when we essay dangerous time journeys.

What precisely is the Bible? The Old Testament is a collection of poems, proverbs, a kind of play (the Book of Job), prophecy, philosophy, theology, and social and military history relating to the trials, triumphs, and aspirations of the Jewish people. It is a massive anthology whose components have in common the theme of a special race chosen by God, for castigation as much as for paternal cosseting, and the manner in which that race fulfilled its obligations, or failed to do so, as the elected bearers of the divine fire. The New Testament, whose Greek is not that of Homer or Aeschylus but the *koine* or common speech of much of the Roman Empire, contains the Gospels, the story of Christ's birth, mission, death and resurrection, and an account of the spreading of the good news (*godspell*) of Christianity by its first propagandists. In addition there are certain books whose origins and authority are obscure or doubtful. These are, when they are addenda to the Old Testament, termed Apocrypha; the addenda to the New Testament are called New Testament Apocrypha. The first consist of fables, historical writing, and philosophy. The second purport to give further details of the birth and resurrection of Christ and the lives of the Apostles. These latter were added to the Gospels and the Acts of the Apostles between A.D. 150 and 500.

The Catholic Church in which I was raised has always insisted that the Word of God is enshrined within itself, as Christ's own foundation. The Protestants have sought the Word in the Bible. An essential aim of the first Protestant reformers was to make the Bible available to all who wished to read it, and this entailed, naturally, translation into the vernacular. The act of translation was, especially in Germany and England, to have profound effects on the language itself. It was to give the national tongue a quasi-divine status, and it was to help determine the way it was used, even for secular purposes.

Medieval Europe knew the Bible in Latin, in that form known as the Vulgate, but there were sporadic attempts to render it, or parts of it, into the vernacular. In England the zeal for translation started early, but the Church was never happy about this. It tolerated translations in the hands of nuns or monks whose Latin was poor or nonexistent. (King Henry VIII knew of these, and cited the case of the priest who used *mumpsimus* instead of *sumpsimus*. When corrected, he said "I will not take your new *sumpsimus* for my old *mumpsimus*.") But in the hands of the laity translations could be dangerous. The common reader might consider that doctrinal authority resided in the written word and not in the Church; he might meditate on the Scriptures and decide on his own interpretation, which could be opposed to that of the bishops and priests. Up to the time of the Reformation, biblical translation was, for the most part, done without the authority, or certainly without the blessing, of the ecclesiastical powers.

John Wycliffe (1330?–1384) was an English priest who may be regarded as a precursor of the great reformers Luther and Calvin. In 1376 he wrote a treatise called *De dominio divino*, which expounded the doctrine that authority is founded on divine grace, and that wicked kings, popes, and priests were automatically debarred from the exercise of power, secular or ecclesiastical. Wycliffe was, as a consequence of this, deprived of sacerdotal authority by Pope Gregory XI, but his response was to condemn the whole Church hierarchy, call the pope "Antichrist," deny the doctrine of transubstantiation, and to declare that every Christian had the right to read the Bible and interpret it according to his own understanding. He was condemned, in turn, by an ecclesiastical court and forced into retirement: why he was not burned has never been well understood. He occupied his retirement with a complete translation of the Vulgate into English—perhaps not all his own work, but certainly all done under his direction—and this first English Bible appeared in 1380 or thereabouts. John Purvey, some eight years later, revised this Wycliffe Bible, bringing its language closer to the spoken tongue of the common people. It was widely read.

In 1408 the Church took violent action. It made episcopal permission—very hard to obtain—the condition for biblical translation. Unauthorized translation would be punished by the excommunication of the offender. William Tyndale (1494?–1536) followed the correct procedure and asked the bishop of London for permission to translate, but this was refused. Tyndale went into exile. Germany, aflame with reform, gave him sanctuary. However the translation of the New Testament he made straight from the Greek, not the Vulgate, ran into trouble when he attempted to print it in Cologne in 1525. He fled to Worms, sanctified Lutheran territory, and brought out what we must regard as the first Modern English version of the New Testament without molestation. This translation is important, since it served as a basis for later translations.

Tyndale worked slowly at the Old Testament, engaging the original Hebrew. In 1535 Miles Coverdale, a faster worker, rushed in with his version, which owed much to Tyndale and not a little to Luther's Bible: there were times when Coverdale found a cognate Teutonic tongue easier going than the originals. He perhaps foolishly attempted to reprint his Bible in Paris in 1538, for the sheets were confiscated by the staunchly unreformed authorities and solemnly burned. He escaped to England, where Henry VIII's Reformation was under way, and a copy of his vernacular Bible was soon ordered to be placed in every church. Tyndale, still on the Continent, fell into the clutches of the papal authorities and, at Antwerp, was condemned to death for heresy. He was strangled and his remains were burned.

Biblical translation in England became a major industry as the Reformation progressed. Matthew's Bible appeared in 1537, the work of John Rogers (1500?–1555), who preferred to publish under the pseudonym of Thomas Matthew. He had been a friend of Tyndale, was converted to Protestantism under his influence, and was burned at Smithfield, London, when Mary Tudor bloodily reimposed Catholicism on the realm. Richard Taverner (1505?–1575) revised Matthew's Bible and Taverner's Bible found favor with the powerful Thomas Cromwell, earl of Essex. But the search for the perfect rendering continued. Coverdale was put in charge of the 1539 translation known as the "Great Bible." With the advent of Catholic Queen Mary, such reformers and Bible scholars who could escape the fires of Smithfield sought refuge in Calvinistic Geneva, where they produced, in 1560, the Geneva Bible that found such favor later with the English Puritans. It is sometimes called the Breeches Bible because, uniquely among the various English translations, which present Adam and Eve as making "aprons" to mask their naked genitals, it dresses them in trousers, or breeches.

It was because of the popularity of the Geneva Bible among English Puritans that in 1568 Archbishop Parker gave his blessing to the so-called Bishops' Bible. The trouble with the Geneva Bible was less the text than the marginal commentary, which disparaged monarchs and implied the need for either a vague republicanism or a powerful oligarchy—or hagiarchy or theocracy—of the saintly or saved. Meanwhile, in Douai, the Catholics had at last yielded to the vernacular vogue and produced an English Bible still in use among anglophone Catholics, although there is a fine modern version made by Monsignor Ronald Knox (1888–1957). Knox was supposed to work only from the Vulgate, but he covertly and disobediently consulted the original languages.

What most English-speaking Protestants mean when they say "the Bible" is the Authorized Version of 1611, produced during the reign of King James I. James, a hater of Calvinism, a loather of the antimonarchial Geneva Bible, convened a conference at Hampton Court in 1604, with a view to the creation of a definitive English version of the Scriptures that should possess final, or kingly, authority. There were to be forty-seven divines and scholars who divided their duties according to their specializations—some dealing with the Old Testament, others with the New, some with the prophetic, others with the poetical. There is a legend, probably apocryphal, to the effect that the poetical books were, in the galley proofs of 1610, handed out to the more reputable professional poets of the day for their verbal embellishment, so long as this did not harm accuracy. This might explain the presence of Shakespeare's name in Psalm 46—"shake" the forty-sixth word from the beginning, "speare" the forty-sixth from the end if you omit the flourish "Selah." The Bard, having no other hope of literary survival, planted his name in the psalm he had polished. There is, unfortunately, little hope of this legend's being true.

The Authorized Version was not strictly a new translation. It was a revision of the Bishops' Bible, with much Tyndale and even some Wycliffe in it, but the revision was made in the light of a close study of the original Hebrew and Greek texts. There were two editions of the work in 1611, one called the He and the other the She Bible. In the first version, chapter 3, verse 15, of the Book of Ruth ran, "And he went into the city." In the second the sex is changed. Later Bibles were based, with certain corrections and variants, on the She Bible. Such terms of designation are quaint but useful. There was once a version of the King James Bible known as the Wicked Bible because the printer had omitted the negative from "Thou shalt not commit adultery." Here we see the possible danger of regarding the Bible as the Word of God.

Between King James's day and our own, the major work in vernacularization has been revisory of the Authorized Version, chiefly in 1881 and 1885: the changes were not well taken by conservative Christians. God had spoken in Jacobean English—a deliberately somewhat archaic dialect of it—and then, the task done, had elected silence. In that the language in which Shakespeare's and Ben Jonson's plays had been written, as well as Bacon's essays and Donne's sermons, remains unsurpassed as a literary medium, there is something in the notion that the tongues of that holy committee were touched with coals of fire. There could not be a better translation from the viewpoint of literary grandeur; scholarly accuracy is a different matter. The literary quality of the King James Version is more remarkable than long habituation to it enables us to realize. For one thing, it admits an Oriental flavor to the native syntax. I referred two chapters back to the lack of subordinating devices in Hebrew. Hence this:

And there was war between Rehoboam and Jeroboam all their days. And Rehoboam slept with his fathers, and was buried with his fathers in the city of David. And his mother's name was Naaman an Ammonitess. And Abijam his son reigned in his stead.

This rhythm is hard to resist, as indeed is the whole Hebrew-Jacobean rhetoric. When the prophetic mood comes on H. G. Wells and George Bernard Shaw, both agnostics, they slip naturally into biblical music. Authors affected by a bigger East than Israel—Kinglake, Doughty, Lawrence of Arabia, to say nothing of Kipling—find their literary precedent back in 1611. But the succinctness and force of the Authorized Version has, for nearly four centuries, affected the speech even of the semiliterate. Phrases like the following are branded into the brain:

And they heard the voice of the Lord God walking in the garden in the cool of the day.

For the imagination of man's heart is evil from his youth.

Who so sheddeth man's blood, by man shall his blood be shed.

I do set my bow in the cloud.

The voice is Jacob's voice, but the hands are the hands of Esau.

And Jacob served seven years for Rachel; and they seemed unto him but a few days, for the love he had to her.

And she caught him by his garment, saying: Lie with me; and he left his garment in her hand, and fled.

Ye shall eat the fat of the land.

Bring down my grey hairs with sorrow to the grave.

Unstable as water, thou shalt not excel.

Unto the utmost bound of the everlasting hills.

I have been a stranger in a strange land.

A land flowing with milk and honey.

I AM THAT I AM.

Life for life, eye for eye, tooth for tooth, hand for hand, foot for foot, burn for burn, wound for wound, stripe for stripe.

If not, blot me, I pray thee, out of the book which thou hast written.

A stiffnecked people.

And these are but a meager selection from the Books of Genesis and of Exodus alone.

In the twentieth century, with the decay of official religion, it seemed to many that the Authorized Version confirmed the view that Christianity, with its premessianic preliminary mythology, was quaint and archaic. Most of the language of the King James Bible was, as Shakespeare's was, intelligible, but its harmonics were those of a remote and dead culture. The archaic personal pronouns, surviving only in dialect, had long faded from Standard English; much of the phraseology was too poetic for a rational society; moreover, Greek and Hebrew scholarship had advanced greatly since the Jacobean time and reluctantly noted inaccuracies in the venerable and venerated version. There have been a number of new translations, and one of the most controversial has been the New English Bible or NEB. The New Testament appeared in 1961 in a language acceptable to modern ears. There were lines at the bookshops to buy it. In 1970 the Old Testament and Apocrypha were published, along with a limited revision of the New Testament. In 1989 there was a total revision, and the Revised English Bible must, we presume, stand for a number of years as a testimony to contemporary scholarship, though not perhaps to contemporary literary genius. Donald Coggan, chairman of the Joint Committee of the enterprise, writes in his Preface as follows:

> Care has been taken to ensure that the style of English used is fluent and of appropriate dignity for liturgical use, while maintaining intelligibility for worshippers of a wide range of ages and backgrounds. The revisers have sought to avoid complex or technical terms where possible, and to provide sentence structure and word order, especially in the Psalms, which will facilitate congregational reading but will not misrepresent the meaning of the original texts. As the "you"-form of address to God is now commonly used, the "thou"-form which was preserved in the language of prayer in the New English Bible has been abandoned. The use of male-oriented language, in passages of traditional versions of the Bible which evidently apply to both genders, has become a sensitive issue in recent years; the revisers have preferred more inclusive gender reference where that has been possible without compromising scholarly integrity or English style.

"Range of ages," "male-oriented": the new divisions in our society are noted and deferred to. There is a timorousness here that would not have been well appreciated by the translators of the 1611 version.

Let us take two representative passages, to see how the King James Bible and the NEB respectively render them. First, the fortieth chapter of Isaiah. Here is the language of 1611, or rather earlier:

> Comfort ye, comfort ye my people, saith your God. Speak ye comfortably to Jerusalem, and cry unto her, that her warfare is accomplished, that her iniquity is pardoned; for she hath received of the Lord's hand double for all her sins.
>   The voice of him that crieth in the wilderness, Prepare ye the way of the Lord, make straight in the desert a highway for our God. Every valley shall be exalted, and every mountain and hill

shall be made low: and the crooked shall be made straight, and the rough places plain:

And the glory of the Lord shall be revealed, and all flesh shall see *it* together: for the mouth of the Lord hath spoken *it*.

Here is the NEB:

Comfort my people; bring comfort to them, says your God; speak kindly to Jerusalem and proclaim to her that her term of bondage is served, her penalty is paid; for she has received at the Lord's hand double measure for all her sins.

A voice cries: Clear a road through the wilderness for the Lord, prepare a highway across the desert for our God. Let every valley be raised, every mountain and hill be brought low, uneven ground be made smooth, and steep places become level. Then will the glory of the Lord be revealed and all mankind together will see it. The Lord himself has spoken.

This is decent English but hardly distinguished. The second paragraph suggests official orders preliminary to the raising of a housing estate. There is a general lack of relish in the prosodic aspect of language: "sin" is more direct than "iniquity" but the repetition of the /ɪ/ in the latter word implies a multitude of wrongs. "Her warfare is accomplished" is less accurate, probably, than the NEB equivalent, but the new implication of serving a stretch, and also paying a fine, is vapid. At the end, the daring physicality of the "mouth of the Lord" is, in deference to the discarding of the anthropomorphic view of God, replaced by something tamer and more timid. On the other hand, we can be assured that this is fairly close to the Hebrew. If we find this translation insufficient—unworthy to be set by a new Handel in a new *Messiah*—we must blame not the translators but the state of the language itself. Let us now look at Saint Paul's First Epistle to the Corinthians (chapter 13). Here, first, the King James Version:

Though I speak with the tongues of men and of angels, and have not charity, I am become *as* sounding brass or a tinkling cymbal.

And though I have the *gift* of prophecy, and understand all mysteries, and all knowledge: and though I have all faith, so that I could remove mountains, and have not charity, I am nothing.

And though I bestow all my goods to feed *the poor*, and though

I give my body to be burned, and have not charity, it profiteth me nothing.

And now the NEB:

I may speak in tongues of men or of angels, but if I have no love, I am a sounding gong or a clanging cymbal. I may have the gift of prophecy and the knowledge of every hidden truth; I may have faith enough to move mountains; but if I have no love, I am nothing. I may give all I possess to the needy, may give my body to be burnt, but if I have no love, I gain nothing by it.

I have no competence in Hebrew, but I am able to read both the original Greek and the Latin of the Vulgate. The *agape* of the one and the *caritas* of the other may be rendered equally as "charity" or "love" (not *amor* or the gift of Eros), and I surmise that the connotations of "charity" in our own age are unacceptable (Dr. Barnado's homes, collecting boxes, "I don't want your charity"). The "sounding gong" particularizes too much the *aes sonans* (literally "sounding brass") of the Vulgate and the *gegona khalkos* of the Greek, the "clanging cymbal" presupposes a modern orchestral instrument, whereas Paul must have had a much smaller round of metal in mind (the *cymbale antique* of Debussy), for the *kymbalon alalazon* and the *cymbalum tinniens* clearly tinkle rather than clang. "Mysteries" is better than "hidden truth": truths may eventually be revealed by inquiry and study, but "mysteries" are elucidated by a very special mentality (they are *mysteria* in both the original and the Latin). On the whole, the NEB does not do badly here. It is dealing with an Indo-European language that behaves like English. But there are renderings in the New Testament section that have aroused fury in some.

T. S. Eliot, for instance, was angry with the new rendering of "Neither cast ye your pearls before swine" (Matt. 7:6): "Do not feed your pearls to pigs." He said: "The substitution of 'feed' for 'cast' makes the figure of speech ludicrous." True: casting is not feeding, and we can imagine the swine grunting and snuffling at the costly offering before rejecting it. "Swine" is not archaic, and the fact that people are sometimes termed swine adds a pejorative layer to the word. Dissatisfaction with the NEB is echoed by the unease with which practicing Christians view the revised prayer book. "Our Father, which art in heaven" became "Our Father in heaven." The marriage vows lost "Thereto I plight thee my troth" and "With all my worldly goods I thee endow" and now have "This is my solemn vow" and "All that I have I share with you." They mean the same thing and are highly intelligible, but a certain solemnity, marked by unusual phraseology, is lost. The pushing of the "thee endow" to the end of the phrase is like the heavy stamping of a seal; the new undertaking seems lighthearted and easily broken.

Having said something of the influence of the Bible on ordinary secular language, I might have added something on the similar power of Shakespeare (King James I was, in one sense, the luckiest of monarchs: the two greatest works of English were published in his lifetime; twelve years after his Bible came the Shakespeare First Folio). I will content myself with the point that though literature is made out of language, language is also made out of literature. Even in this century, and in my own lifetime, the speech and personal letters of the minimally cultivated were busy with Jacobean echoes. The common language of today has to find its mythology in the radio, the television, and the newspapers. A world that looks to the future is not particularly interested in what it regards as the fossils of the past. But language comes out of the past and is not easily separated from it. Semiologists like Umberto Eco seem satisfied with what films like *Casablanca* (an ancient classic to some) and *Star Wars* can feed into our mythological stock. Ignorant of biblical and Latin and Greek myths alike (as Shakespeare was not), we are placed in great difficulty when we come to read the classics of English. There is no consensus anymore about the values that feed the imagination. But our problems as regards the teaching of English to the emerging generations go further than that: they have a great deal to do with the loss of authority, the power of the new media, and the political doctrines of equality. I tackle the teaching problem in my next and last chapter, the Epilogue.

EPILOGUE

WHAT AND HOW SHOULD WE TEACH?

Most of the official and semiofficial directives on the teaching of English, as well as the more tentative advisory documents, are doctrinaire in nature and often have a strong political bias. I propose here certain observations on the subject that have their own bias, as is inevitable, but it is a bias that derives from experience rather than theory.

If my curriculum vitæ is at all impressive, it is because of its variety, and the fact that it covers more than twenty years. I lack firsthand experience of teaching at the infant level, and my knowledge of primary schools has been gained mainly as a supervisor of teaching practice in two training colleges. Cut off, by age and hebetude, from direct knowledge of what happens in the schools of the English-speaking world, I nevertheless hear reports of the dissatisfaction of teachers, an increasing failure of discipline, and a dubiety about what should be taught.

As far as English is concerned, some pundits take the view that it should not be taught at all, since anglophone pupils already know it. This could legitimately apply at the secondary level, granted that the primary school had already taught basic literacy. It is, in fact, the postprimary teaching of English—in all the English-speaking territories—that is the continuing subject of debate. I do not wish now to generalize in the manner of a government white paper. I want instead to suggest what the secondary-school English teacher might do to justify the treating of "English" as a subject at all.

The new pupils assemble, and the teacher confronts them. Their parents ought to have brought them each, as a token of seriousness to come, a copy of the *Collins English Dictionary*. There are far too many matchbox-sized pseudolexica around. I remember once, in an adult class, using the word "ineluctable" and seeing an earnest student search for the word in one of those midgets, naturally not finding it and assuming I had made the word up. The other thing the pupil brings with him (I will use this masculine pronoun, and its other forms, to denote both sexes: deference to feminist grammar is time-wasting) is a name. This cost nothing except its registration not long after birth. The teacher has the practical duty of learning the names of his classes. A name is a linguistic construct fastened for life to the pupil, and it is, to him, the most important item in his linguistic inventory. It deserves to be examined with some care. The study of names is termed onomastics (from the Greek *onoma*, a name). There are four kinds of surname. The first springs from a long-gone family relationship and is either a patronymic or a metronymic. A pupil named William Johnson or Jack Madge or Herbert Margerison is not exhibiting the name of his parent, rather the parent of one of his medieval ancestors. Muslims, of which there may be some in the class, have patronymics (father-names but not metronymics or mother-names) that denote actual parentage, such as Ahmad bin (son of) Abdul Latiff or Rahimah binte (daughter of) Ibrahim. Russians have both a patronymic and a family name: Boris Leonidovich Pasternak, for instance, or Lev (or Leo) Nikolayevich Tolstoy.

The other categories of British or American surname are the place-name—London, Chester, Ireland, Cornish, Scott, either proper noun or adjective from it, or common noun, as with Hill or Field or Rivers, trade name, as with Baker or Butcher or Farrier or Thatcher, and nickname. "Nickname" is a mistaken derivation from *an ekenamer*, an additional name (compare "an orange" and "an adder") and though, as a proper or official name, a frozen form, it goes on exhibiting the original liveliness of its application. Most people are given nicknames, at school or in the services, as a mark of affection or dislike. Regular or family nicknames in English include Armstrong, Redhead, Brown. "Brown" is common in Europe—Braun, Lebrun—but one is not sure whether it refers to hair coloring or to skin. "Browne" is considered more aristocratic than the 'e'-less variety, but it is pronounced the same. In the forces a Brown is a Topper (origin unknown) and a Wilson a Tug ("according to Naval tradition, the name commemorates Admiral of the Fleet Sir Arthur K. Wilson VC, whose original nickname was *Chug*"—Partridge). Anyone in Australia with the name Ashe is nicknamed Oscar after Oscar Ashe (1871–1936), the Australian actor who played in Chu Chin Chow during the First World War. Some origins are relentlessly obscure. Russians with resounding surnames are often very facetiously nicknamed: *Pasternak* means "parsnip" and *Tolstoy* "thick." A jailer had his name adopted by Trotsky; *Gorky* ("bitter") is a name that writer chose for himself. A Victorian gentleman named Bugg changed his name to Norfolk-Howard. For a long time bedbugs were humorously so called.

The *Population Trends* put out by Her Majesty's Stationery Office in 1976 showed, in order of commonness in the United Kingdom, the surnames Smith, Jones, Williams, Brown, Taylor, Davies, Evans, Thomas, Roberts, and Johnson—one nickname, two trade names, the rest patronymics. "Jones" is properly "Johnson"; "Thomas" is the remote paternal name without even a truncated "son"; "Evans" is Welsh, with "Ifan" as the father form. There must once in Britain have been a great number of smiths and tailors. The first three names on the list have maintained their positions in this century, but "Brown" has risen two places, replacing "Taylor" and "Davies," which were once fourth and fifth. Some nicknames shame their owners.

Given or baptismal names enshrine myths—biblical or literary or cinematic or, increasingly, rock-musical. There is a great deal of salutary research to be done here. Who were the mythical Anns, Marys, Deborahs, Johns, Thomases? Why "Pamela"? Ultimately either a novella by Sir Philip Sidney or a novel by Samuel Richardson, in which the name is pronounced with the accent on the second syllable, provides the protonym or original name. Surnames, which are proper nouns, can function as common nouns—"boycott," "lynch," "sandwich." These can also be verbs.

From personal names one can pass to local place-names and to the invented names without which science, technology, and modern marketing could not exist. And there is the whole array of technical terms without which the study of language itself becomes mere amateurish fumbling. A bilabial fricative or glottal stop has as much right to a name as a carburetor or a distributor arm.

The pupil's name is part of his fabric. So is his speech. The sooner the basic principles of phonetics can be taught the better. A language is primarily an auditory system, and the graphic aspect is a mere shadow. Nevertheless, as with any science, a visual notation is needful. The use of the IPA to indicate pronunciation in his dictionary may lead the pupil to think of it as a pure visual code. It must be shown to be, in its narrowest form, the tool of exact description of speech sounds. Children must learn to know, as precisely as possible, what sounds they habitually utter. Speech study has ceased to be prescriptive, in the sense that RP is considered to be the only acceptable dialect, but the notion of what exactly a dialect is is ceasing to be well understood. Certain modes of town speech exhibit not a historical grammatical or phonological system but a debased version of one. By "debased" I mean imperfect articulation of consonants, so that the glottal stop is overprevalent, and reduction of the vowels to a variety of the neutral schwa. The speech of young thugs and street boys is not a dialect with the status of that of Lancashire or Devonshire; it is a travesty of speech with a poverty-stricken vocabulary. When vocabulary is extended, the tendency is for the speech system to approach, if not reach, RP: it is from RP that the new words tend to come. Clarity of speech, whatever its phonemes happen to be, is essential to communication. It has to be fostered.

In the teaching of phonetics, we go beyond the merely phonemic notation of the dictionary. There are varieties of /p/, /b/, and the rest of the consonants that have to be heard clearly, pronounced clearly, notated exactly. The vowels are more complicated and require very close study. The versions of /i:/ that may be heard in the average classroom exhibit degrees of centralization and diphthongization that do not necessarily have to be corrected, but the /i:/ of RP is a norm against which dialectal forms can be measured. Phonetic dictation is valuable, especially of nonsense structures like /mnofkar/ and /gbfgi:gl/. It will be a long time before this scientific approach to the sounds of English is accepted, but it has to be fought for.

As for English as graphemes connected into written or printed constructs, writing must be related to reading. The employment of the language as a quasi-literary implement can be delayed. The printed models should have an informative rather than an aesthetic function: we are concerned with clarity of expression of straightforward ideas. They can be extracts from newspapers and magazines—highly contemporary—indeed, of today's date—and they should never be too long. Extracts from stories or novels need have no aesthetic pretensions. The best sellers of Frederick Forsyth or Jack Higgins are written in correct English: what literary critics hold against them is that the English is not daring enough, since true literature functions in an area where questions of adequate grammatical construction have ceased to be interesting. Secondary-school students are late in reaching an ability to make literary evaluations; some never arrive at all. But they must be able to judge adequacy in putting across information (or indeed propaganda) and attain adequacy themselves in this craft. Art hardly comes into it.

Advertisements are not to be despised, especially when they provoke. Take Mitsubishi. "Introducing a new concept in televisions: they watch you. Are you sitting in a different position in the room? They'll electronically swivel to follow you. Fall asleep in front of them, and they'll turn off automatically." And so on. Now is the time to read aloud part of Orwell's *Nineteen Eighty-Four* and invite comment. Since when has "television" been permitted a plural? A different position in the room from what? Does the advertisement genuinely inform, or does it cheat? Let the class try writing copy for a chocolate bar, a new soft drink, even a computer. It is more difficult than it looks.

A critical approach to pieces of published writing should be encouraged. Transcripts of political speeches are toothsome material. There is a difference between propaganda and plain impartial statement. Newspaper editorials exhibit the bias of the owner's political stance. Letters to the editor have an ax to grind. Like this, from Sara Starkey (*Guardian*, October 29, 1991):

What I really find appalling about London Zoo is its pragmatism towards animals—out with the old, in with the new.

In 1950 three million people queued to see a polar bear cub Brumas, but humans soon got bored. By the late eighties, polar bears were considered unacceptable exhibits for display thanks to much campaigning and research done by the anti-zoo lobby and ZooCheck which proved that polar bears showed psychotic behavior in these prison conditions. London Zoo's answer to the problem was to send, in 1989, two polar bears (polar bears are in the "vulnerable" category, one under "endangered") Mosha and Pipiluk to live out their lives in separate, cramped cages open to the elements. Pipiluk, not surprisingly, has since died. Mosha still languishes there.

But then out of sight is out of mind and everyone can now flock to see London Zoo's latest sentient "turn" before she too becomes just another sad sight that can't bring in the customers.

This, though published in an important newspaper, is not "professional" writing. One is dubious about the use of certain words—"pragmatism," "sentient," "psychotic." "One under 'endangered'" seems clumsy. Anger gets in the way of elegance. It is, however, the sort of letter that anyone with strong feelings about something should be able to write. Literary, or even journalistic, aspirations are not in question.

All pupils can be expected to have strong feelings about something. Otherwise they have little knowledge, limited opinions, unintelligent prejudices, irrational attitudes. An imagined "letter to the editor" represents the summit of what most of them should be expected to write. Poets and novelists will improbably emerge, but not as a result of training. More important than writing, especially in an age of television interviews and radio "phone-ins," is self-expression through speech. What may be termed preparatory writing is an adjunct of that. This means a measure of logic, an avoidance of circularities like "I like arranging flowers because it is a nice thing to do," an opportunity to appraise a written solidity before vaporizing it in the spoken word. The amassing of vocabulary through reading or through browsing in a dictionary must be in the service of a greater fluency of speech.

Formal instruction in grammar, or morphology, is probably necessary because it is an aspect of the study of language, not because it is likely to help self-expression. Jazz pianists can play an augmented dominant thirteenth without knowing the name of the chord. The serious study of music is a different matter. It is necessary to know what a preposition or an adverb is, just as it is necessary to know the difference between a vein and an artery, but it is more necessary to understand the principle of opposition that is at the root of all culture. The free form opposes the bound form, or the autosemanteme the synsemanteme. In a sentence like "I grabbed my shabby old raincoat and rushed out as quickly as I could," the opposition between the meaningful and the purely structural is more important than those slots termed "parts of speech."

I have said nothing about the pleasure principle. This is, as we know, satisfied by reading, or by being read to. One ought to emphasize the contemporary. The confrontation of Shakespeare or Milton has to be a deferred experience if it provokes a groan. We are too pietistic in our concern with transmitting the gems of our national heritage. But one skill of youth ought to be exploited precisely because it fades along with youth—I mean the capacity to learn by heart. Pupils will whine at having to memorize a stanza from Gray's "Elegy" or a speech from *Macbeth* or *Hamlet*. In later years they will be glad to have stocked their minds with the quotable. As for the experience of listening to recited narrative, Friday afternoon was, in my teaching experience, an admirable time for reading aloud *Three Men in a Boat* or *Decline and Fall* or *Nineteen Eighty-Four*. Jerome K. Jerome's chronicle of the Thames is not contemporary, and probably not even literature, but it is funny. Laughter shows that the pleasure principle is at work.

Behind English lies language in general. The aim of this book has been to show that a study that hardly exists in our schools, and is certainly still to be recognized by educational authorities, is important because it deals with the most basic of human faculties. We cannot hope to appreciate what our native language is doing unless we understand what language in general tries to do. Few of us can be expected to be polyglot, and George L. Campbell, editor of the two-volume *Compendium of the World's Languages* (Routledge), certainly knows no more than a tiny percentage of the hundreds of living and dead tongues that he briefly analyzes. But a glance at a language like Abkhaz—of which there are fewer than a hundred thousand speakers in the northwest Caucasian locality that gave it birth—reminds the Anglophone that the rules of his own language are not, as John Stuart Mill seemed to think, a reflection of universal mental reality. For Abkhaz has innumerable consonants but only two vowels, with the /a/ more prevalent than the other, a kind of schwa. Thus, "I" is *sara*, "thou" masculine *wara*, "thou" feminine *bara*, "he" *yara*, "she" *lara*, "we" *hara*, "you" *s'ara*, and "they" *dara*. This might be considered a horrid example to those users of "Yobspeak" who reduce all their vowels to a variety of schwa, but Abkhaz is sane, self-sufficient, and has produced an epic literature.

Students of Latin who find the case system intolerable may expect a "primitive" language like Yidiny, spoken by Australian aborigines, to be easier, only to find that it has more cases than Latin—absolute, ergative, genitive, locative and instrumental, ablative, dative, purposive, and aversive—and that its "this" and "that" forms vary according to distance (close at hand, farther away, remote, not visible). In the companion language Dyirbal a feminine class marker precedes a nominal denoting a bird because its speakers believe that women turn into birds when they die. Language flowers in ways that English will never understand. It is a phenomenon showing an incredible variety of sounds and shapes, and it is all made out of a mouthful of air.

I end with that emphasis. Men and women spoke long before they learned how to write. The signs we inscribe or print should bow down to the sounds we utter. Our highly visual civilization is reversing reality. But language was contrived in the dark, and we remain greatly in the dark about its astonishingly subtle mechanisms. It merits our homage and the devotion of our continued study.

INDEX

Spanish (*cont.*)
Castilian, 75–77, 134
history of, 169, 196–199,
  200–201
sound system of, 41, 74, 77, 80,
  81, 83–84, 88, 93, 94,
  196–199, 200–201
stress in, 100
writing of, 134, 140
Spears, Monroe K., 310–311
speech, rate of, 103–104, 275
speech disorders, 73, 77
speech organs, *see* vocal organs
speech sounds, *see* consonants;
  phonemes; vowels
spelling, *see* English, written
"spiv," 153
Standard English with Received
  Pronunciation (SE with RP),
  8, 22–23, 25
Chaucer and, 251–252
dictionary pronunciation from,
  349
as educational standard, 396
'h' dropping in, 275
importance of, 291, 294
'l' allophones in, 63–64
origin of, 22, 250
'r' dropping in, 98, 136, 268–269,
  274
vowels of, 86, 87, 88, 89, 92, 93,
  96, 274–275, 276–277, 279,
  290
Starkey, Sara, 397–398
Stein, Gertrude, 376
Strang, Barbara, 347
Strauss, Richard, 29
stress, 100–101
in American English, 280
structuralism, 32–33, 39–40
subjunctive mood, 202–203
subtitles, 111, 117
superstition, language and, 19, 220
surface structure, 44
Swahili, 30, 309
Sweden, 111
Swedish, 64, 175, 186–188
Sweeney Agonistes (Eliot), 376
Sweet, Henry, 337, 339–340
"sweetmeat," 152
Sweyn I, king of Denmark, 242
Swift, Jonathan, 255, 334
Swinburne, Algernon Charles,
  363–364

Switzerland, linguistic diversity of,
  203–204
syllabaries, 124–125, 126
syntax, *see* grammar

taboos, language and, 107
Tacitus, 232
Tamil English, 59, 227
Taverner, Richard, 385
"tawdry," 153
"teddy boy," 153
Temiars, 24
Tennyson, Alfred, Lord, 31, 177,
  366
1066 and All That (Sellar and
  Yeatman), 234
Testament of Cresseid, The
  (Henryson), 253
"testimony," 312
Thackeray, William Makepeace, 335
theater, 34
pronunciation in, 268, 272
Yiddish in, 286
Third Man, The, 113
Thomas, Dylan, 380
"Three Sorrowful Things,"
  248–249
Times (London), 19, 20
Timpul, 145
Tolstoy, Leo, 395
tonal languages, 102–103
Tooke, Horne, 335
transformational-generative
  grammar, 43–47
translation:
of Bible, 158, 231, 239–240, 250,
  298–299, 357, 381, 382–392
of classical works, 238, 254–255
errors in, 117
in film dubbing, 110–117
literature and, 156–157, 159, 181
Treichler, Paula A., 312
triphthongs, 69, 98
Troilus and Criseyde (Chaucer), 253
Trubetzkoy, Nikolas, 40
Turco-Tartar languages, 176
Turkish, 151, 173, 176
Turks, whistled language of, 107
Tynan, Kenneth, 320
Tyndale, William, 382–383,
  384–385

Ukrainian, 174
Ulfilas, Bishop, 175